Love Hina

By

Ken Akamatsu

Volume 8

Los Angeles • Tokyo

Translator - Nan Rymer
English Adaption - Adam Arnold
Retouch & Lettering - Krystal Dawson
Cover Layout - Anna Kernbaum

Senior Editor - Luis Reyes
Production Manager - Jennifer Miller
Art Director - Matthew Alford
VP of Production & Manufacturing - Ron Klamert
President & C.O.O. - John Parker
Publisher - Stuart Levy

Email: editor@TOKYOPOP.com
Come visit us online at www.TOKYOPOP.com

A   Manga
TOKYOPOP® is an imprint of Mixx Entertainment Inc.
5900 Wilshire Blvd. Suite 2000, Los Angeles, CA 90036

ISBN: 1-59182-019-7

First TOKYOPOP® printing: January 2003

10   9   8   7
Printed in USA

Love Hina

The Story Thus Far...

Fifteen years ago, Keitaro Urashima made a promise to a girl that the two of them would go to Tokyo University together. For fifteen years, Keitaro Urashima has slaved away at the books, stumbling through academia until the day he could take the entrance exam for Tokyo University. For fifteen years, Keitaro Urashima has been driven by that promise, a drive that has outstripped even his memory of the girl's name. And here he is, fifteen years later, having failed the entrance exam three times already, having readied himself so thoroughly so as to fail again, having discovered that the girl to whom he made that fateful promise might very well be the girl that's now sitting right next to him in the exam hall. All Keitaro Urashima has to do to bring this fifteen-year saga to a close is stay awake. But he can't even handle that. With five minutes left in the exam, Keitaro Urashima wakes to the horror that he has an entire section left to finish. Finishes it he does, and then bolts for the door, leaving a dumbfounded Mutsumi and Naru to trek home alone.

This chapter in Keitaro Urashima's life began a year ago when he inherited from his globe-trotting grandmother the Hinata House, an all-girls dormitory whose clientele is none too pleased that their new, live-in landlord is a man or as close to a man as poor Keitaro can be. The lanky loser incessantly (and accidentally) crashes their sessions in the hot springs, walks in on them changing, and pokes his nose pretty much everywhere that it can get broken, if not by the hot-headed Naru — the mystery girl from fifteen years ago — then by one of the other Hinata inmates — Kitsune, a late-teen alcoholic with a diesel libido; Motoko, a swordsman who struggles with a feminine identity; Shinobu, a pre-teen princess with a colossal crush on Keitaro; Su, a foreign girl with a big appetite; Sarah, an orphaned ward resentful of being left there by her archeologist guardian; Mutsumi, an accident-prone lily also studying for her exams; and Haruka, Keitaro's aunt and de facto matriarch.

Now, Naru has, over the year she's been helping Keitaro study for his exam, developed a bit of a crush on him, though she's loathe to admit it. And Keitaro's crush on Naru, which has reached almost crippling proportions, is one of the main reasons he fled in shame after the exam. So, it's now up to fate to bring them back together, no matter how messy their reunion might be.

CONTENTS

LOVE♡HINA

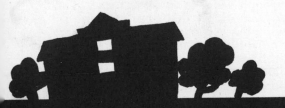

LOVE♡HINA

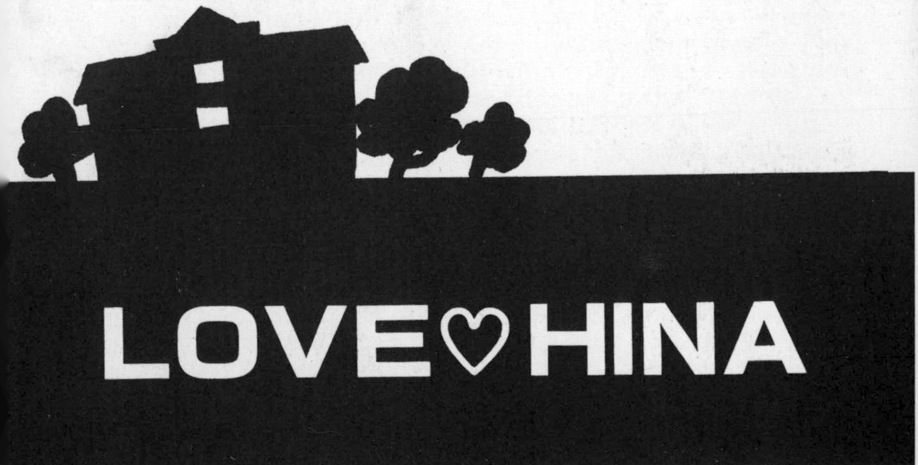

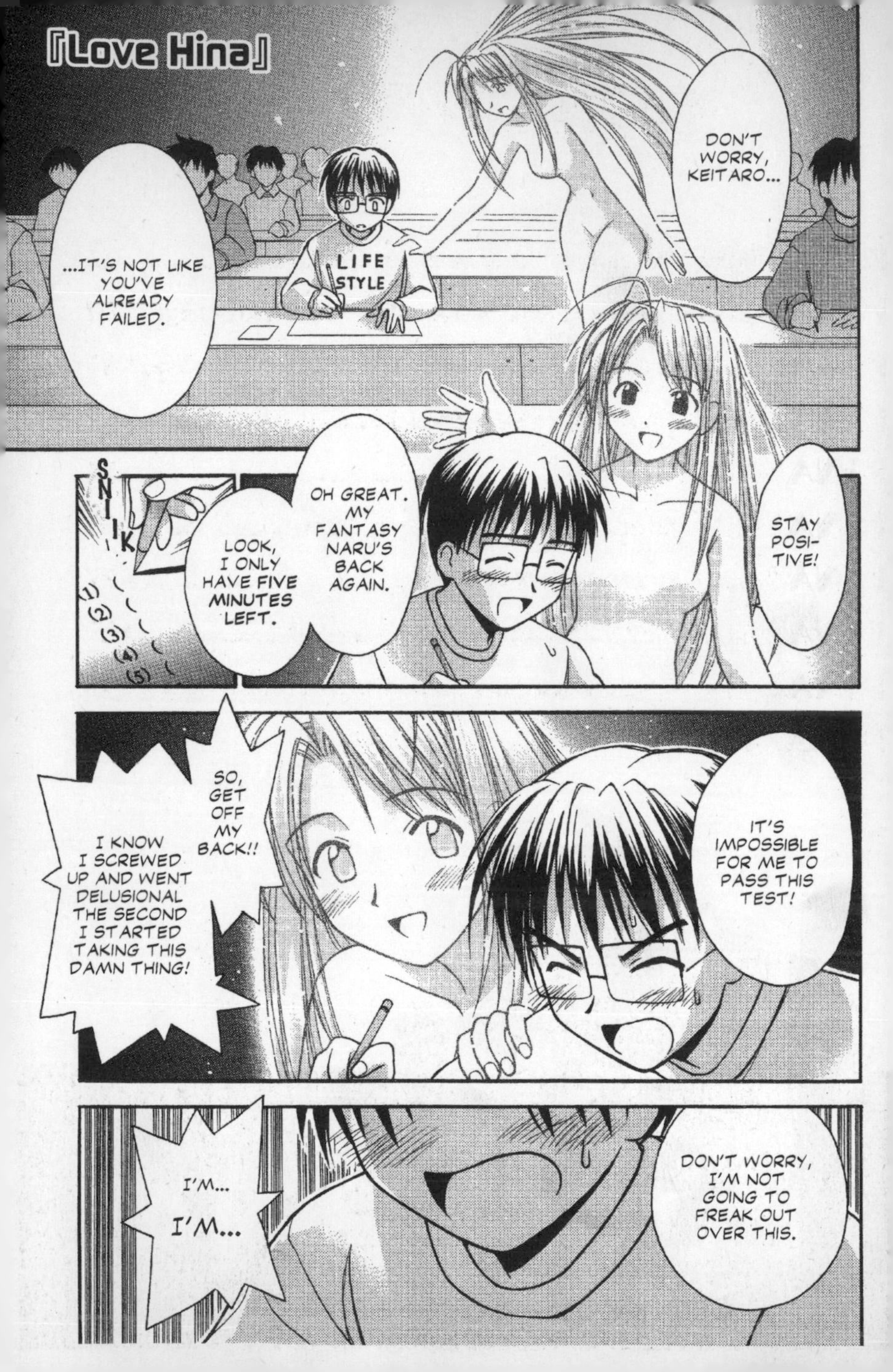
DON'T WORRY, KEITARO...
...IT'S NOT LIKE YOU'VE ALREADY FAILED.
STAY POSI-TIVE!
OH GREAT. MY FANTASY NARU'S BACK AGAIN.
LOOK, I ONLY HAVE FIVE MINUTES LEFT.
SNIIK
(1)
(2)
(3)
(4)
(5)
IT'S IMPOSSIBLE FOR ME TO PASS THIS TEST!
SO, GET OFF MY BACK!!
I KNOW I SCREWED UP AND WENT DELUSIONAL THE SECOND I STARTED TAKING THIS DAMN THING!
DON'T WORRY, I'M NOT GOING TO FREAK OUT OVER THIS.
I'M...
I'M...

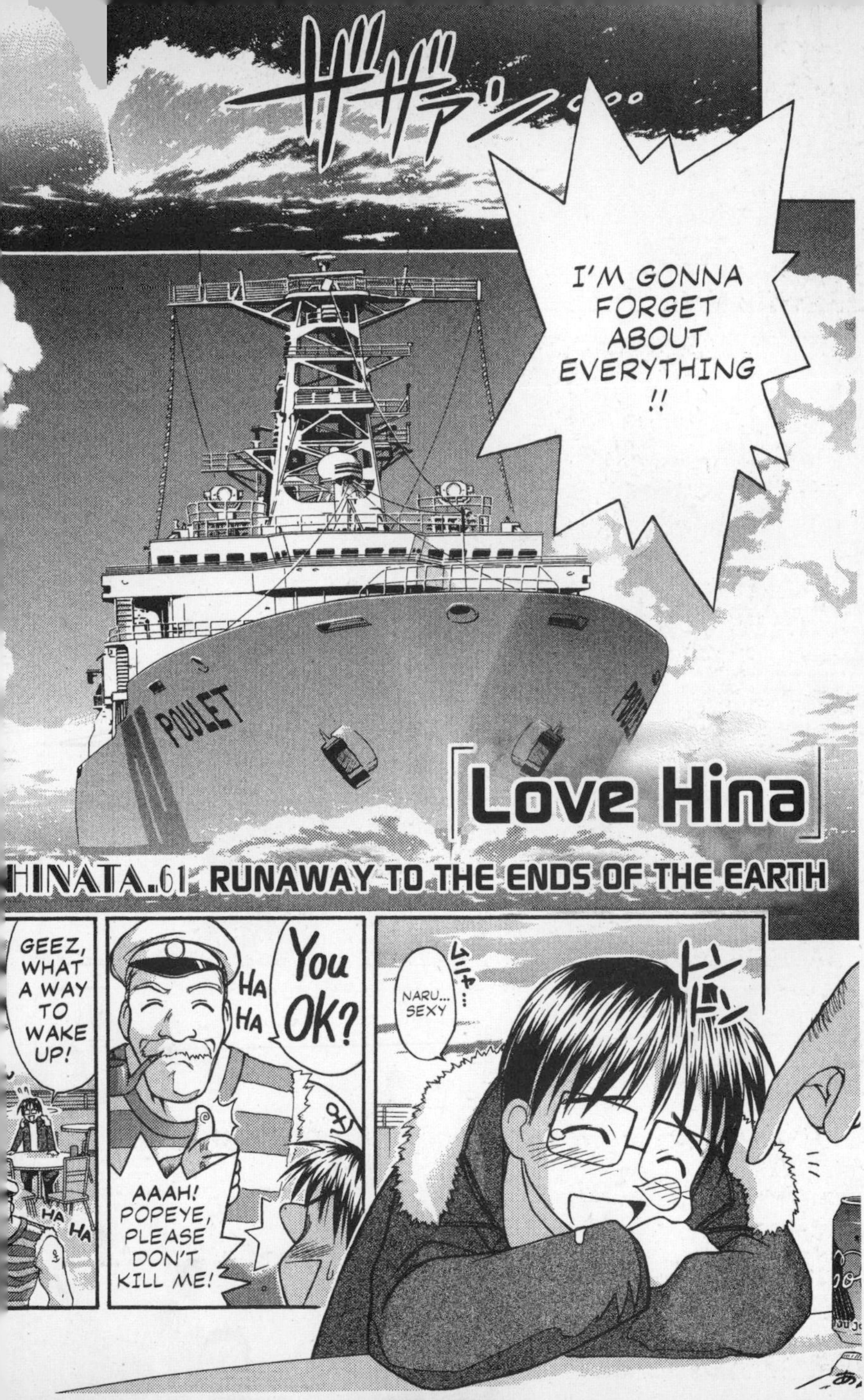
ザザァン。。。
I'M GONNA FORGET ABOUT EVERYTHING !!
POULET
Love Hina
HINATA.61 RUNAWAY TO THE ENDS OF THE EARTH
ムニャ…
NARU... SEXY
You OK?
HA HA
AAAH! POPEYE, PLEASE DON'T KILL ME!
GEEZ, WHAT A WAY TO WAKE UP!
HA HA

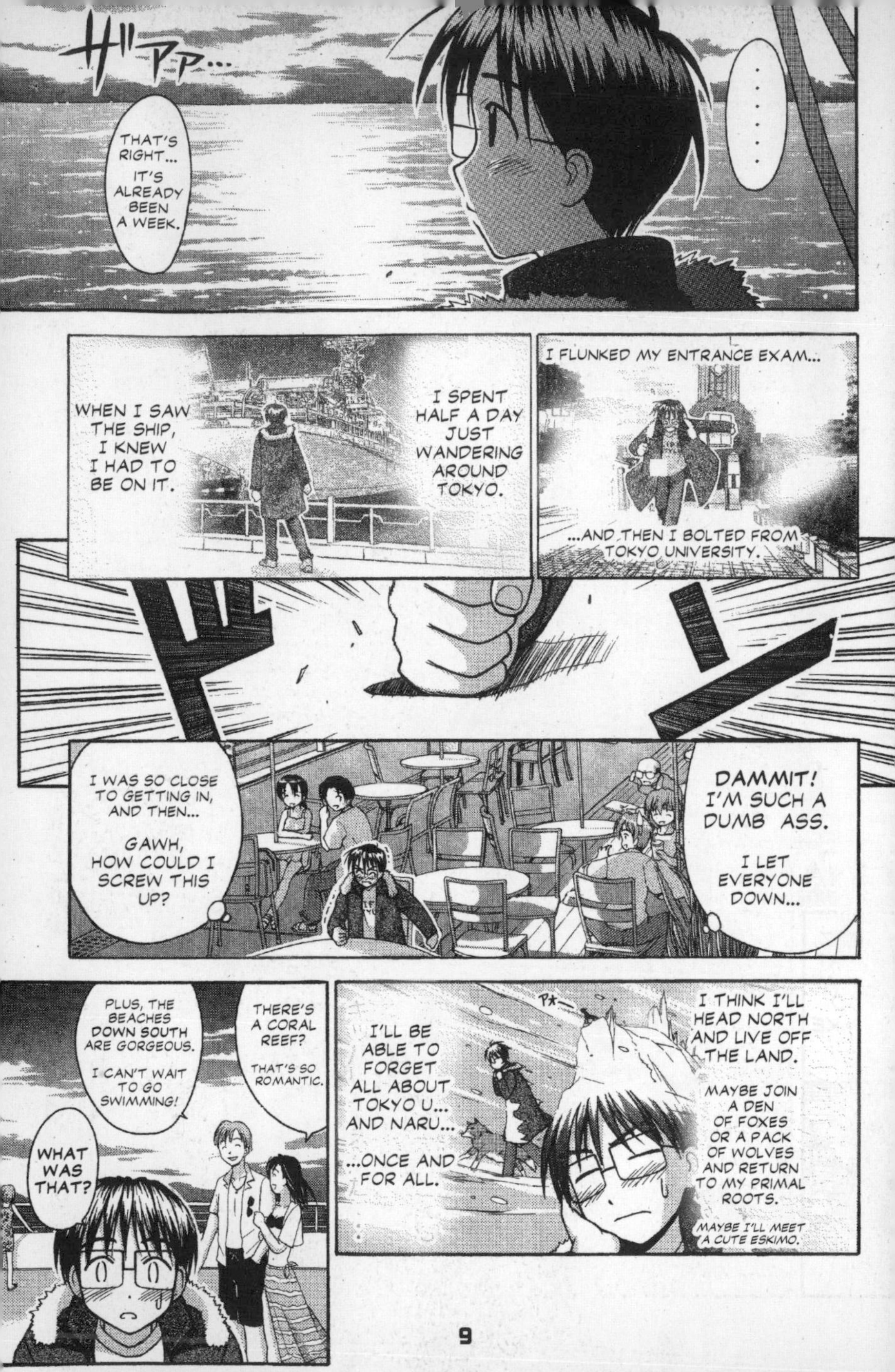
......
ザ"アア...
THAT'S RIGHT... IT'S ALREADY BEEN A WEEK.
I FLUNKED MY ENTRANCE EXAM...
...AND THEN I BOLTED FROM TOKYO UNIVERSITY.
I SPENT HALF A DAY JUST WANDERING AROUND TOKYO.
WHEN I SAW THE SHIP, I KNEW I HAD TO BE ON IT.
DAMMIT! I'M SUCH A DUMB ASS.
I LET EVERYONE DOWN...
I WAS SO CLOSE TO GETTING IN, AND THEN...
GAWH, HOW COULD I SCREW THIS UP?
I THINK I'LL HEAD NORTH AND LIVE OFF THE LAND.
MAYBE JOIN A DEN OF FOXES OR A PACK OF WOLVES AND RETURN TO MY PRIMAL ROOTS.
MAYBE I'LL MEET A CUTE ESKIMO.
I'LL BE ABLE TO FORGET ALL ABOUT TOKYO U... AND NARU...
...ONCE AND FOR ALL.
THERE'S A CORAL REEF?
THAT'S SO ROMANTIC.
PLUS, THE BEACHES DOWN SOUTH ARE GORGEOUS.
I CAN'T WAIT TO GO SWIMMING!
WHAT WAS THAT?

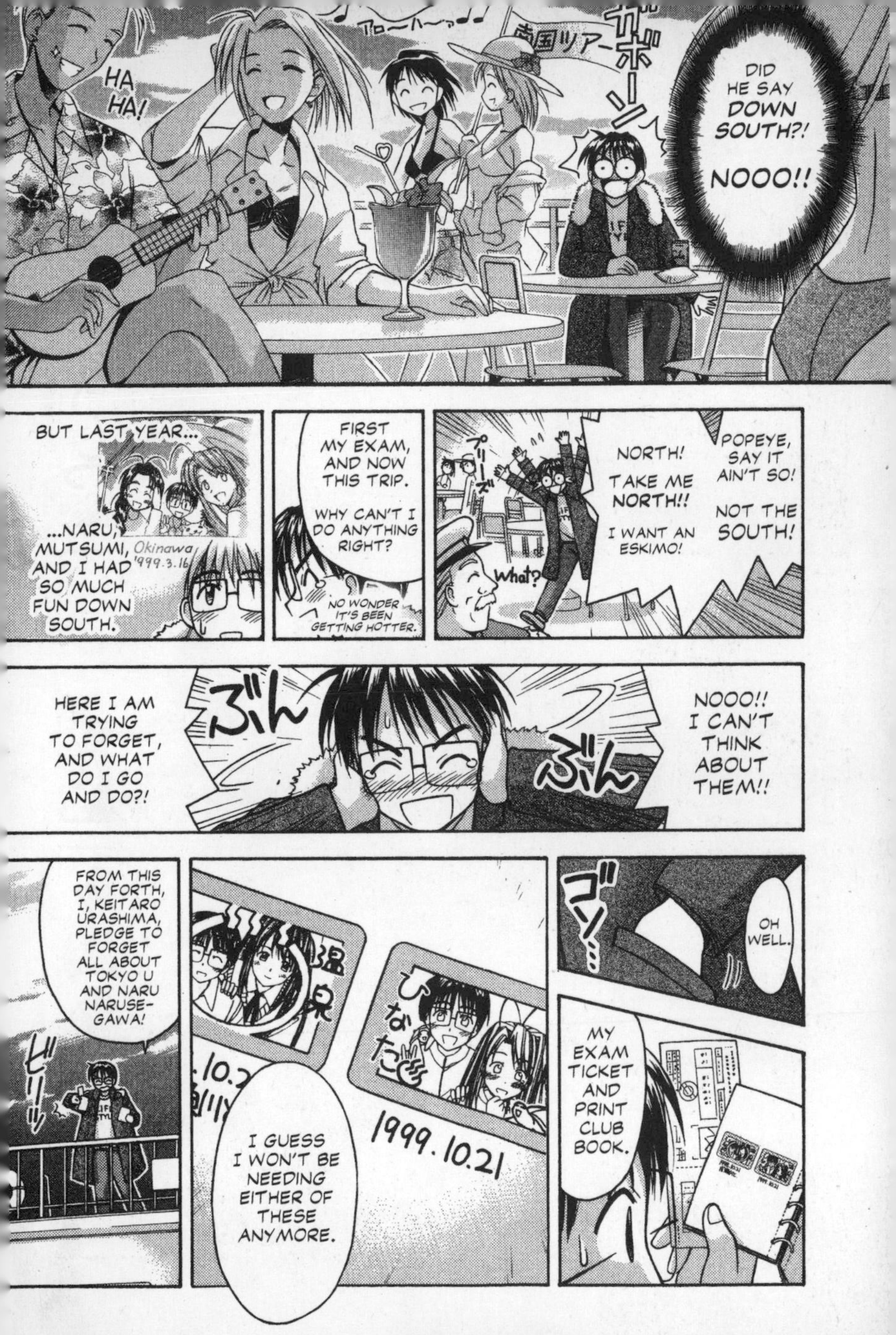

DID HE SAY DOWN SOUTH?!
NOOO!!
ガボーン
南国ツアー
アローハ～ッ♪♪
HA HA!
POPEYE, SAY IT AIN'T SO!
NOT THE SOUTH!
NORTH!
TAKE ME NORTH!!
I WANT AN ESKIMO!
プリーズ
What?
FIRST MY EXAM, AND NOW THIS TRIP.
WHY CAN'T I DO ANYTHING RIGHT?
NO WONDER IT'S BEEN GETTING HOTTER.
BUT LAST YEAR...
Okinawa '999.3.16
...NARU, MUTSUMI, AND I HAD SO MUCH FUN DOWN SOUTH.
NOOO!! I CAN'T THINK ABOUT THEM!!
ぶん
ぶん
HERE I AM TRYING TO FORGET, AND WHAT DO I GO AND DO?!
OH WELL.
ゴソ…
MY EXAM TICKET AND PRINT CLUB BOOK.
ひなた
1999.10.21
I GUESS I WON'T BE NEEDING EITHER OF THESE ANYMORE.
FROM THIS DAY FORTH, I, KEITARO URASHIMA, PLEDGE TO FORGET ALL ABOUT TOKYO U AND NARU NARUSE-GAWA!
ビリーッ

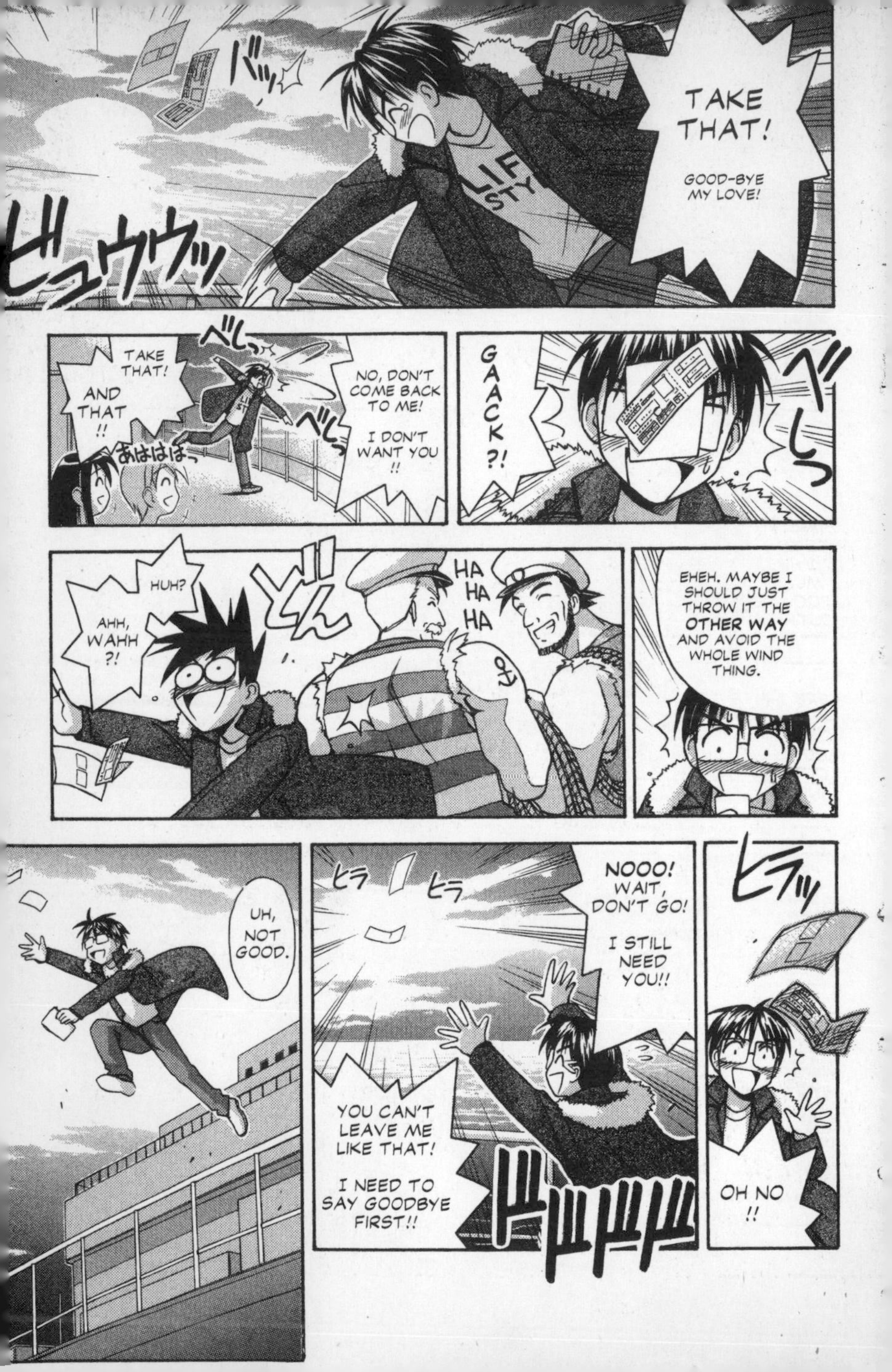
TAKE THAT!
GOOD-BYE MY LOVE!
バッ
ビュウウッ
べしっ
GAACK?!
べしっ
NO, DON'T COME BACK TO ME!
I DON'T WANT YOU!!
TAKE THAT!
AND THAT!!
べしっ
あはははっ
EHEH. MAYBE I SHOULD JUST THROW IT THE OTHER WAY AND AVOID THE WHOLE WIND THING.
HA HA HA
どん
HUH?
AHH, WAHH?!
ヒラッ
OH NO!!
NOOO! WAIT, DON'T GO!
I STILL NEED YOU!!
ヒラ
ヒラ
YOU CAN'T LEAVE ME LIKE THAT!
I NEED TO SAY GOODBYE FIRST!!
UH, NOT GOOD.

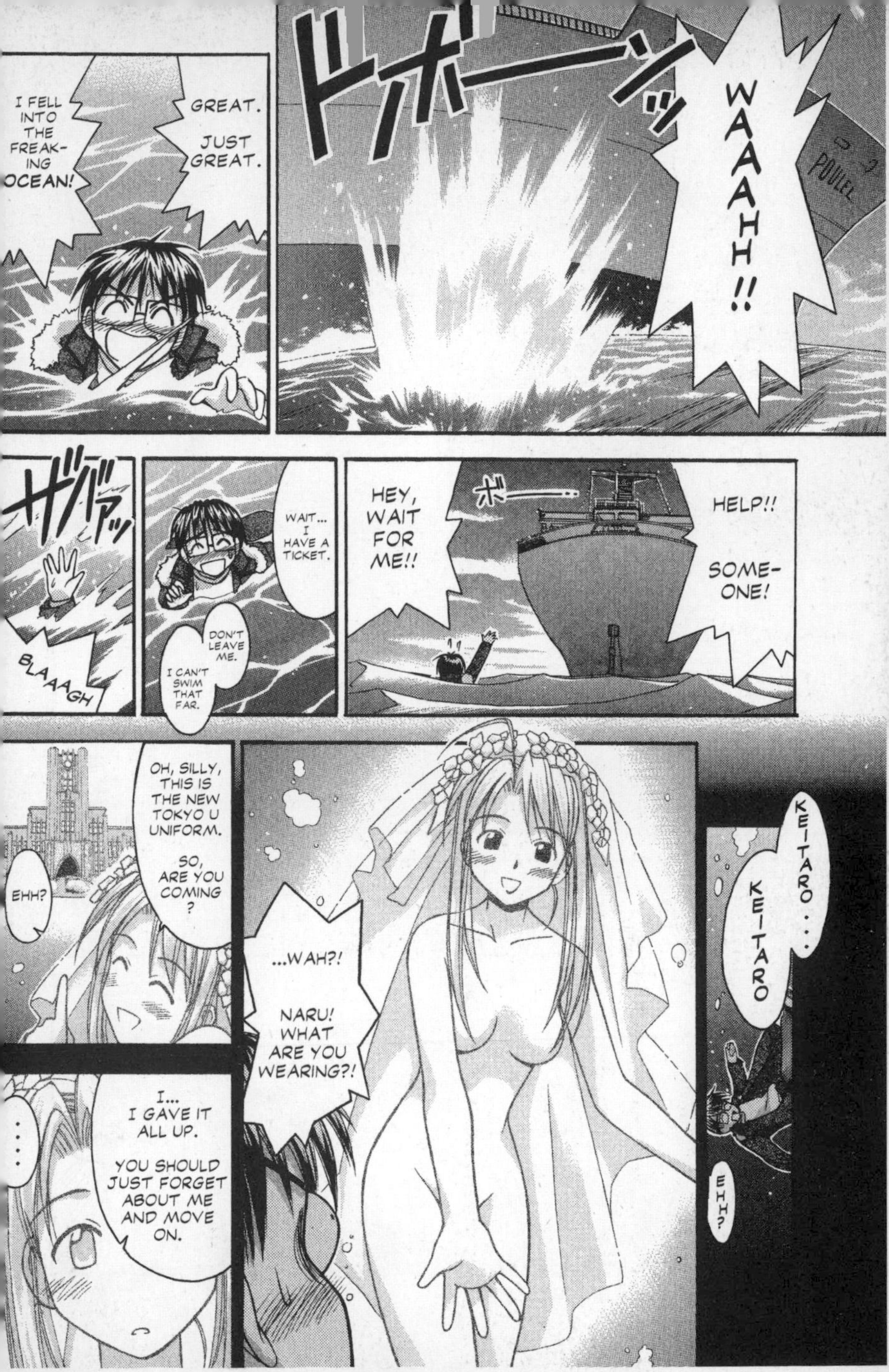
ドボーーッ
WAAAAHH!!
GREAT. JUST GREAT.
I FELL INTO THE FREAKING OCEAN!
HELP!! SOMEONE!
ボーー
HEY, WAIT FOR ME!!
WAIT... I HAVE A TICKET.
DON'T LEAVE ME. I CAN'T SWIM THAT FAR.
ザバァッ
BLAAAGH
KEITARO... KEITARO
EHH?
...WAH?!
NARU! WHAT ARE YOU WEARING?!
OH, SILLY, THIS IS THE NEW TOKYO U UNIFORM.
SO, ARE YOU COMING?
EHH?
I... I GAVE IT ALL UP.
YOU SHOULD JUST FORGET ABOUT ME AND MOVE ON.
....

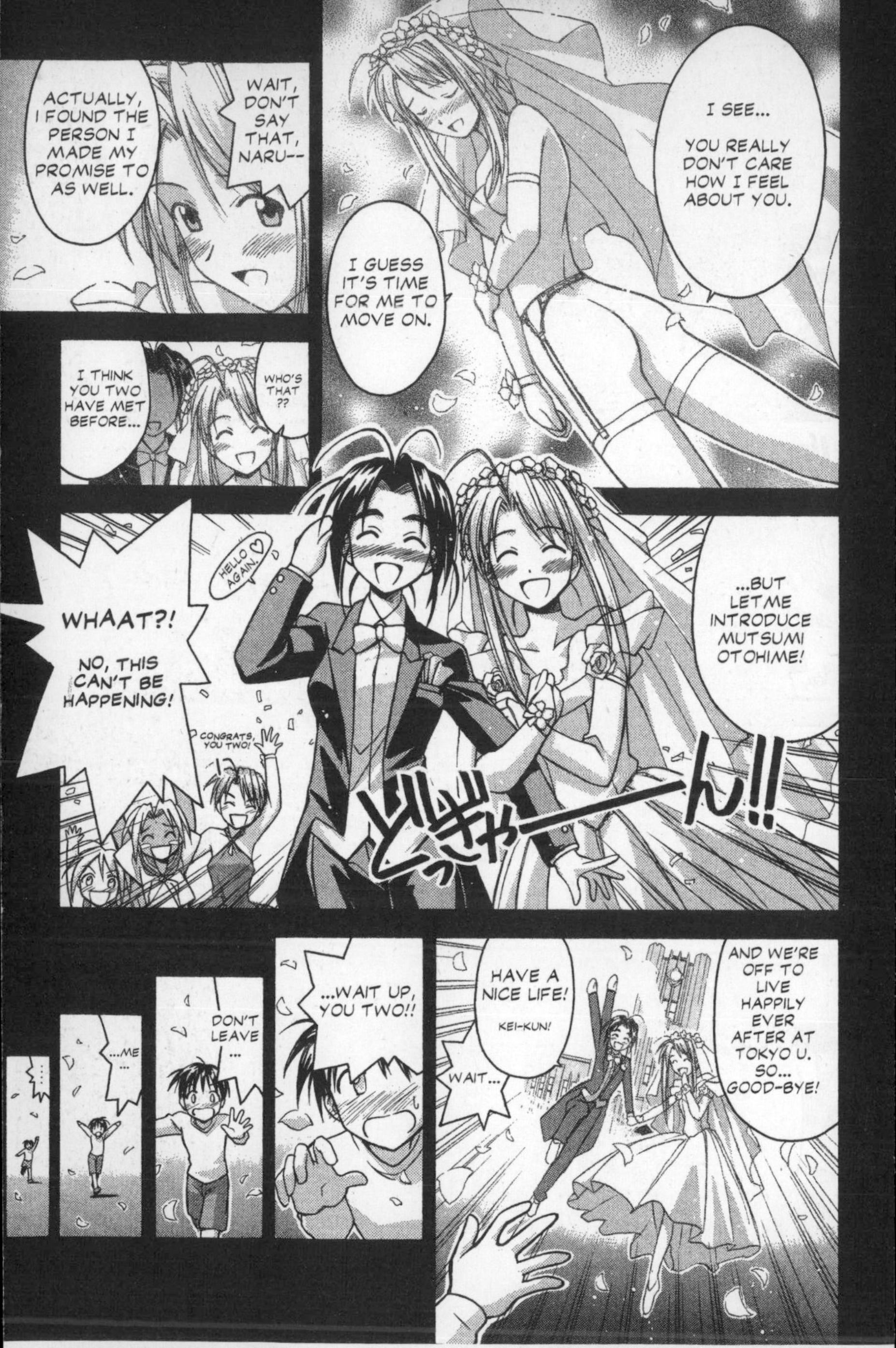
I SEE...
YOU REALLY DON'T CARE HOW I FEEL ABOUT YOU.
I GUESS IT'S TIME FOR ME TO MOVE ON.
ACTUALLY, I FOUND THE PERSON I MADE MY PROMISE TO AS WELL.
WAIT, DON'T SAY THAT, NARU--
I THINK YOU TWO HAVE MET BEFORE...
WHO'S THAT??
...BUT LETME INTRODUCE MUTSUMI OTOHIME!
HELLO AGAIN. ♥
どっぎゃーん!!
WHAAT?!
NO, THIS CAN'T BE HAPPENING!
CONGRATS, YOU TWO!
AND WE'RE OFF TO LIVE HAPPILY EVER AFTER AT TOKYO U. SO... GOOD-BYE!
HAVE A NICE LIFE!
KEI-KUN!
WAIT...
...WAIT UP, YOU TWO!!
DON'T LEAVE ...
...ME ...
......

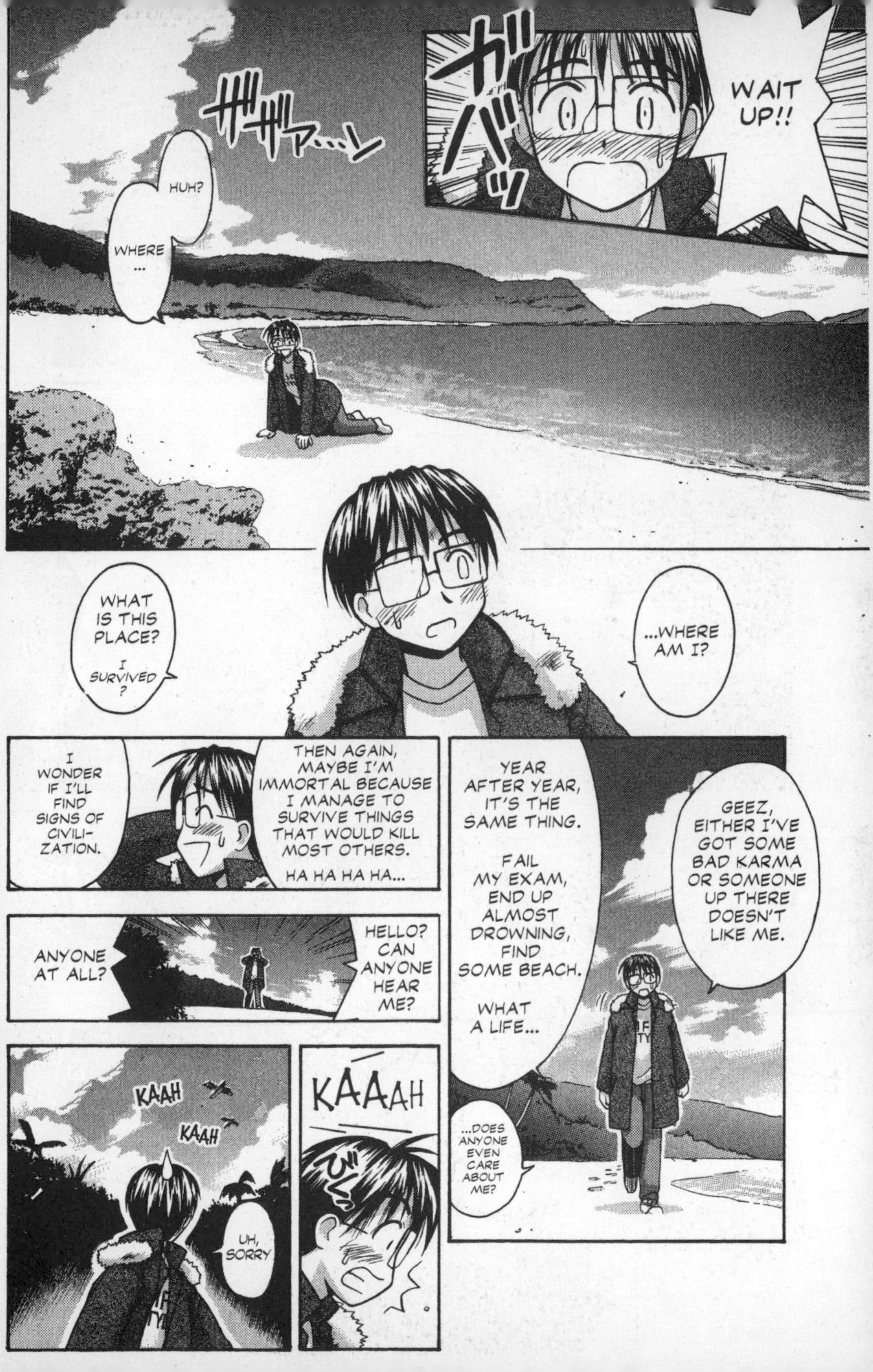
ガバッ
WAIT UP!!
ザザァ…ン
HUH?
WHERE ...
...WHERE AM I?
WHAT IS THIS PLACE?
I SURVIVED?
GEEZ, EITHER I'VE GOT SOME BAD KARMA OR SOMEONE UP THERE DOESN'T LIKE ME.
YEAR AFTER YEAR, IT'S THE SAME THING.
FAIL MY EXAM, END UP ALMOST DROWNING, FIND SOME BEACH.
WHAT A LIFE...
...DOES ANYONE EVEN CARE ABOUT ME?
THEN AGAIN, MAYBE I'M IMMORTAL BECAUSE I MANAGE TO SURVIVE THINGS THAT WOULD KILL MOST OTHERS.
HA HA HA HA...
I WONDER IF I'LL FIND SIGNS OF CIVILI-ZATION.
HELLO? CAN ANYONE HEAR ME?
ANYONE AT ALL?
KAAAH
KAAH
KAAH
UH, SORRY

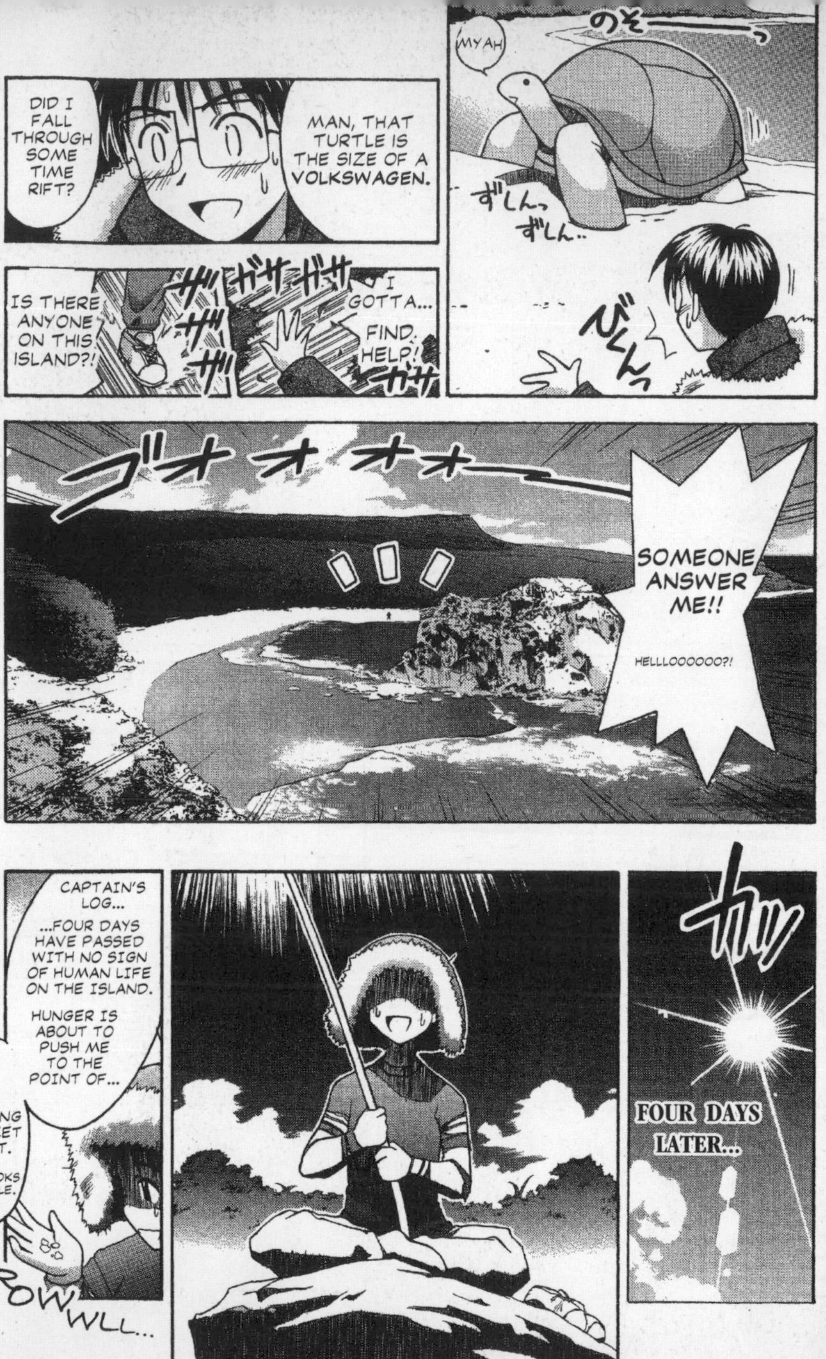
MYAH
のそーーっ
ずしんっ ずしん..
びくんっ
MAN, THAT TURTLE IS THE SIZE OF A VOLKSWAGEN.
DID I FALL THROUGH SOME TIME RIFT?
I GOTTA... FIND. HELP!
ガサ
ガサガサ
ザザザザ
IS THERE ANYONE ON THIS ISLAND?!
ゴオオオオー
SOMEONE ANSWER ME!!
HELLLOOOOOO?!
カッ
FOUR DAYS LATER...
CAPTAIN'S LOG...
...FOUR DAYS HAVE PASSED WITH NO SIGN OF HUMAN LIFE ON THE ISLAND.
HUNGER IS ABOUT TO PUSH ME TO THE POINT OF...
...EATING POCKET LINT.
IT LOOKS EDIBLE.
GRROWWLL...

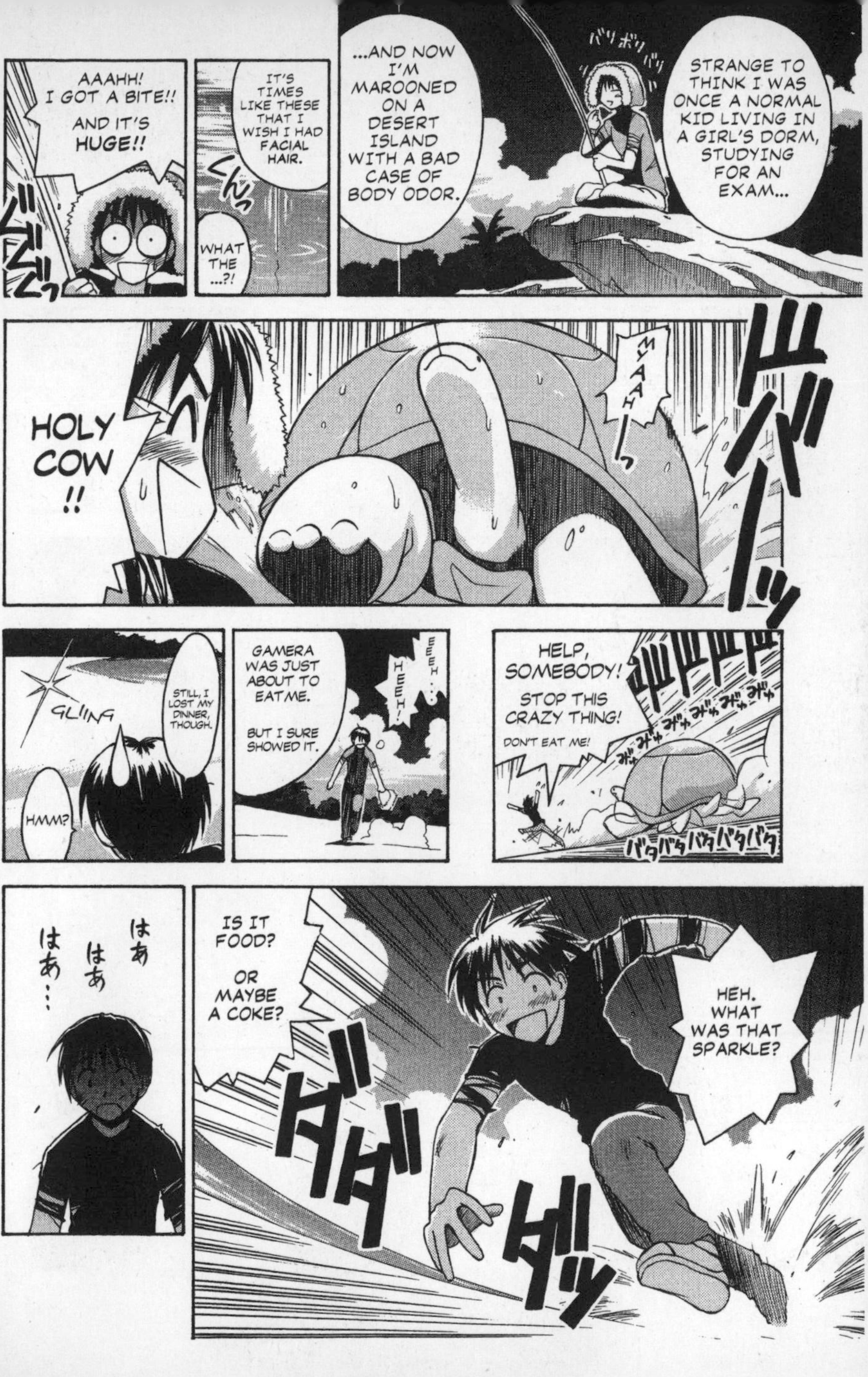
STRANGE TO THINK I WAS ONCE A NORMAL KID LIVING IN A GIRL'S DORM, STUDYING FOR AN EXAM...
...AND NOW I'M MAROONED ON A DESERT ISLAND WITH A BAD CASE OF BODY ODOR.
IT'S TIMES LIKE THESE THAT I WISH I HAD FACIAL HAIR.
くんっ
WHAT THE ...?!
AAAHH! I GOT A BITE!!
AND IT'S HUGE!!
ぐぐぐっ
ザバーッ
MYAAH!~っ
HOLY COW!!
HELP, SOMEBODY!
STOP THIS CRAZY THING!
DON'T EAT ME!
ドドドド
バタバタバタバタ
EEEH... HEEH!
GAMERA WAS JUST ABOUT TO EAT ME.
BUT I SURE SHOWED IT.
STILL, I LOST MY DINNER, THOUGH.
GLIING
HMM?
HEH. WHAT WAS THAT SPARKLE?
IS IT FOOD?
OR MAYBE A COKE?
ダダダッ
はあ はあ はあ…

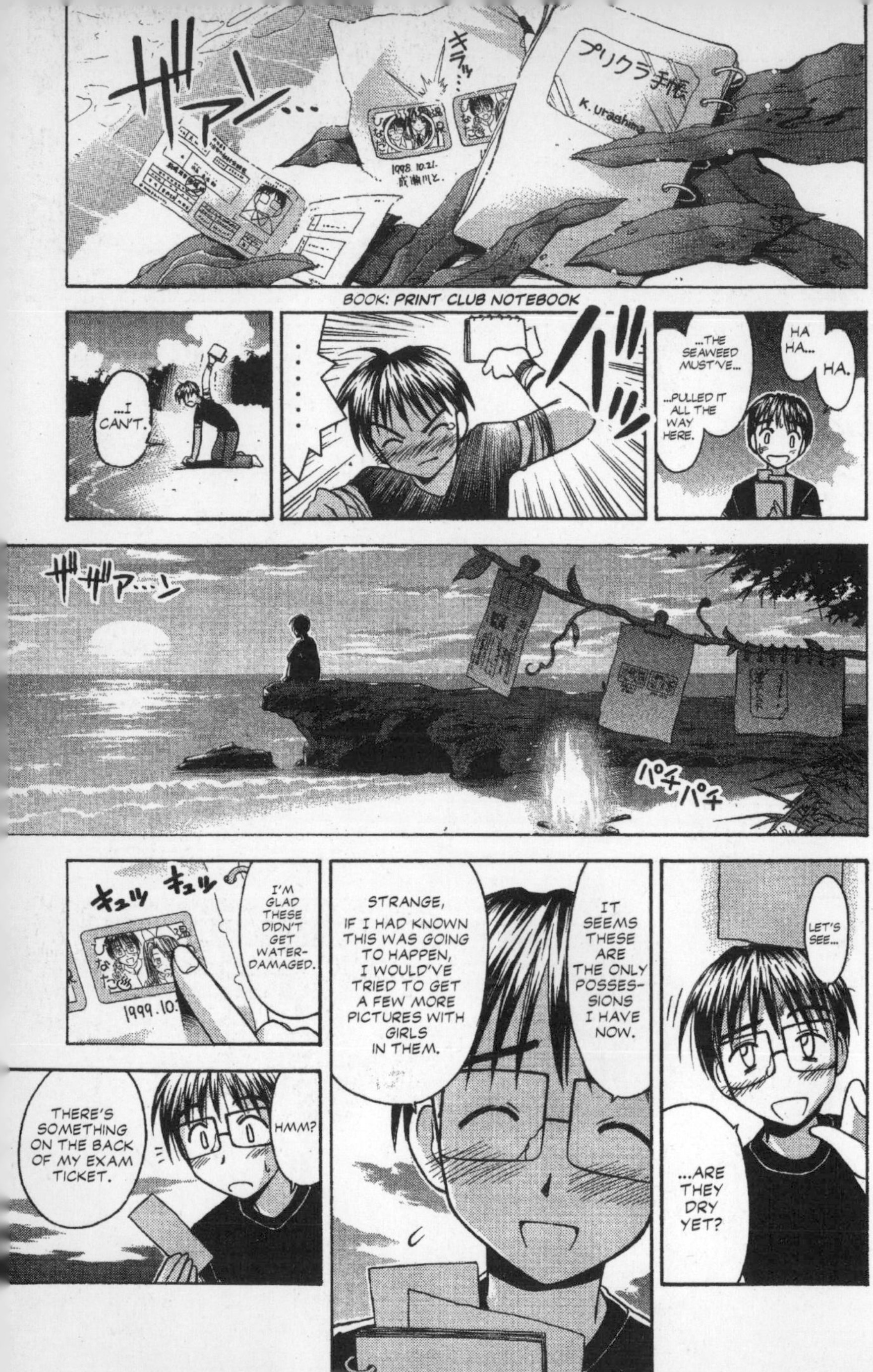

ザァー…
キラッ
プリクラ手帳
K. Urashima
1998.10.21.
成瀬川と.
BOOK: PRINT CLUB NOTEBOOK
HA HA... HA.
...THE SEAWEED MUST'VE...
...PULLED IT ALL THE WAY HERE.
......
バッ
...I CAN'T.
ザザァ…ン
パチパチ
LET'S SEE...
...ARE THEY DRY YET?
IT SEEMS THESE ARE THE ONLY POSSESSIONS I HAVE NOW.
STRANGE, IF I HAD KNOWN THIS WAS GOING TO HAPPEN, I WOULD'VE TRIED TO GET A FEW MORE PICTURES WITH GIRLS IN THEM.
キュッ キュッ
I'M GLAD THESE DIDN'T GET WATER-DAMAGED.
1999.10.
HMM?
THERE'S SOMETHING ON THE BACK OF MY EXAM TICKET.

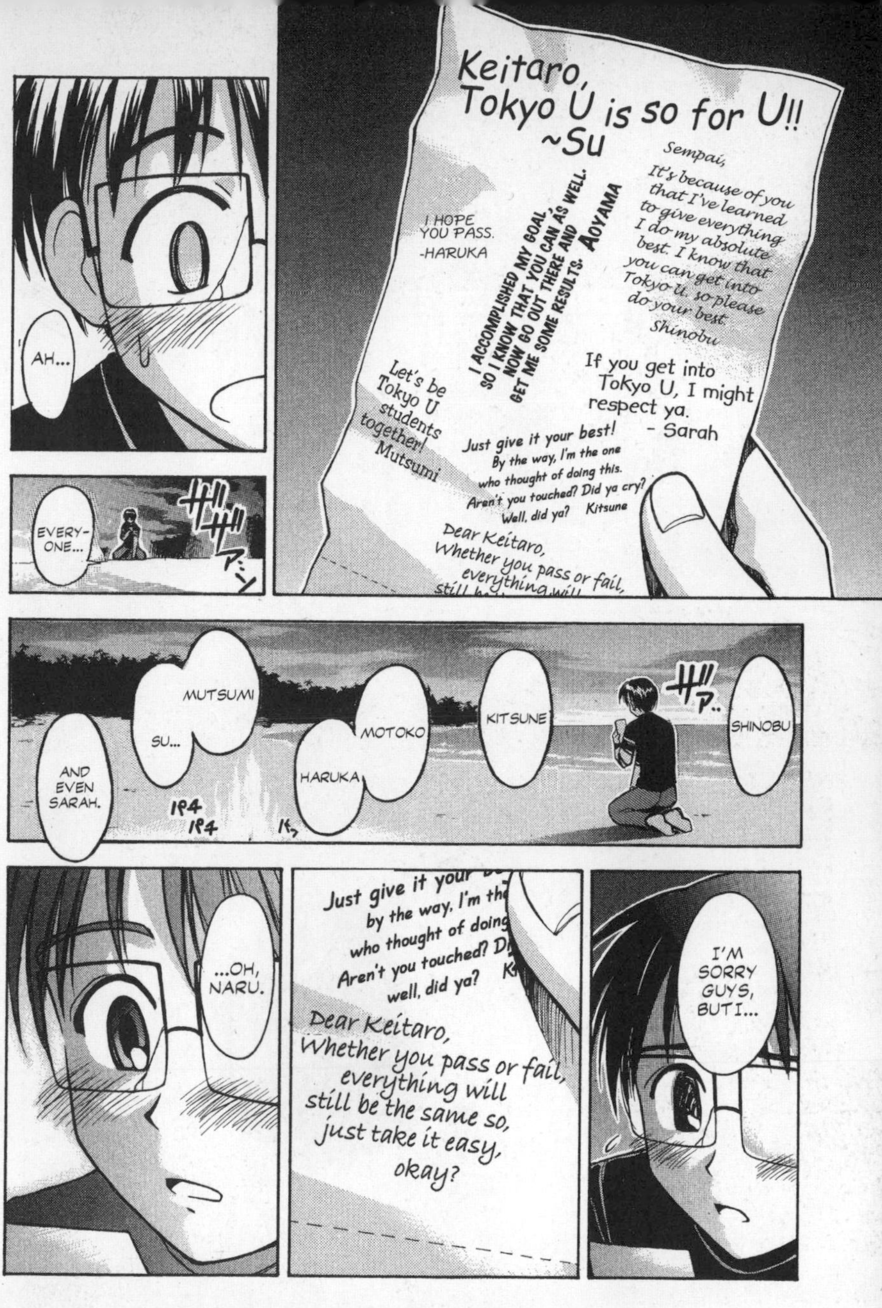
Keitaro, Tokyo U is so for U!! ~Su
Sempai, It's because of you that I've learned to give everything I do my absolute best. I know that you can get into Tokyo U. so please do your best. Shinobu
I ACCOMPLISHED MY GOAL, SO I KNOW THAT YOU CAN AS WELL. NOW GO OUT THERE AND GET ME SOME RESULTS. AOYAMA
I HOPE YOU PASS. -HARUKA
If you get into Tokyo U, I might respect ya. - Sarah
Let's be Tokyo U students together! Mutsumi
Just give it your best! By the way, I'm the one who thought of doing this. Aren't you touched? Did ya cry? Well, did ya? Kitsune
Dear Keitaro, Whether you pass or fail, everything will
AH...
EVERY-ONE...
SHINOBU
KITSUNE
MOTOKO
HARUKA
MUTSUMI
SU...
AND EVEN SARAH.
I'M SORRY GUYS, BUT I...
Dear Keitaro, Whether you pass or fail, everything will still be the same so, just take it easy, okay?
...OH, NARU.

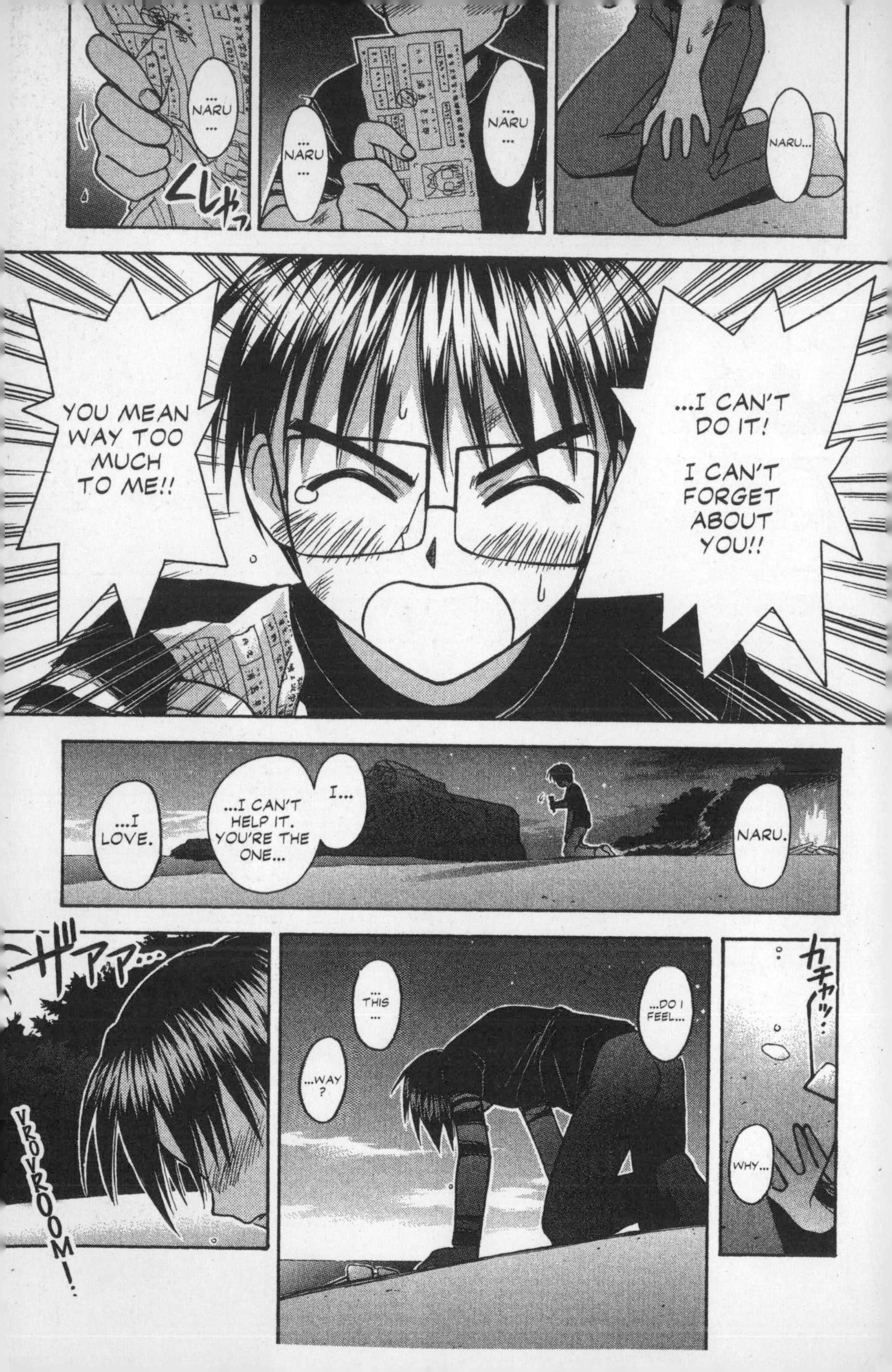
NARU...
...NARU...
...NARU...
...NARU...
くしゃっ
...I CAN'T DO IT!
I CAN'T FORGET ABOUT YOU!!
YOU MEAN WAY TOO MUCH TO ME!!
NARU.
I...
...I CAN'T HELP IT. YOU'RE THE ONE...
...I LOVE.
カチャッ…
WHY...
...DO I FEEL...
...THIS...
...WAY?
ザァァ...
VROVROOM!

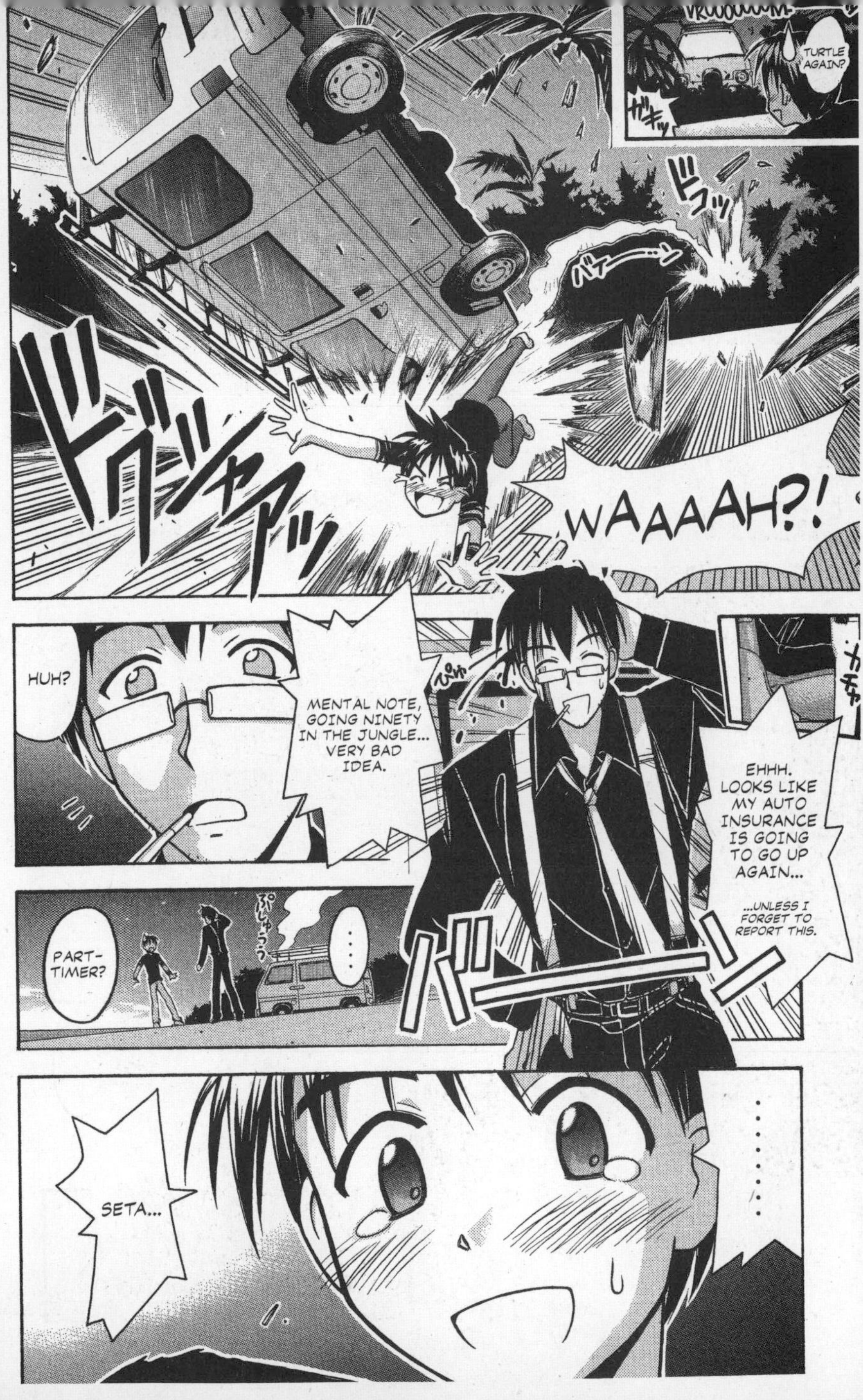
TURTLE AGAIN?
WAAAAH?!
EHHH. LOOKS LIKE MY AUTO INSURANCE IS GOING TO GO UP AGAIN...
...UNLESS I FORGET TO REPORT THIS.
MENTAL NOTE, GOING NINETY IN THE JUNGLE... VERY BAD IDEA.
HUH?
....
PART-TIMER?
....
SETA...

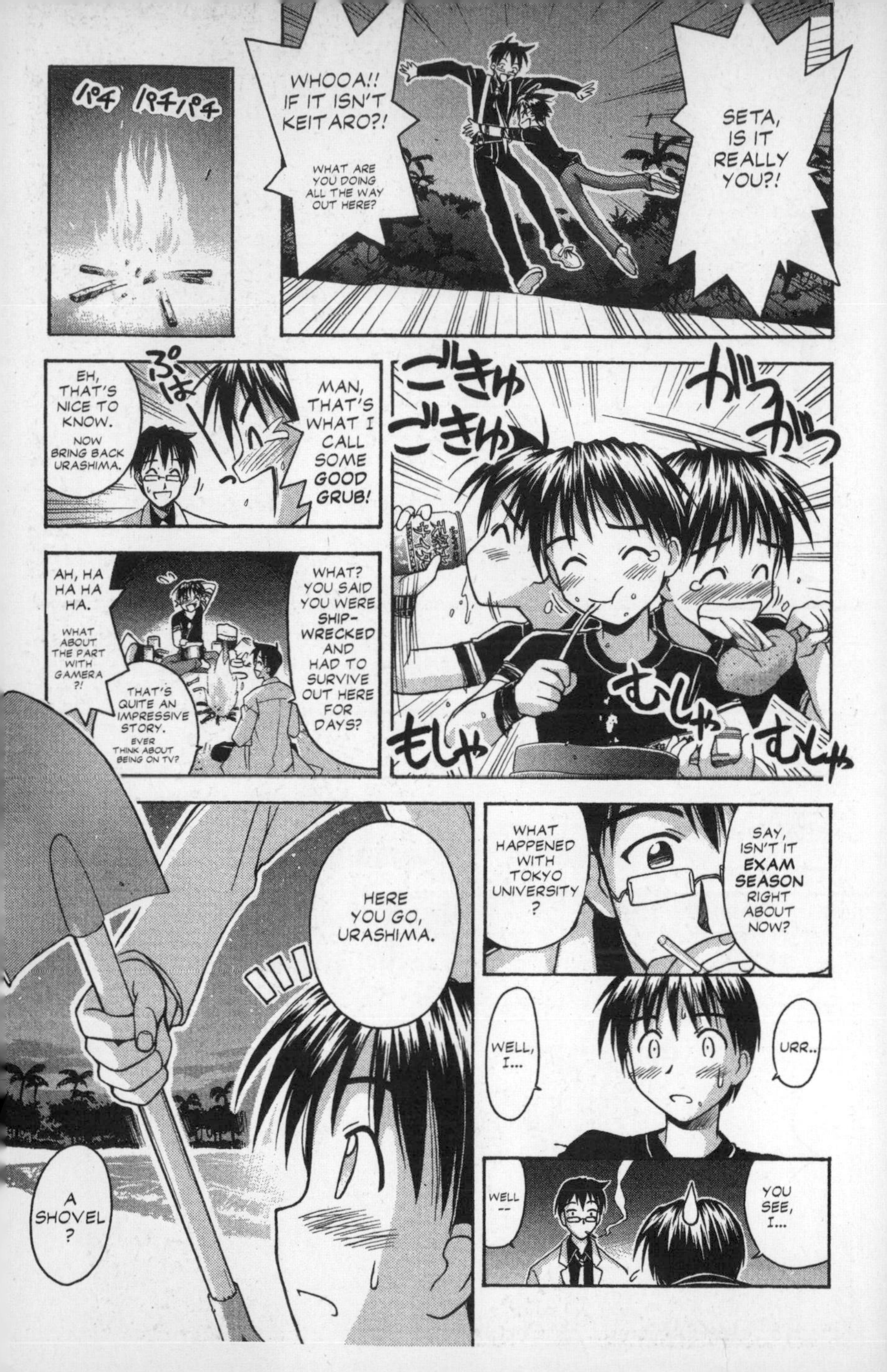
SETA, IS IT REALLY YOU?!
WHOOA!! IF IT ISN'T KEITARO?!
WHAT ARE YOU DOING ALL THE WAY OUT HERE?
パチ パチパチ
がつがつ
ごきゅ ごきゅ
むしゃ むしゃ
もしゃ
MAN, THAT'S WHAT I CALL SOME **GOOD GRUB!**
ぷは
EH, THAT'S NICE TO KNOW.
NOW BRING BACK URASHIMA.
WHAT? YOU SAID YOU WERE **SHIP-WRECKED** AND HAD TO SURVIVE OUT HERE FOR DAYS?
AH, HA HA HA HA.
WHAT ABOUT THE PART WITH GAMERA ?!
THAT'S QUITE AN IMPRESSIVE STORY.
EVER THINK ABOUT BEING ON TV?
SAY, ISN'T IT **EXAM SEASON** RIGHT ABOUT NOW?
WHAT HAPPENED WITH TOKYO UNIVERSITY ?
URR..
WELL, I...
YOU SEE, I...
WELL --
HERE YOU GO, URASHIMA.
A SHOVEL ?

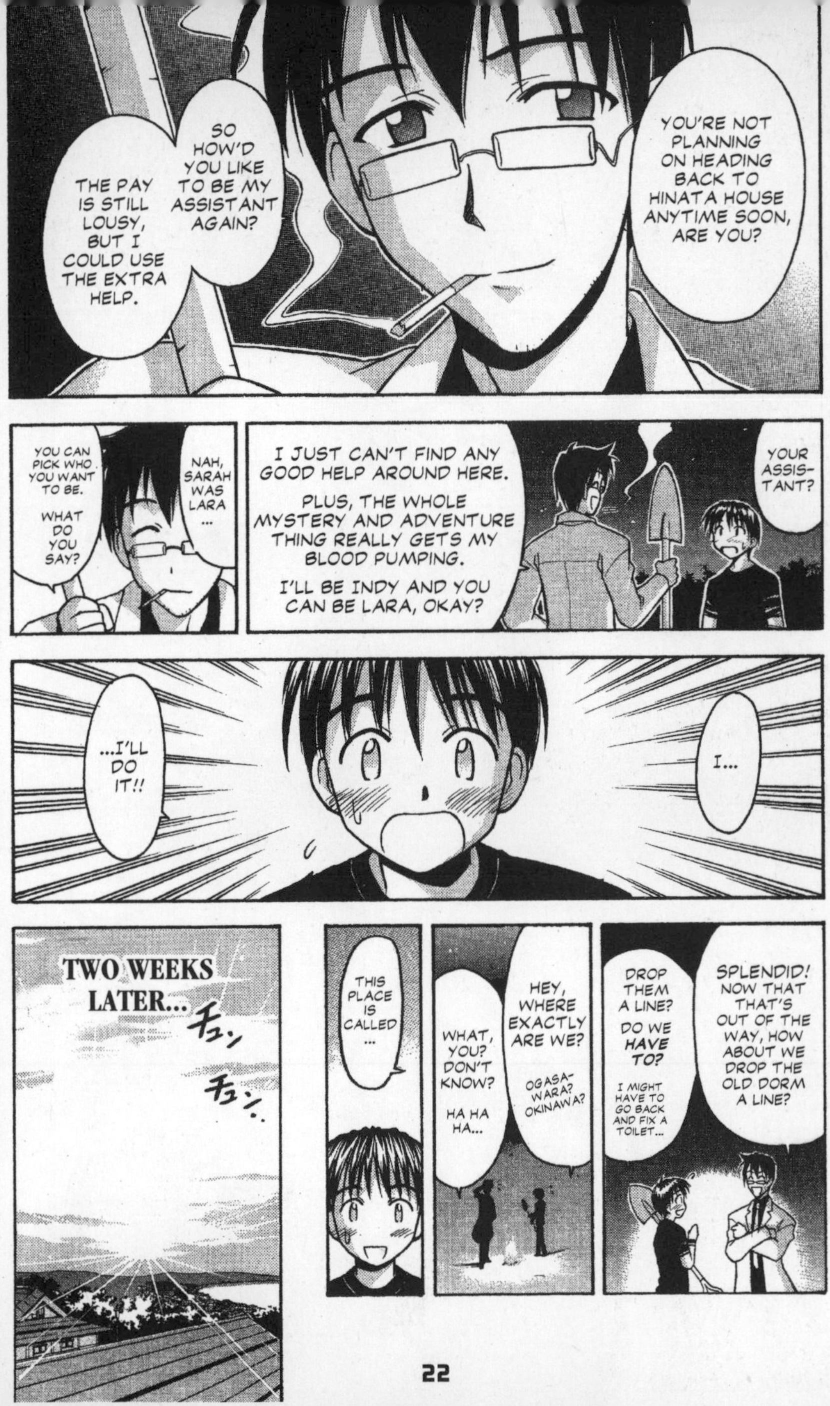
YOU'RE NOT PLANNING ON HEADING BACK TO HINATA HOUSE ANYTIME SOON, ARE YOU?
SO HOW'D YOU LIKE TO BE MY ASSISTANT AGAIN?
THE PAY IS STILL LOUSY, BUT I COULD USE THE EXTRA HELP.
YOUR ASSIS-TANT?
I JUST CAN'T FIND ANY GOOD HELP AROUND HERE.
PLUS, THE WHOLE MYSTERY AND ADVENTURE THING REALLY GETS MY BLOOD PUMPING.
I'LL BE INDY AND YOU CAN BE LARA, OKAY?
NAH, SARAH WAS LARA ...
YOU CAN PICK WHO YOU WANT TO BE.
WHAT DO YOU SAY?
I...
...I'LL DO IT!!
SPLENDID! NOW THAT THAT'S OUT OF THE WAY, HOW ABOUT WE DROP THE OLD DORM A LINE?
DROP THEM A LINE?
DO WE *HAVE TO?*
I MIGHT HAVE TO GO BACK AND FIX A TOILET...
HEY, WHERE EXACTLY ARE WE?
OGASA-WARA? OKINAWA?
WHAT, YOU? DON'T KNOW?
HA HA HA...
THIS PLACE IS CALLED ...
TWO WEEKS LATER...
チュン
チュン..

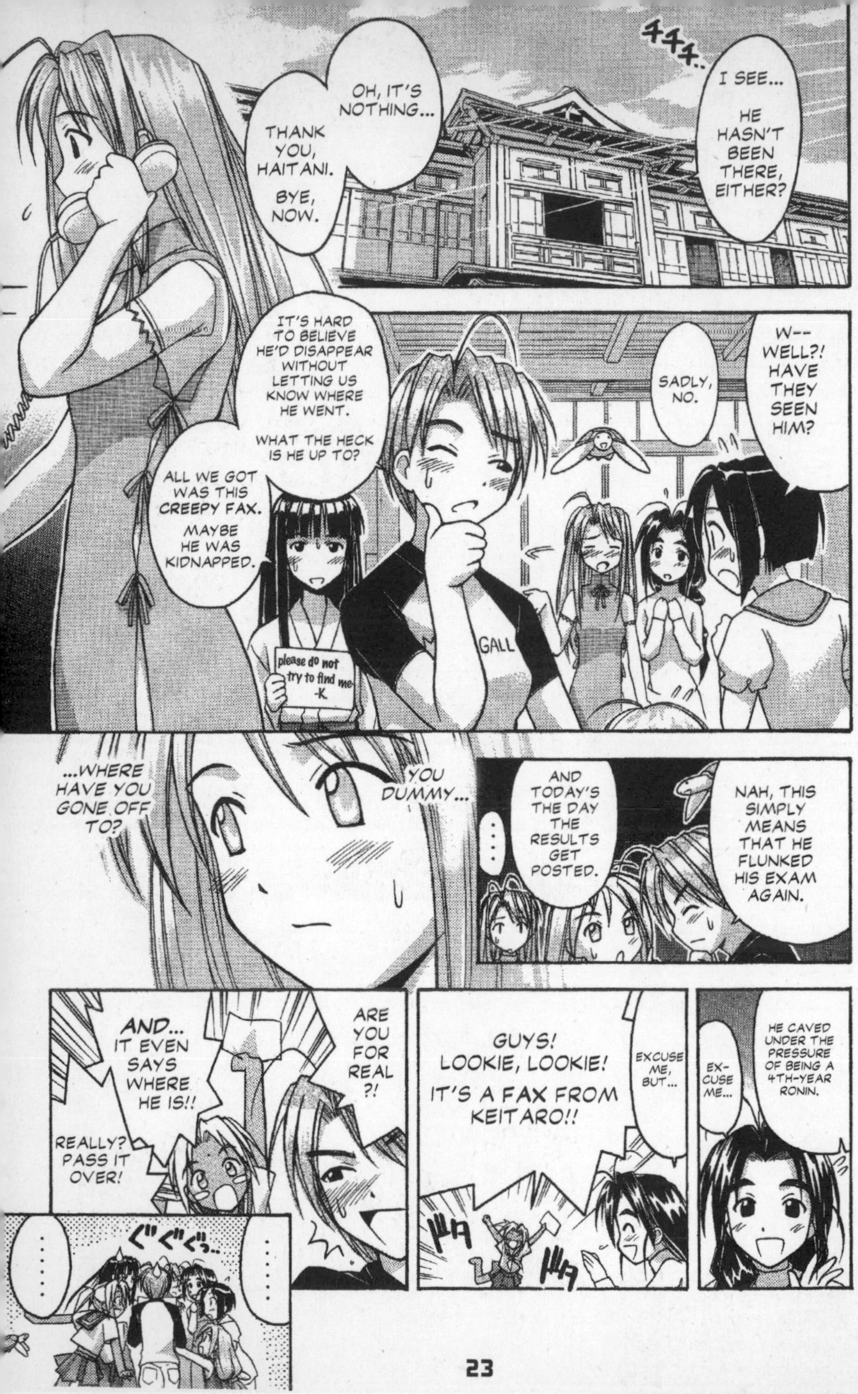
チチチ..
I SEE... HE HASN'T BEEN THERE, EITHER?
OH, IT'S NOTHING... THANK YOU, HAITANI. BYE, NOW.
W-- WELL?! HAVE THEY SEEN HIM?
SADLY, NO.
IT'S HARD TO BELIEVE HE'D DISAPPEAR WITHOUT LETTING US KNOW WHERE HE WENT. WHAT THE HECK IS HE UP TO?
ALL WE GOT WAS THIS CREEPY FAX. MAYBE HE WAS KIDNAPPED.
GALL
please do not try to find me -K.
NAH, THIS SIMPLY MEANS THAT HE FLUNKED HIS EXAM AGAIN.
AND TODAY'S THE DAY THE RESULTS GET POSTED.
....
YOU DUMMY...
...WHERE HAVE YOU GONE OFF TO?
HE CAVED UNDER THE PRESSURE OF BEING A 4TH-YEAR RONIN.
EX-CUSE ME...
EXCUSE ME, BUT...
GUYS! LOOKIE, LOOKIE! IT'S A FAX FROM KEITARO!!
ドタ
ドタ
ARE YOU FOR REAL?!
AND... IT EVEN SAYS WHERE HE IS!!
REALLY? PASS IT OVER!
....
ぐぐぐっ..
....

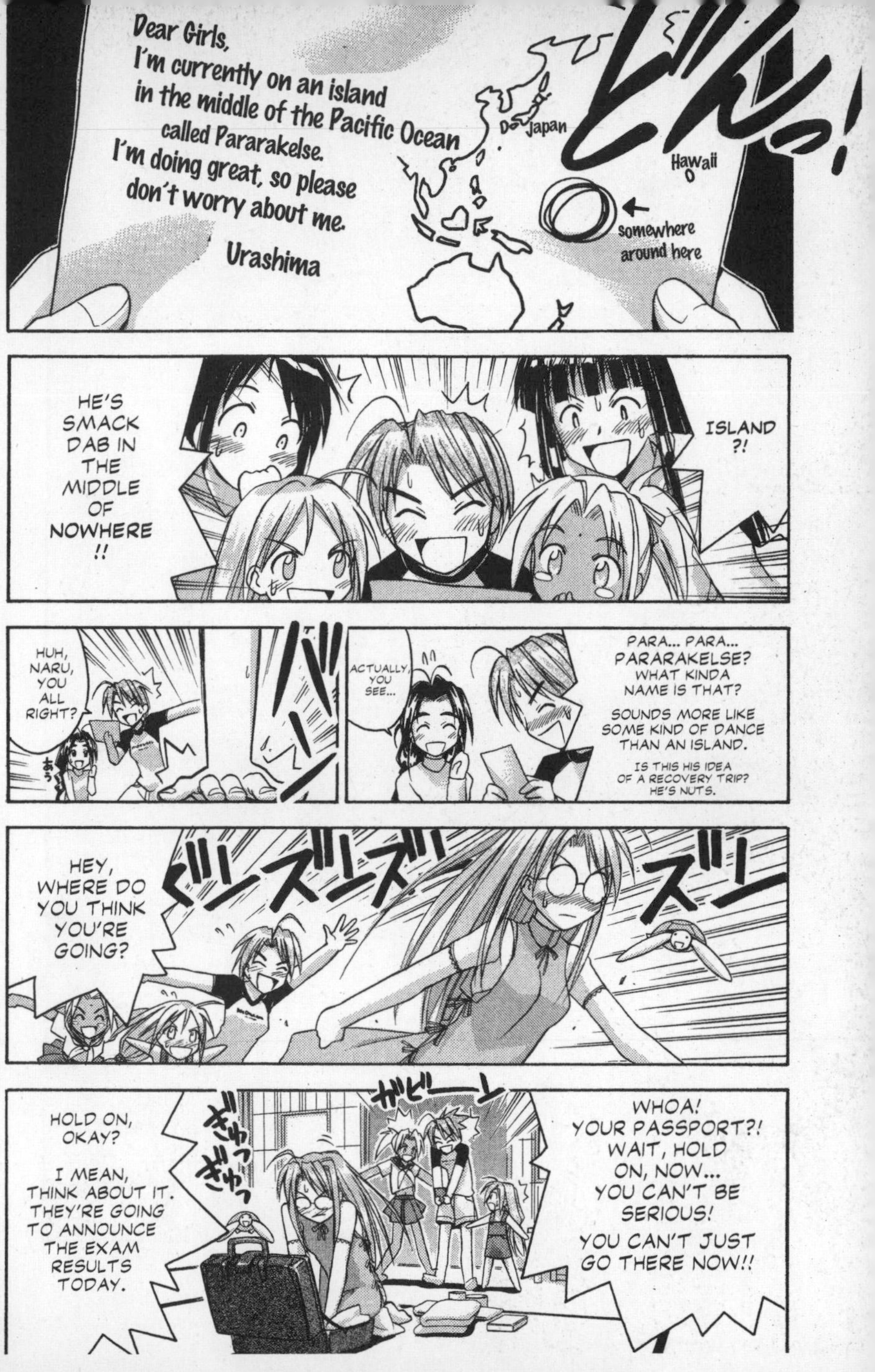
Dear Girls,
I'm currently on an island in the middle of the Pacific Ocean called Pararakelse.
I'm doing great, so please don't worry about me.
Urashima
Japan
Hawaii
somewhere around here
ISLAND ?!
HE'S SMACK DAB IN THE MIDDLE OF NOWHERE !!
PARA... PARA... PARARAKELSE? WHAT KINDA NAME IS THAT?
SOUNDS MORE LIKE SOME KIND OF DANCE THAN AN ISLAND.
IS THIS HIS IDEA OF A RECOVERY TRIP? HE'S NUTS.
ACTUALLY, YOU SEE...
HUH, NARU, YOU ALL RIGHT?
HEY, WHERE DO YOU THINK YOU'RE GOING?
WHOA! YOUR PASSPORT?! WAIT, HOLD ON, NOW... YOU CAN'T BE SERIOUS!
YOU CAN'T JUST GO THERE NOW!!
HOLD ON, OKAY?
I MEAN, THINK ABOUT IT. THEY'RE GOING TO ANNOUNCE THE EXAM RESULTS TODAY.

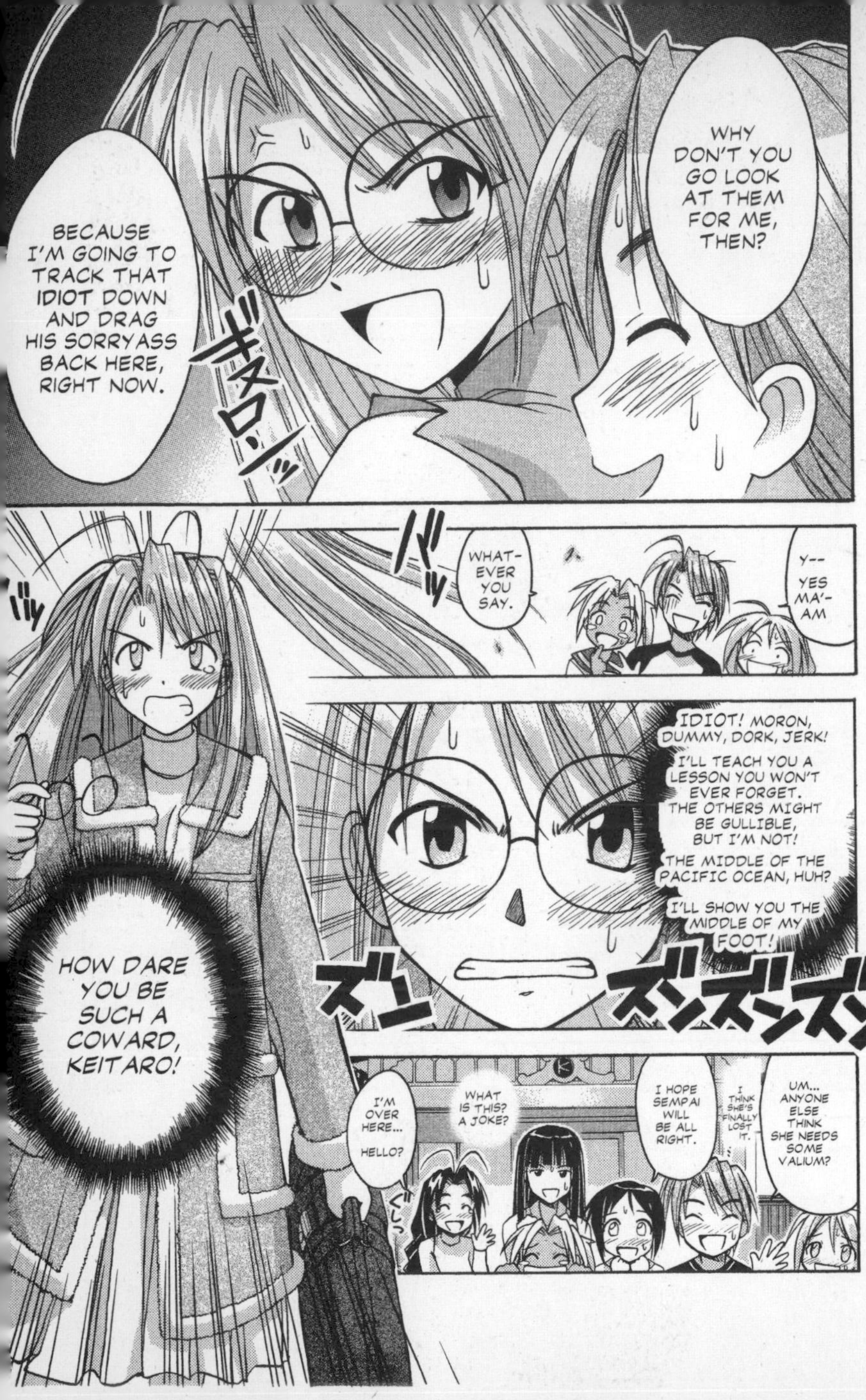
WHY DON'T YOU GO LOOK AT THEM FOR ME, THEN?
BECAUSE I'M GOING TO TRACK THAT IDIOT DOWN AND DRAG HIS SORRYASS BACK HERE, RIGHT NOW.
Y-- YES MA'AM
WHAT-EVER YOU SAY.
IDIOT! MORON, DUMMY, DORK, JERK!
I'LL TEACH YOU A LESSON YOU WON'T EVER FORGET. THE OTHERS MIGHT BE GULLIBLE, BUT I'M NOT!
THE MIDDLE OF THE PACIFIC OCEAN, HUH?
I'LL SHOW YOU THE MIDDLE OF MY FOOT!
UM... ANYONE ELSE THINK SHE NEEDS SOME VALIUM?
I THINK SHE'S FINALLY LOST IT.
I HOPE SEMPAI WILL BE ALL RIGHT.
WHAT IS THIS? A JOKE?
I'M OVER HERE... HELLO?
HOW DARE YOU BE SUCH A COWARD, KEITARO!

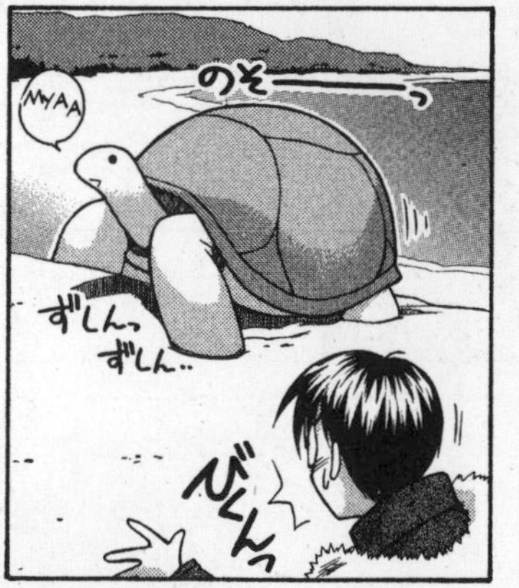
のそーーっ
NYAA
ずしんっ
ずしん‥
びくんっ

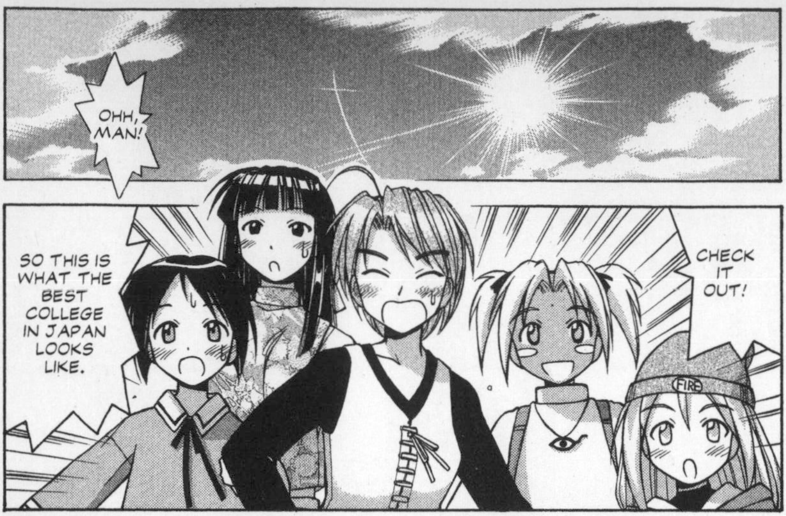
OHH, MAN!
CHECK IT OUT!
SO THIS IS WHAT THE BEST COLLEGE IN JAPAN LOOKS LIKE.
FIRE

Love Hina

HINATA..62 The Cherry Blossoms Are Blooming ...Or Are They?

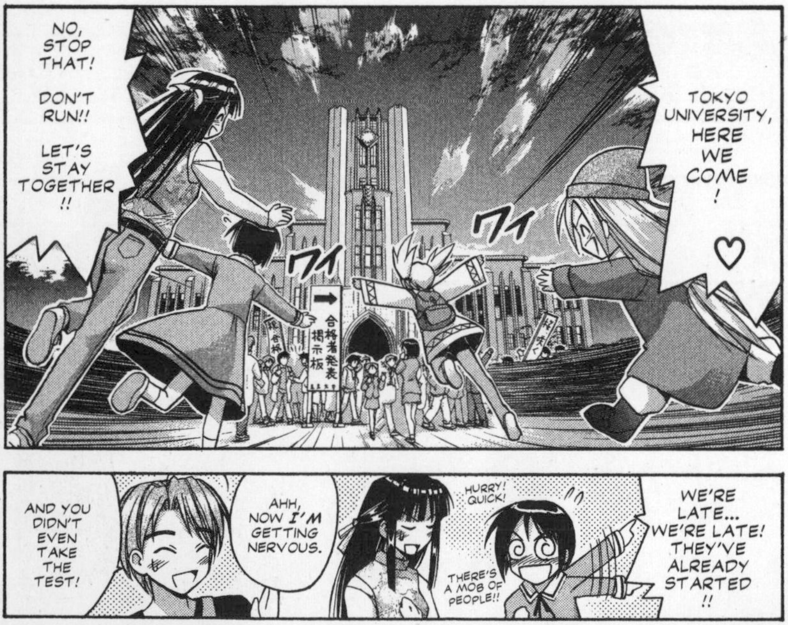
TOKYO UNIVERSITY, HERE WE COME!
♡
ワイ
ワイ
合格者発表掲示板
NO, STOP THAT!
DON'T RUN!!
LET'S STAY TOGETHER!!
WE'RE LATE... WE'RE LATE! THEY'VE ALREADY STARTED!!
HURRY! QUICK!
THERE'S A MOB OF PEOPLE!!
AHH, NOW I'M GETTING NERVOUS.
AND YOU DIDN'T EVEN TAKE THE TEST!

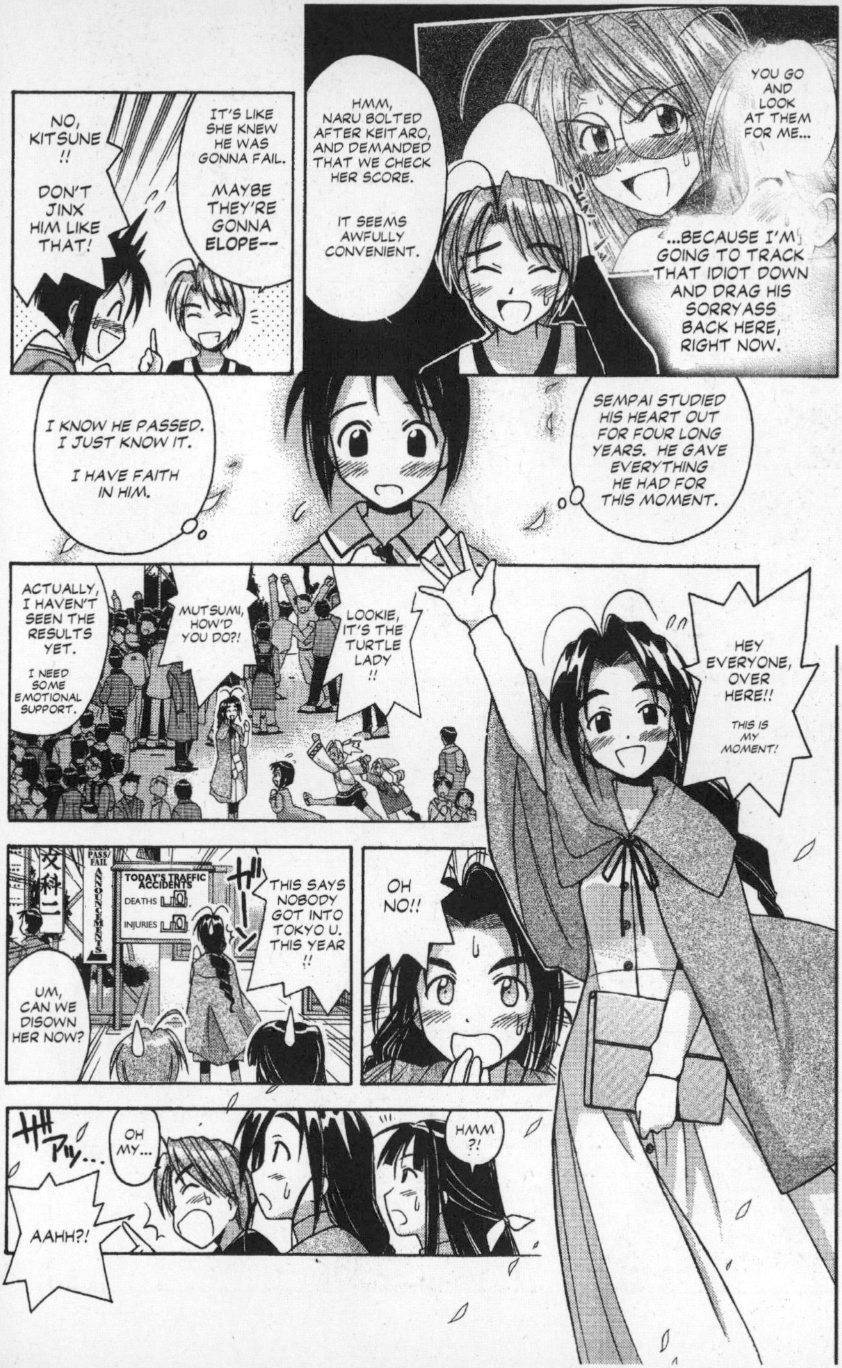
YOU GO AND LOOK AT THEM FOR ME...
...BECAUSE I'M GOING TO TRACK THAT IDIOT DOWN AND DRAG HIS SORRYASS BACK HERE, RIGHT NOW.
HMM, NARU BOLTED AFTER KEITARO, AND DEMANDED THAT WE CHECK HER SCORE.
IT SEEMS AWFULLY CONVENIENT.
IT'S LIKE SHE KNEW HE WAS GONNA FAIL.
MAYBE THEY'RE GONNA ELOPE--
NO, KITSUNE!!
DON'T JINX HIM LIKE THAT!
SEMPAI STUDIED HIS HEART OUT FOR FOUR LONG YEARS. HE GAVE EVERYTHING HE HAD FOR THIS MOMENT.
I KNOW HE PASSED. I JUST KNOW IT.
I HAVE FAITH IN HIM.
HEY EVERYONE, OVER HERE!!
THIS IS MY MOMENT!
LOOKIE, IT'S THE TURTLE LADY!!
MUTSUMI, HOW'D YOU DO?!
ACTUALLY, I HAVEN'T SEEN THE RESULTS YET.
I NEED SOME EMOTIONAL SUPPORT.
OH NO!!
THIS SAYS NOBODY GOT INTO TOKYO U. THIS YEAR!!
TODAY'S TRAFFIC ACCIDENTS
DEATHS 0
INJURIES 0
PASS/FAIL ANNOUNCEMENTS
UM, CAN WE DISOWN HER NOW?
HMM ?!
OH MY...
AAHH?!

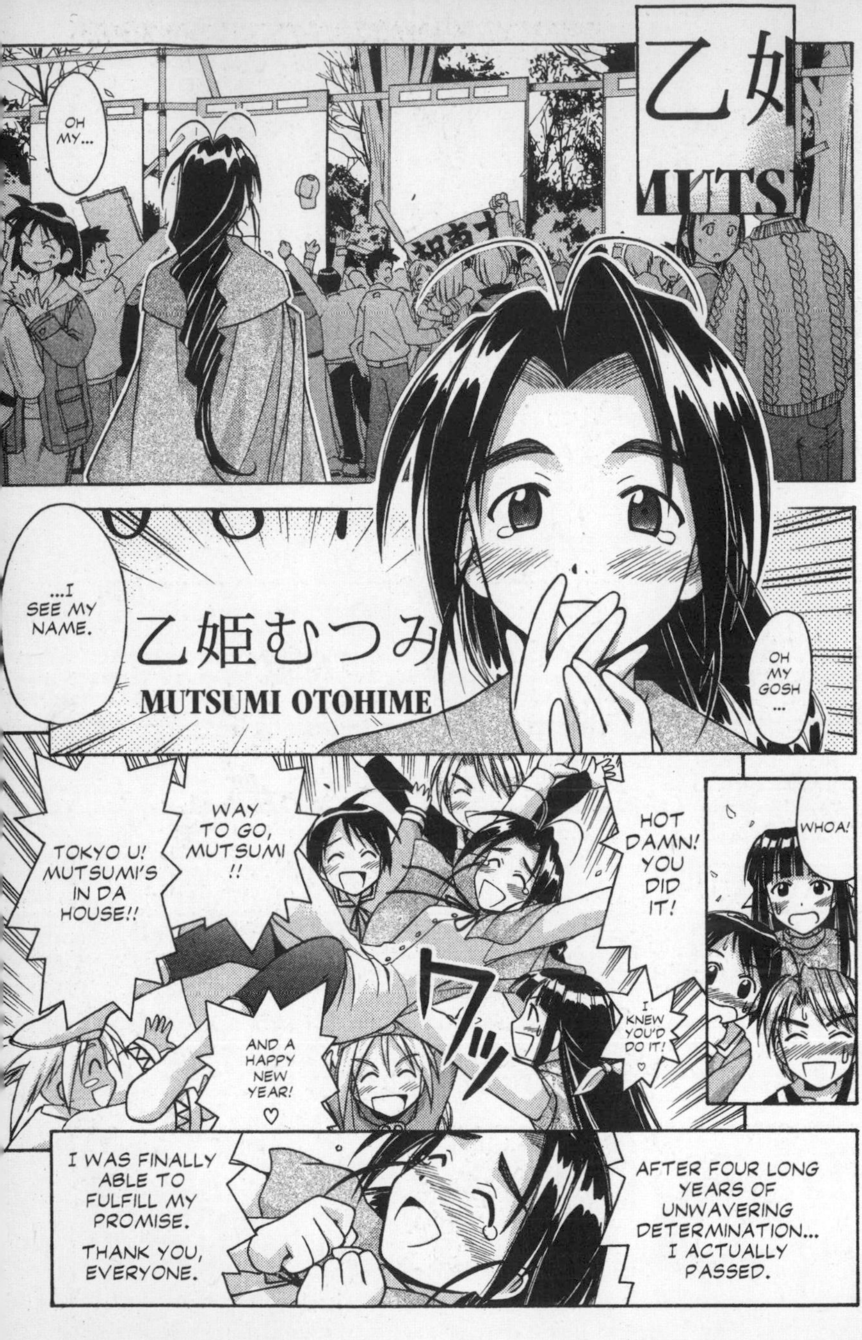
乙姫
MITS
OH MY...
OH MY GOSH...
...I SEE MY NAME.
乙姫むつみ
MUTSUMI OTOHIME
WHOA!
HOT DAMN! YOU DID IT!
I KNEW YOU'D DO IT! ♡
ワッ
WAY TO GO, MUTSUMI!!
TOKYO U! MUTSUMI'S IN DA HOUSE!!
AND A HAPPY NEW YEAR! ♡
AFTER FOUR LONG YEARS OF UNWAVERING DETERMINATION... I ACTUALLY PASSED.
I WAS FINALLY ABLE TO FULFILL MY PROMISE.
THANK YOU, EVERYONE.

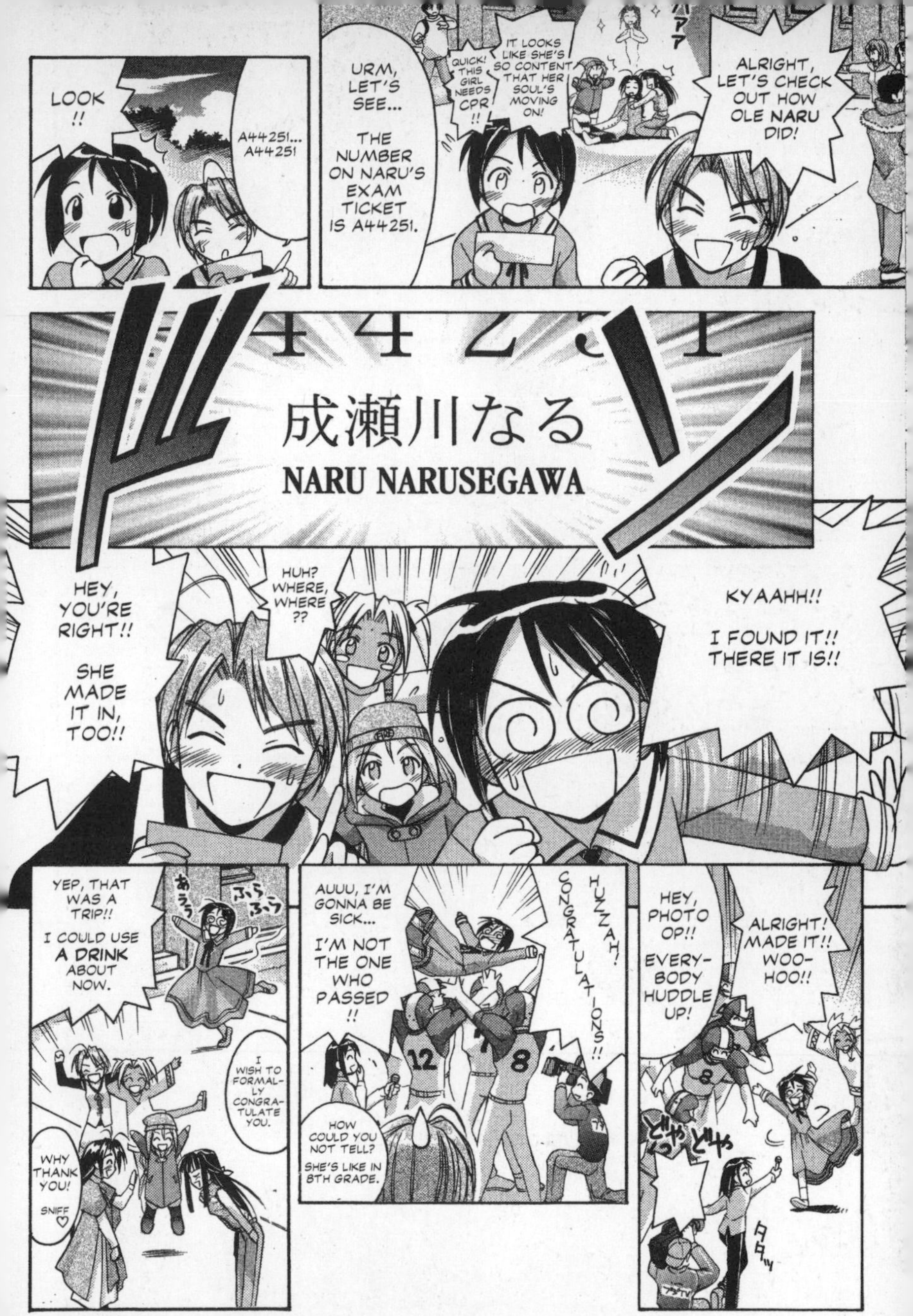
ALRIGHT, LET'S CHECK OUT HOW OLE NARU DID!
IT LOOKS LIKE SHE'S SO CONTENT THAT HER SOUL'S MOVING ON!
QUICK! THIS GIRL NEEDS CPR!!
URM, LET'S SEE... THE NUMBER ON NARU'S EXAM TICKET IS A44251.
A44251... A44251
LOOK !!
ドン
成瀬川なる
NARU NARUSEGAWA
KYAAHH!!
I FOUND IT!! THERE IT IS!!
HUH? WHERE, WHERE ??
HEY, YOU'RE RIGHT!!
SHE MADE IT IN, TOO!!
ALRIGHT! MADE IT!! WOO-HOO!!
HEY, PHOTO OP!! EVERY-BODY HUDDLE UP!
どやどや
タタッ
HUZZAH! CONGRATULATIONS!!
AUUU, I'M GONNA BE SICK...
I'M NOT THE ONE WHO PASSED !!
HOW COULD YOU NOT TELL? SHE'S LIKE IN 8TH GRADE.
ふらふら
あうう
YEP, THAT WAS A TRIP!!
I COULD USE A DRINK ABOUT NOW.
I WISH TO FORMALLY CONGRATULATE YOU.
WHY THANK YOU!
SNIFF ♡

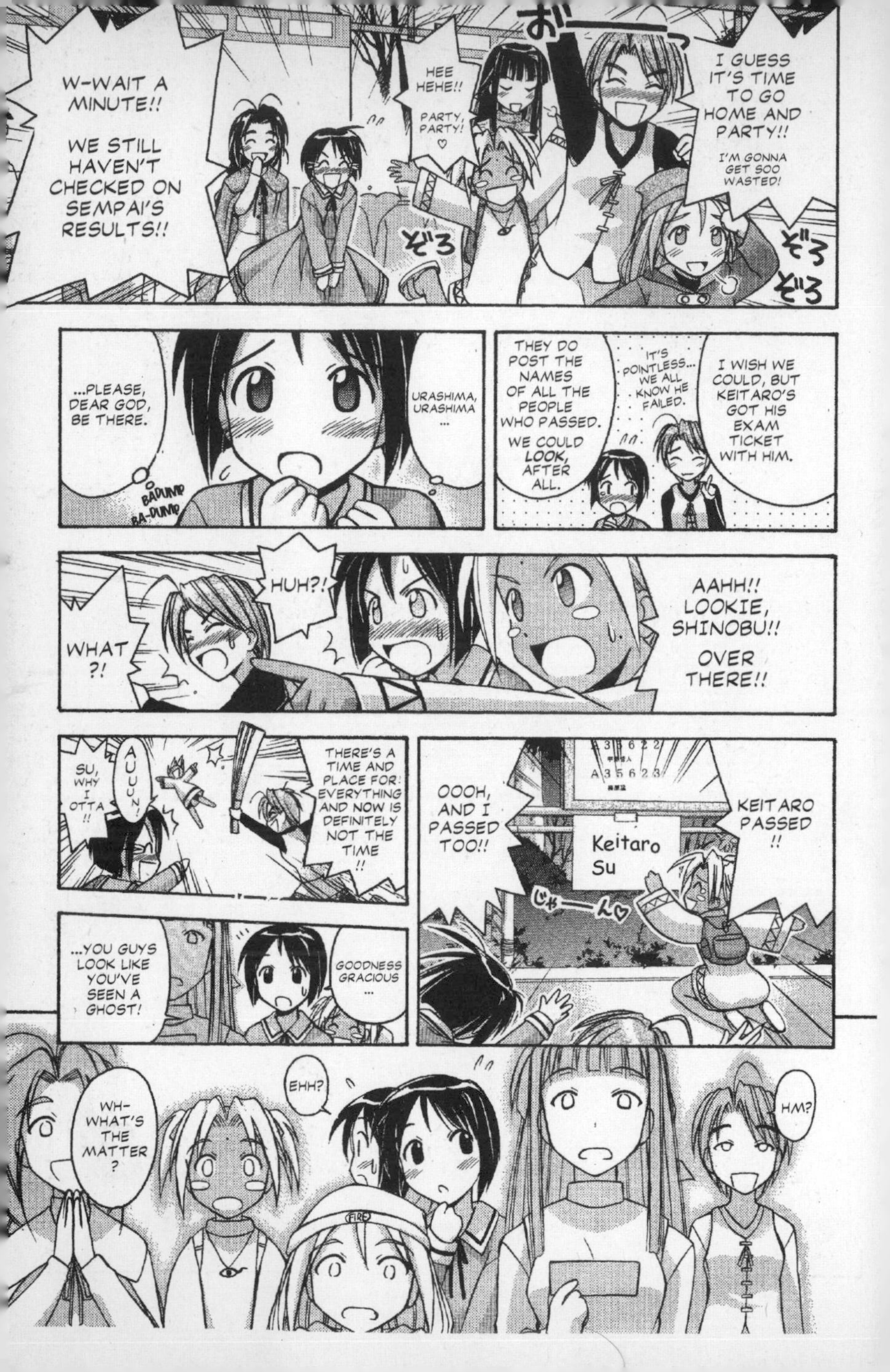
おーーーっ
I GUESS IT'S TIME TO GO HOME AND PARTY!!
I'M GONNA GET SOO WASTED!
ぞろ
ぞろ
HEE HEHE!!
PARTY, PARTY! ♡
W-WAIT A MINUTE!!
WE STILL HAVEN'T CHECKED ON SEMPAI'S RESULTS!!
ぞろ
I WISH WE COULD, BUT KEITARO'S GOT HIS EXAM TICKET WITH HIM.
IT'S POINTLESS... WE ALL KNOW HE FAILED.
THEY DO POST THE NAMES OF ALL THE PEOPLE WHO PASSED.
WE COULD LOOK, AFTER ALL.
URASHIMA, URASHIMA ...
...PLEASE, DEAR GOD, BE THERE.
BADUMP BA-DUMP
AAHH!! LOOKIE, SHINOBU!!
OVER THERE!!
HUH?!
WHAT ?!
KEITARO PASSED !!
A35622
A35623
Keitaro Su
じゃーーん♡
OOOH, AND I PASSED TOO!!
THERE'S A TIME AND PLACE FOR EVERYTHING AND NOW IS DEFINITELY NOT THE TIME !!
AUUUN!
SU, WHY I OTTA !!
GOODNESS GRACIOUS ...
...YOU GUYS LOOK LIKE YOU'VE SEEN A GHOST!
HM?
EHH?
WH-WHAT'S THE MATTER ?
FIRE

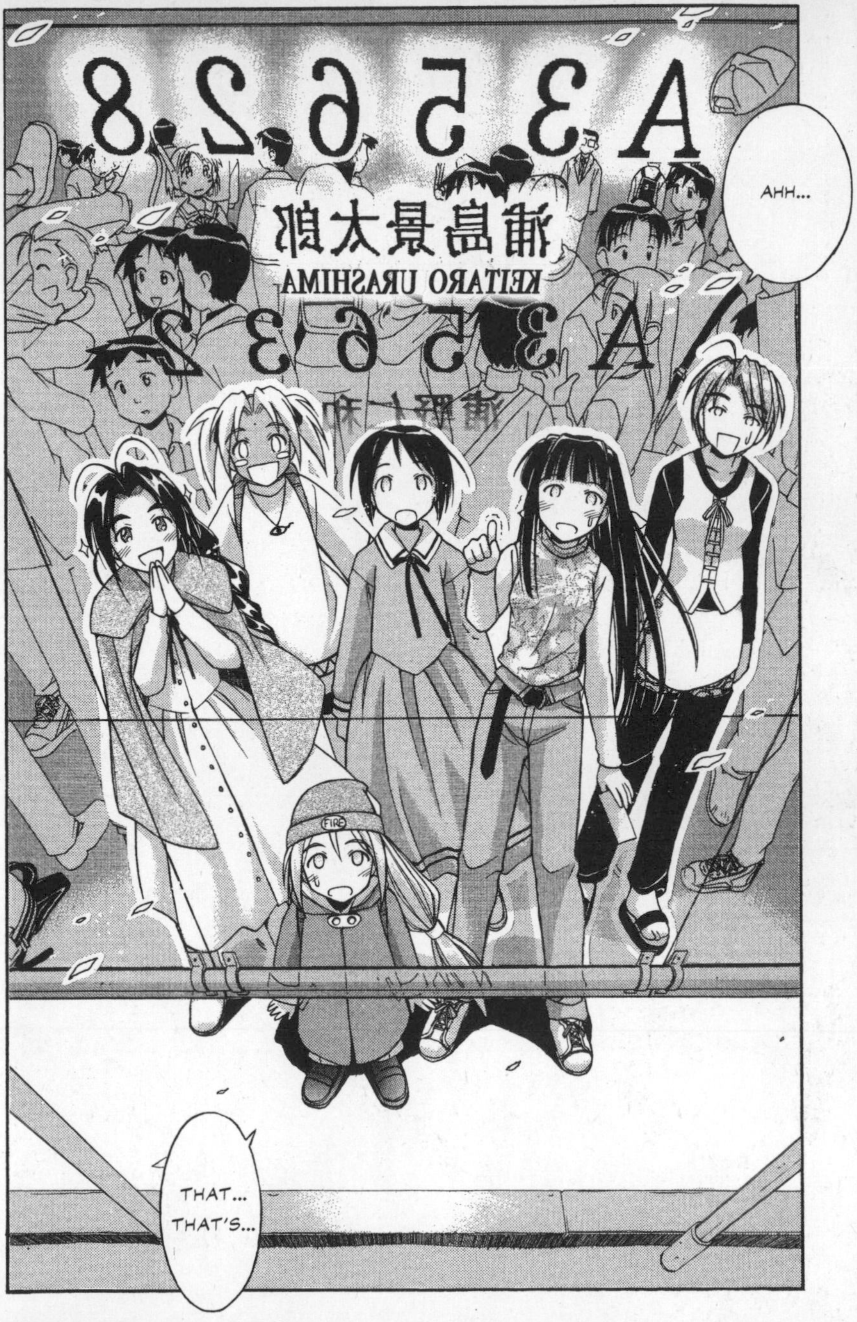
AHH...
THAT...
THAT'S...

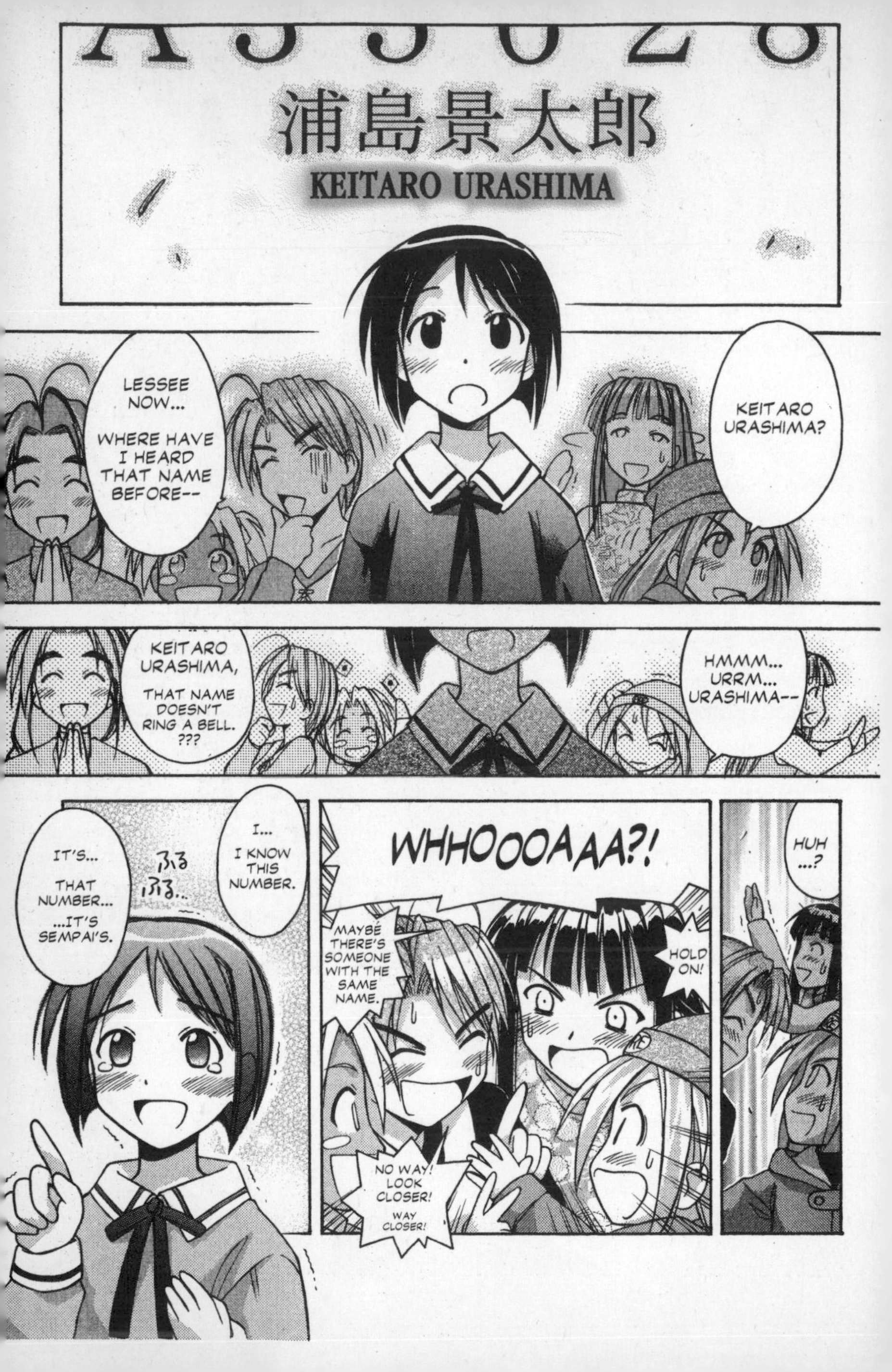

浦島景太郎
KEITARO URASHIMA
KEITARO URASHIMA?
LESSEE NOW... WHERE HAVE I HEARD THAT NAME BEFORE--
HMMM... URRM... URASHIMA--
KEITARO URASHIMA, THAT NAME DOESN'T RING A BELL. ???
HUH ...?
WHHOOOAAA?!
HOLD ON!
MAYBE THERE'S SOMEONE WITH THE SAME NAME.
NO WAY! LOOK CLOSER! WAY CLOSER!
I... I KNOW THIS NUMBER.
ふるふる...
IT'S... THAT NUMBER... ...IT'S SEMPAI'S.

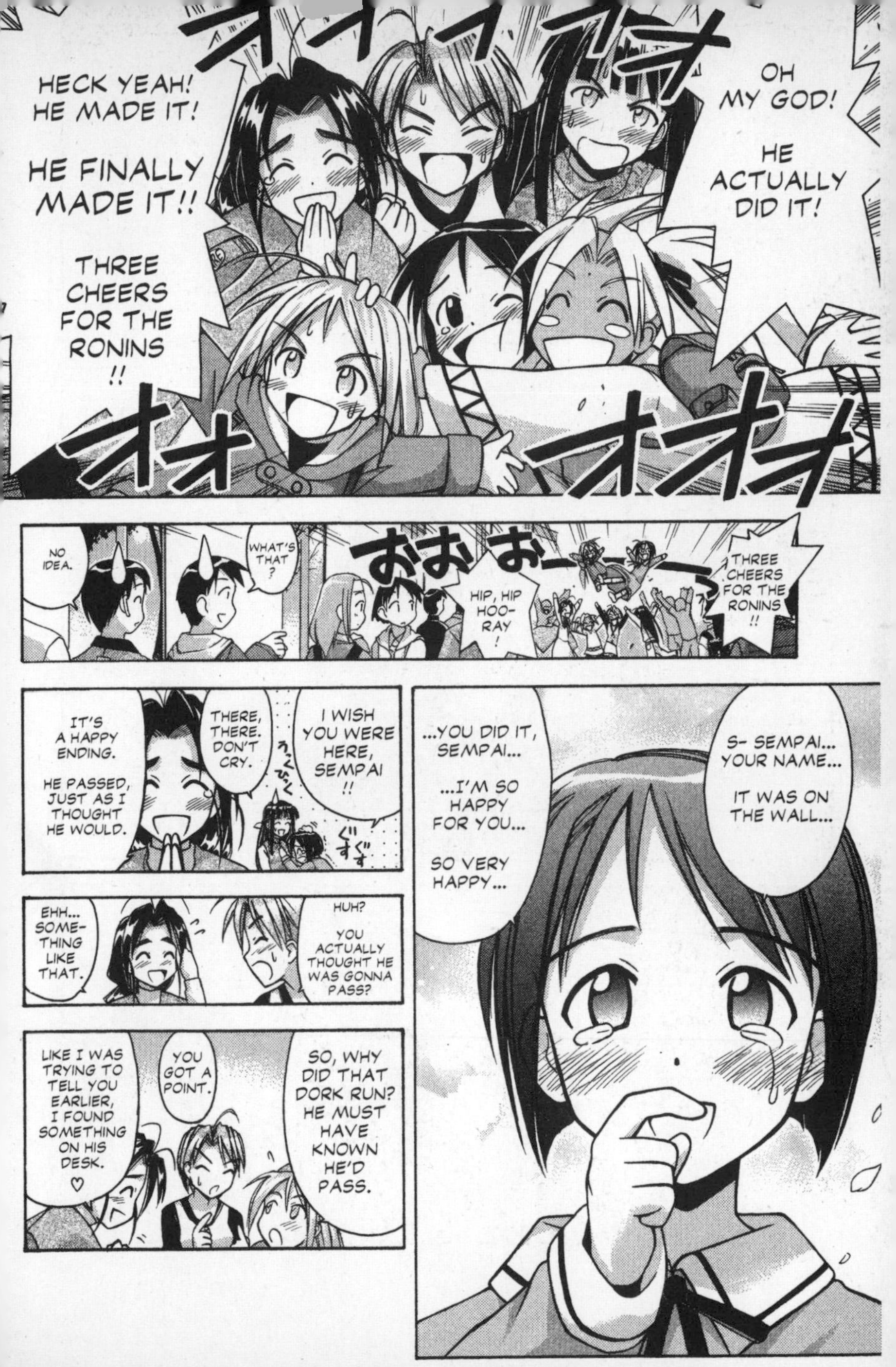
オオオオ
OH MY GOD!
HE ACTUALLY DID IT!
HECK YEAH! HE MADE IT!
HE FINALLY MADE IT!!
THREE CHEERS FOR THE RONINS !!
オオオオ
オオ
THREE CHEERS FOR THE RONINS !!
HIP, HIP HOO-RAY !
おおおー
WHAT'S THAT ?
NO IDEA.
S- SEMPAI... YOUR NAME...
IT WAS ON THE WALL...
...YOU DID IT, SEMPAI...
...I'M SO HAPPY FOR YOU...
SO VERY HAPPY...
I WISH YOU WERE HERE, SEMPAI !!
THERE, THERE. DON'T CRY.
IT'S A HAPPY ENDING.
HE PASSED, JUST AS I THOUGHT HE WOULD.
HUH?
YOU ACTUALLY THOUGHT HE WAS GONNA PASS?
EHH... SOMETHING LIKE THAT.
SO, WHY DID THAT DORK RUN? HE MUST HAVE KNOWN HE'D PASS.
YOU GOT A POINT.
LIKE I WAS TRYING TO TELL YOU EARLIER, I FOUND SOMETHING ON HIS DESK. ♡

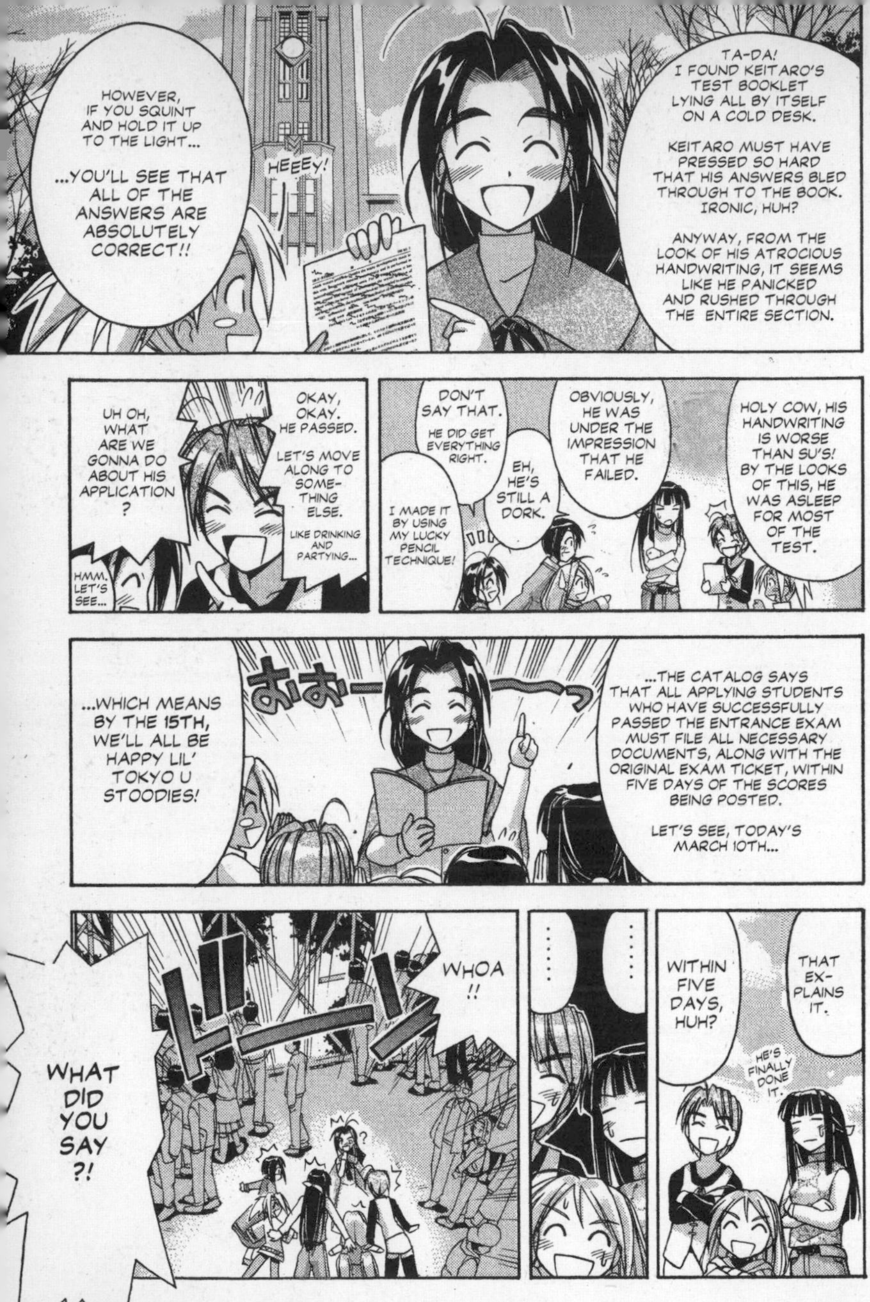
TA-DA! I FOUND KEITARO'S TEST BOOKLET LYING ALL BY ITSELF ON A COLD DESK.
KEITARO MUST HAVE PRESSED SO HARD THAT HIS ANSWERS BLED THROUGH TO THE BOOK. IRONIC, HUH?
ANYWAY, FROM THE LOOK OF HIS ATROCIOUS HANDWRITING, IT SEEMS LIKE HE PANICKED AND RUSHED THROUGH THE ENTIRE SECTION.
HEEEy!
HOWEVER, IF YOU SQUINT AND HOLD IT UP TO THE LIGHT...
...YOU'LL SEE THAT ALL OF THE ANSWERS ARE ABSOLUTELY CORRECT!!
HOLY COW, HIS HANDWRITING IS WORSE THAN SU'S! BY THE LOOKS OF THIS, HE WAS ASLEEP FOR MOST OF THE TEST.
OBVIOUSLY, HE WAS UNDER THE IMPRESSION THAT HE FAILED.
DON'T SAY THAT.
HE DID GET EVERYTHING RIGHT.
EH, HE'S STILL A DORK.
I MADE IT BY USING MY LUCKY PENCIL TECHNIQUE!
OKAY, OKAY. HE PASSED.
LET'S MOVE ALONG TO SOME-THING ELSE.
LIKE DRINKING AND PARTYING...
UH OH, WHAT ARE WE GONNA DO ABOUT HIS APPLICATION ?
HMM. LET'S SEE...
...THE CATALOG SAYS THAT ALL APPLYING STUDENTS WHO HAVE SUCCESSFULLY PASSED THE ENTRANCE EXAM MUST FILE ALL NECESSARY DOCUMENTS, ALONG WITH THE ORIGINAL EXAM TICKET, WITHIN FIVE DAYS OF THE SCORES BEING POSTED.
LET'S SEE, TODAY'S MARCH 10TH...
おおーーーっ
...WHICH MEANS BY THE 15TH, WE'LL ALL BE HAPPY LIL' TOKYO U STOODIES!
THAT EX-PLAINS IT.
WITHIN FIVE DAYS, HUH?
HE'S FINALLY DONE IT.
......
......
WHOA !!
WHAT DID YOU SAY ?!

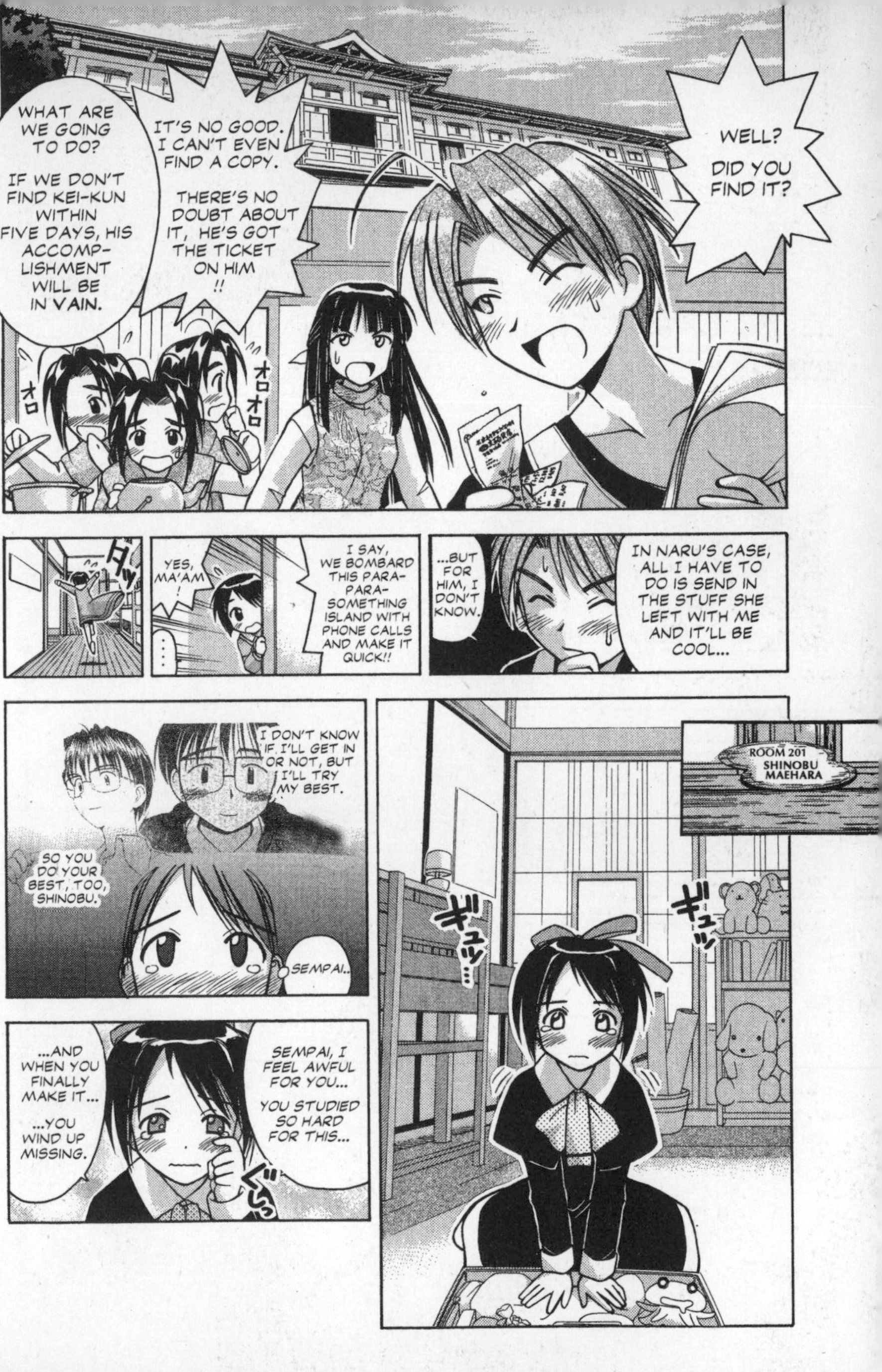
WELL? DID YOU FIND IT?
IT'S NO GOOD. I CAN'T EVEN FIND A COPY. THERE'S NO DOUBT ABOUT IT, HE'S GOT THE TICKET ON HIM !!
WHAT ARE WE GOING TO DO? IF WE DON'T FIND KEI-KUN WITHIN FIVE DAYS, HIS ACCOMPLISHMENT WILL BE IN VAIN.
オロオロ
オロ
IN NARU'S CASE, ALL I HAVE TO DO IS SEND IN THE STUFF SHE LEFT WITH ME AND IT'LL BE COOL...
...BUT FOR HIM, I DON'T KNOW.
I SAY, WE BOMBARD THIS PARA-PARA-SOMETHING ISLAND WITH PHONE CALLS AND MAKE IT QUICK!!
YES, MA'AM!
....
ダッ
ROOM 201 SHINOBU MAEHARA
ギュッ
ギュッ
I DON'T KNOW IF I'LL GET IN OR NOT, BUT I'LL TRY MY BEST.
SO YOU DO YOUR BEST, TOO, SHINOBU.
SEMPAI..
SEMPAI, I FEEL AWFUL FOR YOU... YOU STUDIED SO HARD FOR THIS...
...AND WHEN YOU FINALLY MAKE IT... ...YOU WIND UP MISSING.
ぐらっ

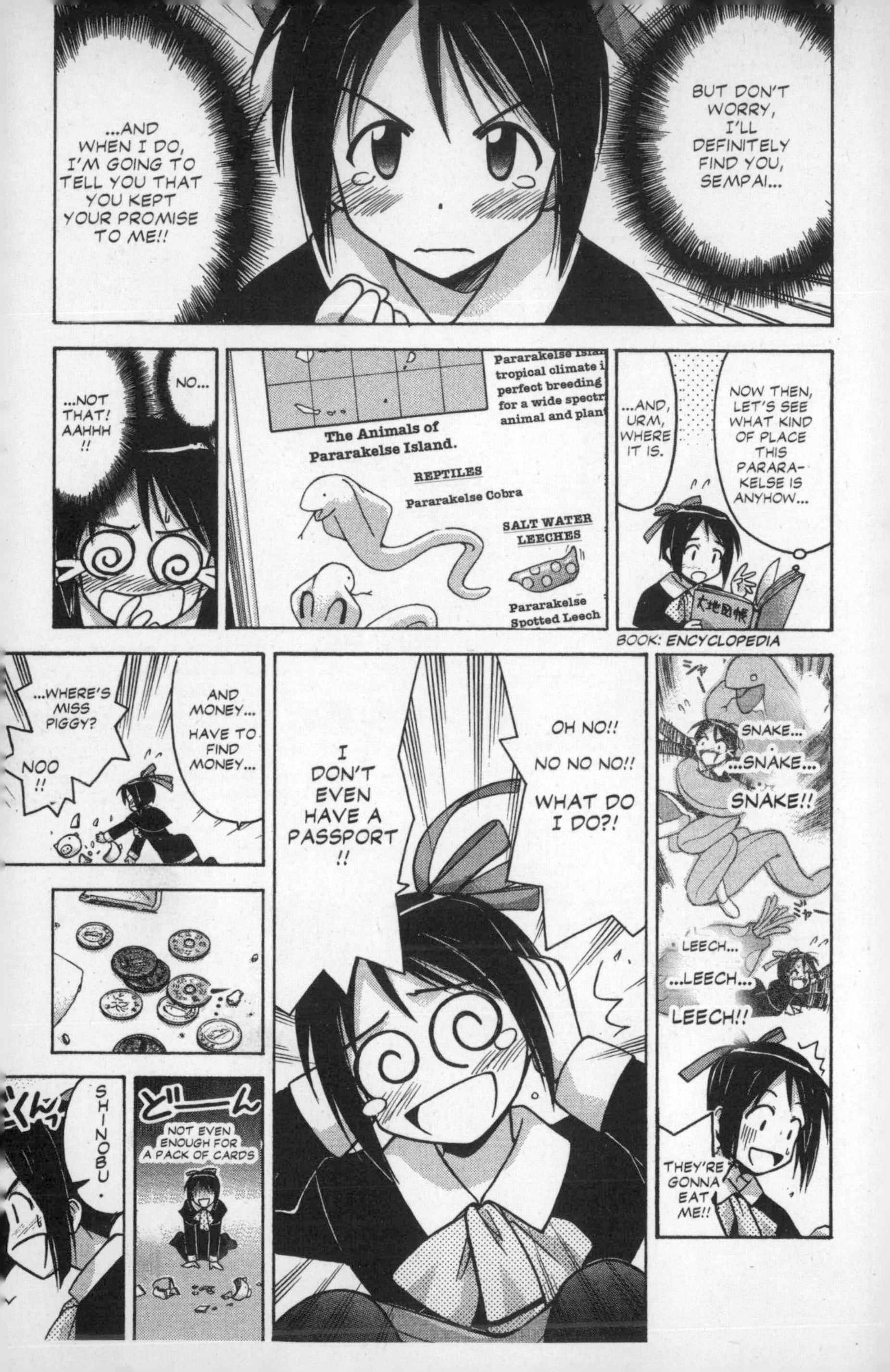

BUT DON'T WORRY, I'LL DEFINITELY FIND YOU, SEMPAI...
...AND WHEN I DO, I'M GOING TO TELL YOU THAT YOU KEPT YOUR PROMISE TO ME!!
NOW THEN, LET'S SEE WHAT KIND OF PLACE THIS PARARAKELSE IS ANYHOW...
...AND, URM, WHERE IT IS.
BOOK: ENCYCLOPEDIA
Pararakelse Islan
tropical climate i
perfect breeding
for a wide spectr
animal and plant
The Animals of Pararakelse Island.
REPTILES
Pararakelse Cobra
SALT WATER LEECHES
Pararakelse Spotted Leech
NO...
...NOT THAT! AAHHH !!
SNAKE...
...SNAKE...
SNAKE!!
LEECH...
...LEECH...
LEECH!!
THEY'RE GONNA EAT ME!!
OH NO!!
NO NO NO!!
WHAT DO I DO?!
I DON'T EVEN HAVE A PASSPORT !!
AND MONEY...
HAVE TO FIND MONEY...
...WHERE'S MISS PIGGY?
NOO !!
どーん
NOT EVEN ENOUGH FOR A PACK OF CARDS
SHINOBU.

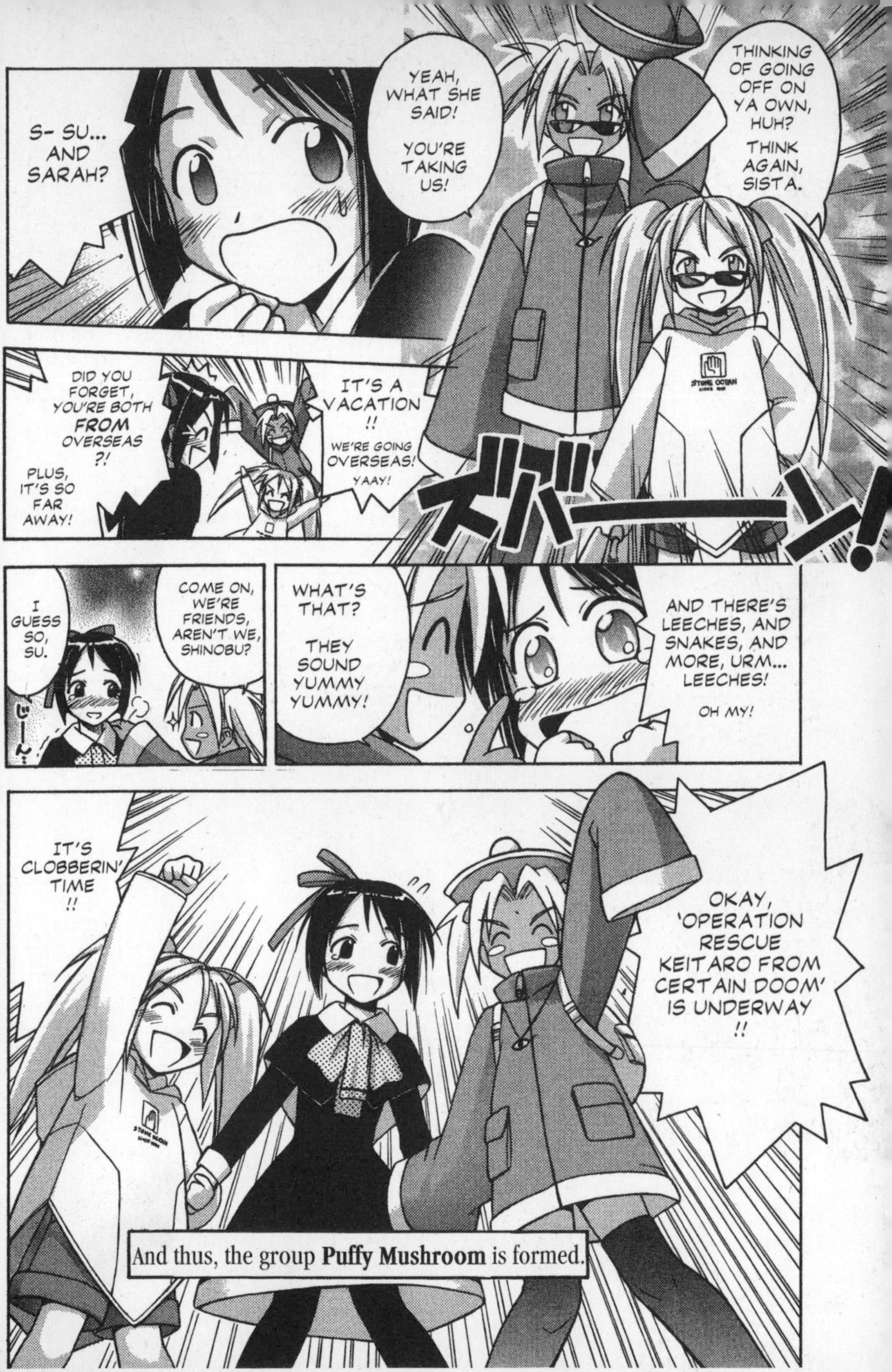
THINKING OF GOING OFF ON YA OWN, HUH?
THINK AGAIN, SISTA.
YEAH, WHAT SHE SAID!
YOU'RE TAKING US!
ズバーーン!
S- SU... AND SARAH?
IT'S A VACATION !!
WE'RE GOING OVERSEAS!
YAAY!
DID YOU FORGET, YOU'RE BOTH FROM OVERSEAS ?!
PLUS, IT'S SO FAR AWAY!
AND THERE'S LEECHES, AND SNAKES, AND MORE, URM... LEECHES!
OH MY!
WHAT'S THAT?
THEY SOUND YUMMY YUMMY!
COME ON, WE'RE FRIENDS, AREN'T WE, SHINOBU?
I GUESS SO, SU.
OKAY, 'OPERATION RESCUE KEITARO FROM CERTAIN DOOM' IS UNDERWAY !!
IT'S CLOBBERIN' TIME !!
And thus, the group Puffy Mushroom is formed.

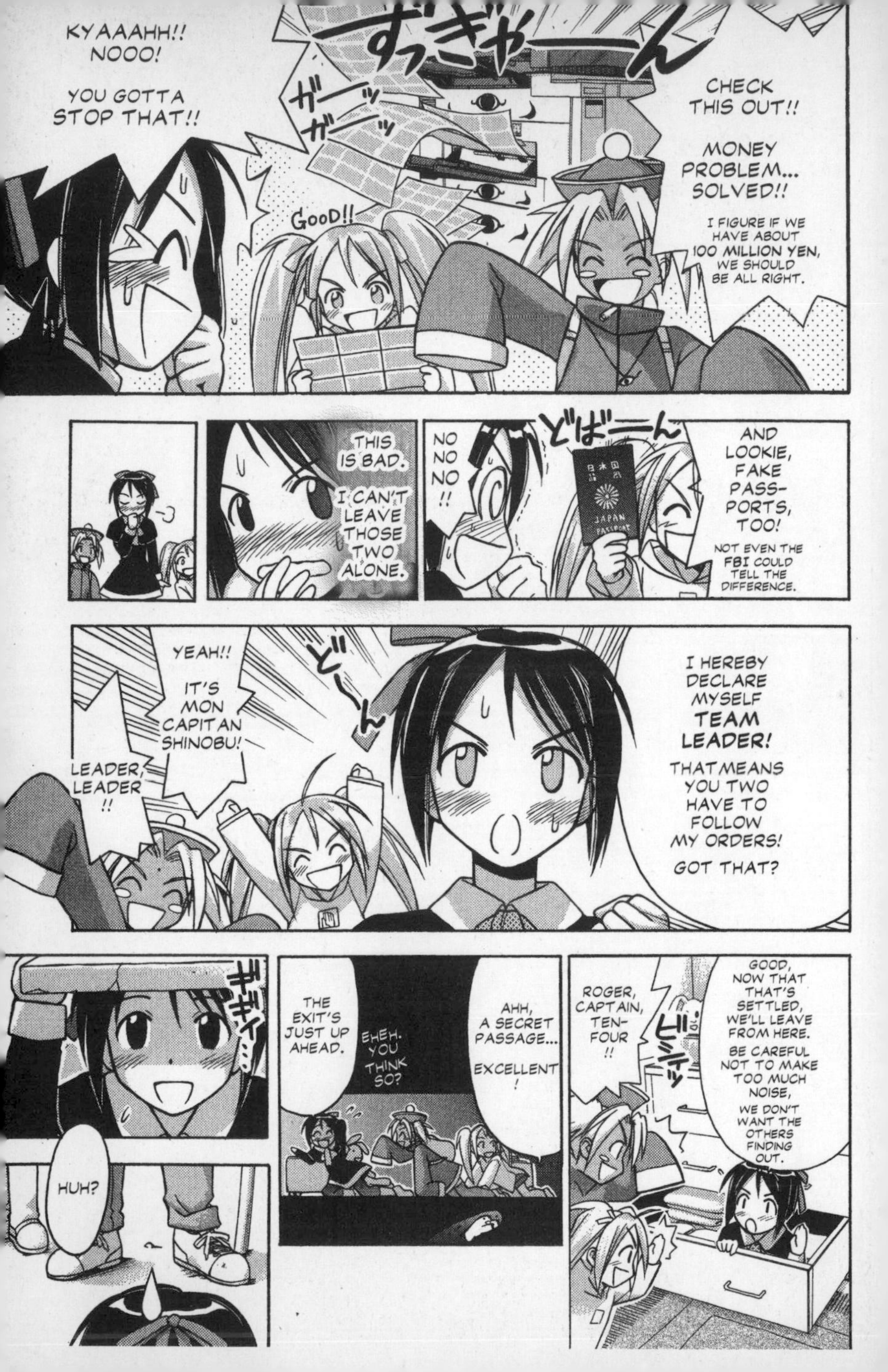

すっぎゃーん
CHECK THIS OUT!!
MONEY PROBLEM... SOLVED!!
I FIGURE IF WE HAVE ABOUT 100 MILLION YEN, WE SHOULD BE ALL RIGHT.
ガーッ
ガーッ
GOOD!!
KYAAAHH!! NOOO!
YOU GOTTA STOP THAT!!
AND LOOKIE, FAKE PASS-PORTS, TOO!
NOT EVEN THE FBI COULD TELL THE DIFFERENCE.
どばーん
NO NO NO !!
THIS IS BAD.
I CAN'T LEAVE THOSE TWO ALONE.
I HEREBY DECLARE MYSELF **TEAM LEADER!**
THATMEANS YOU TWO HAVE TO FOLLOW MY ORDERS!
GOT THAT?
どーん
YEAH!!
IT'S MON CAPITAN SHINOBU!
LEADER, LEADER !!
GOOD, NOW THAT THAT'S SETTLED, WE'LL LEAVE FROM HERE.
BE CAREFUL NOT TO MAKE TOO MUCH NOISE,
WE DON'T WANT THE OTHERS FINDING OUT.
ビシッ
ROGER, CAPTAIN, TEN-FOUR !!
AHH, A SECRET PASSAGE...
EXCELLENT !
EHEH. YOU THINK SO?
THE EXIT'S JUST UP AHEAD.
ギギイ…
HUH?

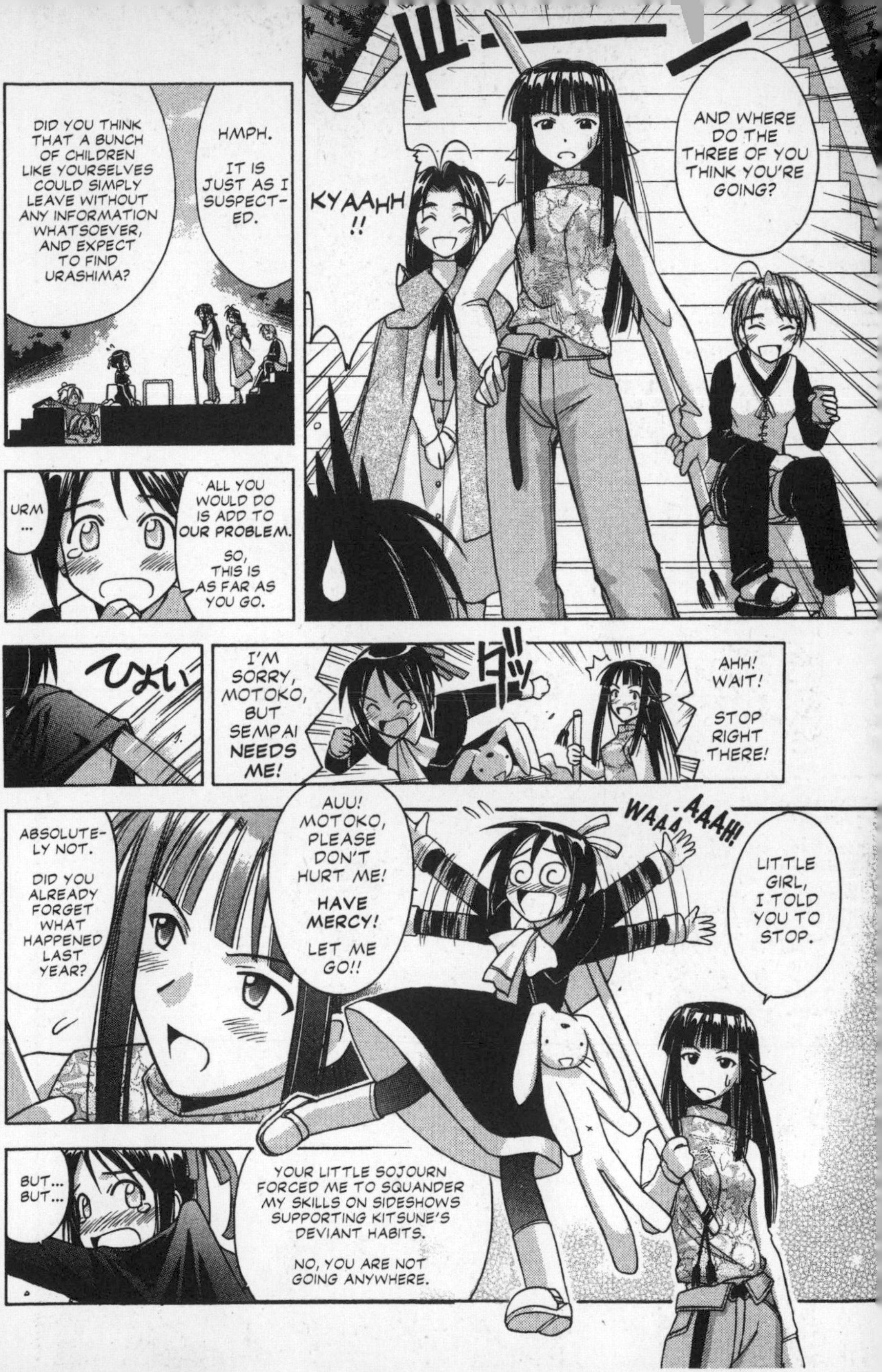
ドーーー
AND WHERE DO THE THREE OF YOU THINK YOU'RE GOING?
KYAAHH !!
HMPH.
IT IS JUST AS I SUSPECT-ED.
DID YOU THINK THAT A BUNCH OF CHILDREN LIKE YOURSELVES COULD SIMPLY LEAVE WITHOUT ANY INFORMATION WHATSOEVER, AND EXPECT TO FIND URASHIMA?
ALL YOU WOULD DO IS ADD TO OUR PROBLEM.
SO, THIS IS AS FAR AS YOU GO.
URM ...
AHH! WAIT!
STOP RIGHT THERE!
ダッ
I'M SORRY, MOTOKO, BUT SEMPAI NEEDS ME!
ひょい
LITTLE GIRL, I TOLD YOU TO STOP.
WAAAAAAH!
AUU! MOTOKO, PLEASE DON'T HURT ME!
HAVE MERCY!
LET ME GO!!
ABSOLUTE-LY NOT.
DID YOU ALREADY FORGET WHAT HAPPENED LAST YEAR?
YOUR LITTLE SOJOURN FORCED ME TO SQUANDER MY SKILLS ON SIDESHOWS SUPPORTING KITSUNE'S DEVIANT HABITS.
NO, YOU ARE NOT GOING ANYWHERE.
BUT... BUT...

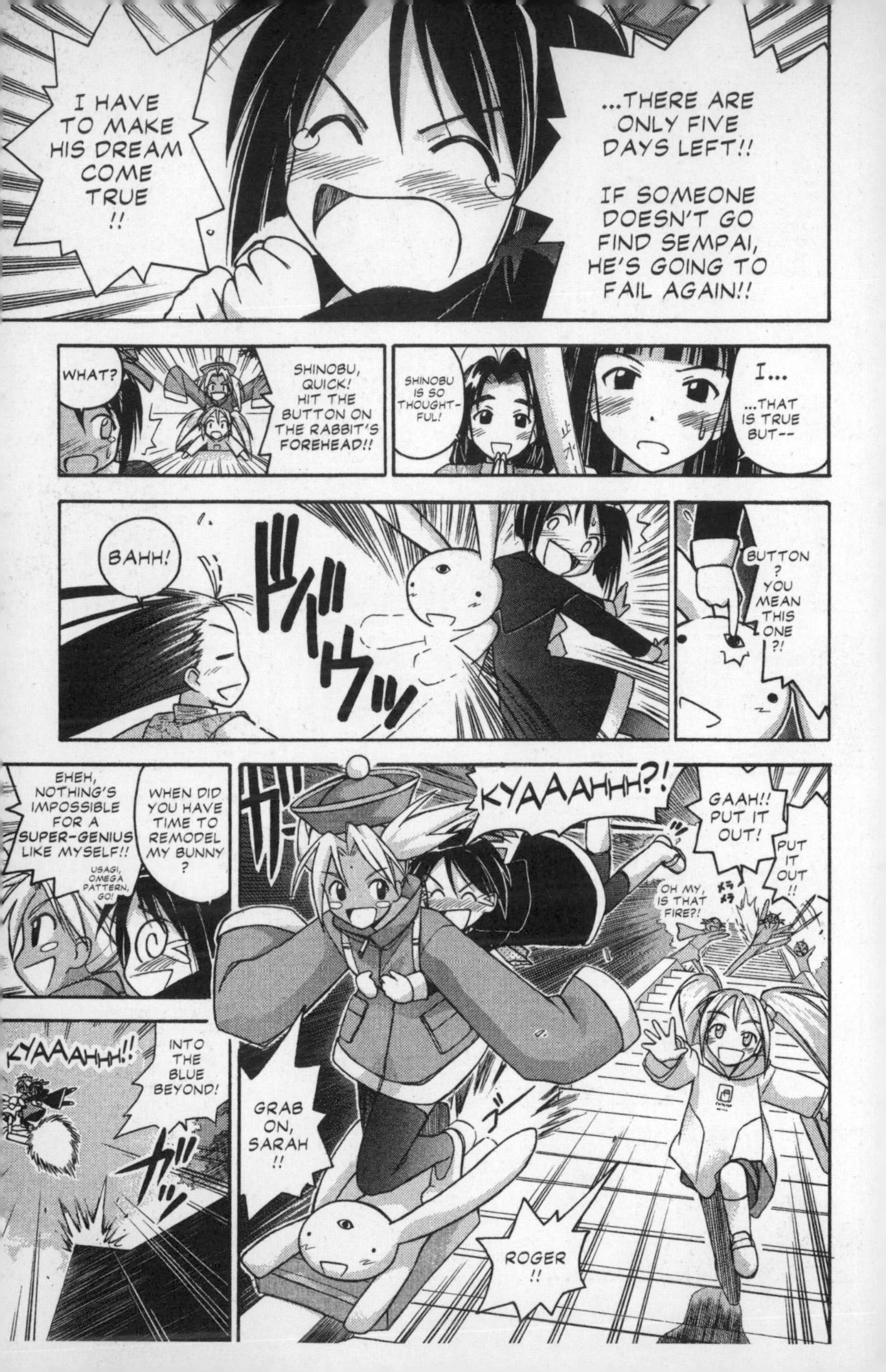
...THERE ARE ONLY FIVE DAYS LEFT!!
IF SOMEONE DOESN'T GO FIND SEMPAI, HE'S GOING TO FAIL AGAIN!!
I HAVE TO MAKE HIS DREAM COME TRUE !!
I...
...THAT IS TRUE BUT--
SHINOBU IS SO THOUGHTFUL!
SHINOBU, QUICK! HIT THE BUTTON ON THE RABBIT'S FOREHEAD!!
WHAT?
BUTTON ? YOU MEAN THIS ONE ?!
ドバウッ
BAHH!
KYAAAHHH?!
GAAH!! PUT IT OUT!
PUT IT OUT !!
OH MY, IS THAT FIRE?!
GRAB ON, SARAH !!
ROGER !!
WHEN DID YOU HAVE TIME TO REMODEL MY BUNNY ?
EHEH, NOTHING'S IMPOSSIBLE FOR A SUPER-GENIUS LIKE MYSELF!!
USAGI, OMEGA PATTERN, GO!
INTO THE BLUE BEYOND!
KYAAAHHH!!

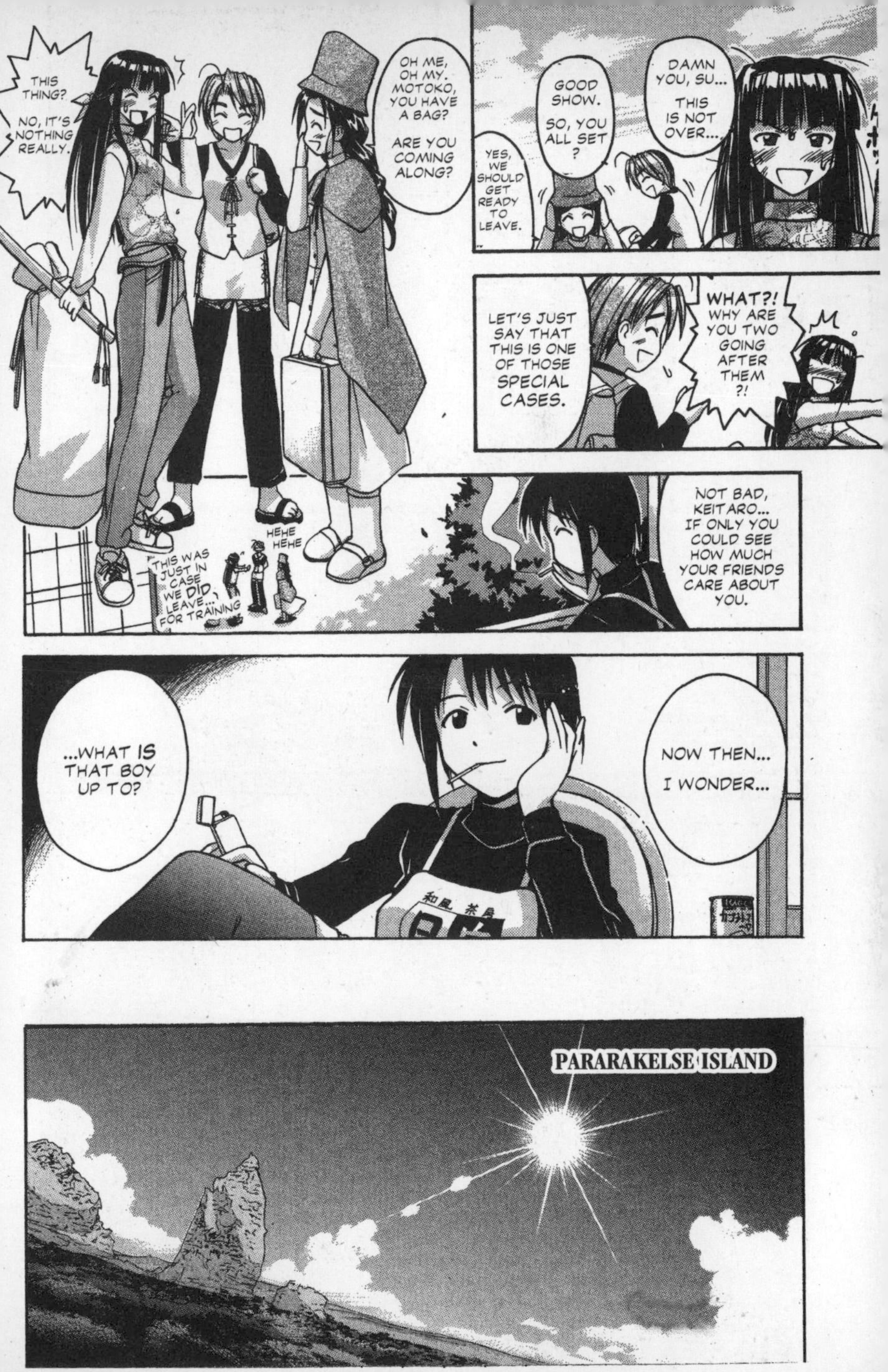
DAMN YOU, SU... THIS IS NOT OVER...
GOOD SHOW. SO, YOU ALL SET?
YES, WE SHOULD GET READY TO LEAVE.
WHAT?! WHY ARE YOU TWO GOING AFTER THEM?!
LET'S JUST SAY THAT THIS IS ONE OF THOSE SPECIAL CASES.
OH ME, OH MY. MOTOKO, YOU HAVE A BAG? ARE YOU COMING ALONG?
THIS THING? NO, IT'S NOTHING REALLY.
HEHE HEHE
THIS WAS JUST IN CASE WE DID LEAVE... FOR TRAINING
NOT BAD, KEITARO... IF ONLY YOU COULD SEE HOW MUCH YOUR FRIENDS CARE ABOUT YOU.
NOW THEN... I WONDER...
...WHAT IS THAT BOY UP TO?
PARARAKELSE ISLAND

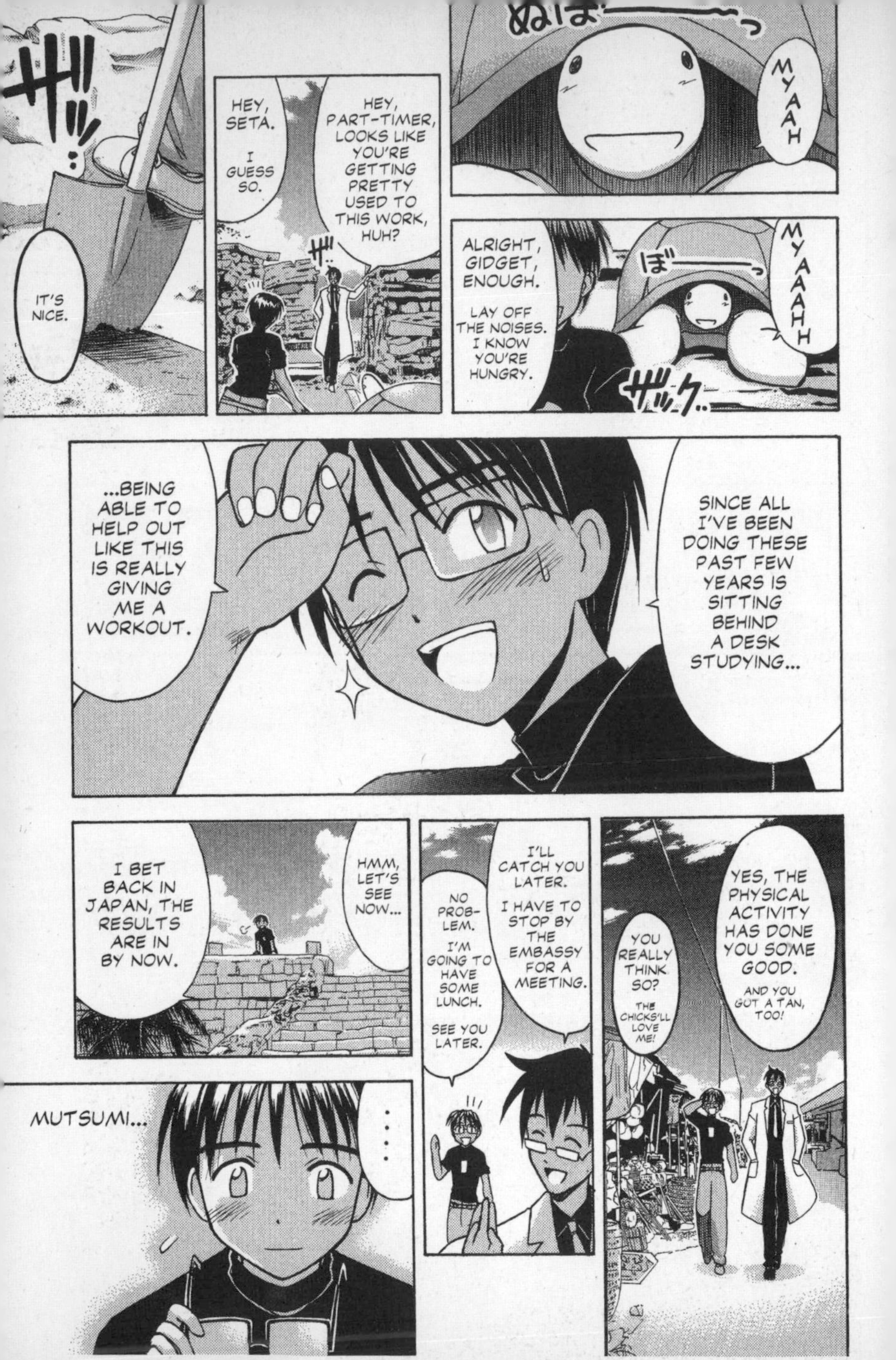
ぬぼーーっ
MYAAH
ALRIGHT, GIDGET, ENOUGH.
LAY OFF THE NOISES. I KNOW YOU'RE HUNGRY.
ぼーーっ
MYAAAH
ザック..
HEY, PART-TIMER, LOOKS LIKE YOU'RE GETTING PRETTY USED TO THIS WORK, HUH?
HEY, SETA.
I GUESS SO.
ザッ..
ザッ!!
IT'S NICE.
SINCE ALL I'VE BEEN DOING THESE PAST FEW YEARS IS SITTING BEHIND A DESK STUDYING...
...BEING ABLE TO HELP OUT LIKE THIS IS REALLY GIVING ME A WORKOUT.
YES, THE PHYSICAL ACTIVITY HAS DONE YOU SOME GOOD.
AND YOU GOT A TAN, TOO!
YOU REALLY THINK SO?
THE CHICKS'LL LOVE ME!
I'LL CATCH YOU LATER.
I HAVE TO STOP BY THE EMBASSY FOR A MEETING.
NO PROBLEM.
I'M GOING TO HAVE SOME LUNCH.
SEE YOU LATER.
HMM, LET'S SEE NOW...
I BET BACK IN JAPAN, THE RESULTS ARE IN BY NOW.
...
MUTSUMI...

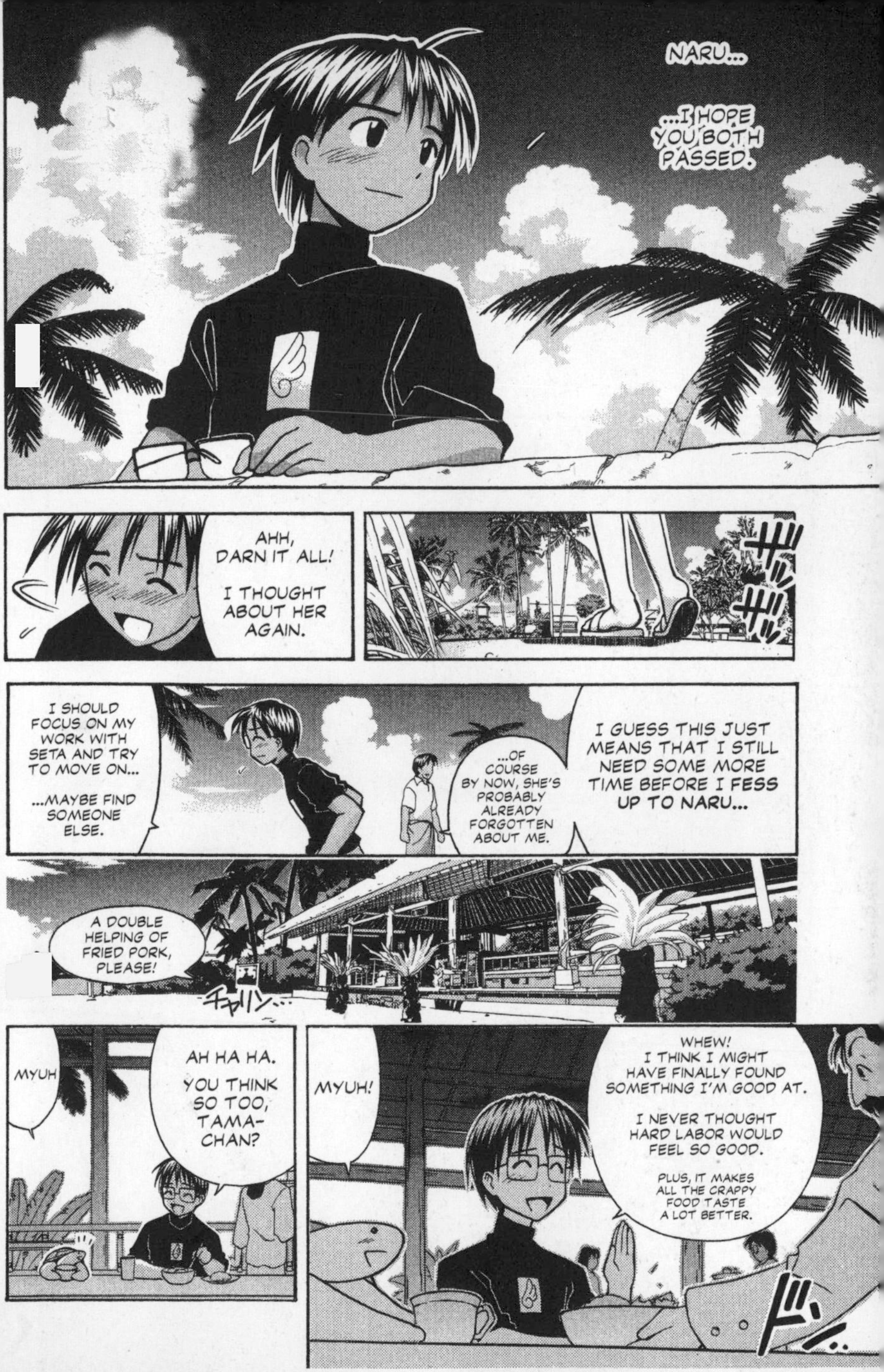
NARU...
...I HOPE YOU BOTH PASSED.
ザッ ザッ
AHH, DARN IT ALL!
I THOUGHT ABOUT HER AGAIN.
I GUESS THIS JUST MEANS THAT I STILL NEED SOME MORE TIME BEFORE I FESS UP TO NARU...
...OF COURSE BY NOW, SHE'S PROBABLY ALREADY FORGOTTEN ABOUT ME.
I SHOULD FOCUS ON MY WORK WITH SETA AND TRY TO MOVE ON...
...MAYBE FIND SOMEONE ELSE.
A DOUBLE HELPING OF FRIED PORK, PLEASE!
チャリン…
WHEW! I THINK I MIGHT HAVE FINALLY FOUND SOMETHING I'M GOOD AT.
I NEVER THOUGHT HARD LABOR WOULD FEEL SO GOOD.
PLUS, IT MAKES ALL THE CRAPPY FOOD TASTE A LOT BETTER.
MYUH!
AH HA HA.
YOU THINK SO TOO, TAMA-CHAN?
MYUH

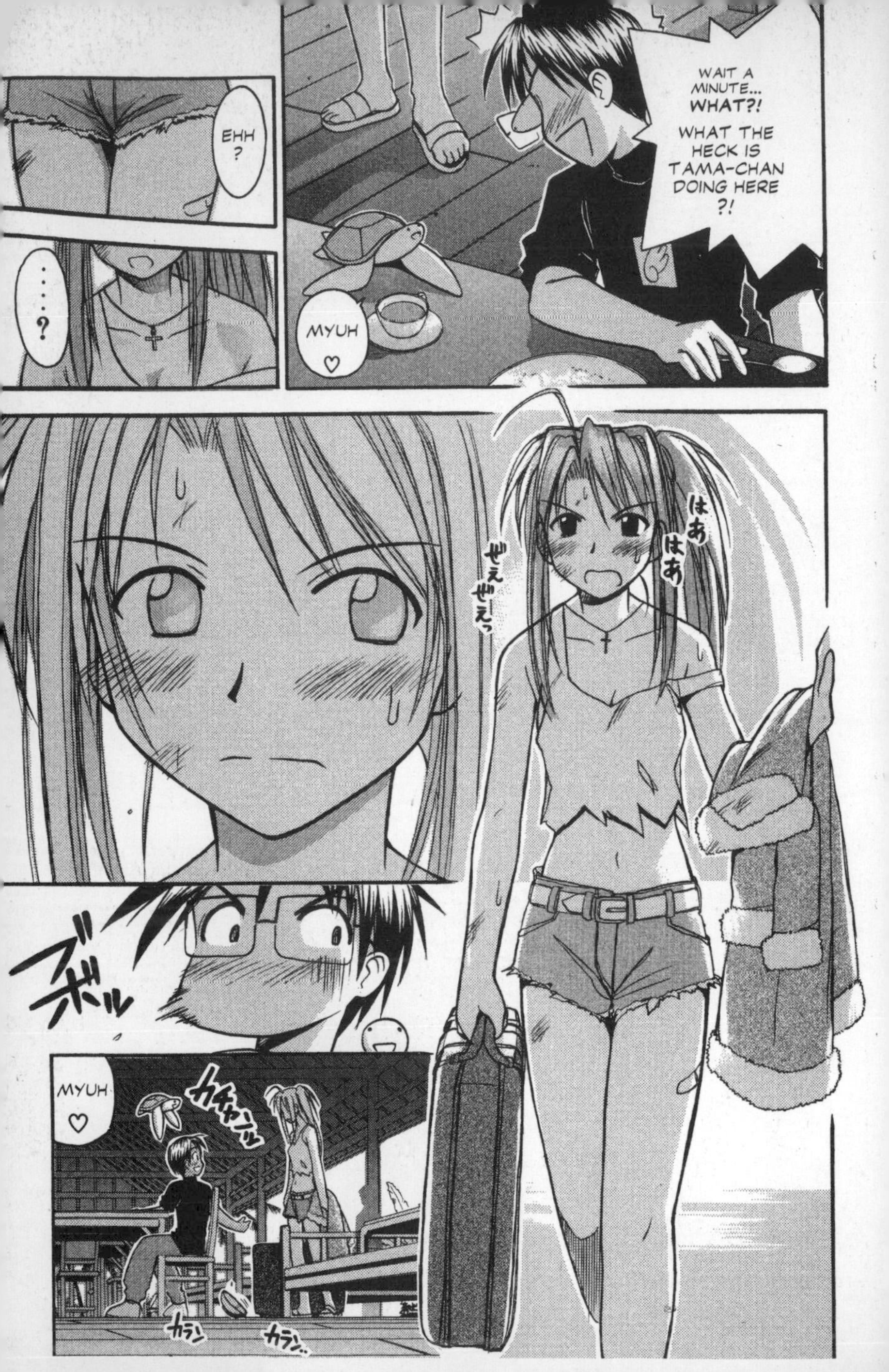
WAIT A MINUTE... WHAT?!
WHAT THE HECK IS TAMA-CHAN DOING HERE ?!
MYUH ♡
EHH ?
...... ?
はあ はあ
ぜぇぜぇっ
MYUH ♡
カラン
カラン..

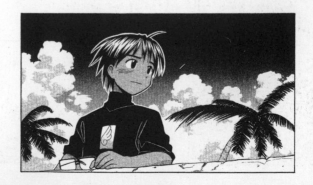

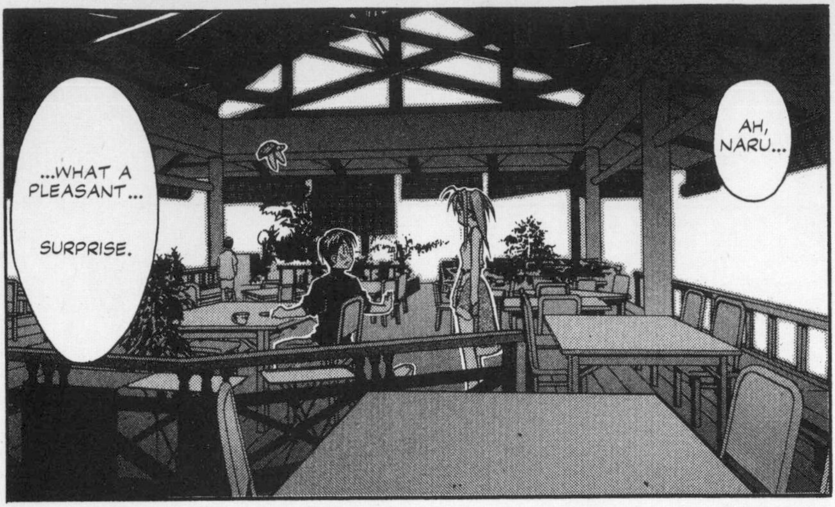
AH, NARU...
...WHAT A PLEASANT...
SURPRISE.

Love Hina

HINATA..63 Follow Me to Pararakelse Island

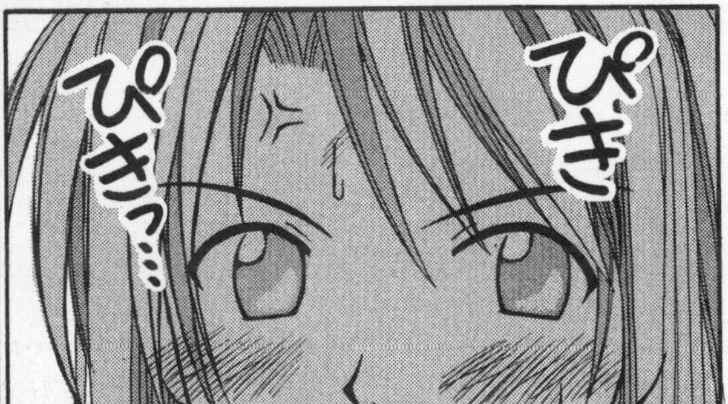
ぴき
ぴきっ…

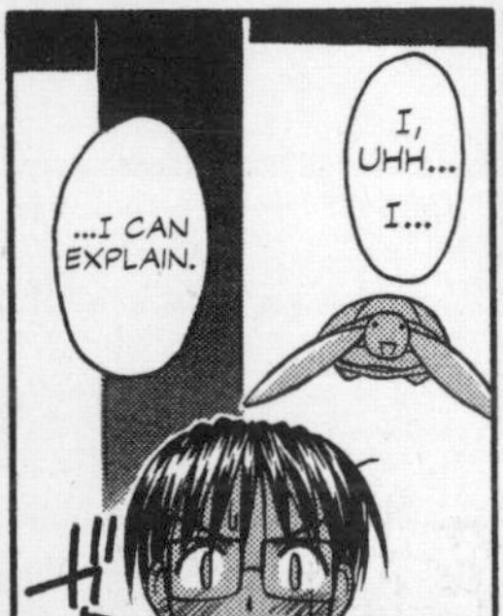
I, UHH... I...
...I CAN EXPLAIN.
ガタッ

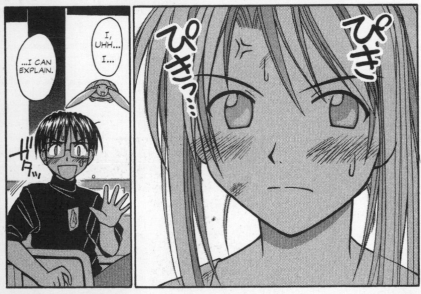

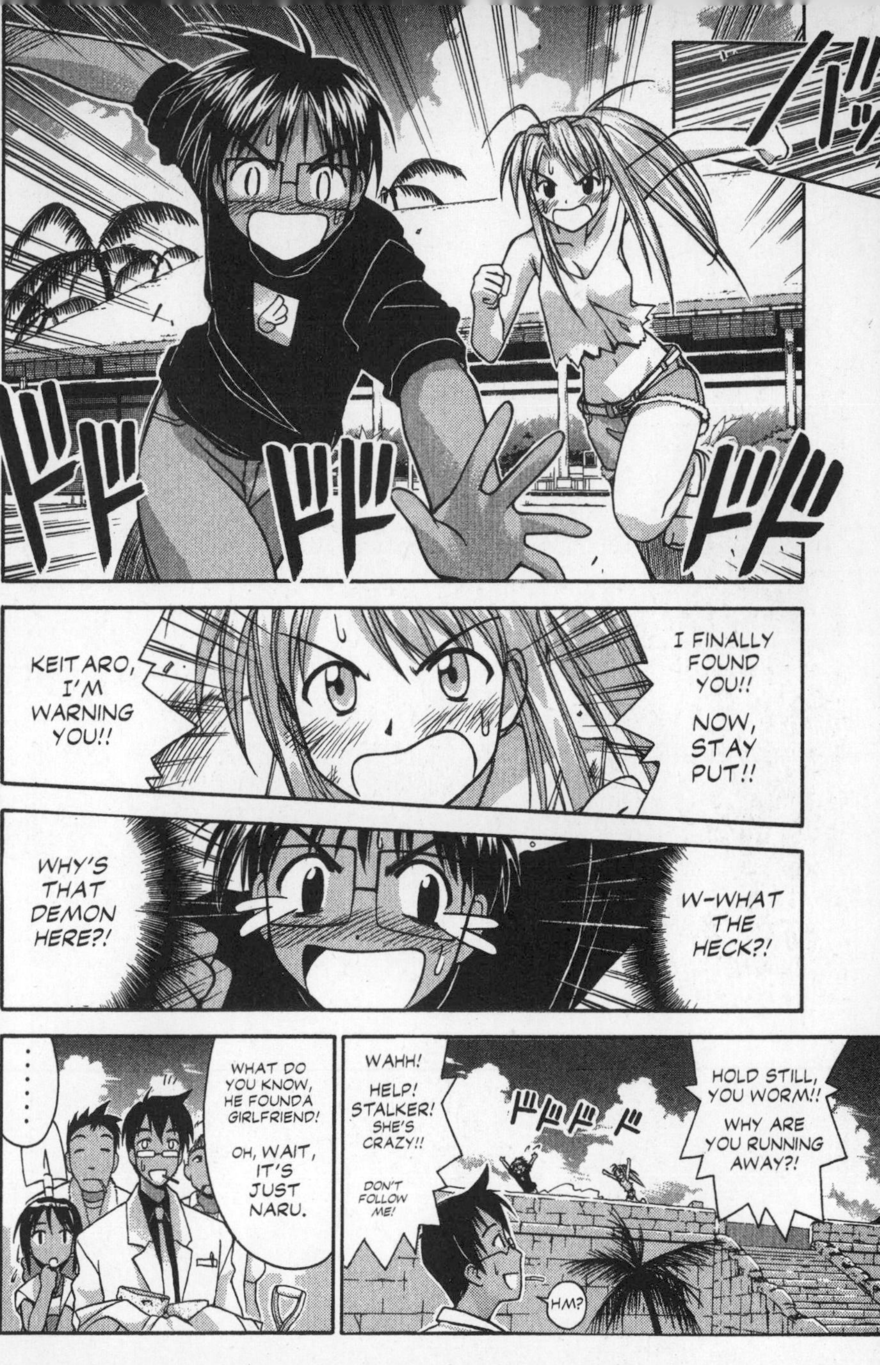
バッ
ドドド
ドドド
ドド
I FINALLY FOUND YOU!!
NOW, STAY PUT!!
KEITARO, I'M WARNING YOU!!
W-WHAT THE HECK?!
WHY'S THAT DEMON HERE?!
HOLD STILL, YOU WORM!!
WHY ARE YOU RUNNING AWAY?!
ドドドド
WAHH!
HELP! STALKER! SHE'S CRAZY!!
DON'T FOLLOW ME!
HM?
WHAT DO YOU KNOW, HE FOUNDA GIRLFRIEND!
OH, WAIT, IT'S JUST NARU.
......

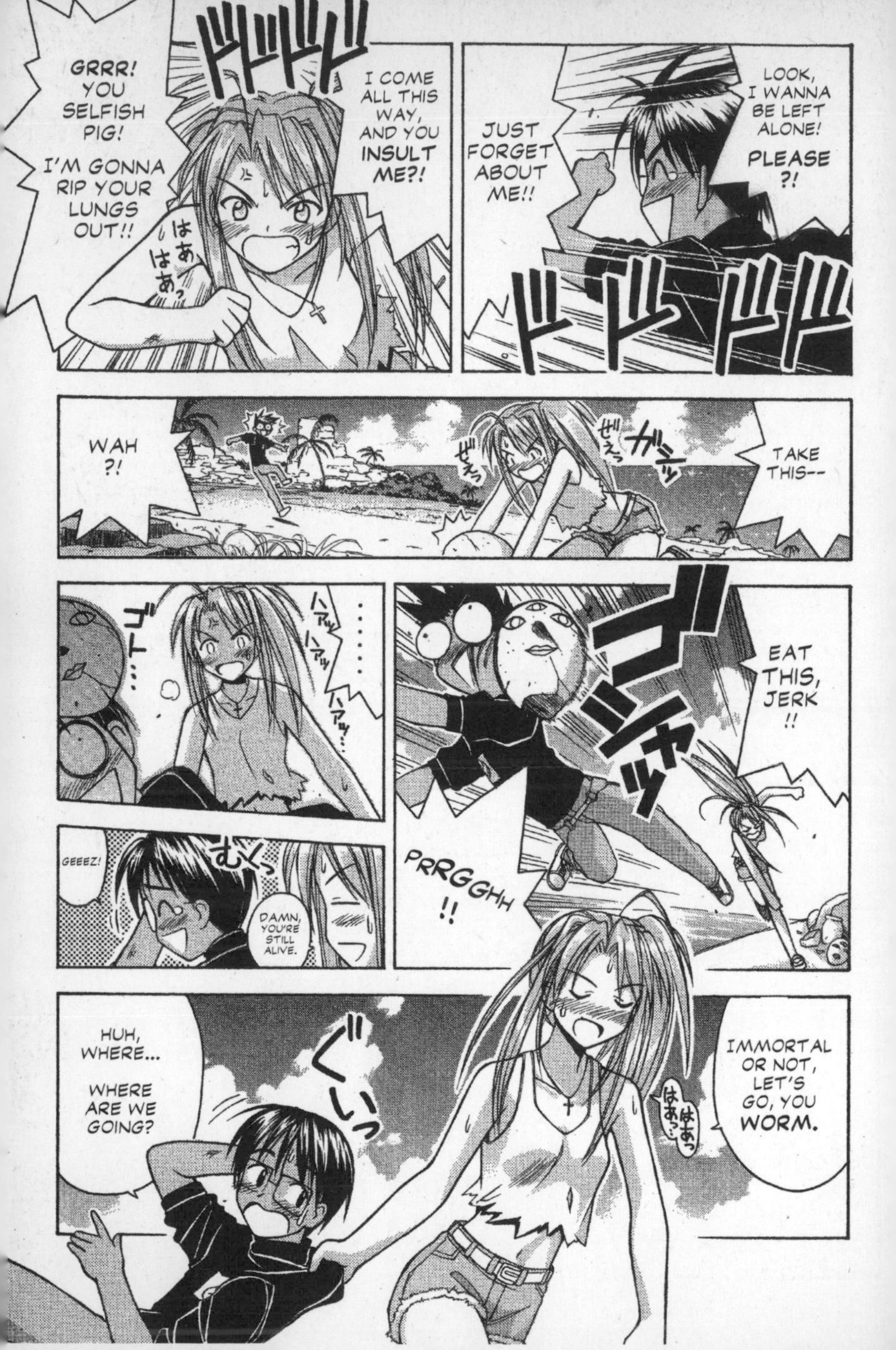
LOOK, I WANNA BE LEFT ALONE! PLEASE?!
JUST FORGET ABOUT ME!!
ドドドド
ドドドド
I COME ALL THIS WAY, AND YOU INSULT ME?!
GRRR! YOU SELFISH PIG!
I'M GONNA RIP YOUR LUNGS OUT!!
はあっはあっ
TAKE THIS--
ガシッ
ぜえっぜえっ
WAH?!
EAT THIS, JERK!!
ゴシャッ
PRRGGHH!!
......
ハァッ ハァッ ハァッ...
ゴト…
DAMN, YOU'RE STILL ALIVE.
むくっ
GEEEZ!
IMMORTAL OR NOT, LET'S GO, YOU WORM.
はあっはあっ
ぐいっ
HUH, WHERE... WHERE ARE WE GOING?

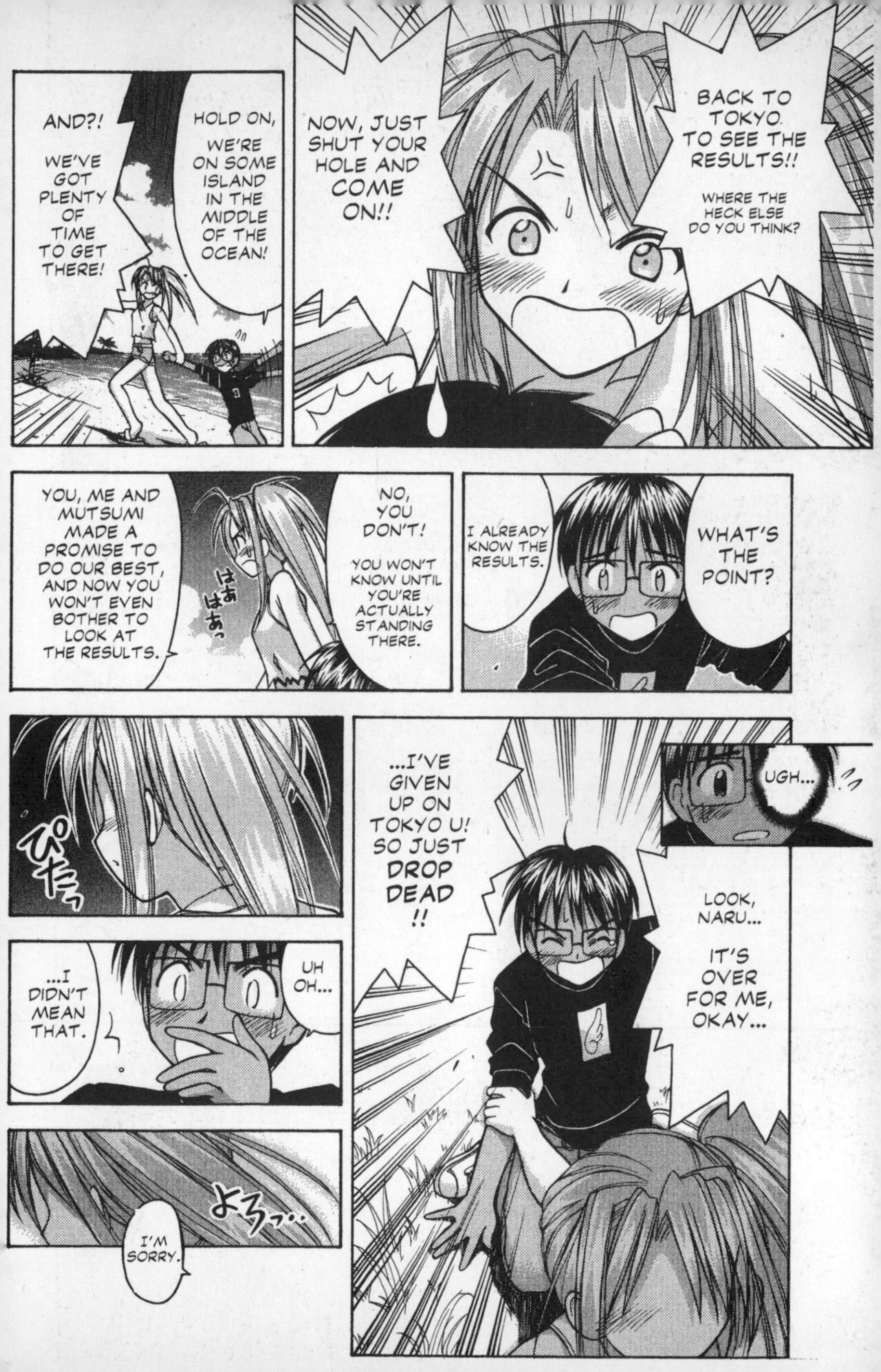
BACK TO TOKYO TO SEE THE RESULTS!!
WHERE THE HECK ELSE DO YOU THINK?
NOW, JUST SHUT YOUR HOLE AND COME ON!!
HOLD ON, WE'RE ON SOME ISLAND IN THE MIDDLE OF THE OCEAN!
AND?! WE'VE GOT PLENTY OF TIME TO GET THERE!
WHAT'S THE POINT?
I ALREADY KNOW THE RESULTS.
NO, YOU DON'T!
YOU WON'T KNOW UNTIL YOU'RE ACTUALLY STANDING THERE.
はあ はあっ
YOU, ME AND MUTSUMI MADE A PROMISE TO DO OUR BEST, AND NOW YOU WON'T EVEN BOTHER TO LOOK AT THE RESULTS.
UGH...
LOOK, NARU...
IT'S OVER FOR ME, OKAY...
...I'VE GIVEN UP ON TOKYO U! SO JUST DROP DEAD!!
ぴたっ
UH OH...
...I DIDN'T MEAN THAT.
よろっ
I'M SORRY.

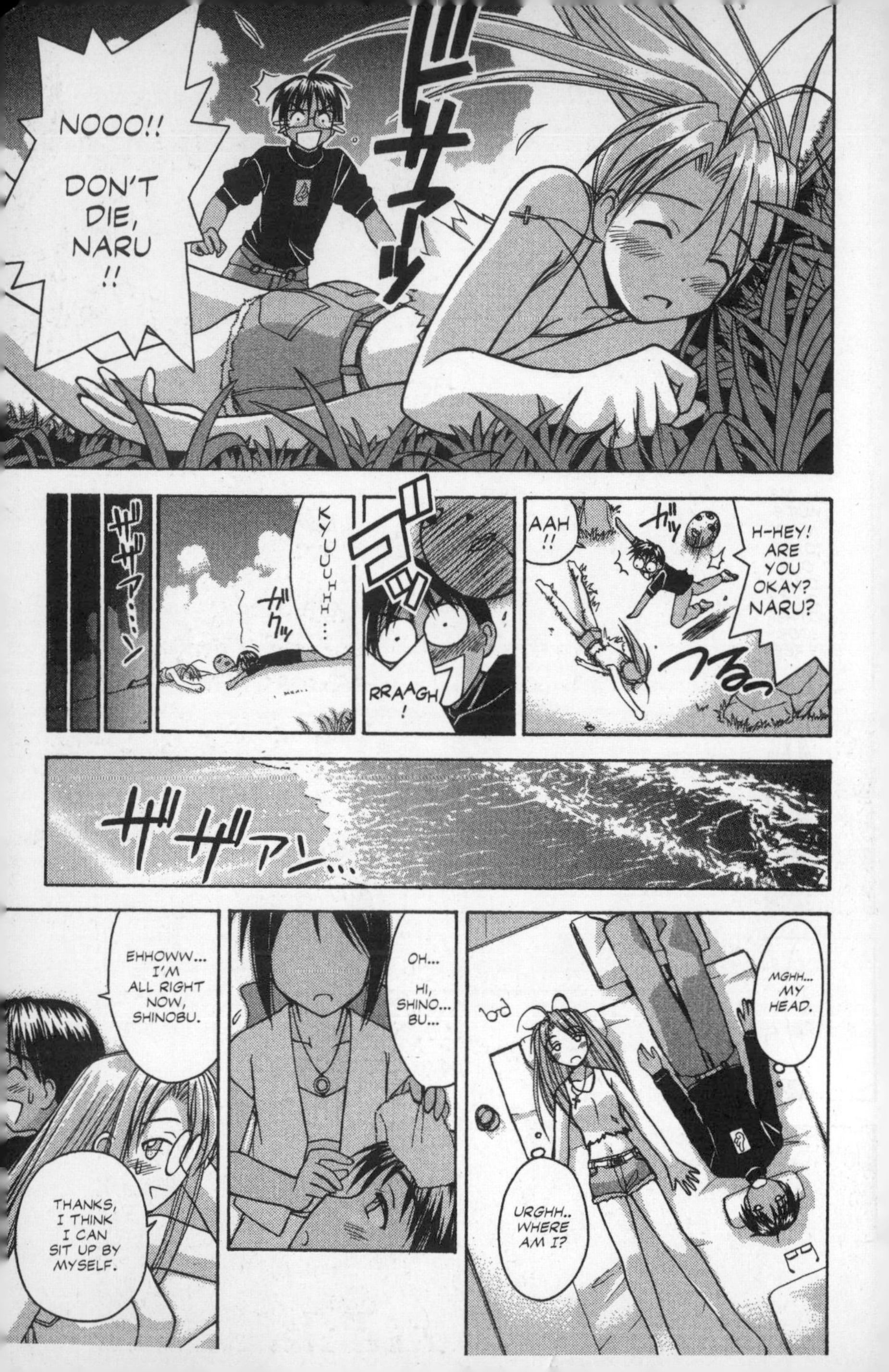
NOOO!! DON'T DIE, NARU!!
H-HEY! ARE YOU OKAY? NARU?
AAH!!
KYUUUHH...
RRAAGH!
MGHH... MY HEAD.
URGHH.. WHERE AM I?
OH... HI, SHINO... BU...
EHHOWW... I'M ALL RIGHT NOW, SHINOBU.
THANKS, I THINK I CAN SIT UP BY MYSELF.

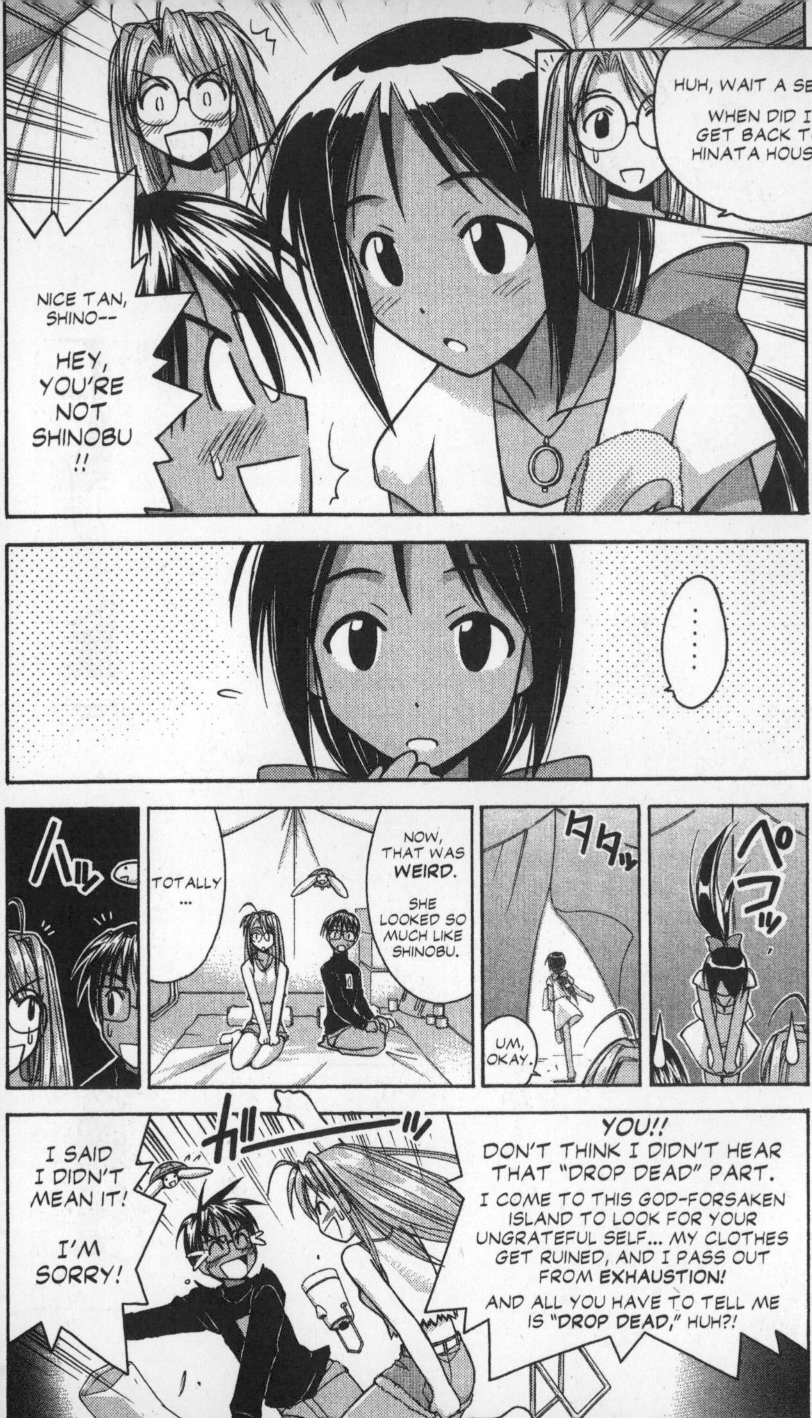
HUH, WAIT A SEC.
WHEN DID I GET BACK TO HINATA HOUSE?
NICE TAN, SHINO--
HEY, YOU'RE NOT SHINOBU!!
......
ペコッ
タタッ
UM, OKAY.
NOW, THAT WAS WEIRD.
SHE LOOKED SO MUCH LIKE SHINOBU.
TOTALLY...
ハッ
YOU!!
DON'T THINK I DIDN'T HEAR THAT "DROP DEAD" PART.
I COME TO THIS GOD-FORSAKEN ISLAND TO LOOK FOR YOUR UNGRATEFUL SELF... MY CLOTHES GET RUINED, AND I PASS OUT FROM EXHAUSTION!
AND ALL YOU HAVE TO TELL ME IS "DROP DEAD," HUH?!
I SAID I DIDN'T MEAN IT!
I'M SORRY!

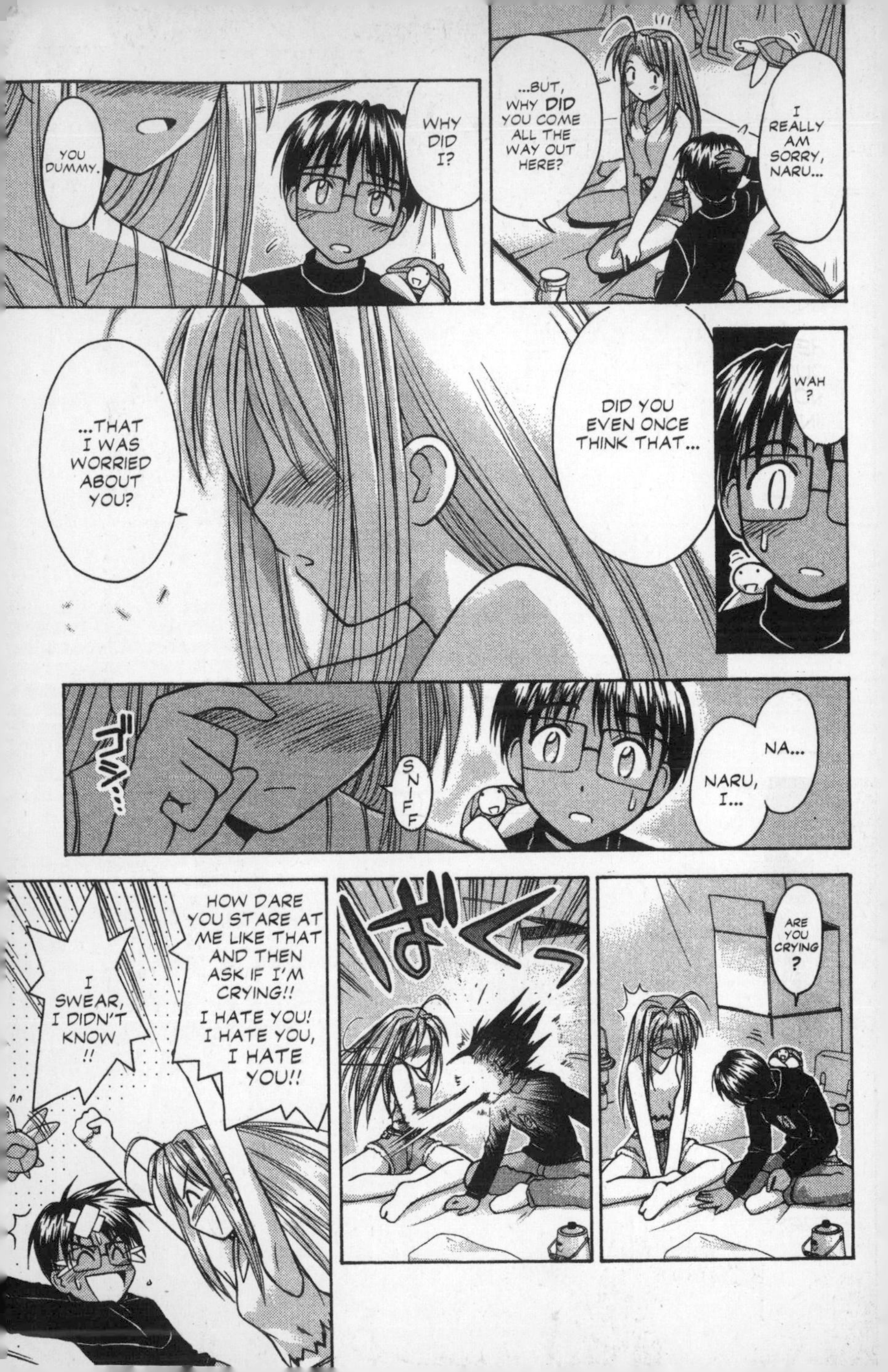
I REALLY AM SORRY, NARU...
...BUT, WHY DID YOU COME ALL THE WAY OUT HERE?
WHY DID I?
YOU DUMMY.
WAH?
DID YOU EVEN ONCE THINK THAT...
...THAT I WAS WORRIED ABOUT YOU?
NA...
NARU, I...
SNIFF
ARE YOU CRYING?
HOW DARE YOU STARE AT ME LIKE THAT AND THEN ASK IF I'M CRYING!!
I HATE YOU! I HATE YOU, I HATE YOU!!
I SWEAR, I DIDN'T KNOW!!

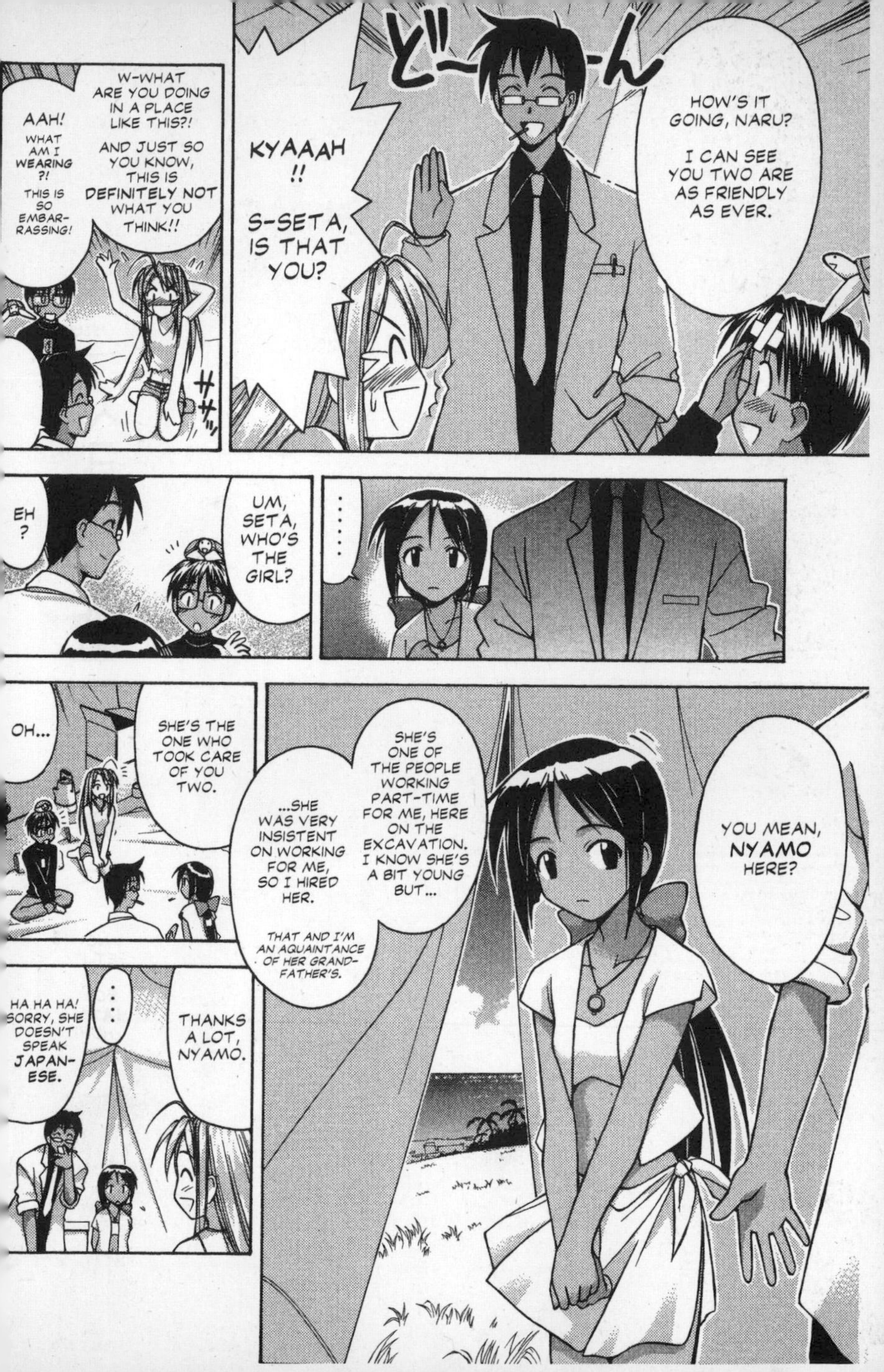
どど～ん
HOW'S IT GOING, NARU?
I CAN SEE YOU TWO ARE AS FRIENDLY AS EVER.
KYAAAH!!
S-SETA, IS THAT YOU?
W-WHAT ARE YOU DOING IN A PLACE LIKE THIS?!
AND JUST SO YOU KNOW, THIS IS DEFINITELY NOT WHAT YOU THINK!!
AAH!
WHAT AM I WEARING?!
THIS IS SO EMBARRASSING!
......
UM, SETA, WHO'S THE GIRL?
EH?
YOU MEAN, NYAMO HERE?
SHE'S ONE OF THE PEOPLE WORKING PART-TIME FOR ME, HERE ON THE EXCAVATION. I KNOW SHE'S A BIT YOUNG BUT...
...SHE WAS VERY INSISTENT ON WORKING FOR ME, SO I HIRED HER.
THAT AND I'M AN AQUAINTANCE OF HER GRAND-FATHER'S.
SHE'S THE ONE WHO TOOK CARE OF YOU TWO.
OH...
THANKS A LOT, NYAMO.
....
HA HA HA! SORRY, SHE DOESN'T SPEAK JAPAN-ESE.

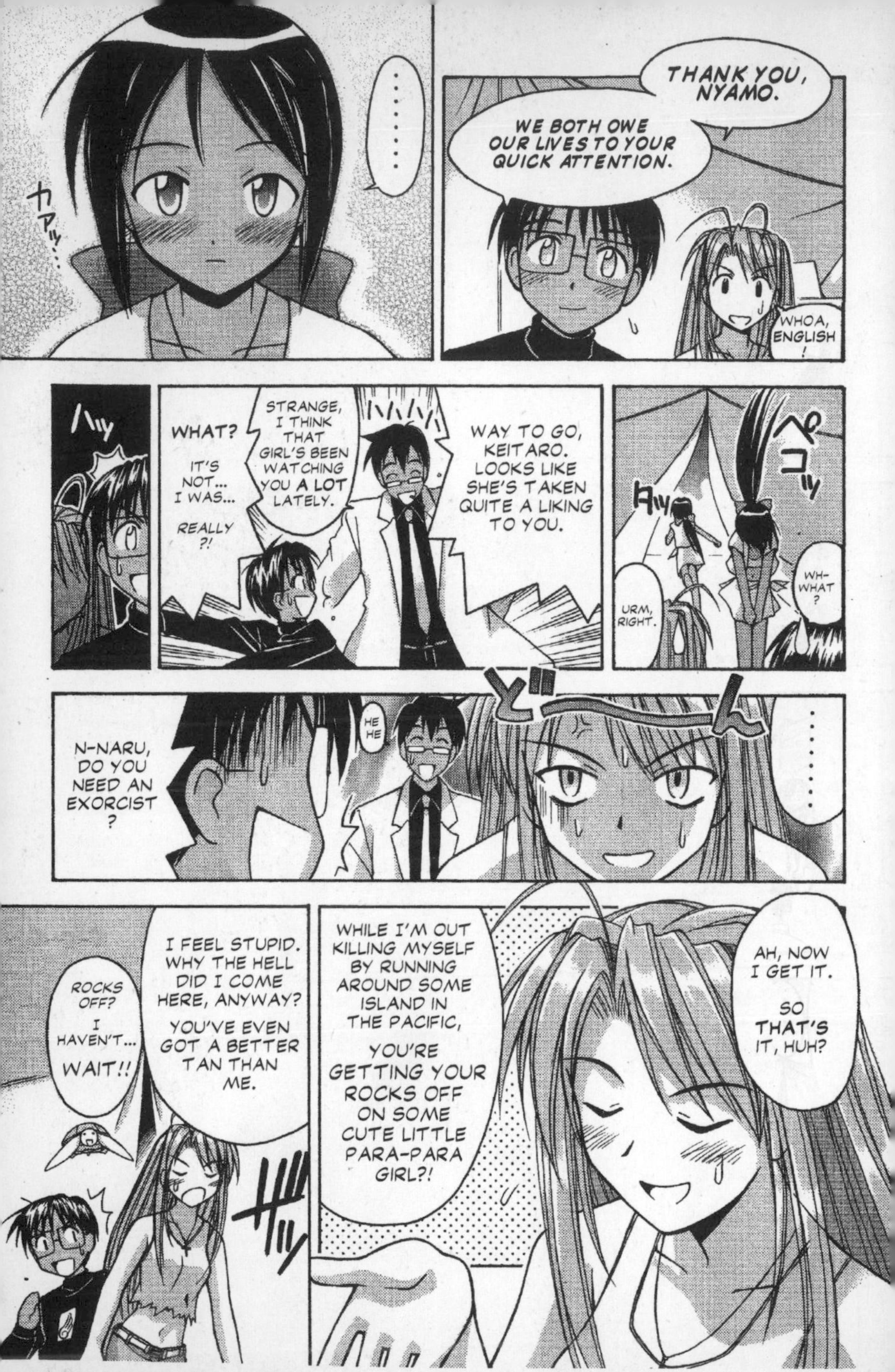
THANK YOU, NYAMO.
WE BOTH OWE OUR LIVES TO YOUR QUICK ATTENTION.
WHOA, ENGLISH!
......
WH-WHAT?
URM, RIGHT.
WAY TO GO, KEITARO. LOOKS LIKE SHE'S TAKEN QUITE A LIKING TO YOU.
STRANGE, I THINK THAT GIRL'S BEEN WATCHING YOU **A LOT** LATELY.
WHAT?
IT'S NOT... I WAS...
REALLY?!
......
HE HE
N-NARU, DO YOU NEED AN EXORCIST?
AH, NOW I GET IT.
SO **THAT'S** IT, HUH?
WHILE I'M OUT KILLING MYSELF BY RUNNING AROUND SOME ISLAND IN THE PACIFIC,
YOU'RE GETTING YOUR ROCKS OFF ON SOME CUTE LITTLE PARA-PARA GIRL?!
I FEEL STUPID. WHY THE HELL DID I COME HERE, ANYWAY?
YOU'VE EVEN GOT A BETTER TAN THAN ME.
ROCKS OFF? I HAVEN'T... WAIT!!

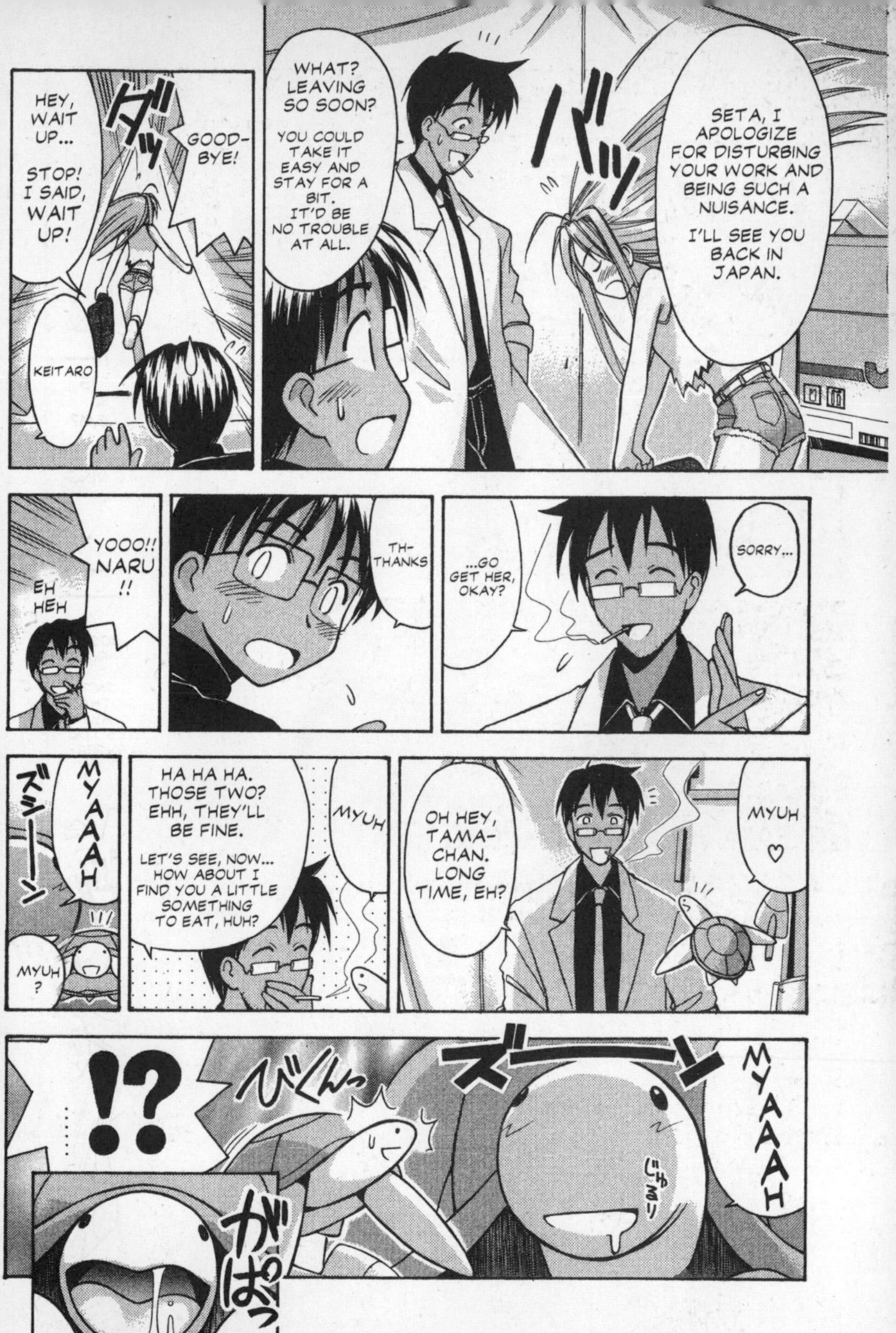
SETA, I APOLOGIZE FOR DISTURBING YOUR WORK AND BEING SUCH A NUISANCE.
I'LL SEE YOU BACK IN JAPAN.
バッ
WHAT? LEAVING SO SOON?
YOU COULD TAKE IT EASY AND STAY FOR A BIT. IT'D BE NO TROUBLE AT ALL.
GOOD-BYE!
ダッ
HEY, WAIT UP...
STOP! I SAID, WAIT UP!
KEITARO
SORRY...
...GO GET HER, OKAY?
TH-THANKS
YOOO!! NARU!!
EH HEH
MYUH ♡
OH HEY, TAMA-CHAN. LONG TIME, EH?
MYUH
HA HA HA. THOSE TWO? EHH, THEY'LL BE FINE.
LET'S SEE, NOW... HOW ABOUT I FIND YOU A LITTLE SOMETHING TO EAT, HUH?
MYAAAH
ズシーン
MYUH ?
MYAAAH
ズーン
じゅるり
びくんっ
!?
......
がぱっ

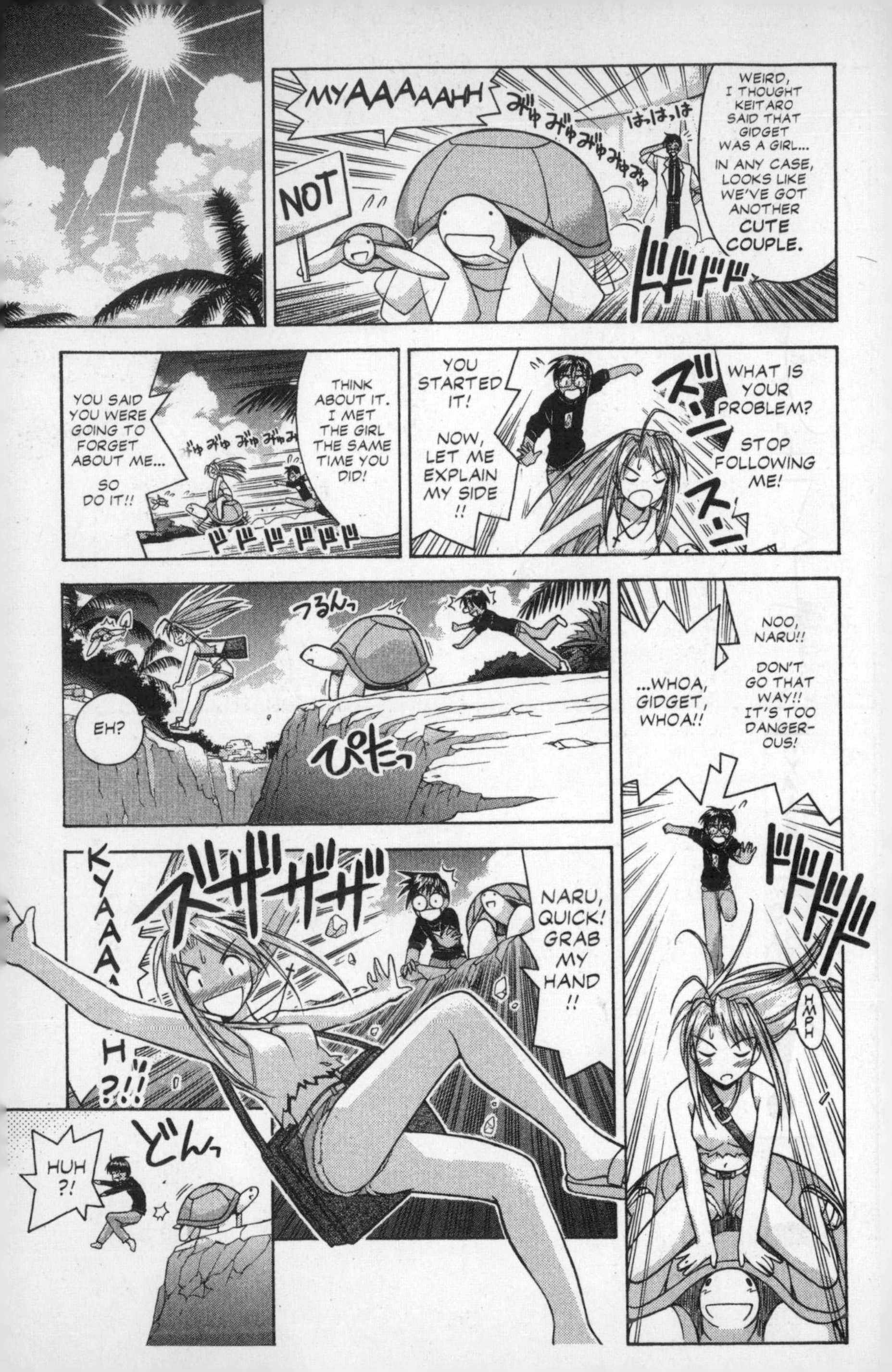
WEIRD, I THOUGHT KEITARO SAID THAT GIDGET WAS A GIRL... IN ANY CASE, LOOKS LIKE WE'VE GOT ANOTHER CUTE COUPLE.
はっはっは
みゅ みゅ みゅ みゅ みゅ みゅ みゅ
MYAAAAAHH
NOT
ドドドド
WHAT IS YOUR PROBLEM?
STOP FOLLOWING ME!
ズン ズン
YOU STARTED IT!
NOW, LET ME EXPLAIN MY SIDE!!
THINK ABOUT IT. I MET THE GIRL THE SAME TIME YOU DID!
YOU SAID YOU WERE GOING TO FORGET ABOUT ME...
SO DO IT!!
みゅ みゅ みゅ みゅ みゅ
ドドドドドド
NOO, NARU!!
DON'T GO THAT WAY!! IT'S TOO DANGER-OUS!
...WHOA, GIDGET, WHOA!!
ドドドド
HMPH
つるんっ
EH?
ぴたっ
NARU, QUICK! GRAB MY HAND!!
ズザザザ
KYAAAAH?!!
HUH?!
どんっ

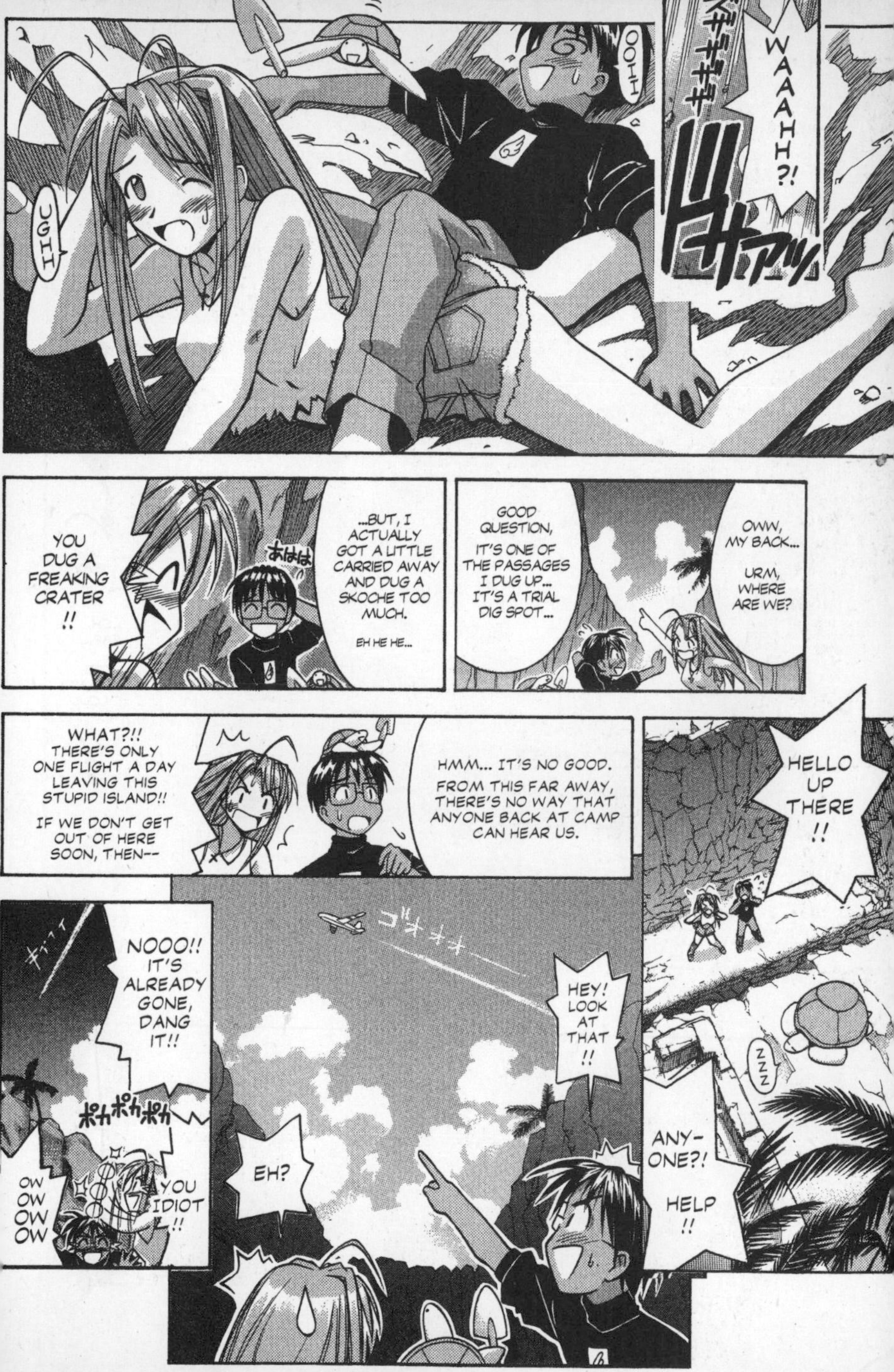

WAAAHH?!
ズザザザ
ドサァッ
OOIII
UGHH
OWW, MY BACK... URM, WHERE ARE WE?
GOOD QUESTION, IT'S ONE OF THE PASSAGES I DUG UP... IT'S A TRIAL DIG SPOT...
...BUT, I ACTUALLY GOT A LITTLE CARRIED AWAY AND DUG A SKOCHE TOO MUCH.
EH HE HE...
あはは
YOU DUG A FREAKING CRATER!!
HELLO UP THERE!!
ANY-ONE?! HELP!!
ZZZ
HMM... IT'S NO GOOD. FROM THIS FAR AWAY, THERE'S NO WAY THAT ANYONE BACK AT CAMP CAN HEAR US.
WHAT?!! THERE'S ONLY ONE FLIGHT A DAY LEAVING THIS STUPID ISLAND!! IF WE DON'T GET OUT OF HERE SOON, THEN--
HEY! LOOK AT THAT!!
EH?
NOOO!! IT'S ALREADY GONE, DANG IT!!
ポカポカポカ
YOU IDIOT!!
OW OW OW OW

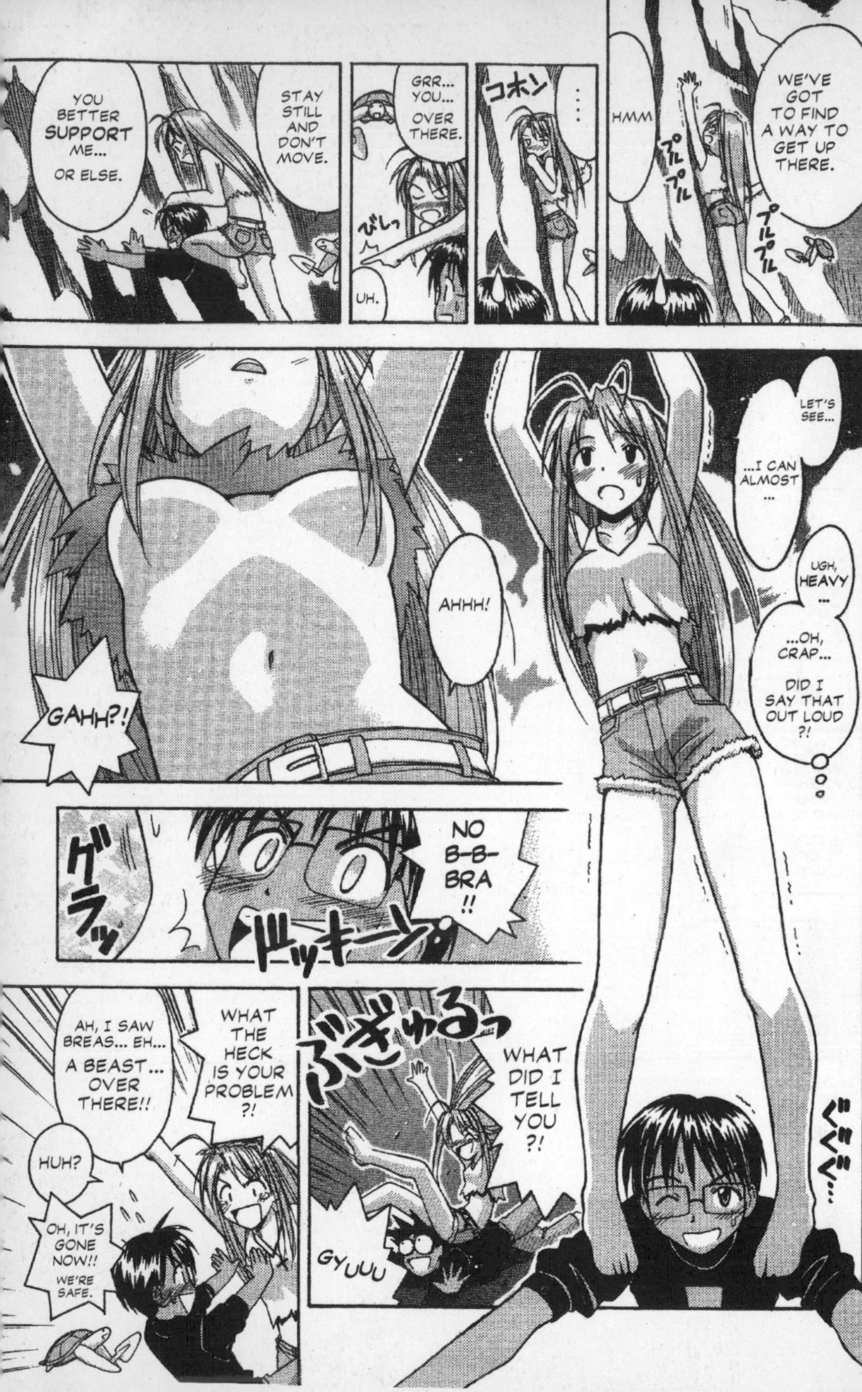

WE'VE GOT TO FIND A WAY TO GET UP THERE.
HMM
プルプル
プルプル
....
コホン
GRR... YOU... OVER THERE.
びしっ
UH.
STAY STILL AND DON'T MOVE.
YOU BETTER SUPPORT ME... OR ELSE.
LET'S SEE...
...I CAN ALMOST...
UGH, HEAVY...
...OH, CRAP...
DID I SAY THAT OUT LOUD?!
じじじ...
AHHH!
GAHH?!
NO B-B-BRA!!
グラッ
ドッキーン
WHAT DID I TELL YOU?!
ぶぎゅるっ
WHAT THE HECK IS YOUR PROBLEM?!
GYUUU
AH, I SAW BREAS... EH... A BEAST... OVER THERE!!
HUH?
OH, IT'S GONE NOW!! WE'RE SAFE.

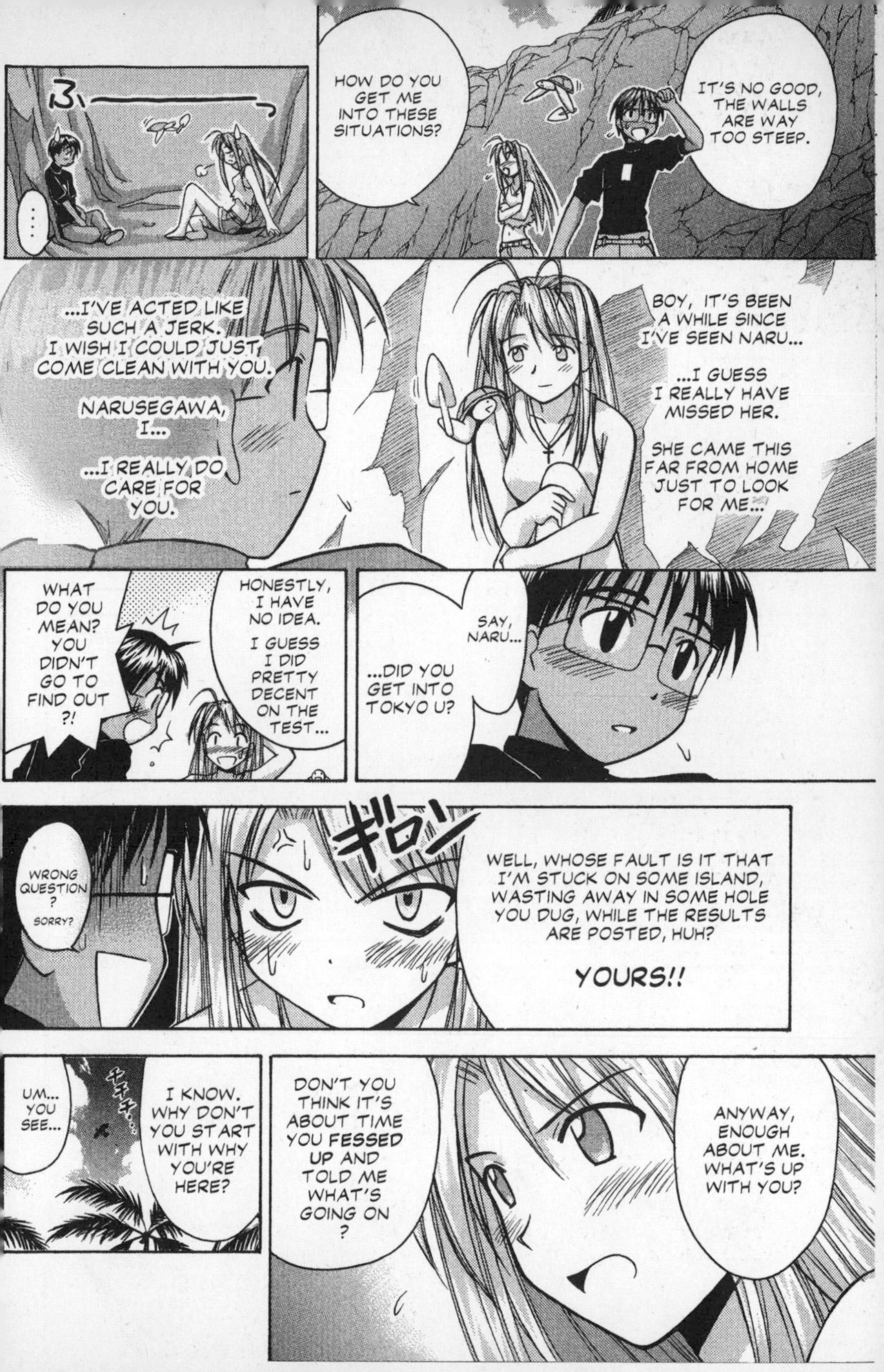
IT'S NO GOOD, THE WALLS ARE WAY TOO STEEP.
HOW DO YOU GET ME INTO THESE SITUATIONS?
ふ—————
....
BOY, IT'S BEEN A WHILE SINCE I'VE SEEN NARU...
...I GUESS I REALLY HAVE MISSED HER.
SHE CAME THIS FAR FROM HOME JUST TO LOOK FOR ME...
...I'VE ACTED LIKE SUCH A JERK. I WISH I COULD JUST COME CLEAN WITH YOU.
NARUSEGAWA, I...
...I REALLY DO CARE FOR YOU.
SAY, NARU...
...DID YOU GET INTO TOKYO U?
HONESTLY, I HAVE NO IDEA.
I GUESS I DID PRETTY DECENT ON THE TEST...
WHAT DO YOU MEAN? YOU DIDN'T GO TO FIND OUT ?!
ギロン
WELL, WHOSE FAULT IS IT THAT I'M STUCK ON SOME ISLAND, WASTING AWAY IN SOME HOLE YOU DUG, WHILE THE RESULTS ARE POSTED, HUH?
YOURS!!
WRONG QUESTION ?
SORRY?
ANYWAY, ENOUGH ABOUT ME. WHAT'S UP WITH YOU?
DON'T YOU THINK IT'S ABOUT TIME YOU FESSED UP AND TOLD ME WHAT'S GOING ON ?
I KNOW. WHY DON'T YOU START WITH WHY YOU'RE HERE?
UM... YOU SEE...

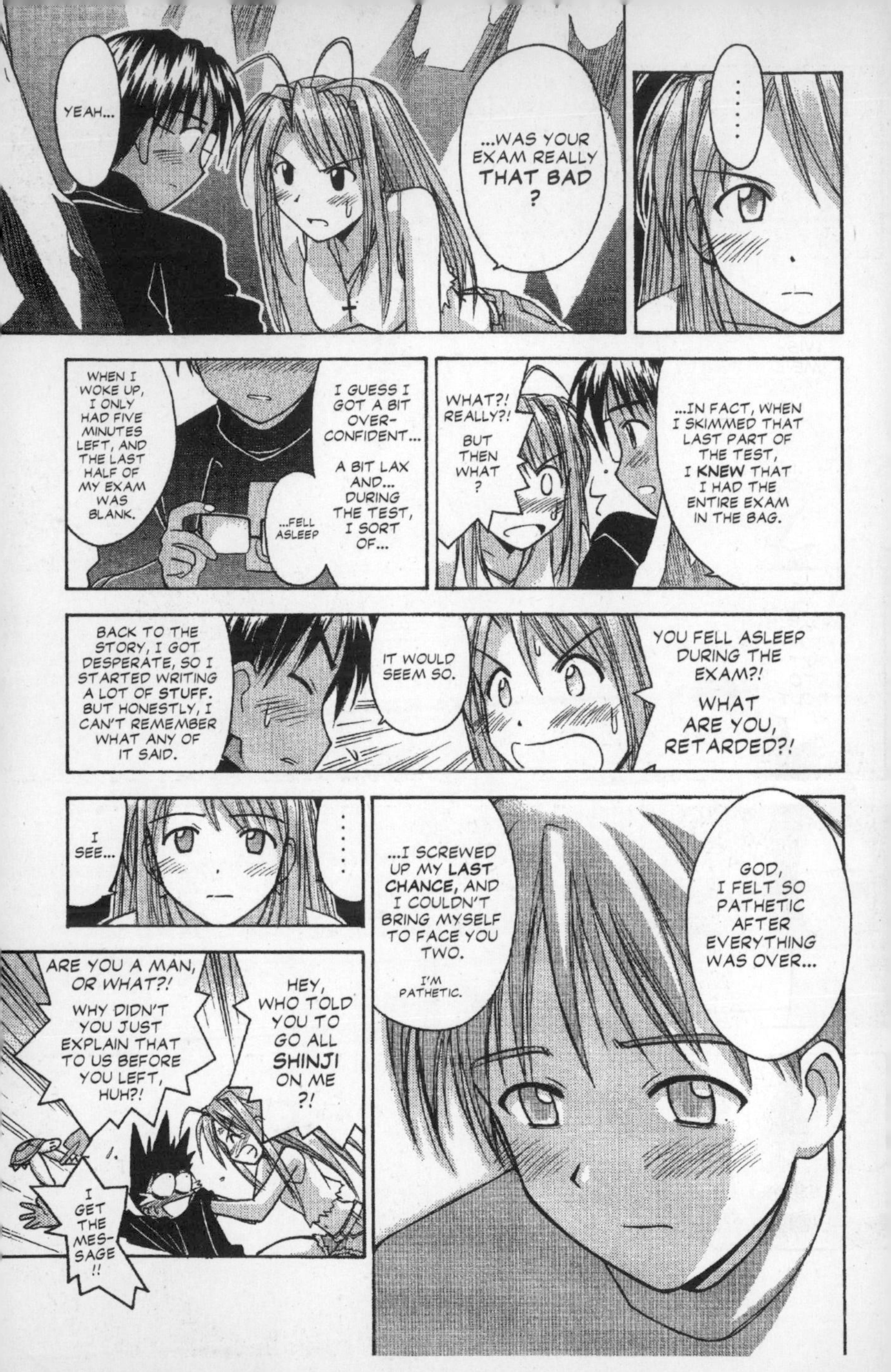
......
...WAS YOUR EXAM REALLY THAT BAD ?
YEAH...
...IN FACT, WHEN I SKIMMED THAT LAST PART OF THE TEST, I KNEW THAT I HAD THE ENTIRE EXAM IN THE BAG.
WHAT?! REALLY?!
BUT THEN WHAT ?
I GUESS I GOT A BIT OVER-CONFIDENT...
A BIT LAX AND... DURING THE TEST, I SORT OF...
...FELL ASLEEP
WHEN I WOKE UP, I ONLY HAD FIVE MINUTES LEFT, AND THE LAST HALF OF MY EXAM WAS BLANK.
YOU FELL ASLEEP DURING THE EXAM?!
WHAT ARE YOU, RETARDED?!
IT WOULD SEEM SO.
BACK TO THE STORY, I GOT DESPERATE, SO I STARTED WRITING A LOT OF STUFF. BUT HONESTLY, I CAN'T REMEMBER WHAT ANY OF IT SAID.
GOD, I FELT SO PATHETIC AFTER EVERYTHING WAS OVER...
...I SCREWED UP MY LAST CHANCE, AND I COULDN'T BRING MYSELF TO FACE YOU TWO.
I'M PATHETIC.
......
I SEE...
HEY, WHO TOLD YOU TO GO ALL SHINJI ON ME ?!
ARE YOU A MAN, OR WHAT?!
WHY DIDN'T YOU JUST EXPLAIN THAT TO US BEFORE YOU LEFT, HUH?!
I GET THE MES-SAGE !!

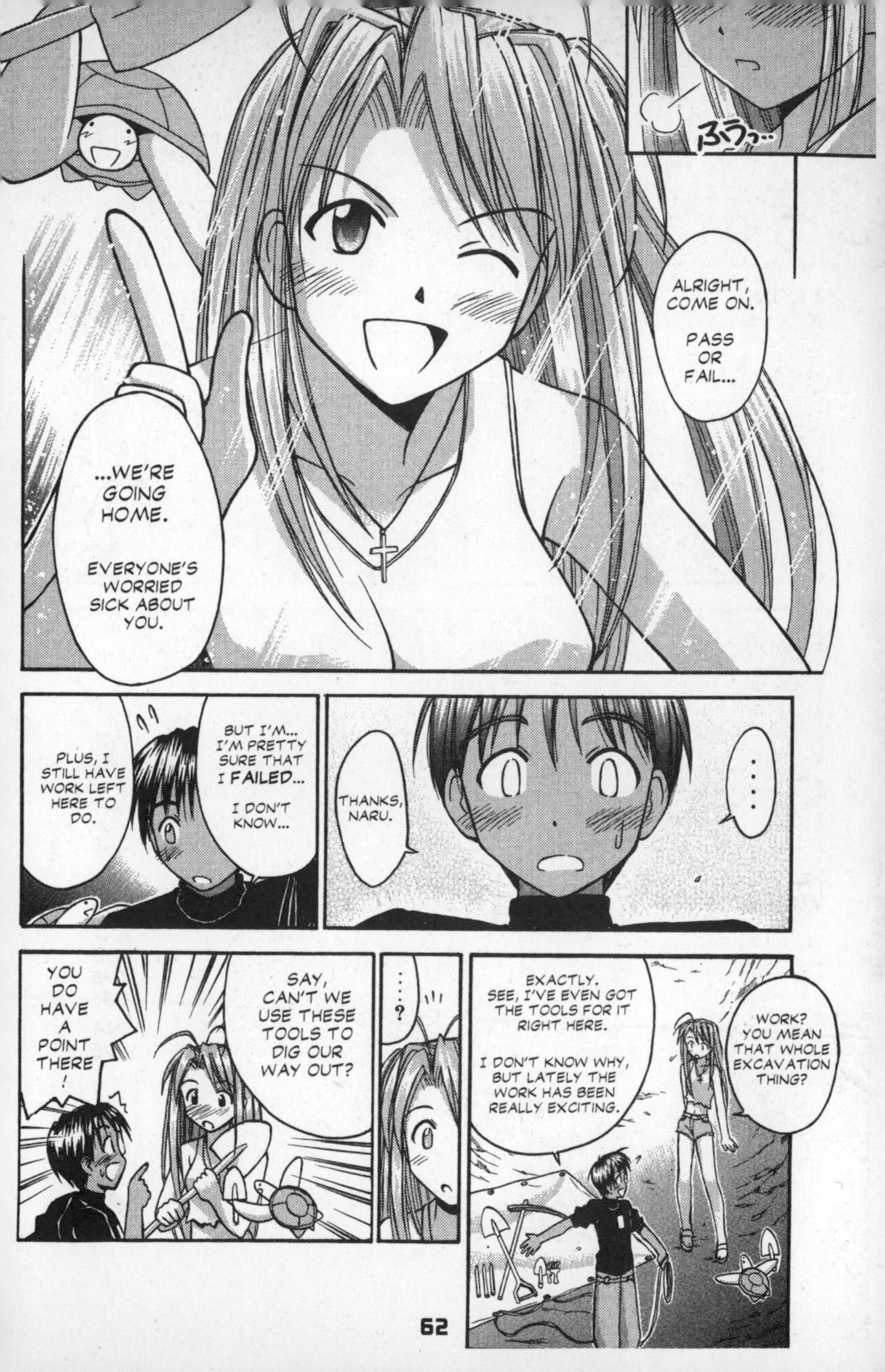
ふうっ...
ALRIGHT, COME ON.
PASS OR FAIL...
...WE'RE GOING HOME.
EVERYONE'S WORRIED SICK ABOUT YOU.
.....
THANKS, NARU.
BUT I'M... I'M PRETTY SURE THAT I **FAILED**...
I DON'T KNOW...
PLUS, I STILL HAVE WORK LEFT HERE TO DO.
WORK? YOU MEAN THAT WHOLE EXCAVATION THING?
EXACTLY. SEE, I'VE EVEN GOT THE TOOLS FOR IT RIGHT HERE.
I DON'T KNOW WHY, BUT LATELY THE WORK HAS BEEN REALLY EXCITING.
...?
SAY, CAN'T WE USE THESE TOOLS TO DIG OUR WAY OUT?
YOU DO HAVE A POINT THERE!

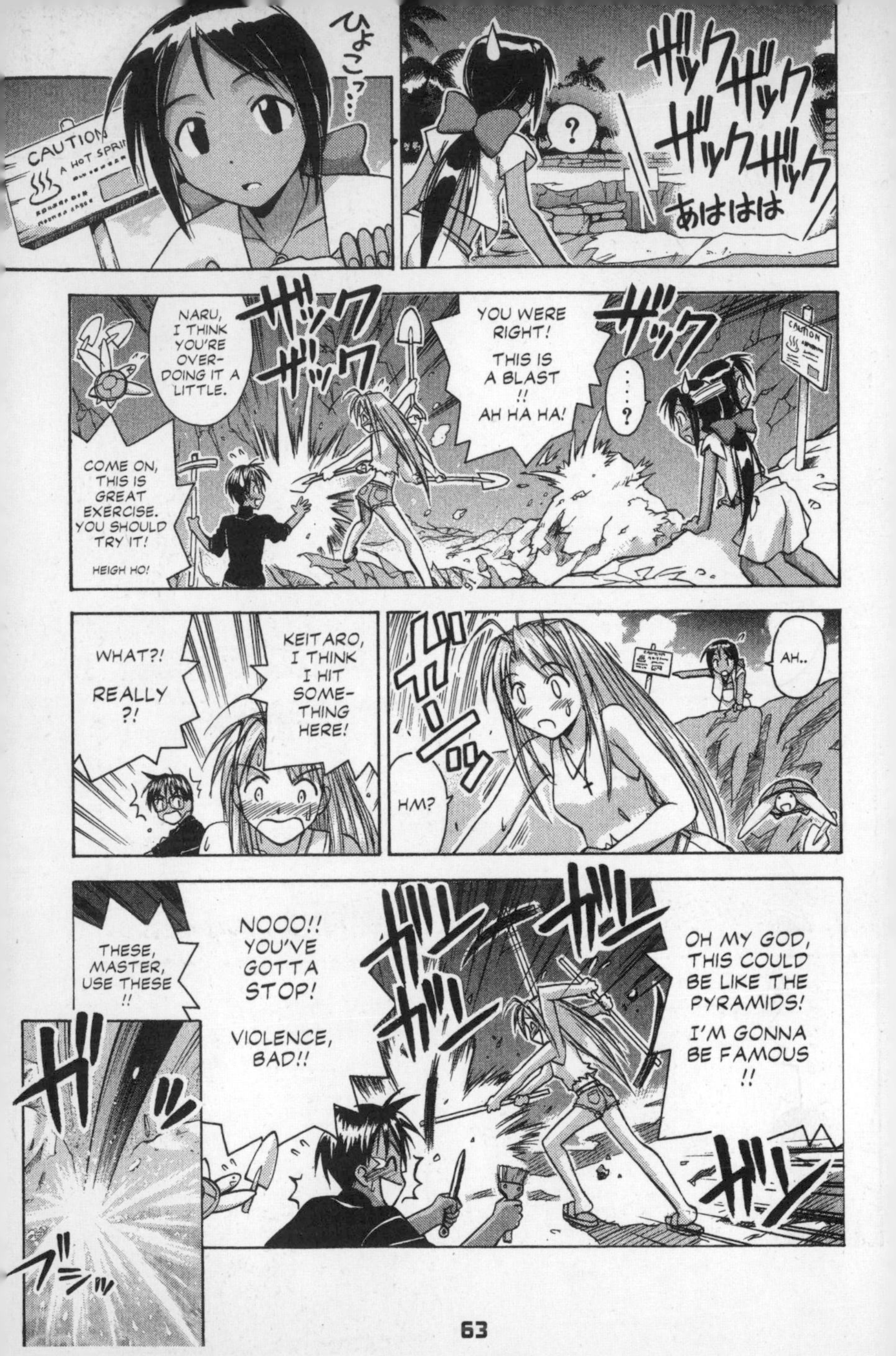
ザックザック
ザックザック
あははは
?
ひよこっ…
CAUTION
A HOT SPRIN
ザック
....?
YOU WERE RIGHT!
THIS IS A BLAST!! AH HA HA!
ザック ザック
NARU, I THINK YOU'RE OVER-DOING IT A LITTLE.
COME ON, THIS IS GREAT EXERCISE. YOU SHOULD TRY IT!
HEIGH HO!
CAUTION
AH..
HM?
KEITARO, I THINK I HIT SOME-THING HERE!
WHAT?!
REALLY?!
OH MY GOD, THIS COULD BE LIKE THE PYRAMIDS!
I'M GONNA BE FAMOUS!!
NOOO!! YOU'VE GOTTA STOP!
VIOLENCE, BAD!!
THESE, MASTER, USE THESE!!

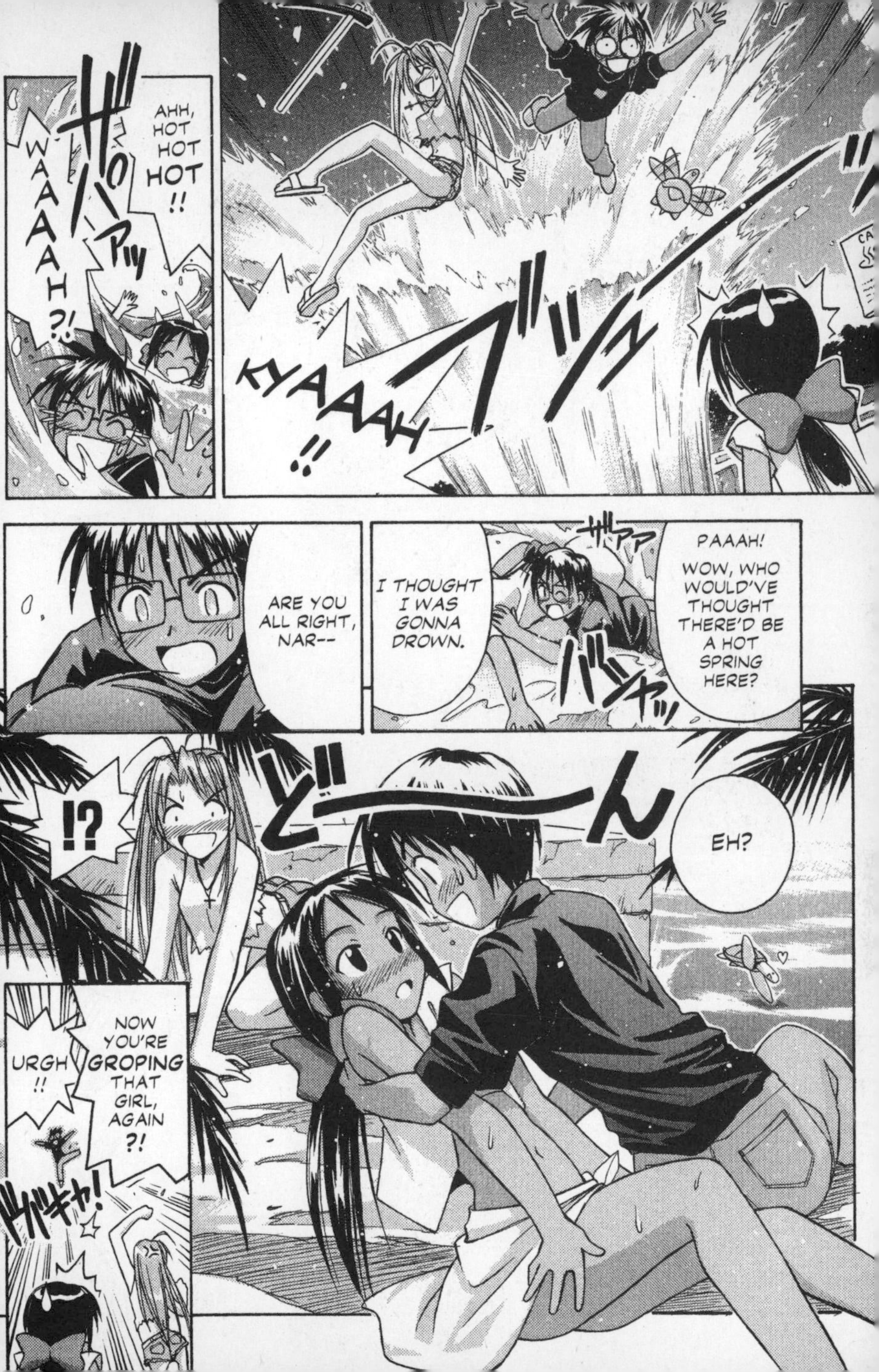

KYAAAAH!!
AHH, HOT HOT HOT!!
WAAAAAH?!
PAAAH!
WOW, WHO WOULD'VE THOUGHT THERE'D BE A HOT SPRING HERE?
I THOUGHT I WAS GONNA DROWN.
ARE YOU ALL RIGHT, NAR--
EH?
!?
NOW YOU'RE GROPING THAT GIRL, AGAIN?!
URGH!!

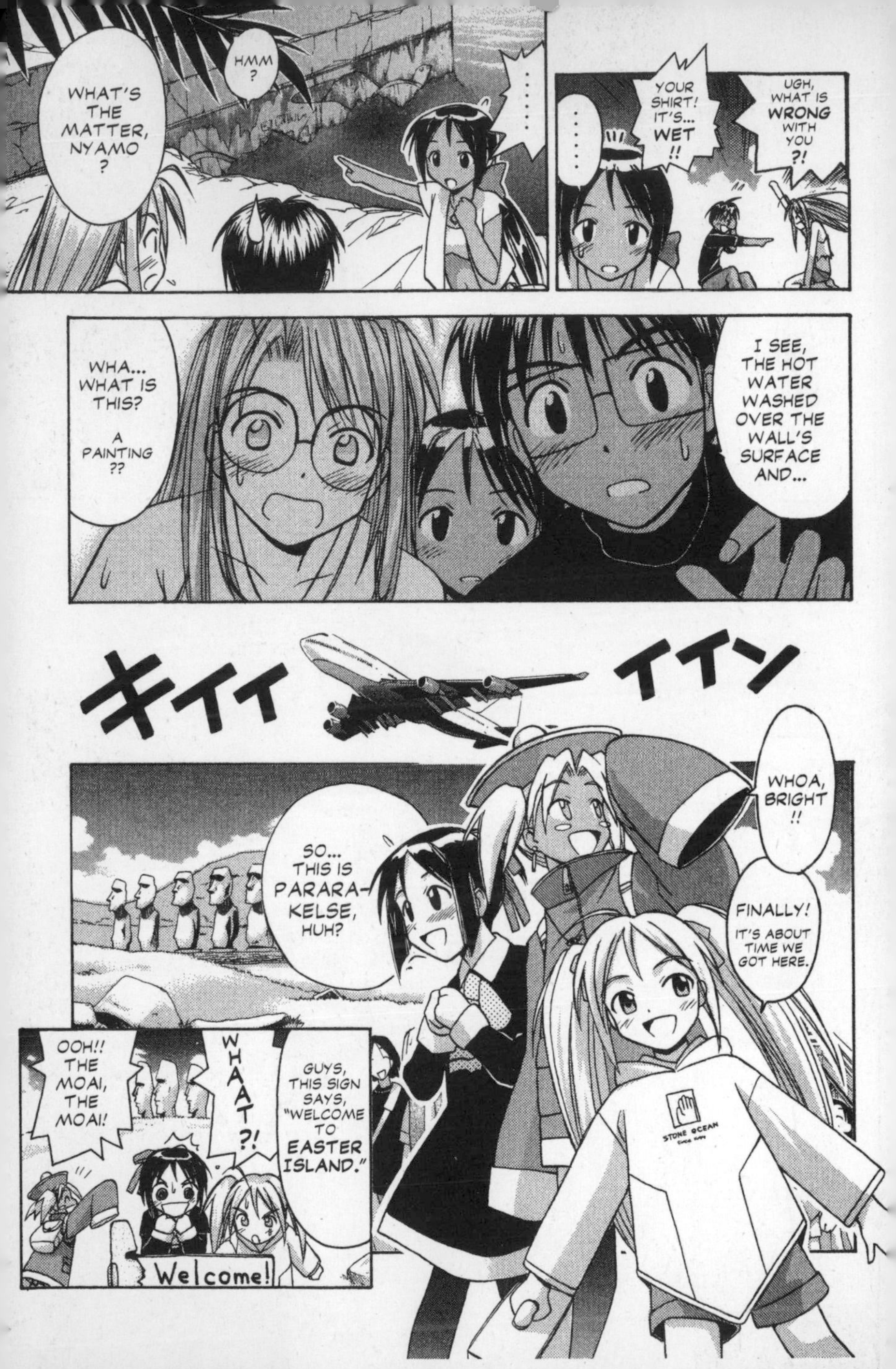

UGH, WHAT IS WRONG WITH YOU?!
YOUR SHIRT! IT'S... WET!!
......
....
HMM?
WHAT'S THE MATTER, NYAMO?
I SEE, THE HOT WATER WASHED OVER THE WALL'S SURFACE AND...
WHA... WHAT IS THIS? A PAINTING??
キイイ イイン
WHOA, BRIGHT!!
FINALLY! IT'S ABOUT TIME WE GOT HERE.
SO... THIS IS PARARA-KELSE, HUH?
STONE OCEAN
GUYS, THIS SIGN SAYS, "WELCOME TO EASTER ISLAND."
WHAAT?!
OOH!! THE MOAI, THE MOAI!
Welcome!

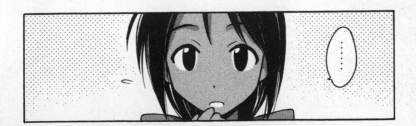

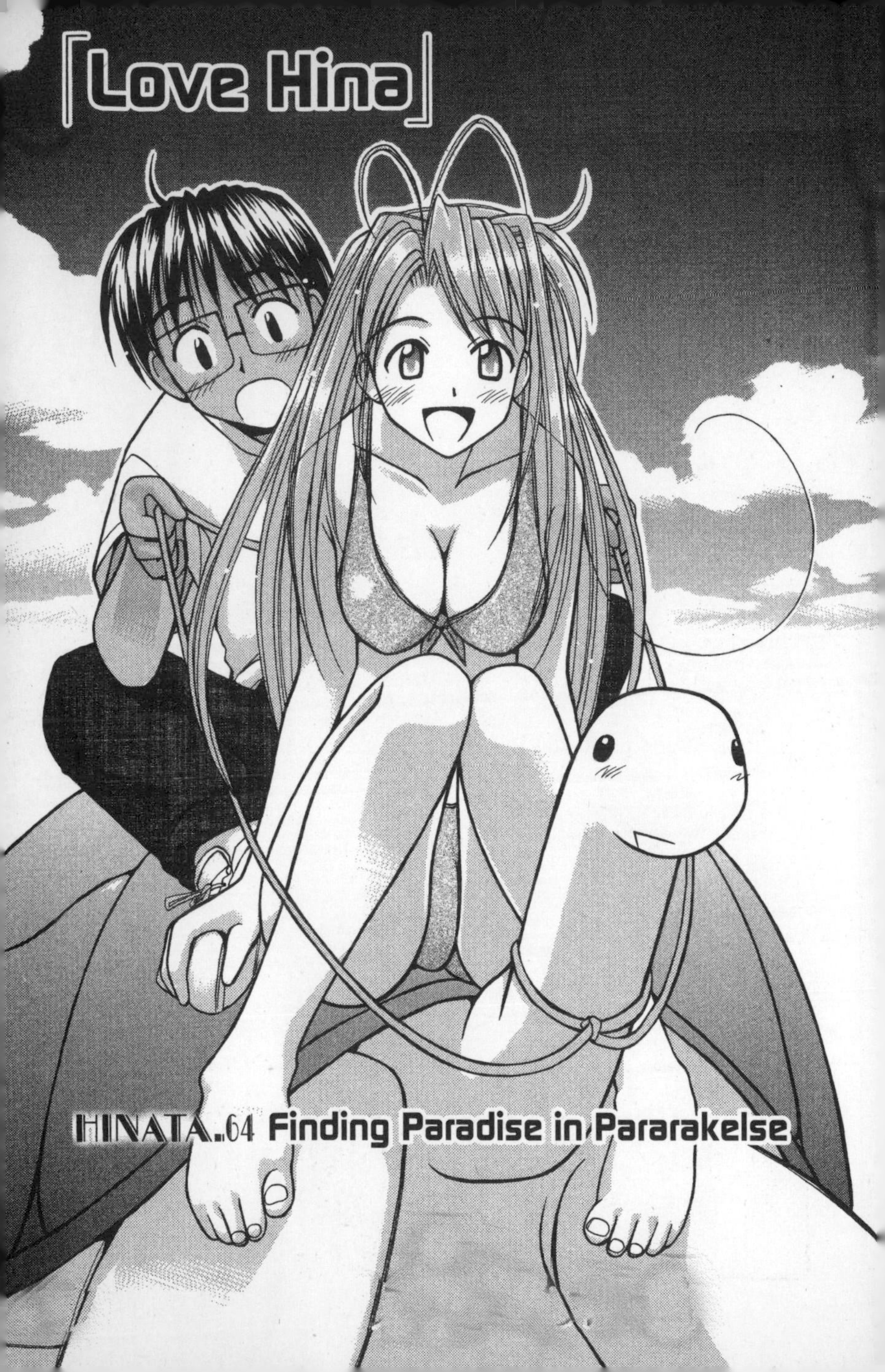
「Love Hina」
HINATA.64 Finding Paradise in Pararakelse

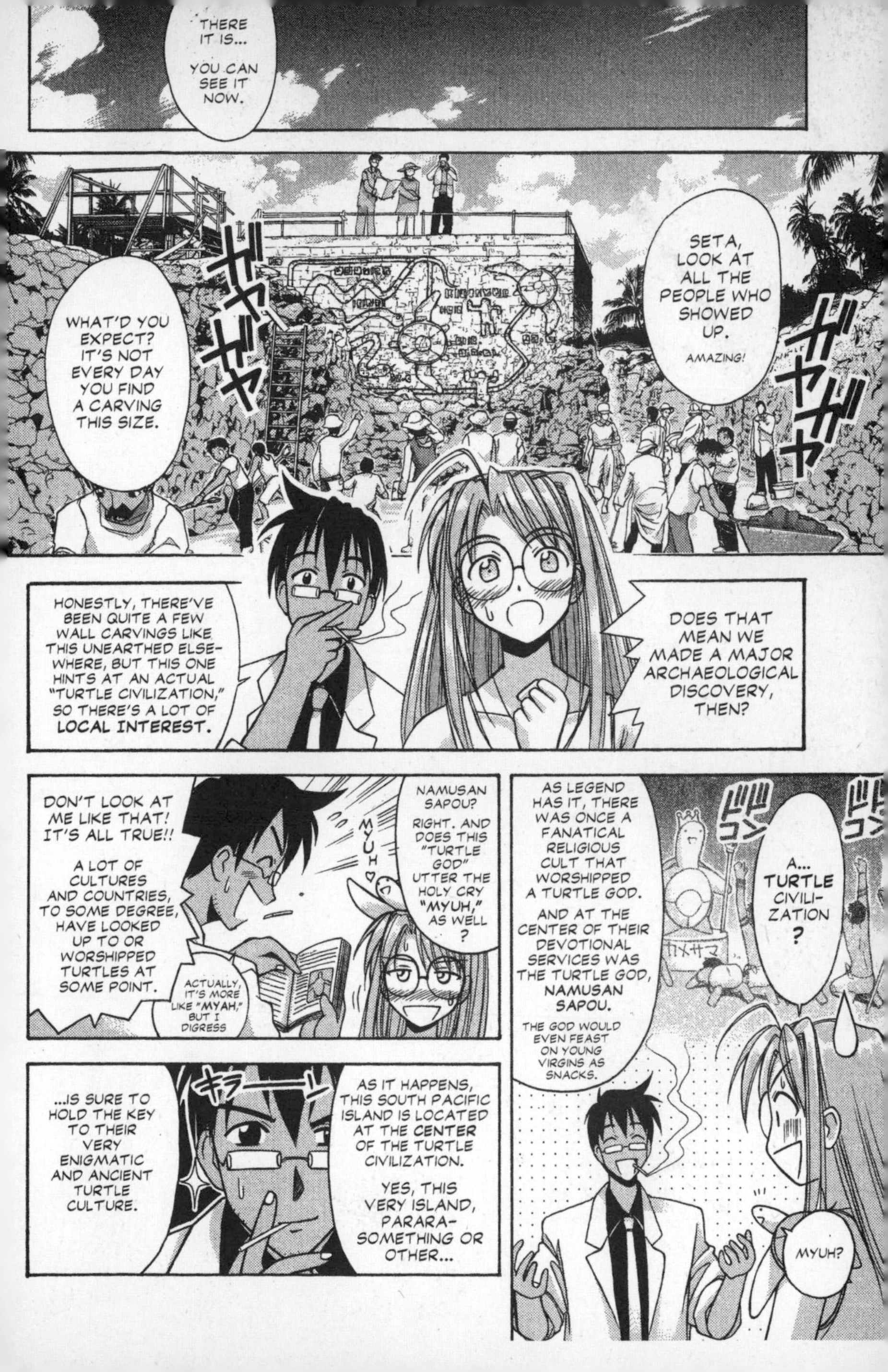
THERE IT IS... YOU CAN SEE IT NOW.
SETA, LOOK AT ALL THE PEOPLE WHO SHOWED UP.
AMAZING!
ガヤガヤ
ガヤガヤ
WHAT'D YOU EXPECT? IT'S NOT EVERY DAY YOU FIND A CARVING THIS SIZE.
DOES THAT MEAN WE MADE A MAJOR ARCHAEOLOGICAL DISCOVERY, THEN?
HONESTLY, THERE'VE BEEN QUITE A FEW WALL CARVINGS LIKE THIS UNEARTHED ELSE-WHERE, BUT THIS ONE HINTS AT AN ACTUAL "TURTLE CIVILIZATION," SO THERE'S A LOT OF LOCAL INTEREST.
ドン
ドン
A... TURTLE CIVILI-ZATION?
AS LEGEND HAS IT, THERE WAS ONCE A FANATICAL RELIGIOUS CULT THAT WORSHIPPED A TURTLE GOD.
AND AT THE CENTER OF THEIR DEVOTIONAL SERVICES WAS THE TURTLE GOD, NAMUSAN SAPOU.
THE GOD WOULD EVEN FEAST ON YOUNG VIRGINS AS SNACKS.
MYUH?
NAMUSAN SAPOU?
RIGHT. AND DOES THIS "TURTLE GOD" UTTER THE HOLY CRY "MYUH," AS WELL?
MYUH
DON'T LOOK AT ME LIKE THAT! IT'S ALL TRUE!!
A LOT OF CULTURES AND COUNTRIES, TO SOME DEGREE, HAVE LOOKED UP TO OR WORSHIPPED TURTLES AT SOME POINT.
ACTUALLY, IT'S MORE LIKE "MYAH," BUT I DIGRESS
AS IT HAPPENS, THIS SOUTH PACIFIC ISLAND IS LOCATED AT THE CENTER OF THE TURTLE CIVILIZATION.
YES, THIS VERY ISLAND, PARARA-SOMETHING OR OTHER...
...IS SURE TO HOLD THE KEY TO THEIR VERY ENIGMATIC AND ANCIENT TURTLE CULTURE.

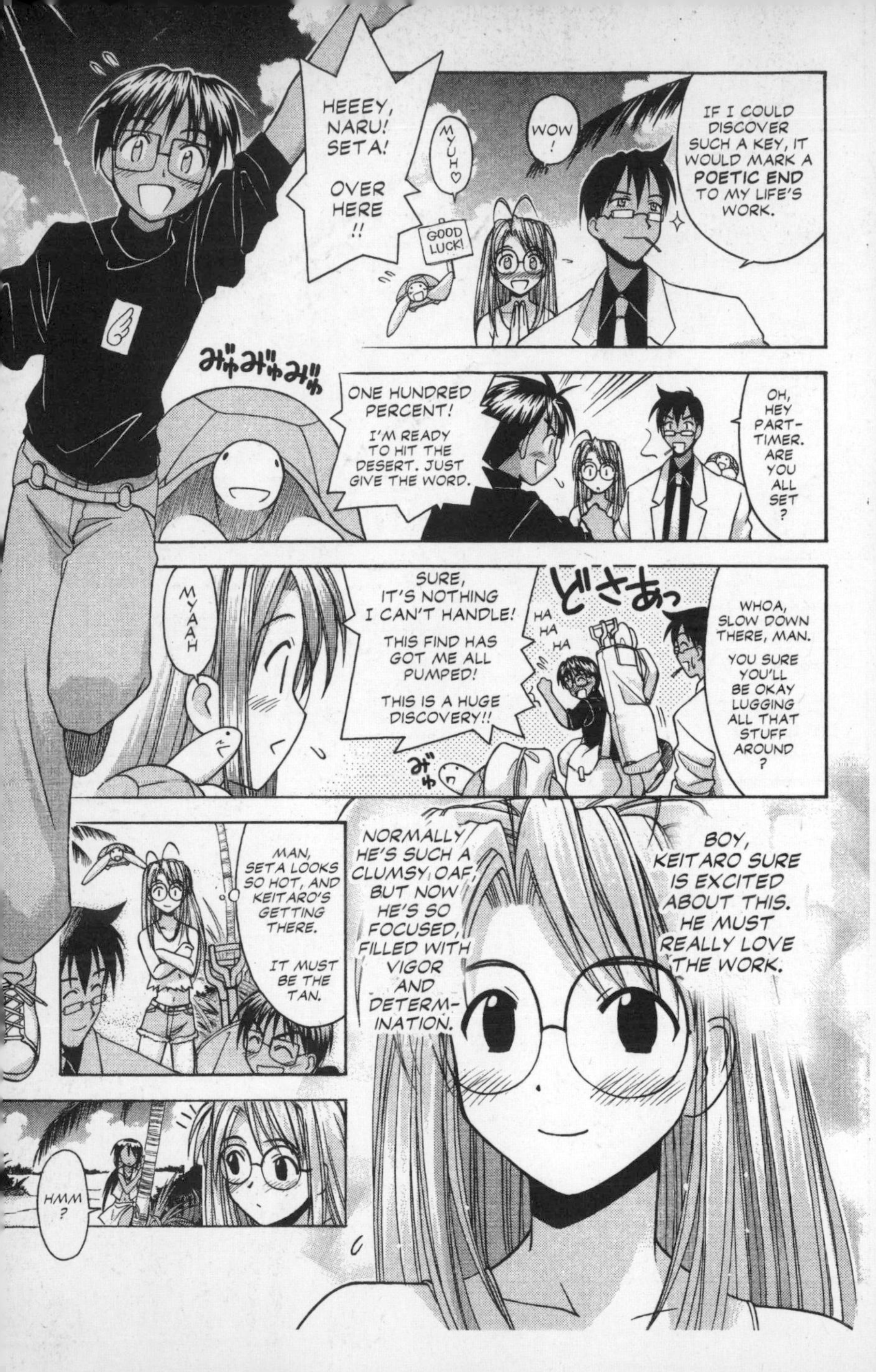
IF I COULD DISCOVER SUCH A KEY, IT WOULD MARK A **POETIC END** TO MY LIFE'S WORK.
WOW!
MYUH♡
GOOD LUCK!
HEEEY, NARU! SETA! OVER HERE!!
OH, HEY PART-TIMER. ARE YOU ALL SET?
ONE HUNDRED PERCENT! I'M READY TO HIT THE DESERT. JUST GIVE THE WORD.
みゅみゅみゅ
WHOA, SLOW DOWN THERE, MAN. YOU SURE YOU'LL BE OKAY LUGGING ALL THAT STUFF AROUND?
どさあっ
HA HA HA
SURE, IT'S NOTHING I CAN'T HANDLE! THIS FIND HAS GOT ME ALL PUMPED! THIS IS A HUGE DISCOVERY!!
みゅ
MYAAH
BOY, KEITARO SURE IS EXCITED ABOUT THIS. HE MUST REALLY LOVE THE WORK.
NORMALLY HE'S SUCH A CLUMSY OAF, BUT NOW HE'S SO FOCUSED, FILLED WITH VIGOR AND DETERMINATION.
MAN, SETA LOOKS SO HOT, AND KEITARO'S GETTING THERE. IT MUST BE THE TAN.
HMM?

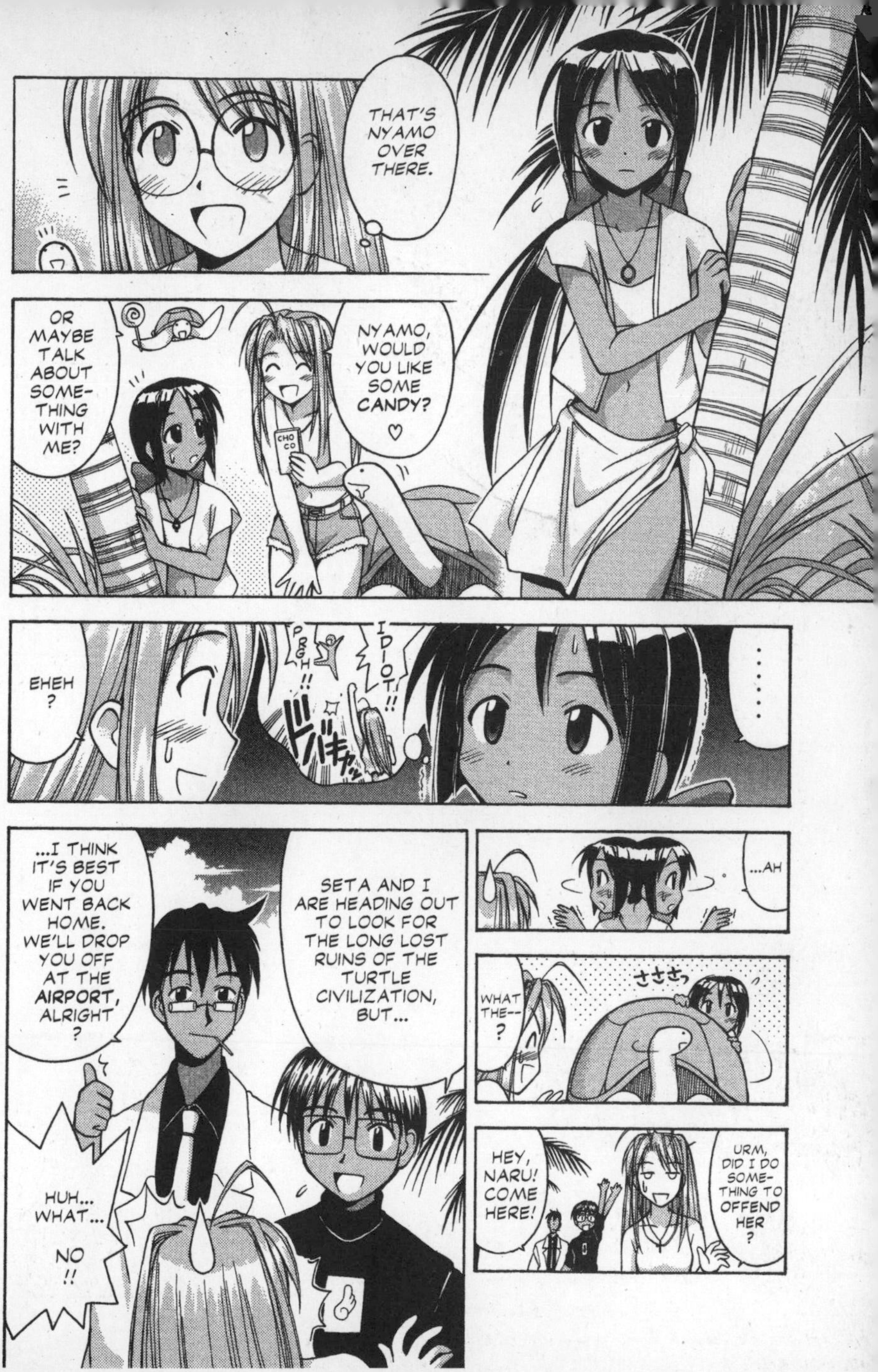
THAT'S NYAMO OVER THERE.
NYAMO, WOULD YOU LIKE SOME CANDY? ♡
CHOCO
OR MAYBE TALK ABOUT SOME-THING WITH ME?
......
IDIOT!!
PRGH!!
ドバキャッ
EHEH?
...AH
さささっ
WHAT THE--?
URM, DID I DO SOME-THING TO OFFEND HER?
HEY, NARU! COME HERE!
SETA AND I ARE HEADING OUT TO LOOK FOR THE LONG LOST RUINS OF THE TURTLE CIVILIZATION, BUT...
...I THINK IT'S BEST IF YOU WENT BACK HOME. WE'LL DROP YOU OFF AT THE AIRPORT, ALRIGHT?
HUH... WHAT...
NO!!

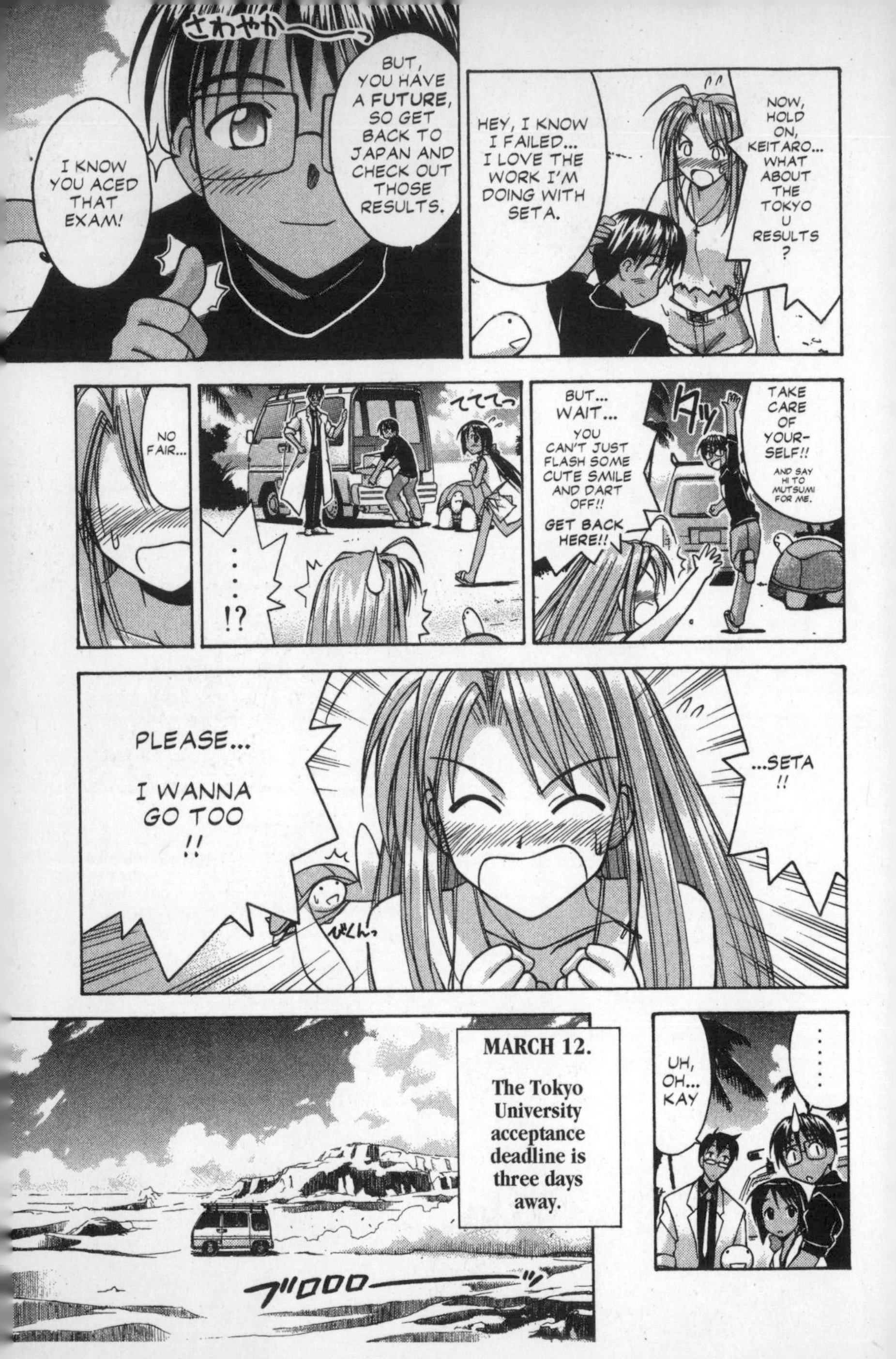
NOW, HOLD ON, KEITARO... WHAT ABOUT THE TOKYO U RESULTS?
HEY, I KNOW I FAILED... I LOVE THE WORK I'M DOING WITH SETA.
さわやか〜
BUT, YOU HAVE A FUTURE, SO GET BACK TO JAPAN AND CHECK OUT THOSE RESULTS.
I KNOW YOU ACED THAT EXAM!
TAKE CARE OF YOURSELF!!
AND SAY HI TO MUTSUMI FOR ME.
ダッ
BUT... WAIT... YOU CAN'T JUST FLASH SOME CUTE SMILE AND DART OFF!! GET BACK HERE!!
てててっ
......!?
NO FAIR...
...SETA!!
PLEASE... I WANNA GO TOO!!
びくんっ
......
UH, OH... KAY
MARCH 12.
The Tokyo University acceptance deadline is three days away.
ブロロロ

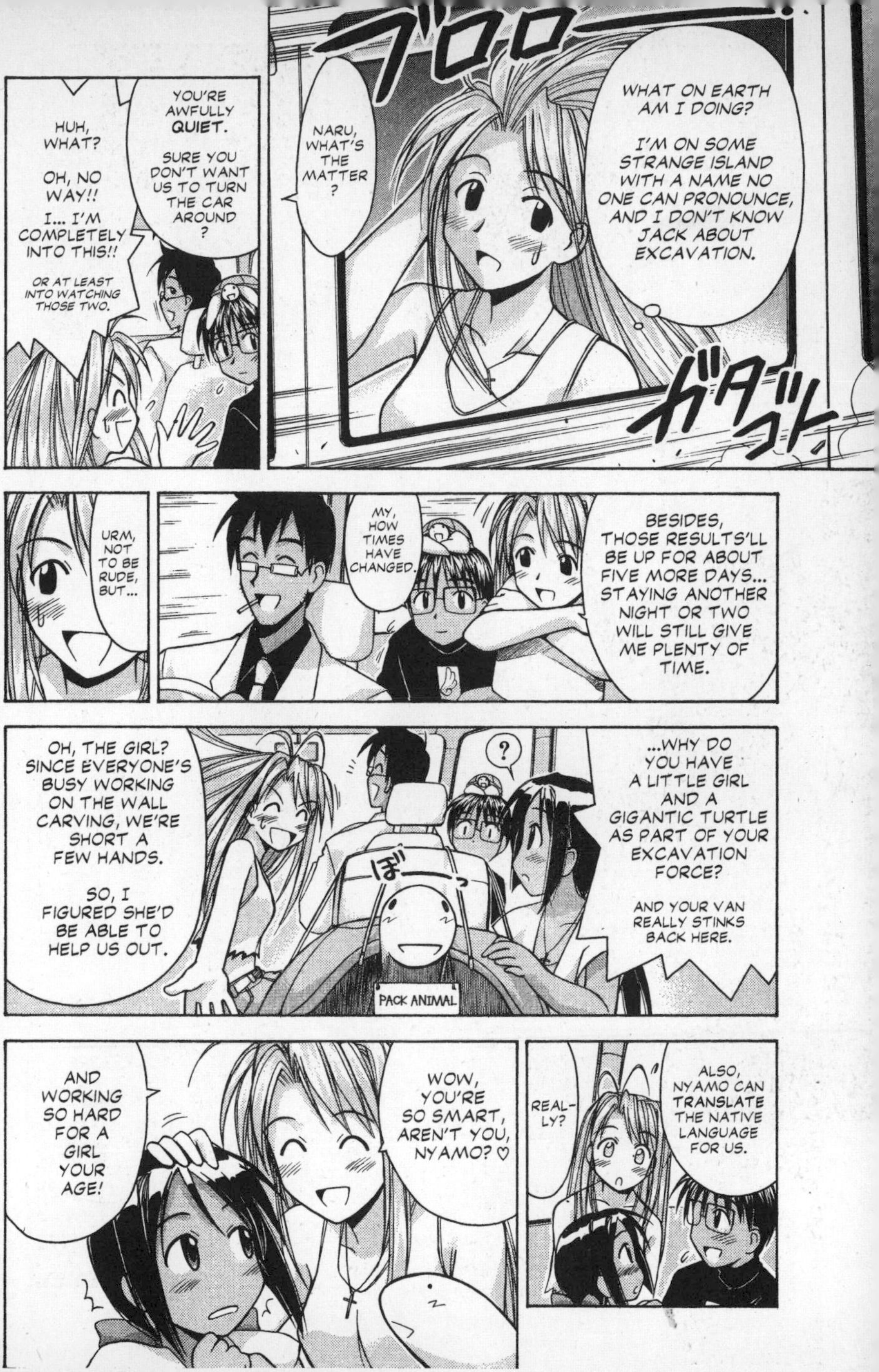
ブロロー
WHAT ON EARTH AM I DOING? I'M ON SOME STRANGE ISLAND WITH A NAME NO ONE CAN PRONOUNCE, AND I DON'T KNOW JACK ABOUT EXCAVATION.
NARU, WHAT'S THE MATTER?
ガタゴト
YOU'RE AWFULLY QUIET. SURE YOU DON'T WANT US TO TURN THE CAR AROUND?
HUH, WHAT? OH, NO WAY!! I... I'M COMPLETELY INTO THIS!!
OR AT LEAST INTO WATCHING THOSE TWO.
BESIDES, THOSE RESULTS'LL BE UP FOR ABOUT FIVE MORE DAYS... STAYING ANOTHER NIGHT OR TWO WILL STILL GIVE ME PLENTY OF TIME.
MY, HOW TIMES HAVE CHANGED.
URM, NOT TO BE RUDE, BUT...
...WHY DO YOU HAVE A LITTLE GIRL AND A GIGANTIC TURTLE AS PART OF YOUR EXCAVATION FORCE?
AND YOUR VAN REALLY STINKS BACK HERE.
?
ぼー
PACK ANIMAL
OH, THE GIRL? SINCE EVERYONE'S BUSY WORKING ON THE WALL CARVING, WE'RE SHORT A FEW HANDS.
SO, I FIGURED SHE'D BE ABLE TO HELP US OUT.
ALSO, NYAMO CAN TRANSLATE THE NATIVE LANGUAGE FOR US.
REAL-LY?
WOW, YOU'RE SO SMART, AREN'T YOU, NYAMO? ♡
AND WORKING SO HARD FOR A GIRL YOUR AGE!

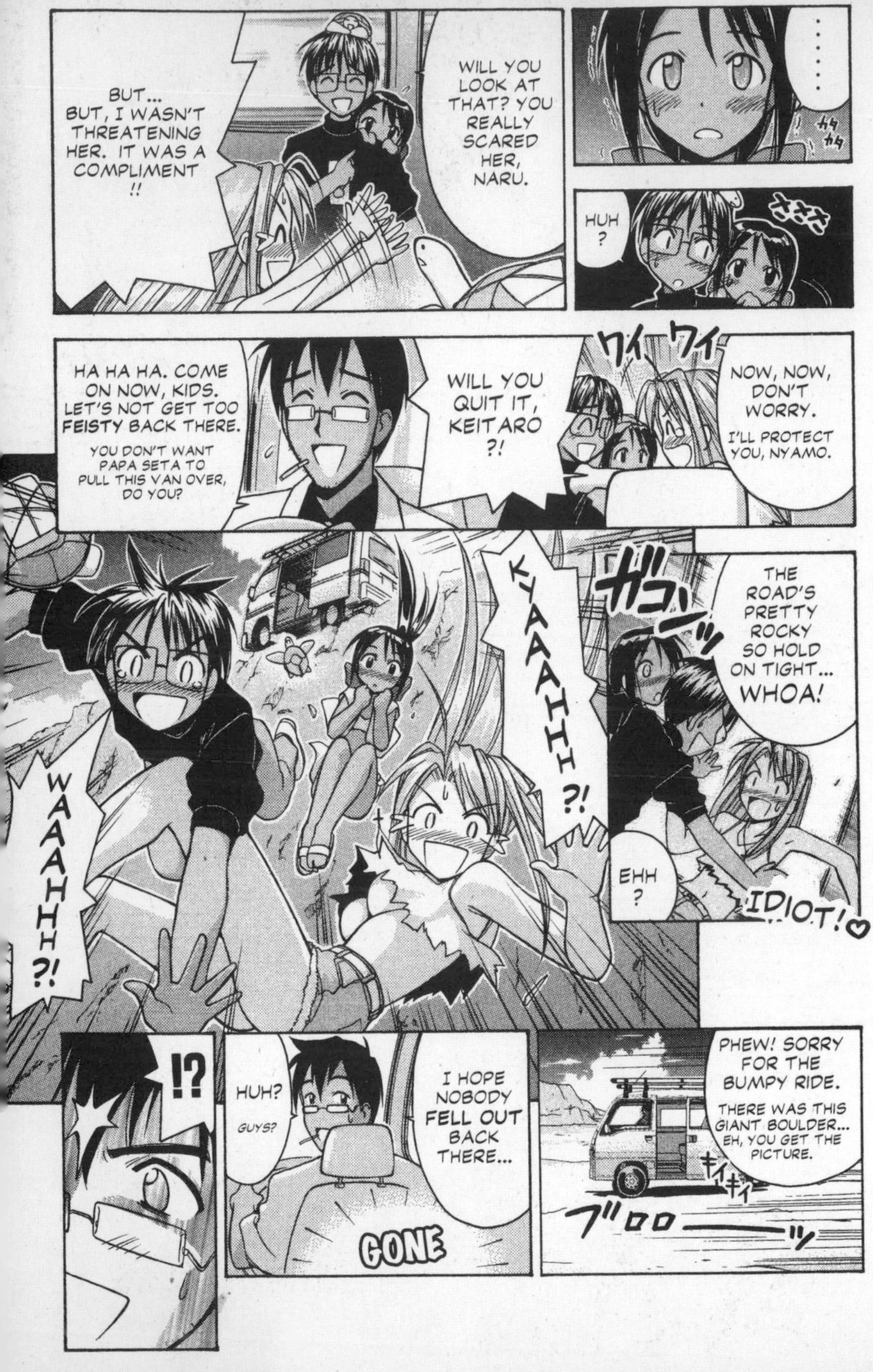
......
HUH ?
WILL YOU LOOK AT THAT? YOU REALLY SCARED HER, NARU.
BUT... BUT, I WASN'T THREATENING HER. IT WAS A COMPLIMENT !!
ワイ ワイ
NOW, NOW, DON'T WORRY.
I'LL PROTECT YOU, NYAMO.
WILL YOU QUIT IT, KEITARO ?!
HA HA HA. COME ON NOW, KIDS. LET'S NOT GET TOO FEISTY BACK THERE.
YOU DON'T WANT PAPA SETA TO PULL THIS VAN OVER, DO YOU?
ガコン
THE ROAD'S PRETTY ROCKY SO HOLD ON TIGHT... WHOA!
EHH ?
IDIOT! ♡
KYAAAAHHH ?!
WAAAAHHH ?!
PHEW! SORRY FOR THE BUMPY RIDE.
THERE WAS THIS GIANT BOULDER... EH, YOU GET THE PICTURE.
キィ キィ
ブロロ――ッ
I HOPE NOBODY FELL OUT BACK THERE...
HUH?
GUYS?
GONE
!?

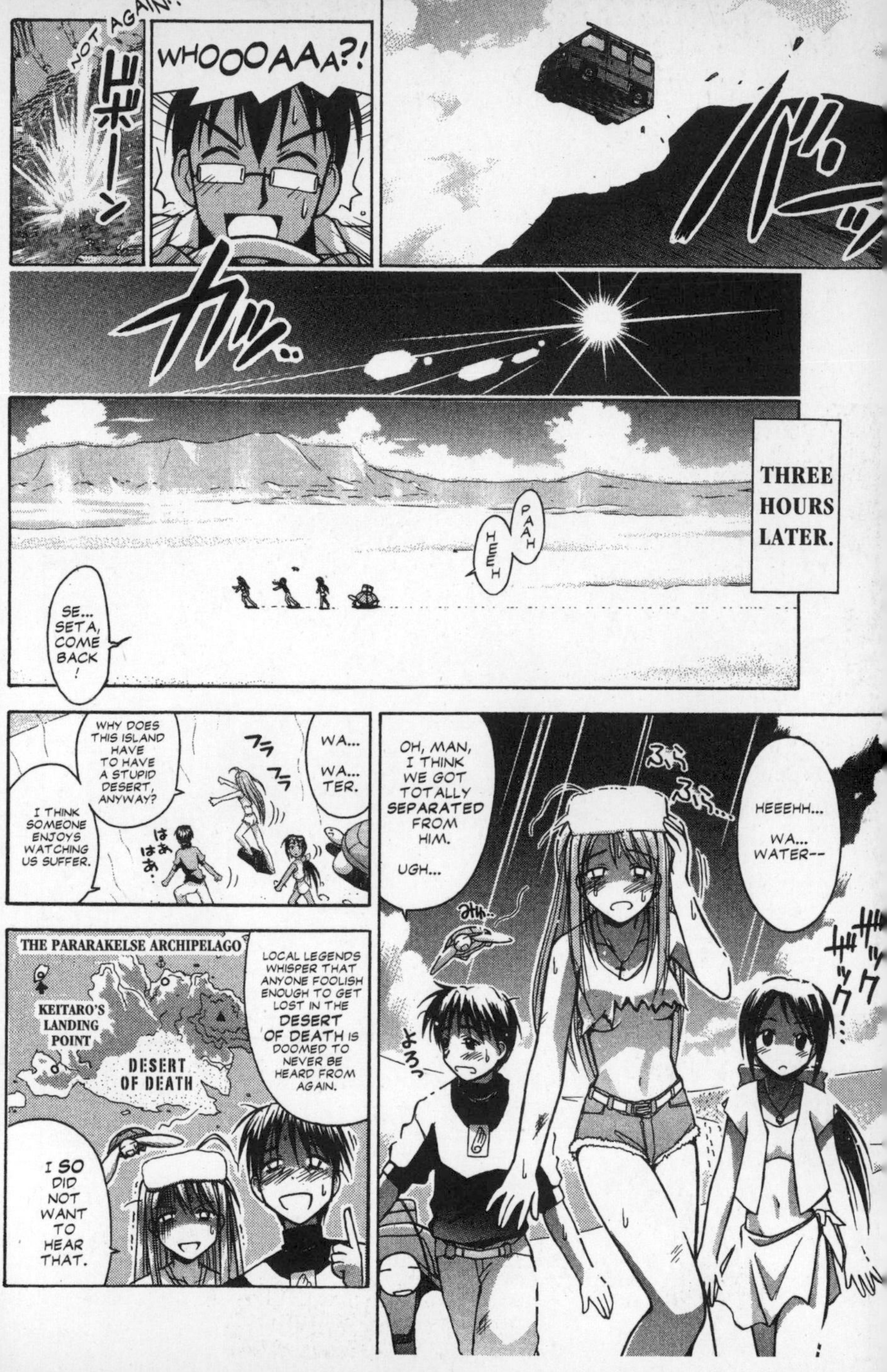
WHOOOAAA?!
NOT AGAIN!!
THREE HOURS LATER.
PAAH HEEH
SE... SETA, COME BACK!
HEEEHH... WA... WATER--
OH, MAN, I THINK WE GOT TOTALLY SEPARATED FROM HIM. UGH...
WA... WA... TER.
WHY DOES THIS ISLAND HAVE TO HAVE A STUPID DESERT, ANYWAY?
I THINK SOMEONE ENJOYS WATCHING US SUFFER.
THE PARARAKELSE ARCHIPELAGO
KEITARO'S LANDING POINT
DESERT OF DEATH
LOCAL LEGENDS WHISPER THAT ANYONE FOOLISH ENOUGH TO GET LOST IN THE DESERT OF DEATH IS DOOMED TO NEVER BE HEARD FROM AGAIN.
I SO DID NOT WANT TO HEAR THAT.

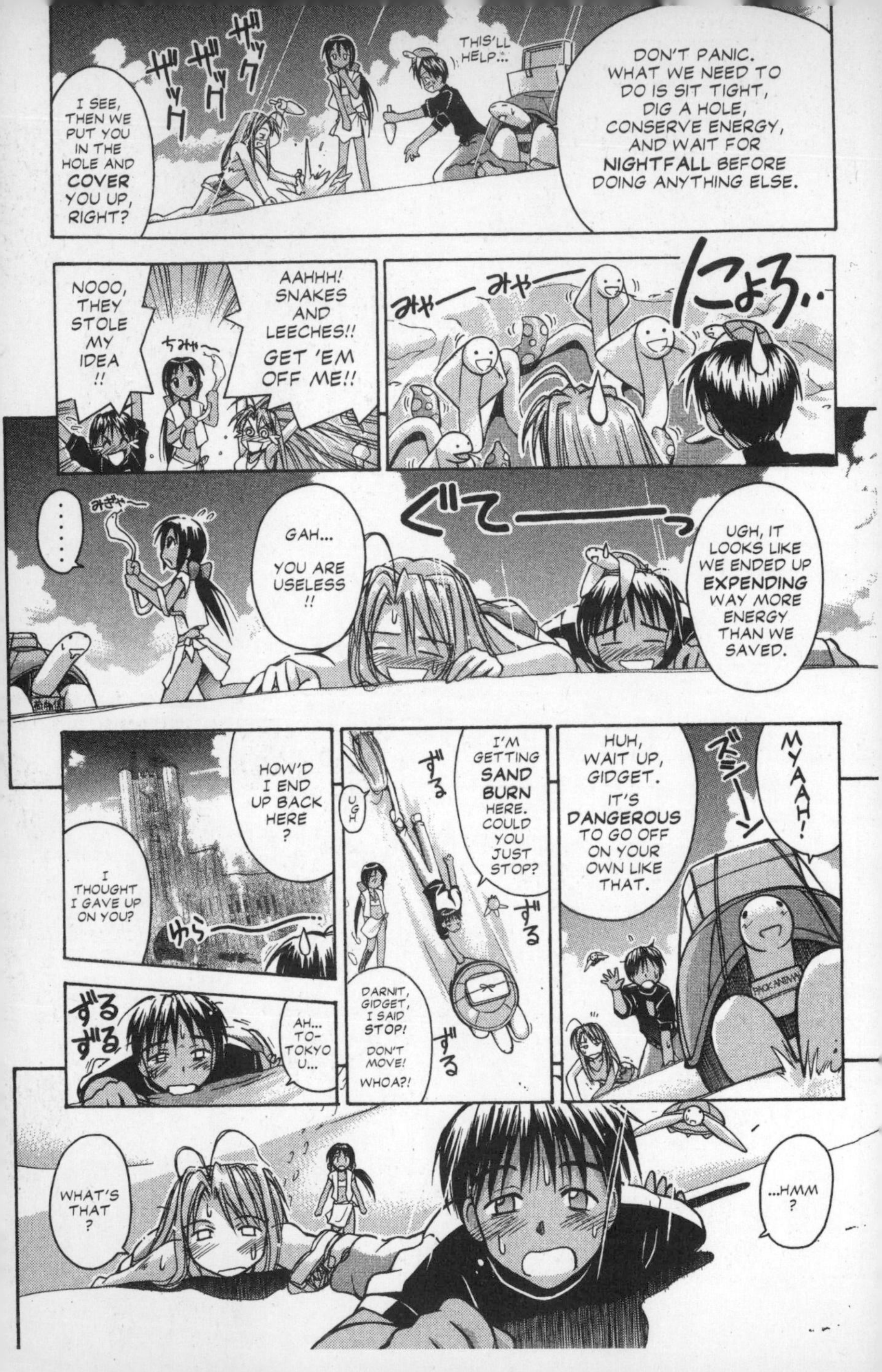
DON'T PANIC. WHAT WE NEED TO DO IS SIT TIGHT, DIG A HOLE, CONSERVE ENERGY, AND WAIT FOR NIGHTFALL BEFORE DOING ANYTHING ELSE.
THIS'LL HELP...
ザック
ザック
ザック
I SEE, THEN WE PUT YOU IN THE HOLE AND COVER YOU UP, RIGHT?
にょろ..
みゃー みゃー
AAHHH! SNAKES AND LEECHES!! GET 'EM OFF ME!!
ちみゃ～
NOOO, THEY STOLE MY IDEA!!
UGH, IT LOOKS LIKE WE ENDED UP EXPENDING WAY MORE ENERGY THAN WE SAVED.
ぐでーーっ
GAH... YOU ARE USELESS!!
みぎゃ～
......
MYAAH!
ズシーン
HUH, WAIT UP, GIDGET. IT'S DANGEROUS TO GO OFF ON YOUR OWN LIKE THAT.
I'M GETTING SAND BURN HERE. COULD YOU JUST STOP?
ずる
UGH
ずる
DARNIT, GIDGET, I SAID STOP! DON'T MOVE! WHOA?!
ずる
HOW'D I END UP BACK HERE?
I THOUGHT I GAVE UP ON YOU?
ゆら
AH... TO-TOKYO U...
ずる ずる
...HMM?
WHAT'S THAT?

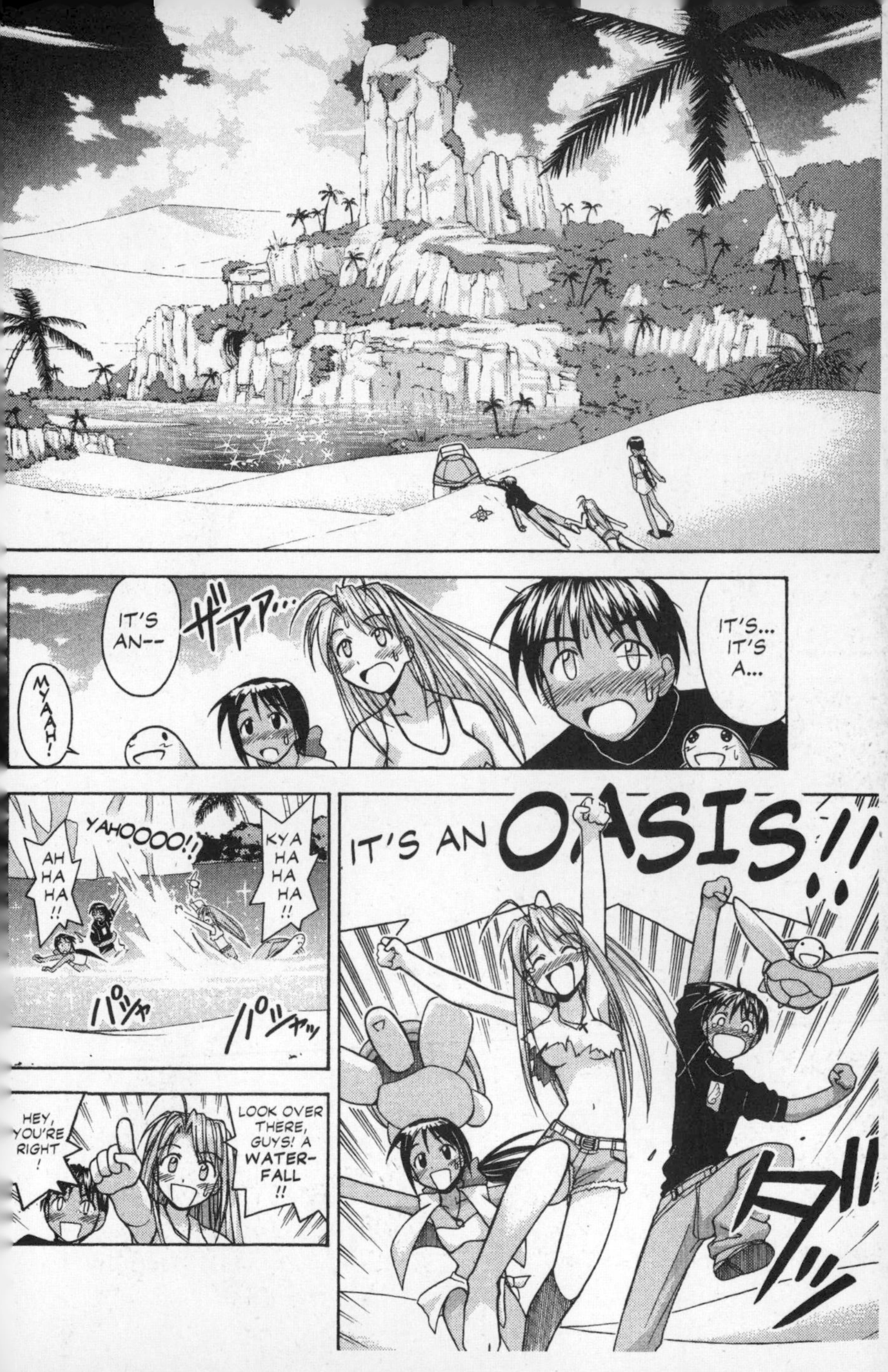

IT'S... IT'S A...
IT'S AN--
ザァァ...
MYAAH!
IT'S AN OASIS!!
ダッ
KYA HA HA HA HA!!
YAHOOOO!!
AH HA HA HA!!
パシャッ
パシャ
LOOK OVER THERE, GUYS! A WATERFALL!!
HEY, YOU'RE RIGHT!

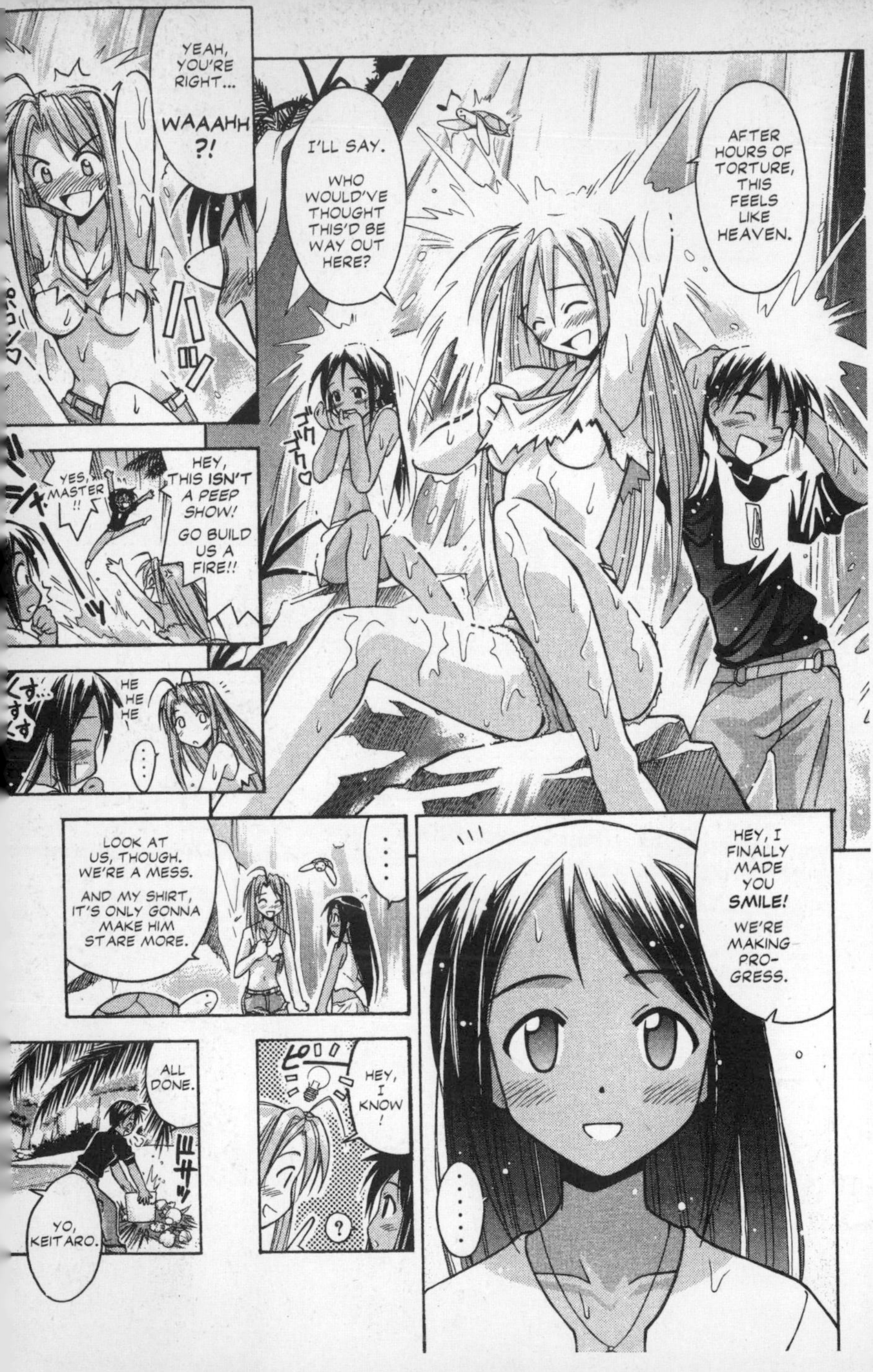
AFTER HOURS OF TORTURE, THIS FEELS LIKE HEAVEN.
I'LL SAY.
WHO WOULD'VE THOUGHT THIS'D BE WAY OUT HERE?
YEAH, YOU'RE RIGHT...
WAAAHH ?!
HEY, THIS ISN'T A PEEP SHOW!
GO BUILD US A FIRE!!
YES, MASTER !!
HE HE HE
......
HEY, I FINALLY MADE YOU SMILE!
WE'RE MAKING PRO-GRESS.
....
LOOK AT US, THOUGH. WE'RE A MESS.
AND MY SHIRT, IT'S ONLY GONNA MAKE HIM STARE MORE.
HEY, I KNOW!
......
?
ALL DONE.
YO, KEITARO.

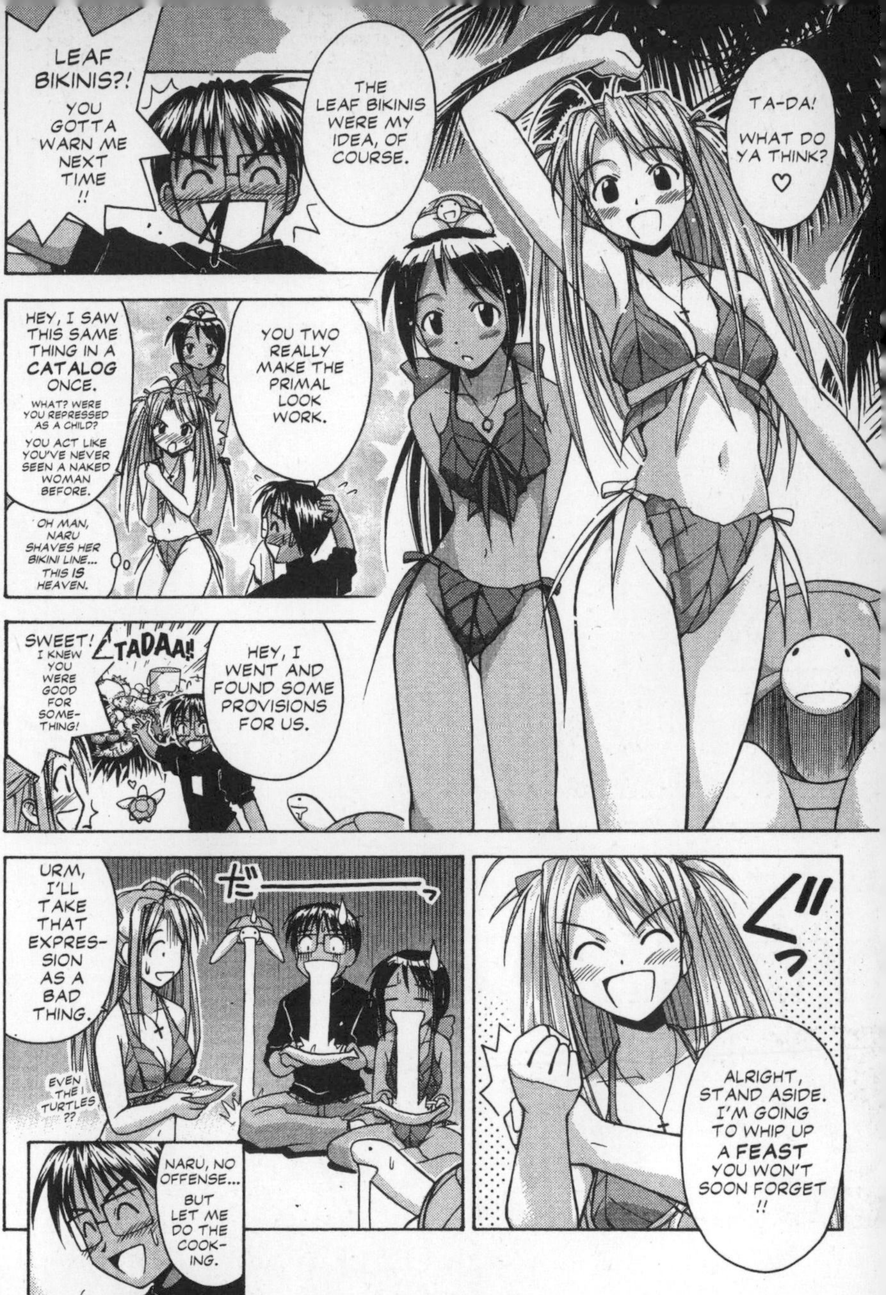
TA-DA! WHAT DO YA THINK? ♡
THE LEAF BIKINIS WERE MY IDEA, OF COURSE.
LEAF BIKINIS?! YOU GOTTA WARN ME NEXT TIME !!
YOU TWO REALLY MAKE THE PRIMAL LOOK WORK.
HEY, I SAW THIS SAME THING IN A CATALOG ONCE.
WHAT? WERE YOU REPRESSED AS A CHILD? YOU ACT LIKE YOU'VE NEVER SEEN A NAKED WOMAN BEFORE.
OH MAN, NARU SHAVES HER BIKINI LINE... THIS IS HEAVEN.
HEY, I WENT AND FOUND SOME PROVISIONS FOR US.
TADAA!!
SWEET! I KNEW YOU WERE GOOD FOR SOME-THING!
ALRIGHT, STAND ASIDE. I'M GOING TO WHIP UP A FEAST YOU WON'T SOON FORGET !!
URM, I'LL TAKE THAT EXPRES-SION AS A BAD THING.
EVEN THE TURTLES ??
NARU, NO OFFENSE... BUT LET ME DO THE COOK-ING.

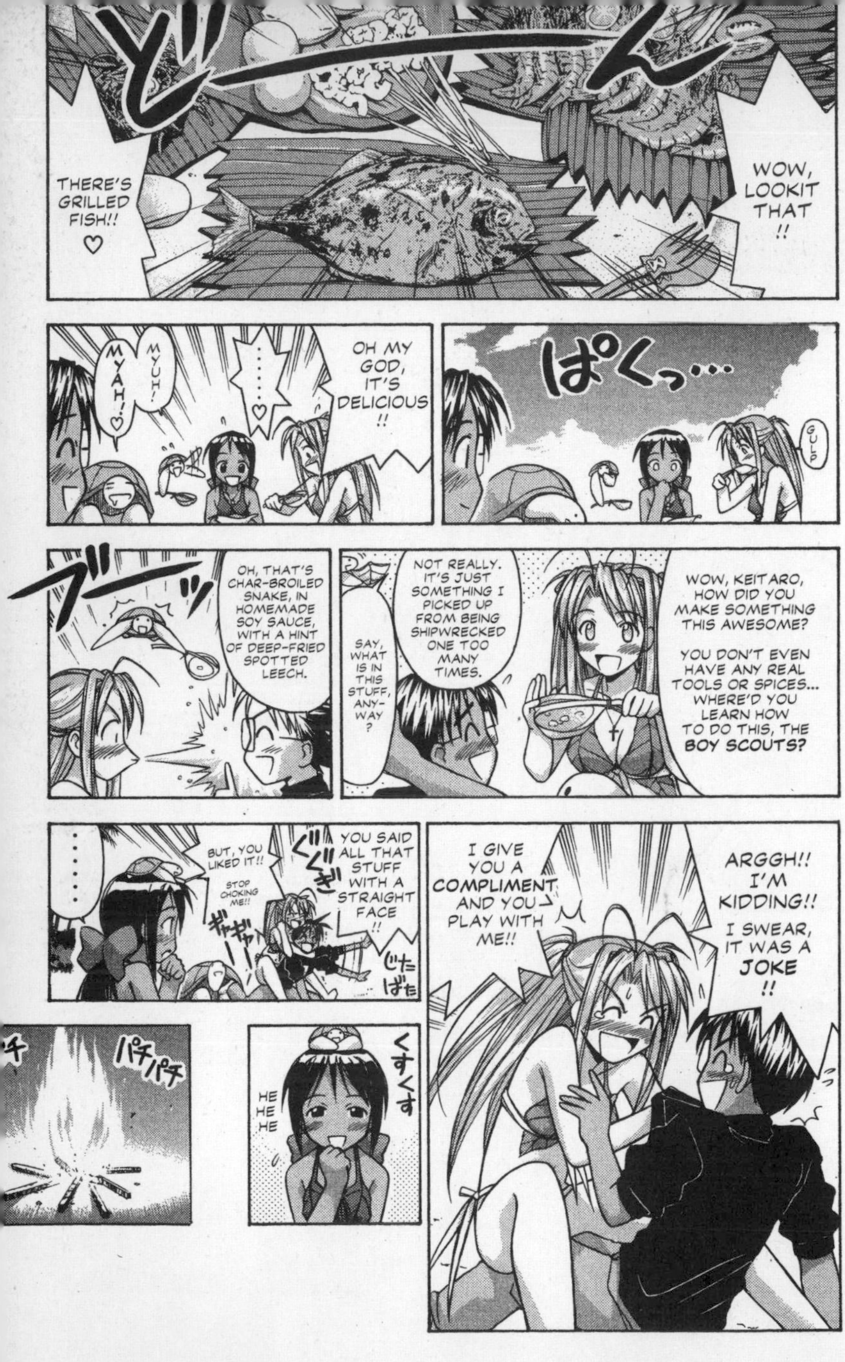
どーん
WOW, LOOKIT THAT !!
THERE'S GRILLED FISH!! ♡
ぱくっ…
GULP
OH MY GOD, IT'S DELICIOUS !!
......♡
MYUH!
MYAH!!♡
WOW, KEITARO, HOW DID YOU MAKE SOMETHING THIS AWESOME?
YOU DON'T EVEN HAVE ANY REAL TOOLS OR SPICES... WHERE'D YOU LEARN HOW TO DO THIS, THE **BOY SCOUTS?**
NOT REALLY. IT'S JUST SOMETHING I PICKED UP FROM BEING SHIPWRECKED ONE TOO MANY TIMES.
SAY, WHAT IS IN THIS STUFF, ANY-WAY?
OH, THAT'S CHAR-BROILED SNAKE, IN HOMEMADE SOY SAUCE, WITH A HINT OF DEEP-FRIED SPOTTED LEECH.
ブーーッ
ARGGH!! I'M KIDDING!!
I SWEAR, IT WAS A **JOKE** !!
I GIVE YOU A **COMPLIMENT** AND YOU PLAY WITH ME!!
YOU SAID ALL THAT STUFF WITH A STRAIGHT FACE !!
ぐぎぐぎ
BUT, YOU LIKED IT!!
STOP CHOKING ME!!
ギャギャー
じたばた
......
くすくす
HE HE HE
パチパチ

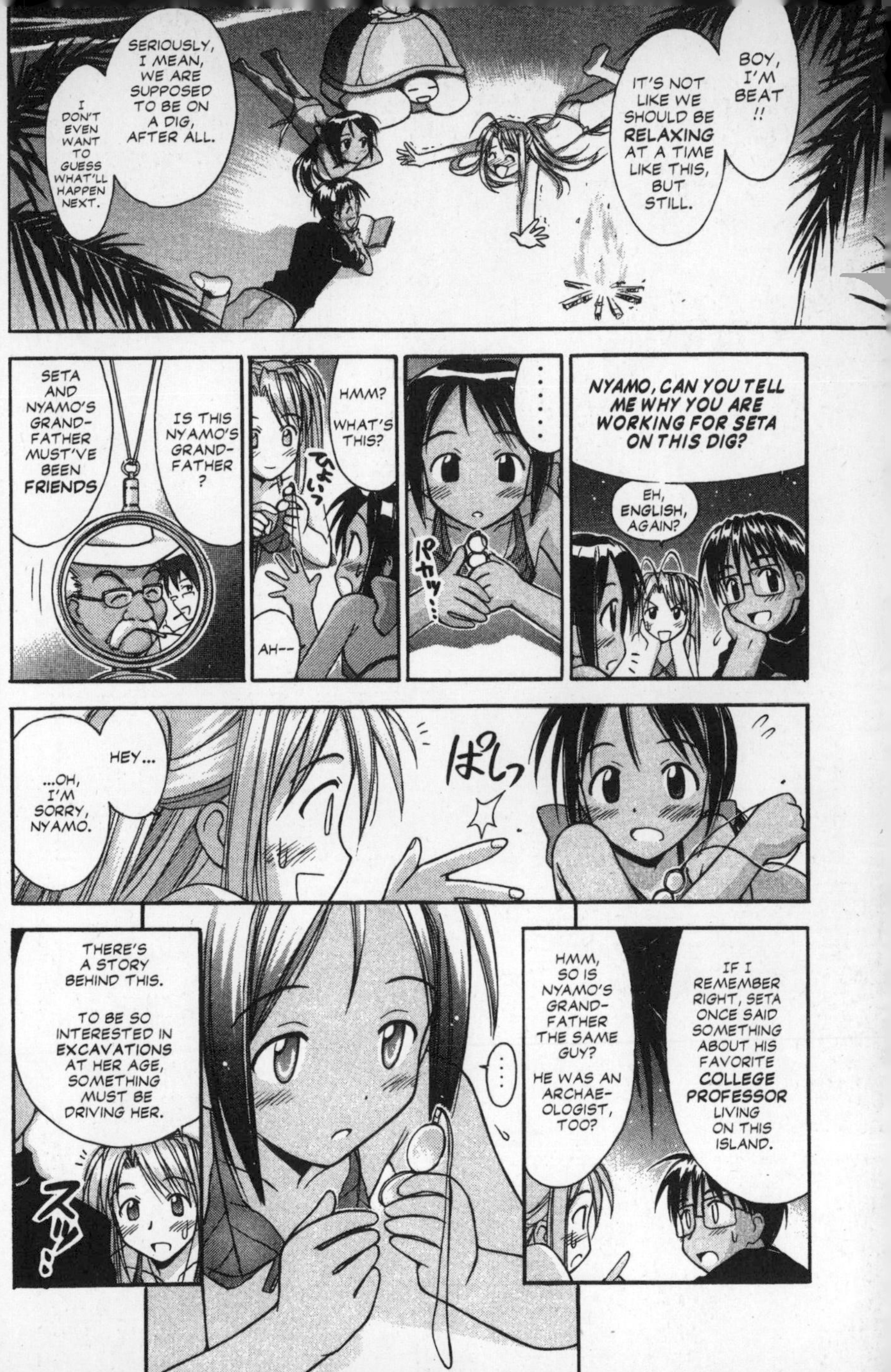
BOY, I'M BEAT!!
IT'S NOT LIKE WE SHOULD BE RELAXING AT A TIME LIKE THIS, BUT STILL.
SERIOUSLY, I MEAN, WE ARE SUPPOSED TO BE ON A DIG, AFTER ALL.
I DON'T EVEN WANT TO GUESS WHAT'LL HAPPEN NEXT.
NYAMO, CAN YOU TELL ME WHY YOU ARE WORKING FOR SETA ON THIS DIG?
EH, ENGLISH, AGAIN?
......
パカッ...
HMM? WHAT'S THIS?
AH--
IS THIS NYAMO'S GRANDFATHER?
SETA AND NYAMO'S GRANDFATHER MUST'VE BEEN FRIENDS
ぱしっ
HEY...
...OH, I'M SORRY, NYAMO.
IF I REMEMBER RIGHT, SETA ONCE SAID SOMETHING ABOUT HIS FAVORITE COLLEGE PROFESSOR LIVING ON THIS ISLAND.
HMM, SO IS NYAMO'S GRANDFATHER THE SAME GUY? HE WAS AN ARCHAEOLOGIST, TOO?
.....
THERE'S A STORY BEHIND THIS. TO BE SO INTERESTED IN EXCAVATIONS AT HER AGE, SOMETHING MUST BE DRIVING HER.

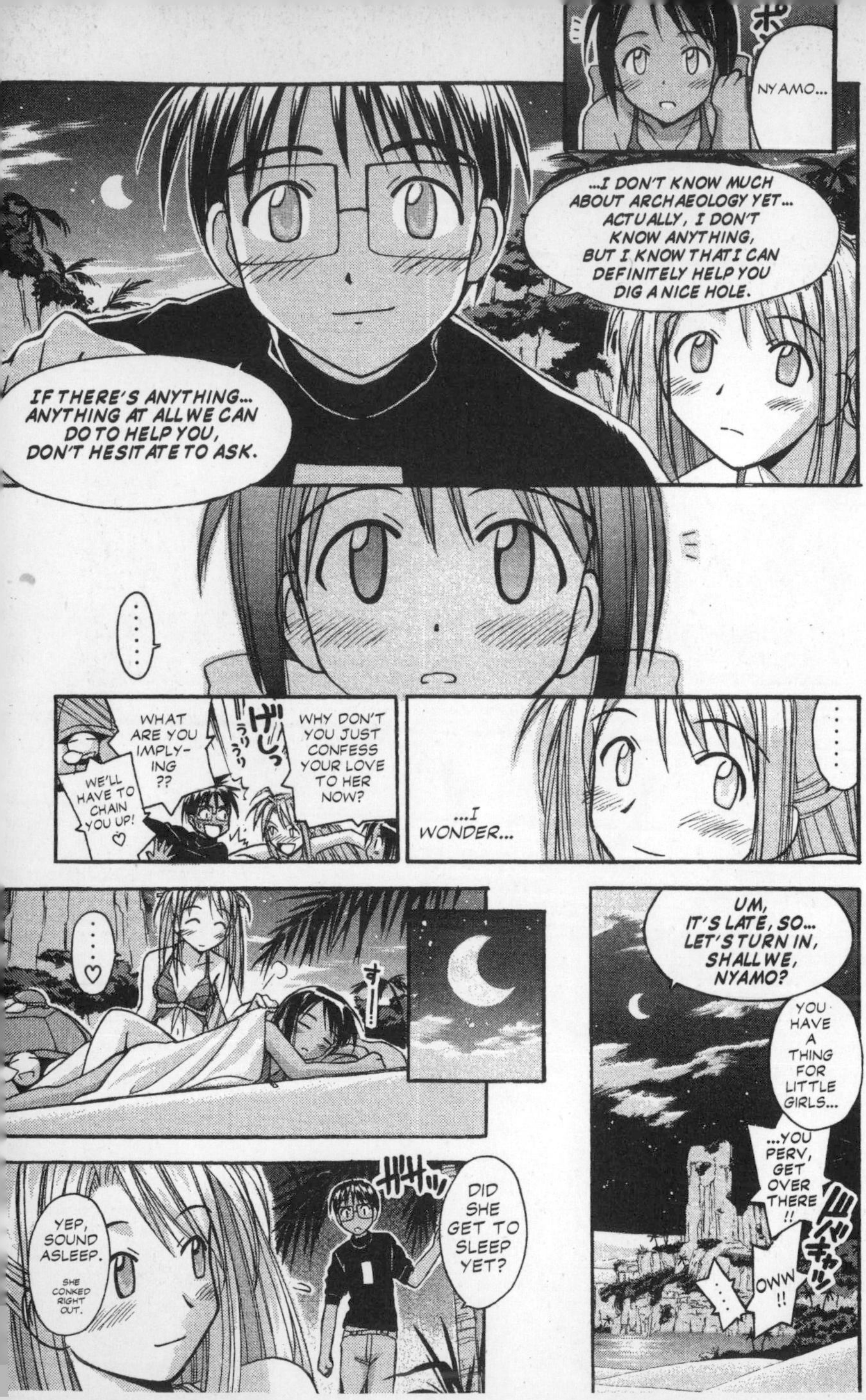
ポ
NYAMO...
...I DON'T KNOW MUCH ABOUT ARCHAEOLOGY YET... ACTUALLY, I DON'T KNOW ANYTHING, BUT I KNOW THAT I CAN DEFINITELY HELP YOU DIG A NICE HOLE.
IF THERE'S ANYTHING... ANYTHING AT ALL WE CAN DO TO HELP YOU, DON'T HESITATE TO ASK.
......
......
...I WONDER...
WHY DON'T YOU JUST CONFESS YOUR LOVE TO HER NOW?
げしっ
うりうり
WHAT ARE YOU IMPLYING??
WE'LL HAVE TO CHAIN YOU UP! ♡
UM, IT'S LATE, SO... LET'S TURN IN, SHALL WE, NYAMO?
YOU HAVE A THING FOR LITTLE GIRLS...
...YOU PERV, GET OVER THERE!!
バギャッ
OWW!!
......
......♡
す…
ガサッ
DID SHE GET TO SLEEP YET?
YEP, SOUND ASLEEP.
SHE CONKED RIGHT OUT.

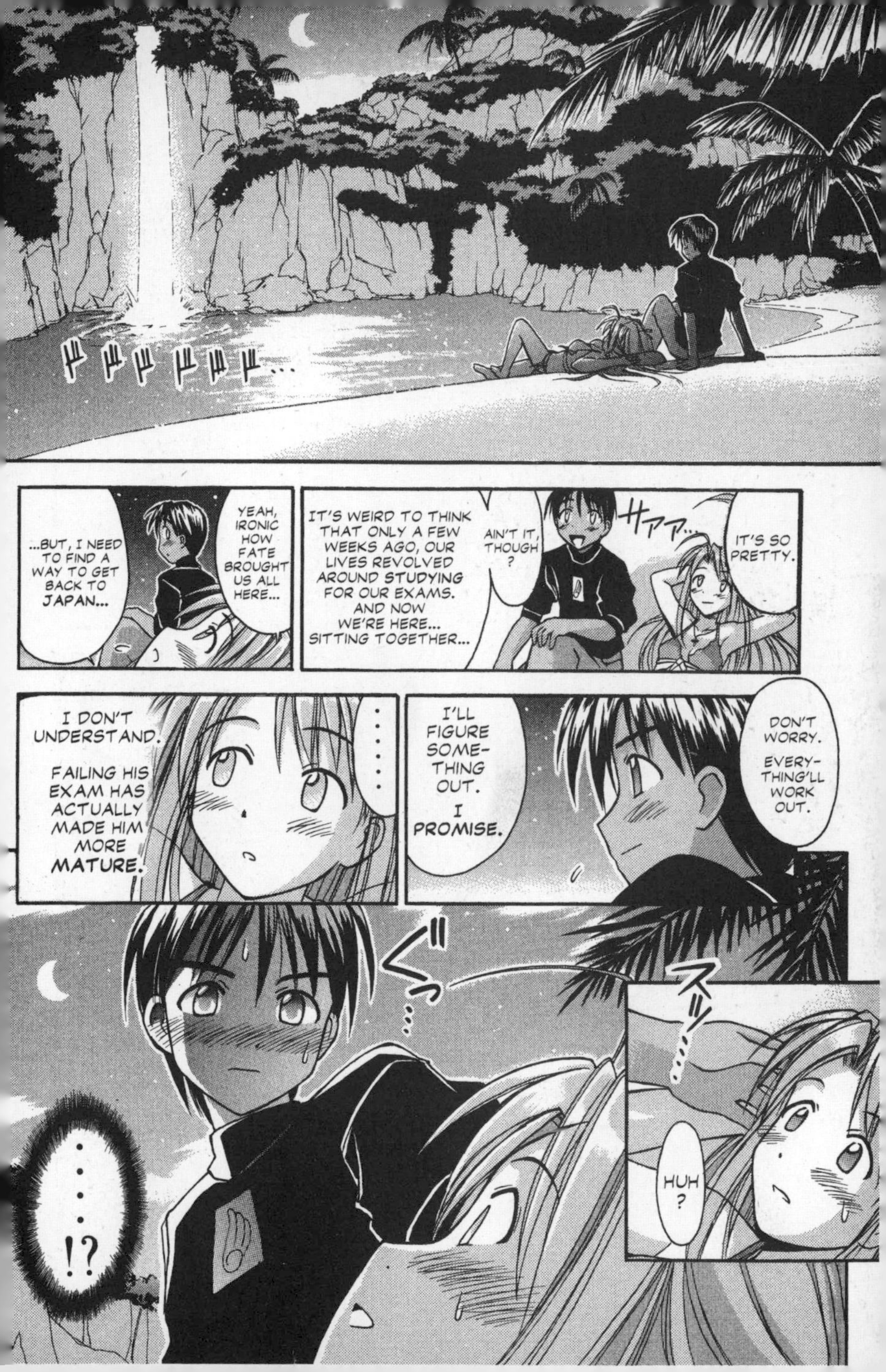
ドドドドドド…
IT'S SO PRETTY.
サァァ…
AIN'T IT, THOUGH?
IT'S WEIRD TO THINK THAT ONLY A FEW WEEKS AGO, OUR LIVES REVOLVED AROUND STUDYING FOR OUR EXAMS. AND NOW WE'RE HERE... SITTING TOGETHER...
YEAH, IRONIC HOW FATE BROUGHT US ALL HERE...
...BUT, I NEED TO FIND A WAY TO GET BACK TO JAPAN...
DON'T WORRY. EVERYTHING'LL WORK OUT.
I'LL FIGURE SOMETHING OUT. I PROMISE.
......
I DON'T UNDERSTAND. FAILING HIS EXAM HAS ACTUALLY MADE HIM MORE MATURE.
スッ....
HUH?
ぐっ...
......!?

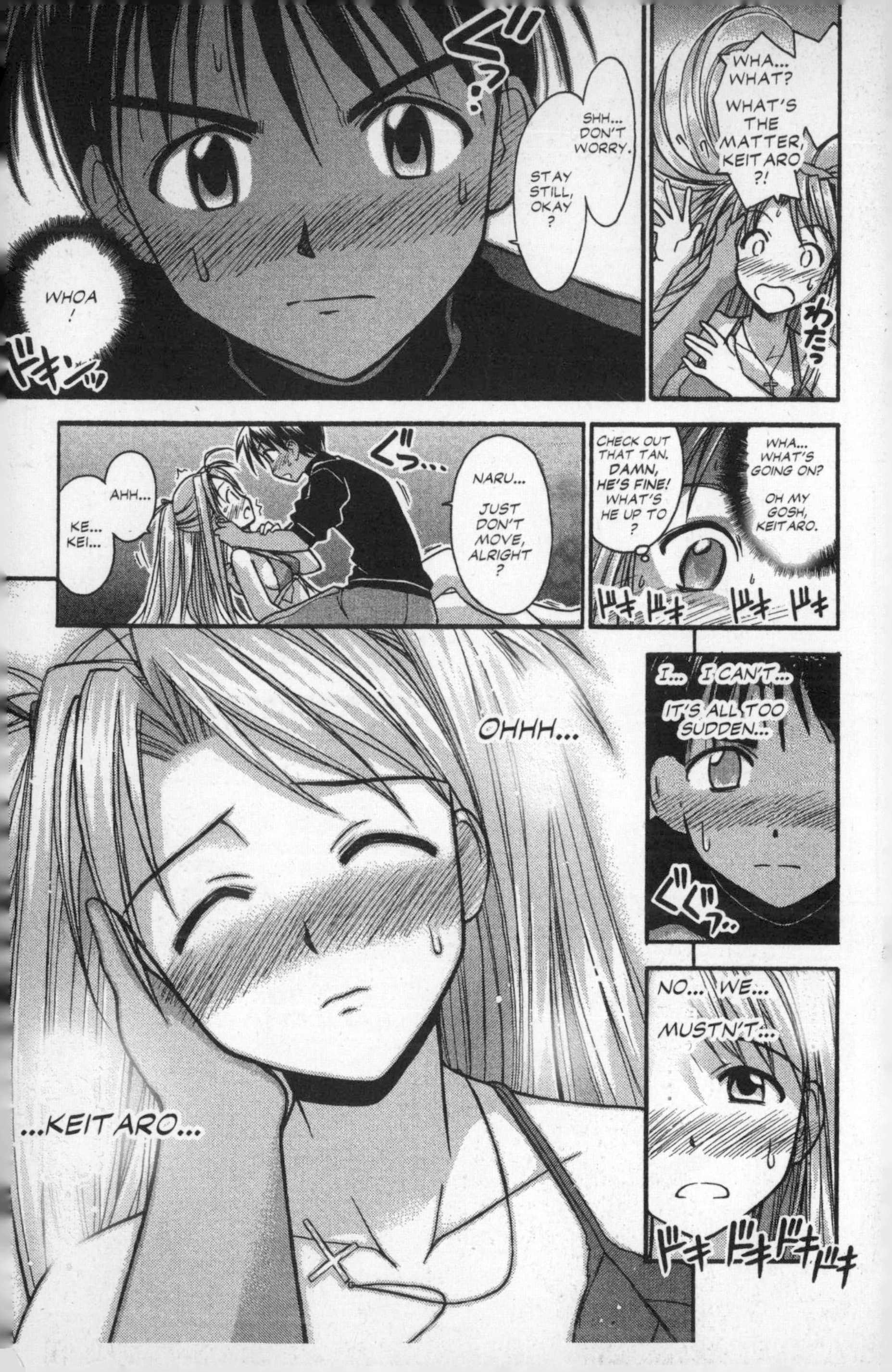
WHA... WHAT?
WHAT'S THE MATTER, KEITARO ?!
わたっ
ぐっ..
SHH... DON'T WORRY.
STAY STILL, OKAY ?
WHOA !
ドキンッ
WHA... WHAT'S GOING ON?
OH MY GOSH, KEITARO.
CHECK OUT THAT TAN. DAMN, HE'S FINE! WHAT'S HE UP TO ?
ドキ ドキ ドキ ドキ
ぐっ...
NARU...
JUST DON'T MOVE, ALRIGHT ?
AHH...
KE... KEI...
I... I CAN'T...
IT'S ALL TOO SUDDEN...
ぐぐっ..
NO... WE...
MUSTN'T...
ドキドキドキドキ
OHHH...
...KEITARO...

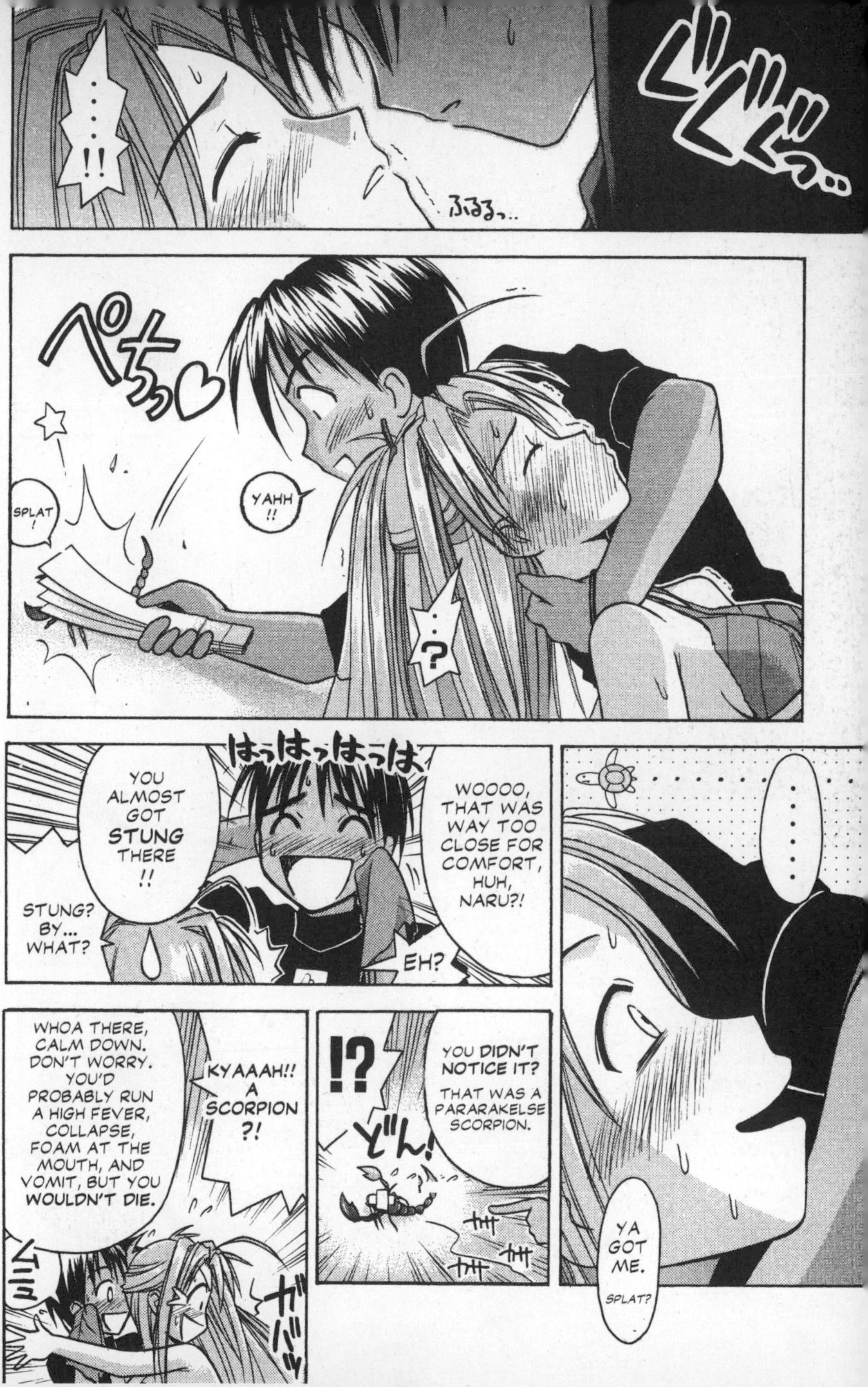
ぐぐぐっ..
...!!
ふるるっ..
ぺちっ♡
YAHH!!
SPLAT!
...?
...
YA GOT ME.
SPLAT?
はっはっはっは
WOOOO, THAT WAS WAY TOO CLOSE FOR COMFORT, HUH, NARU?!
YOU ALMOST GOT STUNG THERE!!
STUNG? BY... WHAT?
EH?
YOU DIDN'T NOTICE IT? THAT WAS A PARARAKELSE SCORPION.
!?
どん!
カサ
カサ
カサ
KYAAAH!! A SCORPION?!
WHOA THERE, CALM DOWN. DON'T WORRY. YOU'D PROBABLY RUN A HIGH FEVER, COLLAPSE, FOAM AT THE MOUTH, AND VOMIT, BUT YOU WOULDN'T DIE.
ガバッ
ムニュ

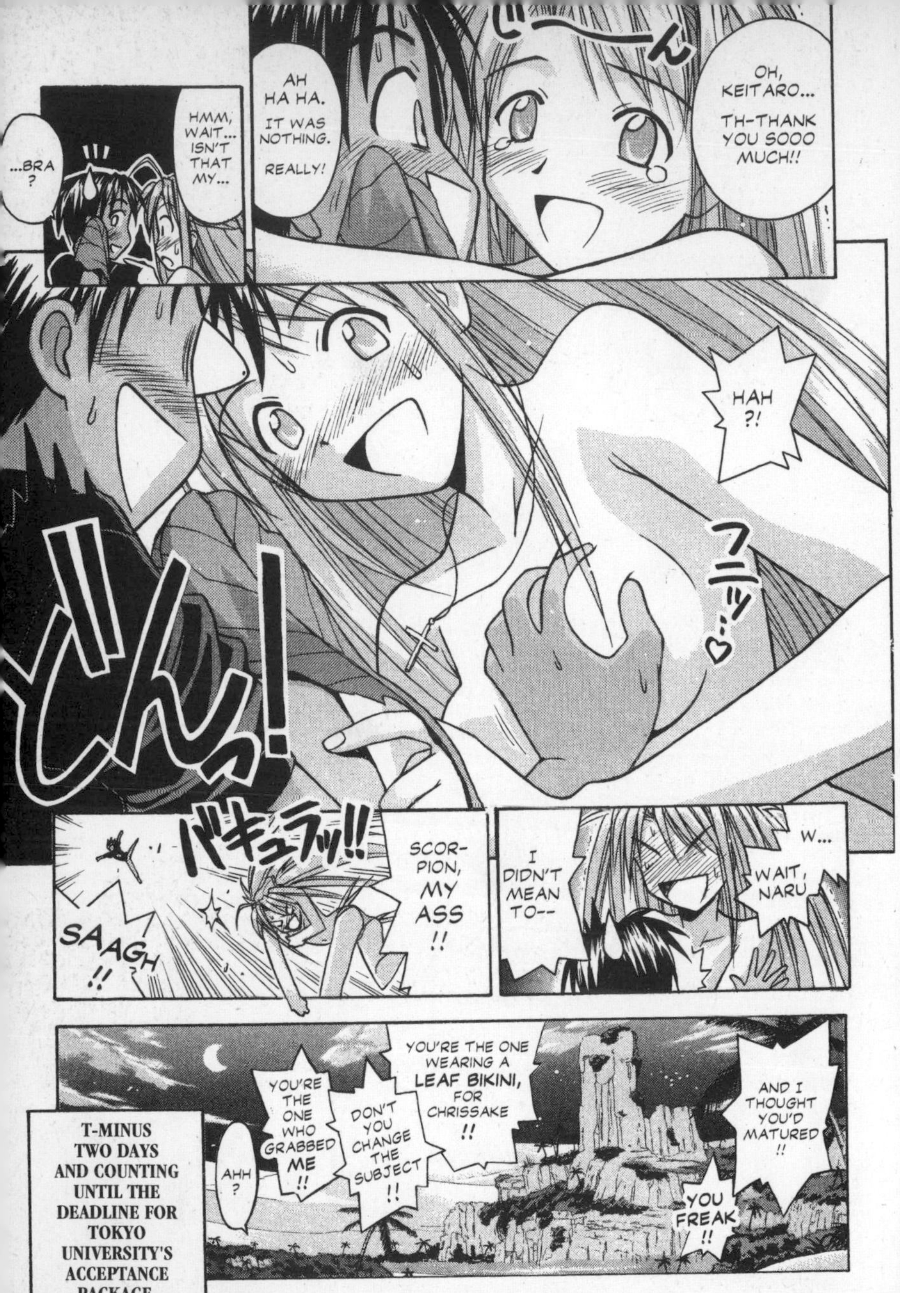
OH, KEITARO... TH-THANK YOU SOOO MUCH!!
じーーん
AH HA HA. IT WAS NOTHING. REALLY!
HMM, WAIT... ISN'T THAT MY...
...BRA?
HAH?!
フニッ..♡
どんっ!
W... WAIT, NARU
I DIDN'T MEAN TO--
SCORPION, MY ASS!!
バキュラッ!!
SAAGH!!
AND I THOUGHT YOU'D MATURED!!
YOU FREAK!!
YOU'RE THE ONE WEARING A LEAF BIKINI, FOR CHRISSAKE!!
DON'T YOU CHANGE THE SUBJECT!!
YOU'RE THE ONE WHO GRABBED ME!!
AHH?
T-MINUS TWO DAYS AND COUNTING UNTIL THE DEADLINE FOR TOKYO UNIVERSITY'S ACCEPTANCE PACKAGE.

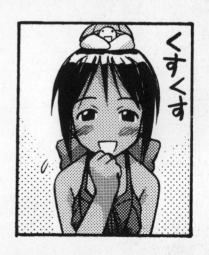

くすくす

Love Hina

HINATA.65 Go, Shinobu Go!

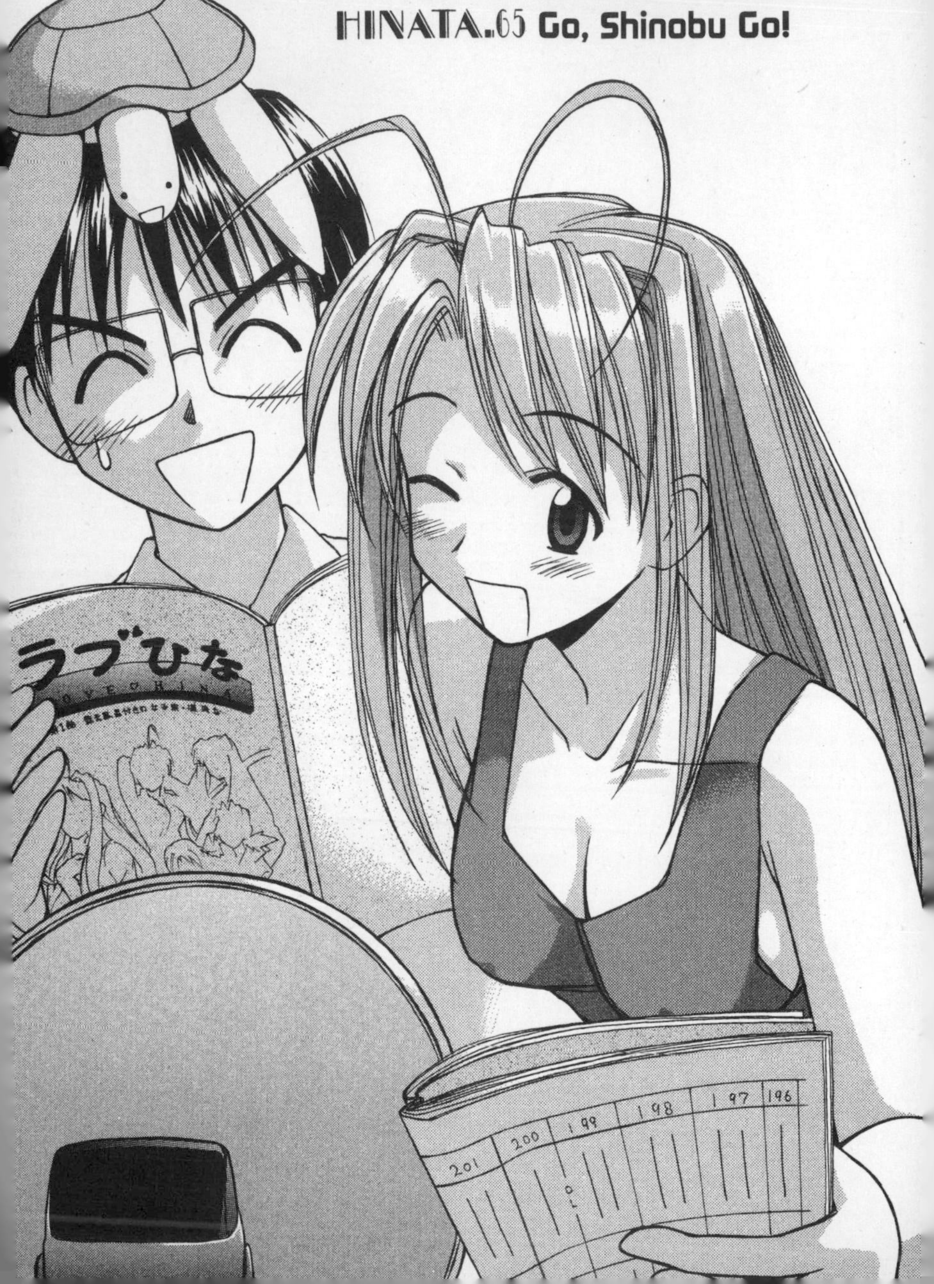
ラブひな
201
200
199
198
197
196

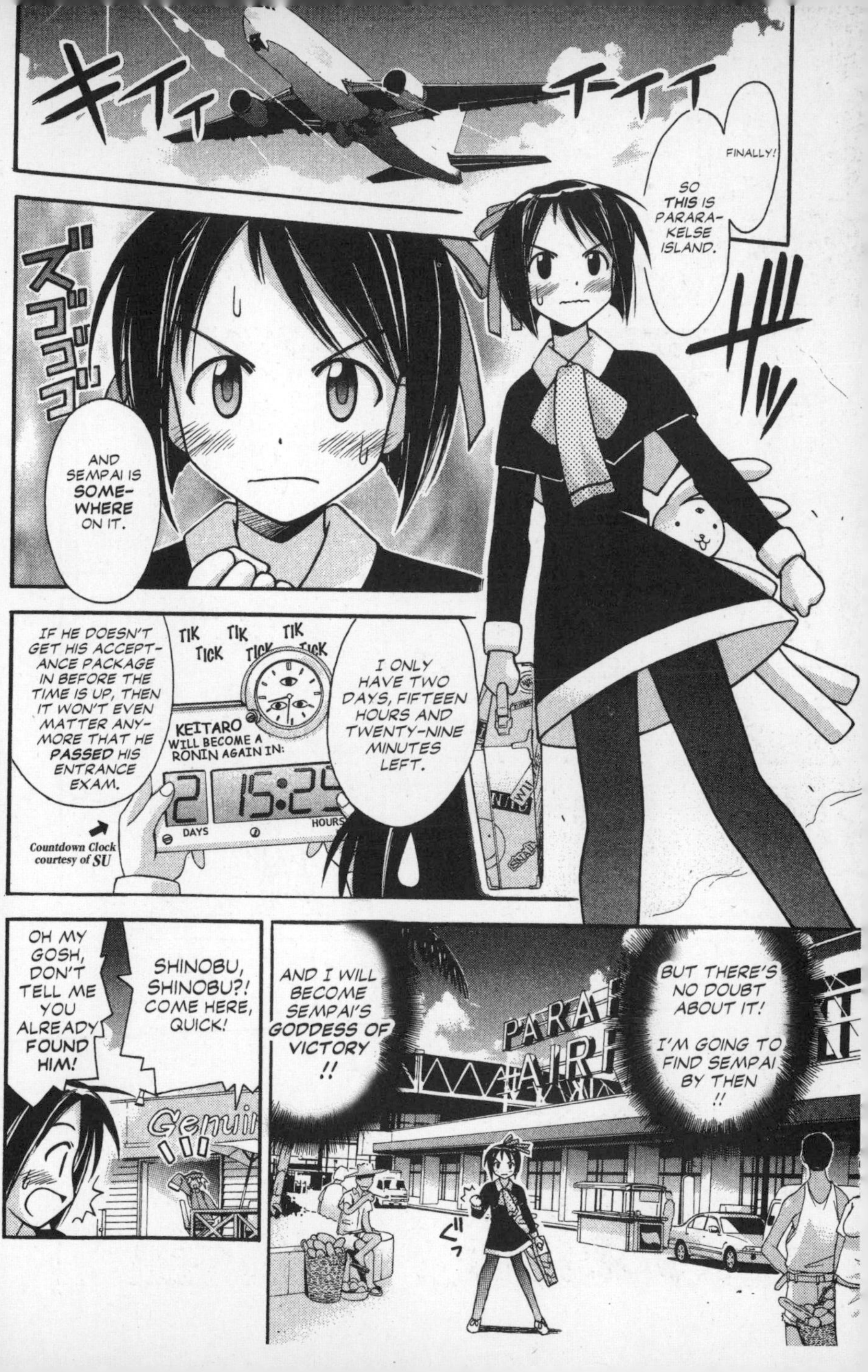

FINALLY!
SO THIS IS PARARA-KELSE ISLAND.
AND SEMPAI IS SOME-WHERE ON IT.
I ONLY HAVE TWO DAYS, FIFTEEN HOURS AND TWENTY-NINE MINUTES LEFT.
TIK TICK TIK TICK TIK TICK
KEITARO WILL BECOME A RONIN AGAIN IN:
2 15:29
DAYS HOURS
IF HE DOESN'T GET HIS ACCEPT-ANCE PACKAGE IN BEFORE THE TIME IS UP, THEN IT WON'T EVEN MATTER ANY-MORE THAT HE PASSED HIS ENTRANCE EXAM.
Countdown Clock courtesy of SU
BUT THERE'S NO DOUBT ABOUT IT!
I'M GOING TO FIND SEMPAI BY THEN !!
AND I WILL BECOME SEMPAI'S GODDESS OF VICTORY !!
SHINOBU, SHINOBU?! COME HERE, QUICK!
OH MY GOSH, DON'T TELL ME YOU ALREADY FOUND HIM!

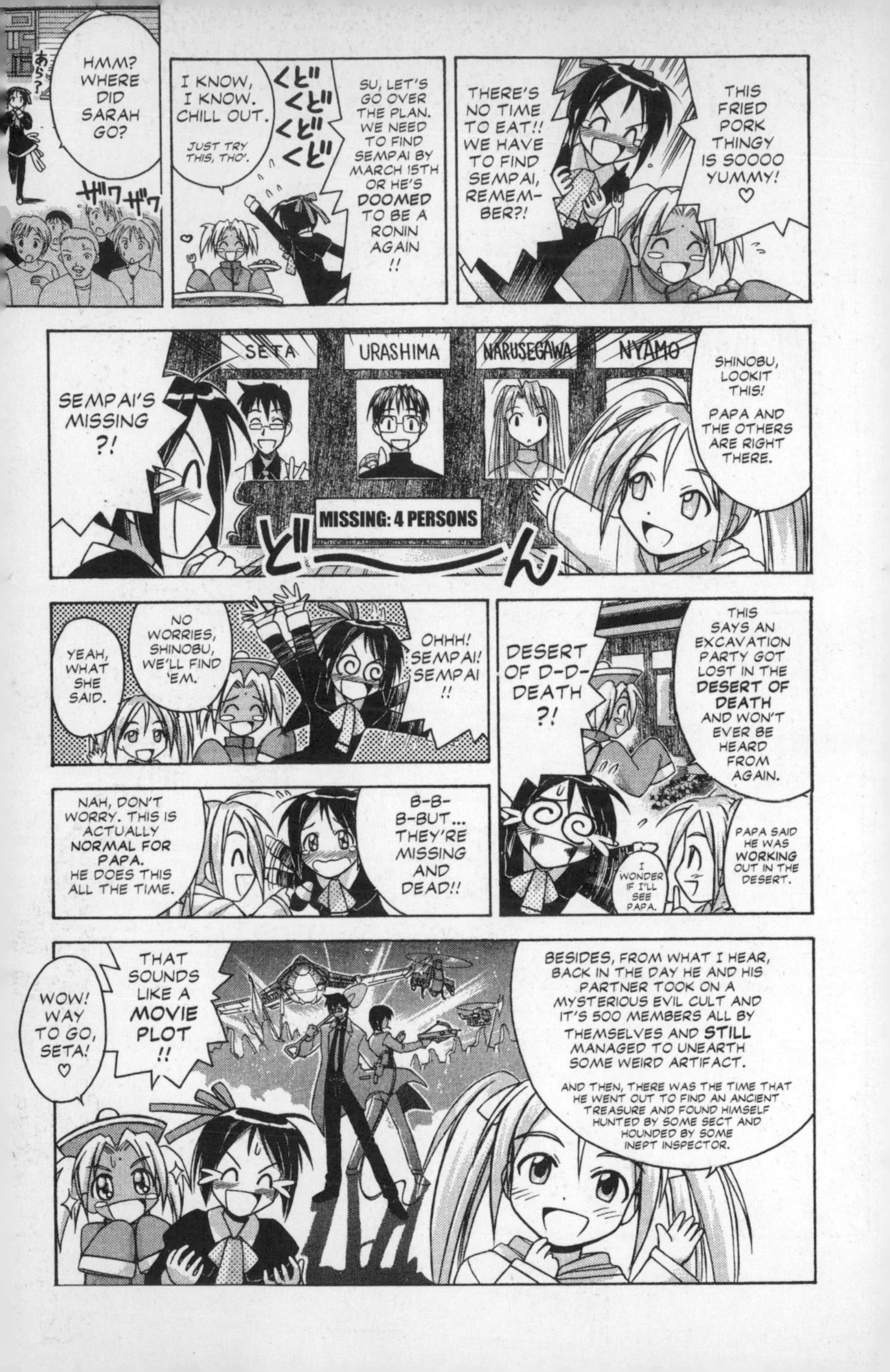
THIS FRIED PORK THINGY IS SOOOO YUMMY! ♡
THERE'S NO TIME TO EAT!! WE HAVE TO FIND SEMPAI, REMEMBER?!
SU, LET'S GO OVER THE PLAN. WE NEED TO FIND SEMPAI BY MARCH 15TH OR HE'S DOOMED TO BE A RONIN AGAIN!!
くどくどくどくど
I KNOW, I KNOW. CHILL OUT.
JUST TRY THIS, THO'.
HMM? WHERE DID SARAH GO?
あら?
ザワザワ
SHINOBU, LOOKIT THIS! PAPA AND THE OTHERS ARE RIGHT THERE.
NYAMO
NARUSEGAWA
URASHIMA
SETA
SEMPAI'S MISSING?!
MISSING: 4 PERSONS
どーーん
THIS SAYS AN EXCAVATION PARTY GOT LOST IN THE DESERT OF DEATH AND WON'T EVER BE HEARD FROM AGAIN.
DESERT OF D-D-DEATH?!
PAPA SAID HE WAS WORKING OUT IN THE DESERT.
I WONDER IF I'LL SEE PAPA.
OHHH! SEMPAI! SEMPAI!!
NO WORRIES, SHINOBU, WE'LL FIND 'EM.
YEAH, WHAT SHE SAID.
B-B-B-BUT... THEY'RE MISSING AND DEAD!!
NAH, DON'T WORRY. THIS IS ACTUALLY NORMAL FOR PAPA. HE DOES THIS ALL THE TIME.
BESIDES, FROM WHAT I HEAR, BACK IN THE DAY HE AND HIS PARTNER TOOK ON A MYSTERIOUS EVIL CULT AND IT'S 500 MEMBERS ALL BY THEMSELVES AND STILL MANAGED TO UNEARTH SOME WEIRD ARTIFACT.
AND THEN, THERE WAS THE TIME THAT HE WENT OUT TO FIND AN ANCIENT TREASURE AND FOUND HIMSELF HUNTED BY SOME SECT AND HOUNDED BY SOME INEPT INSPECTOR.
THAT SOUNDS LIKE A MOVIE PLOT!!
WOW! WAY TO GO, SETA! ♡

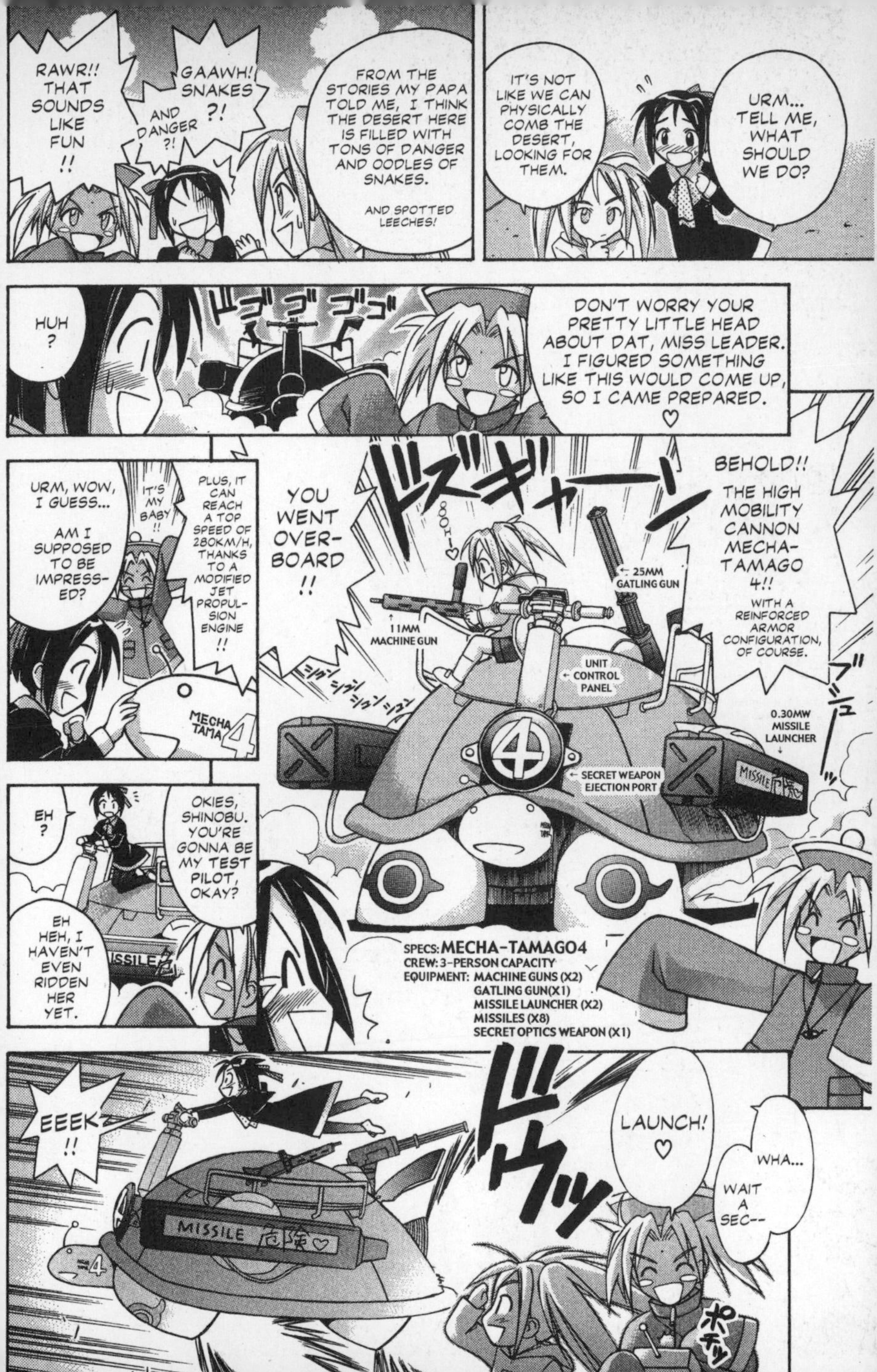
URM... TELL ME, WHAT SHOULD WE DO?
IT'S NOT LIKE WE CAN PHYSICALLY COMB THE DESERT, LOOKING FOR THEM.
FROM THE STORIES MY PAPA TOLD ME, I THINK THE DESERT HERE IS FILLED WITH TONS OF DANGER AND OODLES OF SNAKES.
AND SPOTTED LEECHES!
GAAWH! SNAKES?!
AND DANGER?!
RAWR!! THAT SOUNDS LIKE FUN!!
DON'T WORRY YOUR PRETTY LITTLE HEAD ABOUT DAT, MISS LEADER. I FIGURED SOMETHING LIKE THIS WOULD COME UP, SO I CAME PREPARED. ♡
HUH?
BEHOLD!!
THE HIGH MOBILITY CANNON MECHA-TAMAGO 4!!
WITH A REINFORCED ARMOR CONFIGURATION, OF COURSE.
ドズギャーン
OOOH ♡
YOU WENT OVERBOARD!!
← 25MM GATLING GUN
11MM MACHINE GUN
← UNIT CONTROL PANEL
0.30MW MISSILE LAUNCHER
← SECRET WEAPON EJECTION PORT
MISSILE 危険
PLUS, IT CAN REACH A TOP SPEED OF 280KM/H, THANKS TO A MODIFIED JET PROPULSION ENGINE!!
IT'S MY BABY!!
URM, WOW, I GUESS...
AM I SUPPOSED TO BE IMPRESSED?
MECHA TAMA 4
OKIES, SHINOBU. YOU'RE GONNA BE MY TEST PILOT, OKAY?
EH?
EH HEH, I HAVEN'T EVEN RIDDEN HER YET.
SPECS: MECHA-TAMAGO4
CREW: 3-PERSON CAPACITY
EQUIPMENT: MACHINE GUNS (X2)
GATLING GUN(X1)
MISSILE LAUNCHER (X2)
MISSILES (X8)
SECRET OPTICS WEAPON (X1)
WHA...
WAIT A SEC--
LAUNCH! ♡
ドゥッ
EEEKZ!!
MISSILE 危険 ♡
ポチッ

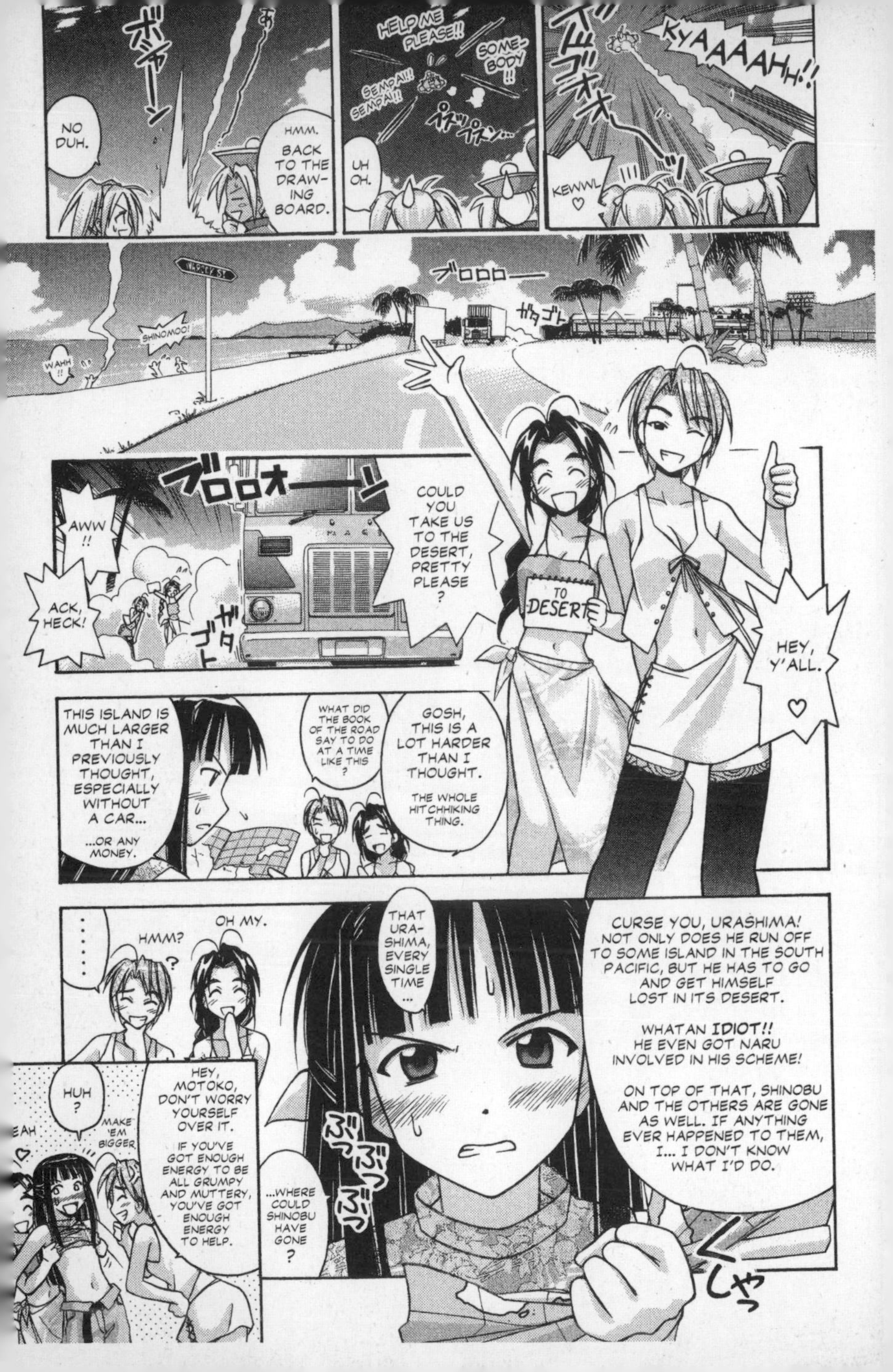
KYAAAAAHH!!
KEWWL ♡
HELP ME PLEASE!!
SOME-BODY!!
SEMPAI!! SEMPAI!!
UH OH.
HMM. BACK TO THE DRAWING BOARD.
NO DUH.
ボシャーン
ブロロロー
ガタゴト
SHINOMOO!
WAHH!!
HEY, Y'ALL. ♡
TO DESERT
COULD YOU TAKE US TO THE DESERT, PRETTY PLEASE?
ブロロオーー
AWW!!
ACK, HECK!
GOSH, THIS IS A LOT HARDER THAN I THOUGHT.
THE WHOLE HITCHHIKING THING.
WHAT DID THE BOOK OF THE ROAD SAY TO DO AT A TIME LIKE THIS?
THIS ISLAND IS MUCH LARGER THAN I PREVIOUSLY THOUGHT, ESPECIALLY WITHOUT A CAR...
...OR ANY MONEY.
CURSE YOU, URASHIMA! NOT ONLY DOES HE RUN OFF TO SOME ISLAND IN THE SOUTH PACIFIC, BUT HE HAS TO GO AND GET HIMSELF LOST IN ITS DESERT.
WHATAN IDIOT!! HE EVEN GOT NARU INVOLVED IN HIS SCHEME!
ON TOP OF THAT, SHINOBU AND THE OTHERS ARE GONE AS WELL. IF ANYTHING EVER HAPPENED TO THEM, I... I DON'T KNOW WHAT I'D DO.
THAT URASHIMA, EVERY SINGLE TIME...
OH MY.
HMM?
......
...WHERE COULD SHINOBU HAVE GONE?
HEY, MOTOKO, DON'T WORRY YOURSELF OVER IT.
IF YOU'VE GOT ENOUGH ENERGY TO BE ALL GRUMPY AND MUTTERY, YOU'VE GOT ENOUGH ENERGY TO HELP.
MAKE 'EM BIGGER
HUH?

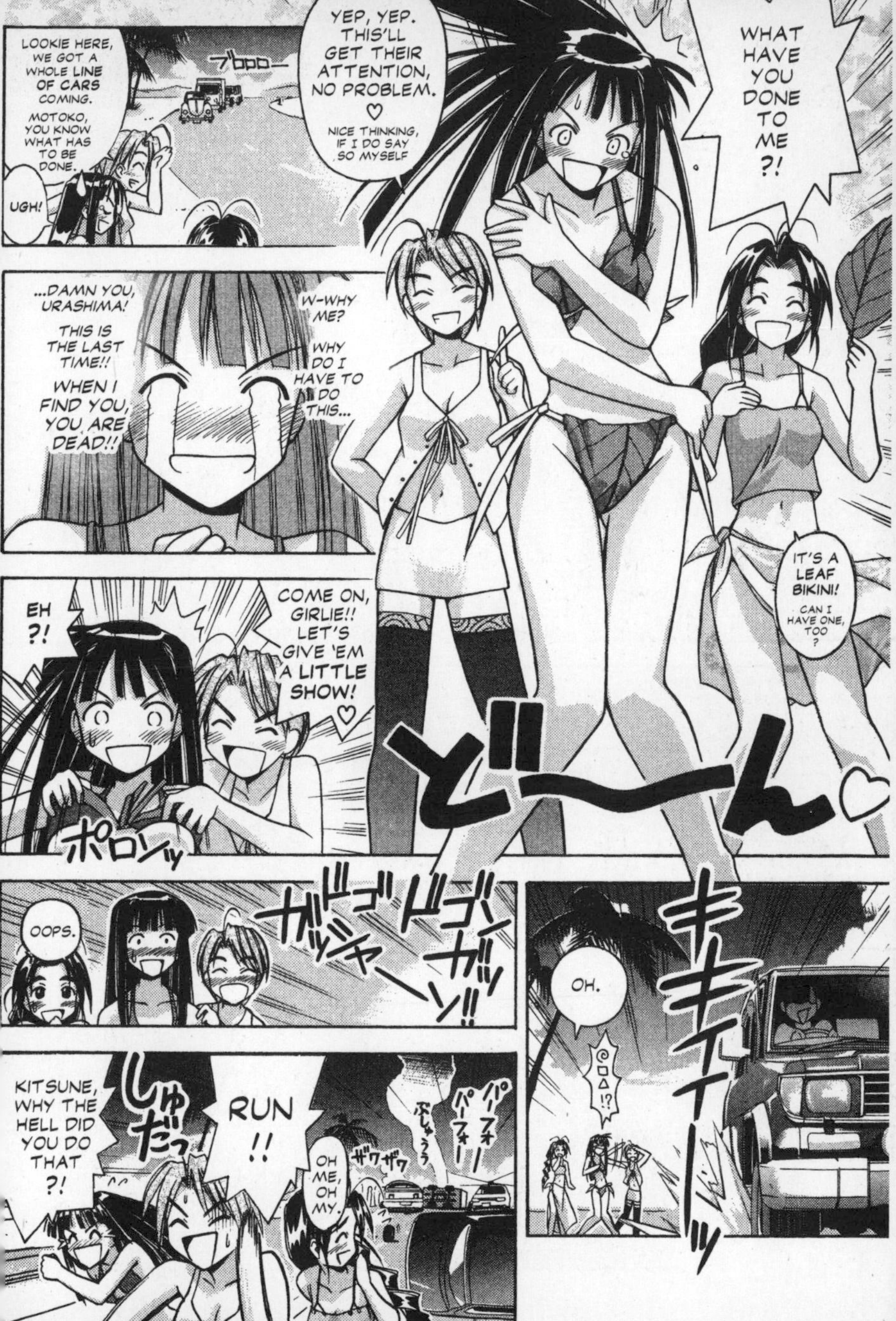
WHAT HAVE YOU DONE TO ME ?!
YEP, YEP. THIS'LL GET THEIR ATTENTION, NO PROBLEM. ♡
NICE THINKING, IF I DO SAY SO MYSELF
W-WHY ME?
WHY DO I HAVE TO DO THIS...
IT'S A LEAF BIKINI!
CAN I HAVE ONE, TOO ?
どーん♡
LOOKIE HERE, WE GOT A WHOLE LINE OF CARS COMING.
ブロロー
MOTOKO, YOU KNOW WHAT HAS TO BE DONE.
UGH!
...DAMN YOU, URASHIMA!
THIS IS THE LAST TIME!!
WHEN I FIND YOU, YOU ARE DEAD!!
COME ON, GIRLIE!! LET'S GIVE 'EM A LITTLE SHOW! ♡
EH ?!
ポロンッ
キキーッ
OH.
@ロ△!?
ドゴン
ガッシャーン!!
OOPS.
パーフォー パーフォー
ぷしゅううう
ザワザワ
OH ME, OH MY.
RUN !!
しゅだっ
KITSUNE, WHY THE HELL DID YOU DO THAT ?!

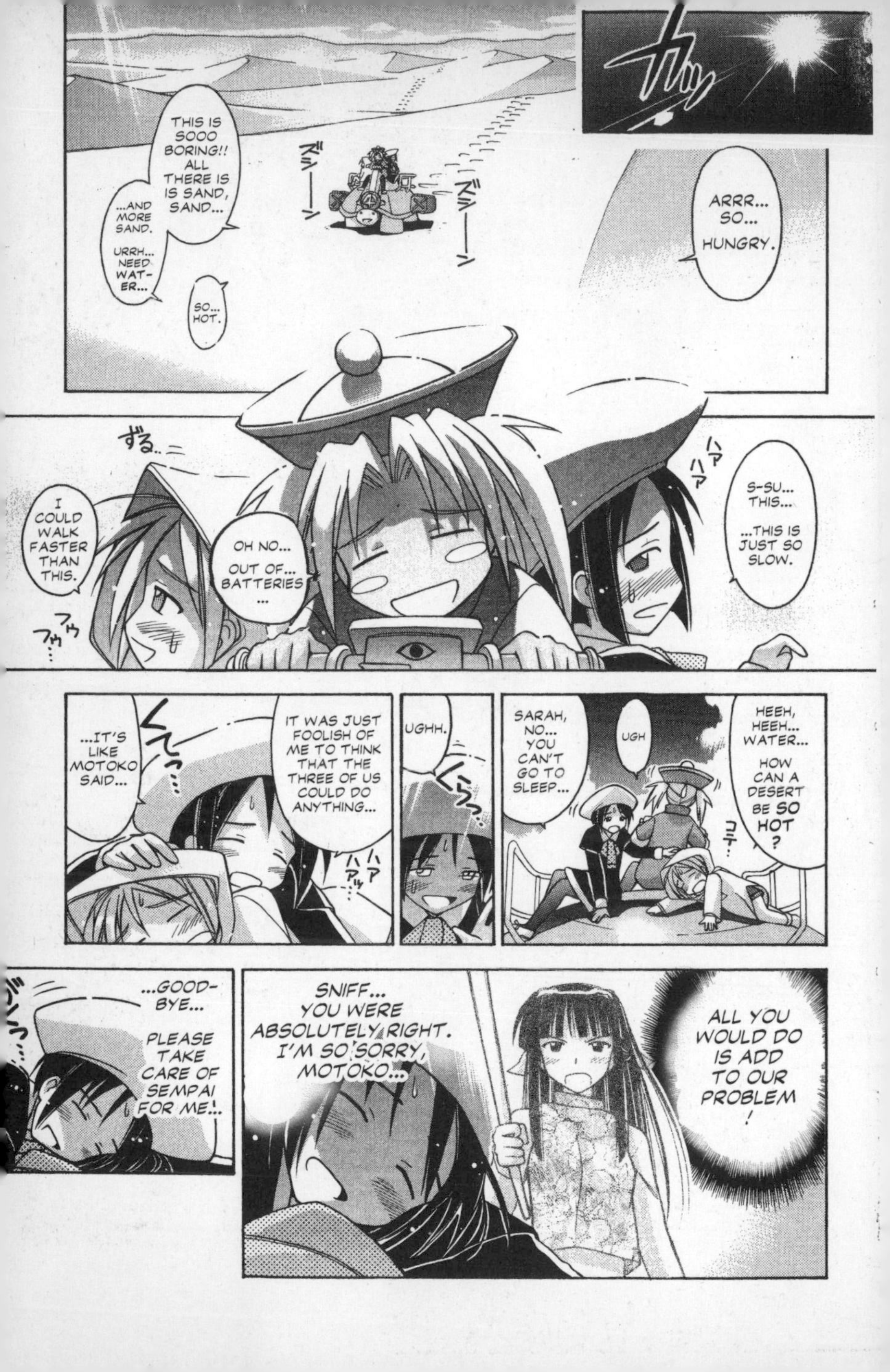
ARRR... SO... HUNGRY.
THIS IS SOOO BORING!! ALL THERE IS IS SAND, SAND...
...AND MORE SAND.
URRH... NEED WATER...
SO... HOT.
S-SU... THIS...
...THIS IS JUST SO SLOW.
OH NO... OUT OF... BATTERIES ...
I COULD WALK FASTER THAN THIS.
ずる...
HEEH, HEEH... WATER...
HOW CAN A DESERT BE SO HOT?
UGH
SARAH, NO... YOU CAN'T GO TO SLEEP...
UGHH.
IT WAS JUST FOOLISH OF ME TO THINK THAT THE THREE OF US COULD DO ANYTHING...
...IT'S LIKE MOTOKO SAID...
ALL YOU WOULD DO IS ADD TO OUR PROBLEM!
SNIFF... YOU WERE ABSOLUTELY RIGHT. I'M SO SORRY, MOTOKO...
...GOOD-BYE...
PLEASE TAKE CARE OF SEMPAI FOR ME!...

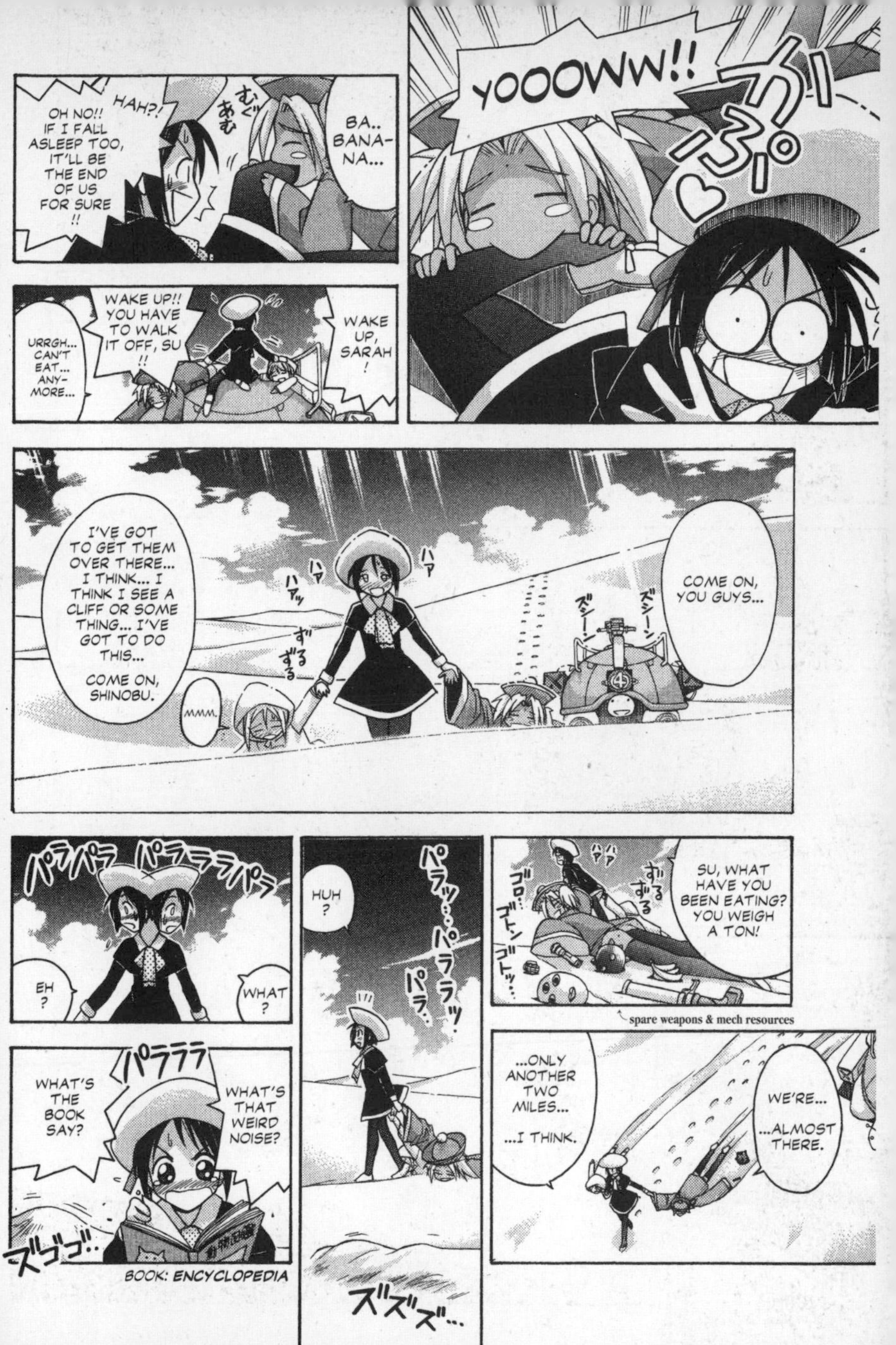

YOOOWW!!
かーぷー
BA.. BANANA...
むぐ あむ
HAH?!
OH NO!! IF I FALL ASLEEP TOO, IT'LL BE THE END OF US FOR SURE!!
WAKE UP, SARAH!
WAKE UP!! YOU HAVE TO WALK IT OFF, SU!!
URRGH... CAN'T EAT... ANY-MORE...
COME ON, YOU GUYS...
ズシーン
ズシーン
ハァ
ハァ
ハァッ
I'VE GOT TO GET THEM OVER THERE... I THINK... I THINK I SEE A CLIFF OR SOME THING... I'VE GOT TO DO THIS...
COME ON, SHINOBU.
ずる ずる
MMM.
SU, WHAT HAVE YOU BEEN EATING? YOU WEIGH A TON!
ハァ ハァ
ずる ずる
ゴロ... ゴトン ゴトッ...
spare weapons & mech resources
WE'RE... ...ALMOST THERE.
...ONLY ANOTHER TWO MILES... ...I THINK.
パラッ... パララッ パラ..
HUH?
ズズズ...
パラパラ パラララパラ
WHAT?
EH?
パラララ
WHAT'S THAT WEIRD NOISE?
WHAT'S THE BOOK SAY?
ズゴゴ..
BOOK: ENCYCLOPEDIA

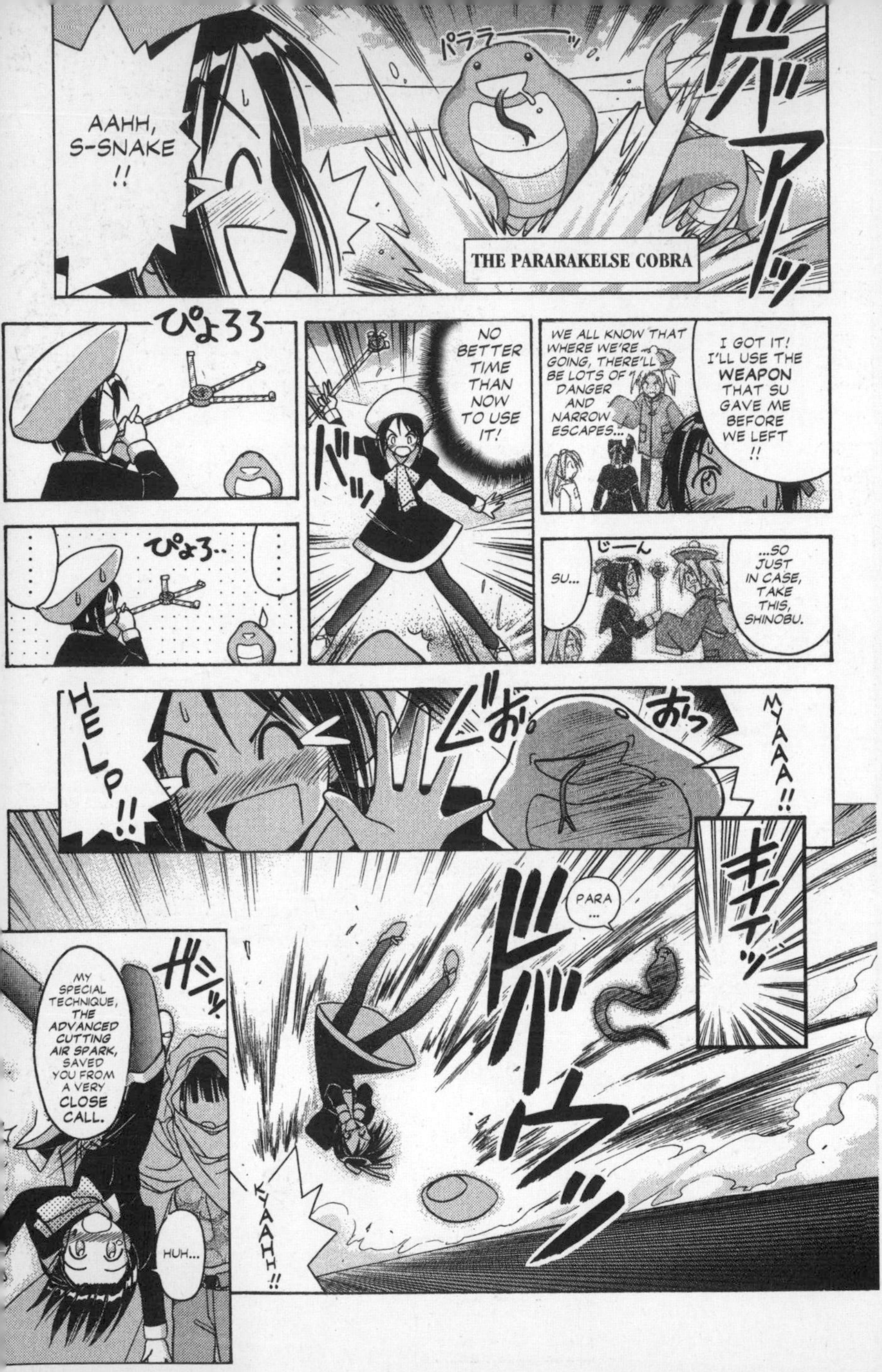

ドバァーッ
パララーッ
THE PARARAKELSE COBRA
AAHH, S-SNAKE !!
I GOT IT! I'LL USE THE WEAPON THAT SU GAVE ME BEFORE WE LEFT !!
WE ALL KNOW THAT WHERE WE'RE GOING, THERE'LL BE LOTS OF DANGER AND NARROW ESCAPES...
...SO JUST IN CASE, TAKE THIS, SHINOBU.
じーん
SU...
NO BETTER TIME THAN NOW TO USE IT!
バッ
ぴょろろ
ぴょろ..
MYAAA!!
おっ
ぐお
HELP!!
ギィッ
PARA ...
ドバウッ
KYAAHH!!
ザン!!
MY SPECIAL TECHNIQUE, THE ADVANCED CUTTING AIR SPARK, SAVED YOU FROM A VERY CLOSE CALL.
HUH...

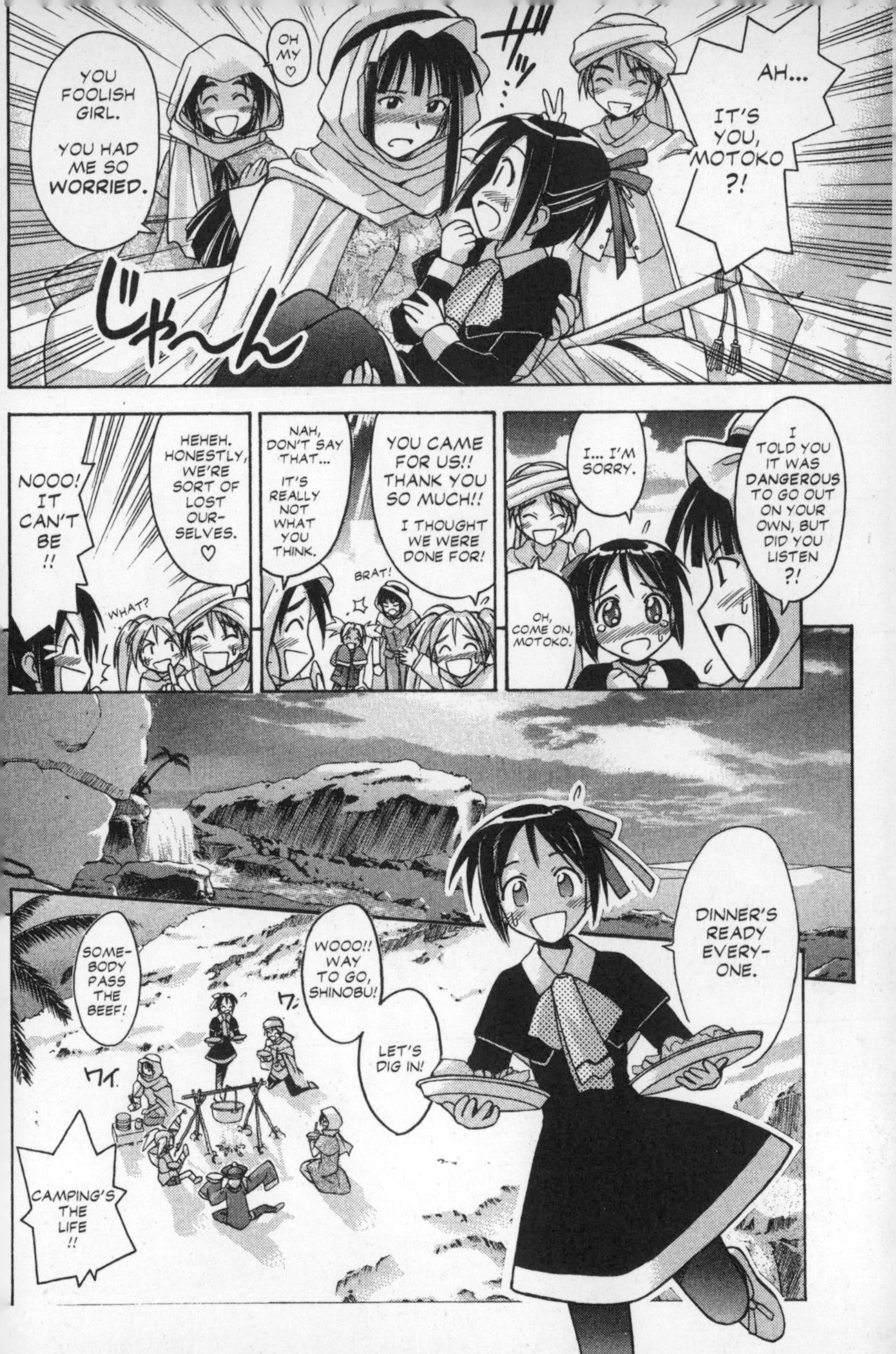
ザッ
AH... IT'S YOU, MOTOKO?!
OH MY ♡
YOU FOOLISH GIRL. YOU HAD ME SO WORRIED.
じゃ〜ん
I TOLD YOU IT WAS DANGEROUS TO GO OUT ON YOUR OWN, BUT DID YOU LISTEN?!
I... I'M SORRY.
OH, COME ON, MOTOKO.
YOU CAME FOR US!! THANK YOU SO MUCH!! I THOUGHT WE WERE DONE FOR!
NAH, DON'T SAY THAT... IT'S REALLY NOT WHAT YOU THINK.
BRAT!
HEHEH. HONESTLY, WE'RE SORT OF LOST OURSELVES. ♡
NOOO! IT CAN'T BE!!
WHAT?
DINNER'S READY EVERYONE.
WOOO!! WAY TO GO, SHINOBU!
LET'S DIG IN!
ワ
SOMEBODY PASS THE BEEF!
ワイ
CAMPING'S THE LIFE!!

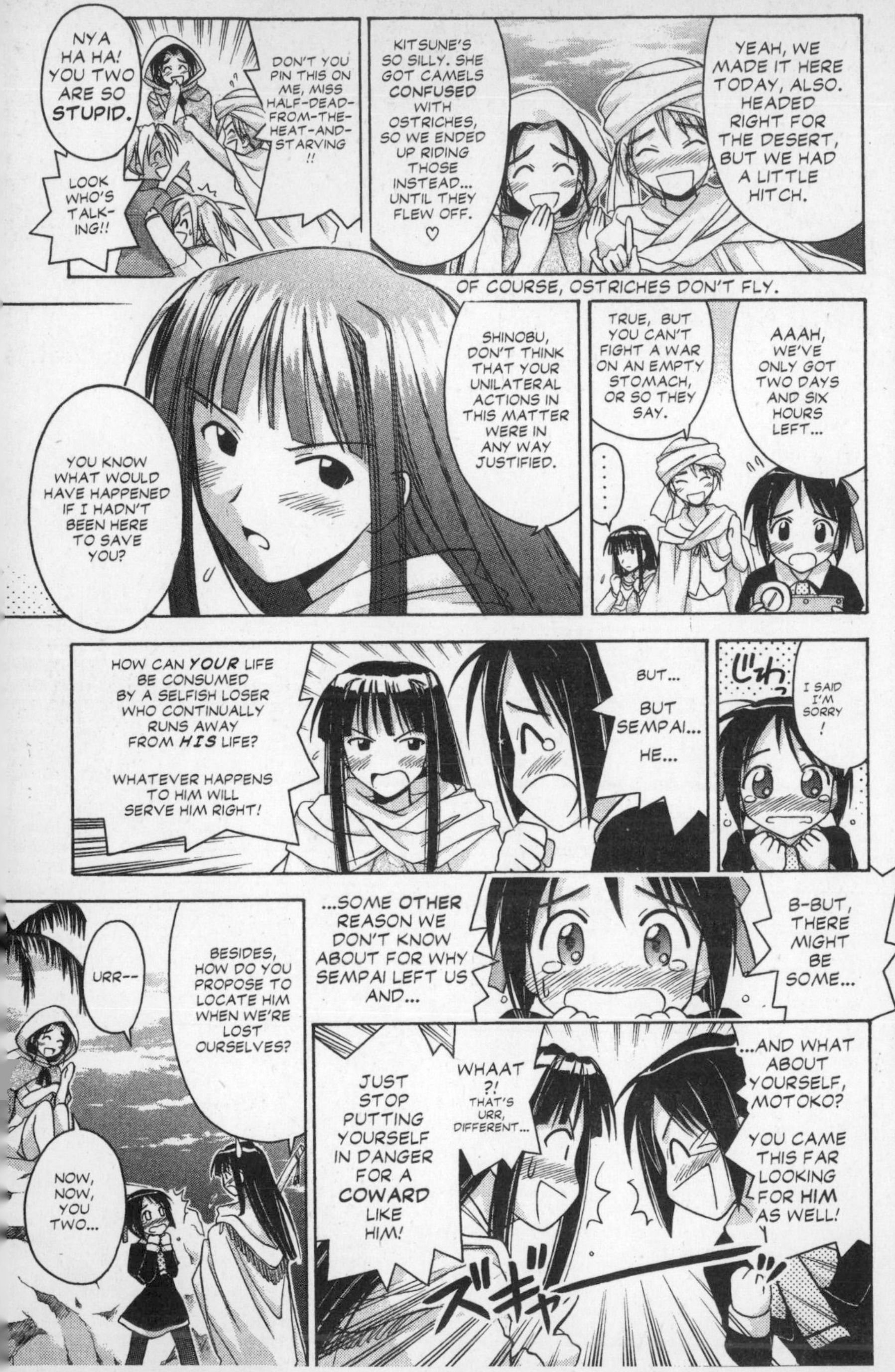
YEAH, WE MADE IT HERE TODAY, ALSO. HEADED RIGHT FOR THE DESERT, BUT WE HAD A LITTLE HITCH.
KITSUNE'S SO SILLY. SHE GOT CAMELS CONFUSED WITH OSTRICHES, SO WE ENDED UP RIDING THOSE INSTEAD... UNTIL THEY FLEW OFF. ♡
NYA HA HA! YOU TWO ARE SO STUPID.
DON'T YOU PIN THIS ON ME, MISS HALF-DEAD-FROM-THE-HEAT-AND-STARVING!!
LOOK WHO'S TALKING!!
OF COURSE, OSTRICHES DON'T FLY.
AAAH, WE'VE ONLY GOT TWO DAYS AND SIX HOURS LEFT...
TRUE, BUT YOU CAN'T FIGHT A WAR ON AN EMPTY STOMACH, OR SO THEY SAY.
......
SHINOBU, DON'T THINK THAT YOUR UNILATERAL ACTIONS IN THIS MATTER WERE IN ANY WAY JUSTIFIED.
YOU KNOW WHAT WOULD HAVE HAPPENED IF I HADN'T BEEN HERE TO SAVE YOU?
じわっ
I SAID I'M SORRY!
BUT... BUT SEMPAI... HE...
HOW CAN YOUR LIFE BE CONSUMED BY A SELFISH LOSER WHO CONTINUALLY RUNS AWAY FROM HIS LIFE?
WHATEVER HAPPENS TO HIM WILL SERVE HIM RIGHT!
B-BUT, THERE MIGHT BE SOME...
...SOME OTHER REASON WE DON'T KNOW ABOUT FOR WHY SEMPAI LEFT US AND...
...AND WHAT ABOUT YOURSELF, MOTOKO?
YOU CAME THIS FAR LOOKING FOR HIM AS WELL!
WHAAT?! THAT'S URR, DIFFERENT...
JUST STOP PUTTING YOURSELF IN DANGER FOR A COWARD LIKE HIM!
ズギャ
BESIDES, HOW DO YOU PROPOSE TO LOCATE HIM WHEN WE'RE LOST OURSELVES?
URR--
NOW, NOW, YOU TWO...

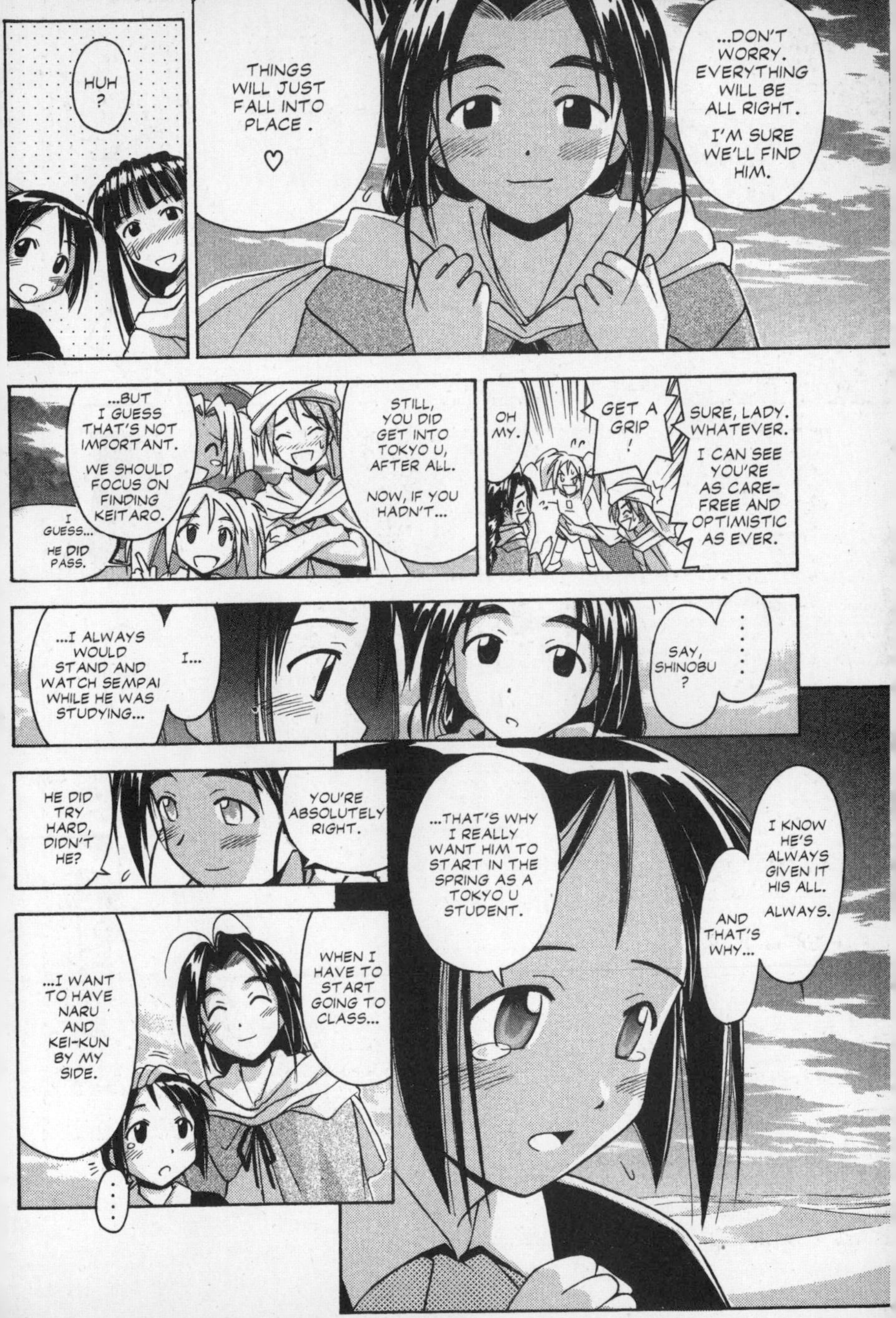
...DON'T WORRY. EVERYTHING WILL BE ALL RIGHT.
I'M SURE WE'LL FIND HIM.
THINGS WILL JUST FALL INTO PLACE. ♡
HUH ?
SURE, LADY. WHATEVER. I CAN SEE YOU'RE AS CAREFREE AND OPTIMISTIC AS EVER.
GET A GRIP !
OH MY.
STILL, YOU DID GET INTO TOKYO U, AFTER ALL.
NOW, IF YOU HADN'T...
...BUT I GUESS THAT'S NOT IMPORTANT.
WE SHOULD FOCUS ON FINDING KEITARO.
I GUESS... HE DID PASS.
......
SAY, SHINOBU ?
I...
...I ALWAYS WOULD STAND AND WATCH SEMPAI WHILE HE WAS STUDYING...
I KNOW HE'S ALWAYS GIVEN IT HIS ALL.
ALWAYS.
AND THAT'S WHY...
...THAT'S WHY I REALLY WANT HIM TO START IN THE SPRING AS A TOKYO U STUDENT.
YOU'RE ABSOLUTELY RIGHT.
HE DID TRY HARD, DIDN'T HE?
WHEN I HAVE TO START GOING TO CLASS...
...I WANT TO HAVE NARU AND KEI-KUN BY MY SIDE.
....

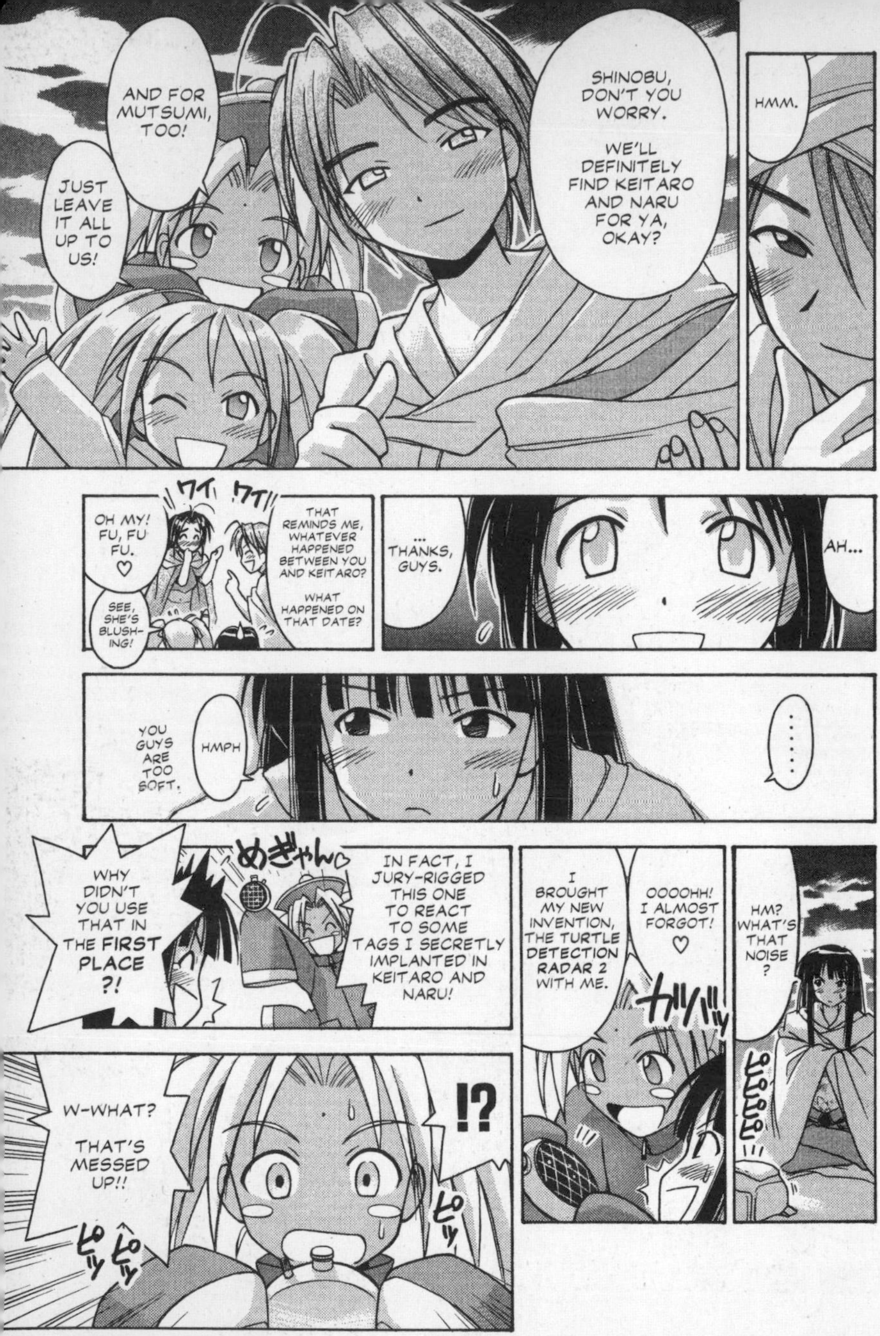

HMM.
SHINOBU, DON'T YOU WORRY.
WE'LL DEFINITELY FIND KEITARO AND NARU FOR YA, OKAY?
AND FOR MUTSUMI, TOO!
JUST LEAVE IT ALL UP TO US!
AH...
... THANKS, GUYS.
ワイ ワイ
THAT REMINDS ME, WHATEVER HAPPENED BETWEEN YOU AND KEITARO?
WHAT HAPPENED ON THAT DATE?
OH MY! FU, FU FU. ♡
SEE, SHE'S BLUSHING!
......
HMPH
YOU GUYS ARE TOO SOFT.
HM? WHAT'S THAT NOISE?
ピピピピ
OOOOHH! I ALMOST FORGOT! ♡
ガバッ
I BROUGHT MY NEW INVENTION, THE TURTLE DETECTION RADAR 2 WITH ME.
IN FACT, I JURY-RIGGED THIS ONE TO REACT TO SOME TAGS I SECRETLY IMPLANTED IN KEITARO AND NARU!
めぎゃん♡
WHY DIDN'T YOU USE THAT IN THE FIRST PLACE?!
!?
ピッ
W-WHAT?
THAT'S MESSED UP!!
ピッ ピッ

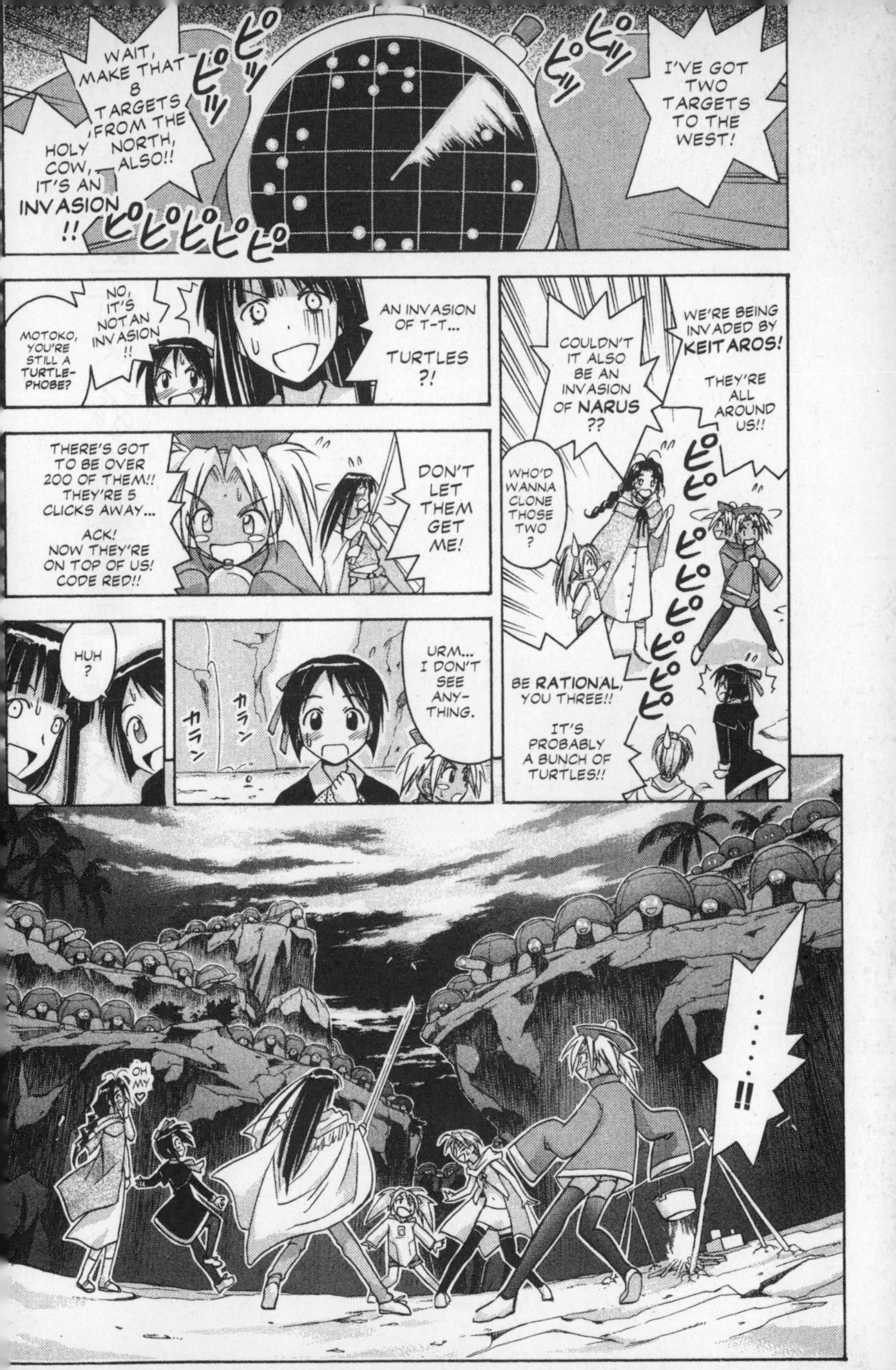

I'VE GOT TWO TARGETS TO THE WEST!
ピピッ
WAIT, MAKE THAT 8 TARGETS FROM THE NORTH, ALSO!!
ピッピッ
HOLY COW, IT'S AN INVASION!!
ピピピピピピ
WE'RE BEING INVADED BY KEITAROS!
THEY'RE ALL AROUND US!!
COULDN'T IT ALSO BE AN INVASION OF NARUS??
WHO'D WANNA CLONE THOSE TWO?
ピピピピピピピピ
BE RATIONAL, YOU THREE!!
IT'S PROBABLY A BUNCH OF TURTLES!!
AN INVASION OF T-T...
TURTLES?!
NO, IT'S NOT AN INVASION!!
MOTOKO, YOU'RE STILL A TURTLE-PHOBE?
DON'T LET THEM GET ME!
THERE'S GOT TO BE OVER 200 OF THEM!! THEY'RE 5 CLICKS AWAY...
ACK! NOW THEY'RE ON TOP OF US! CODE RED!!
URM... I DON'T SEE ANYTHING.
カラン
カラン
HUH?
......!!
OH MY ♥

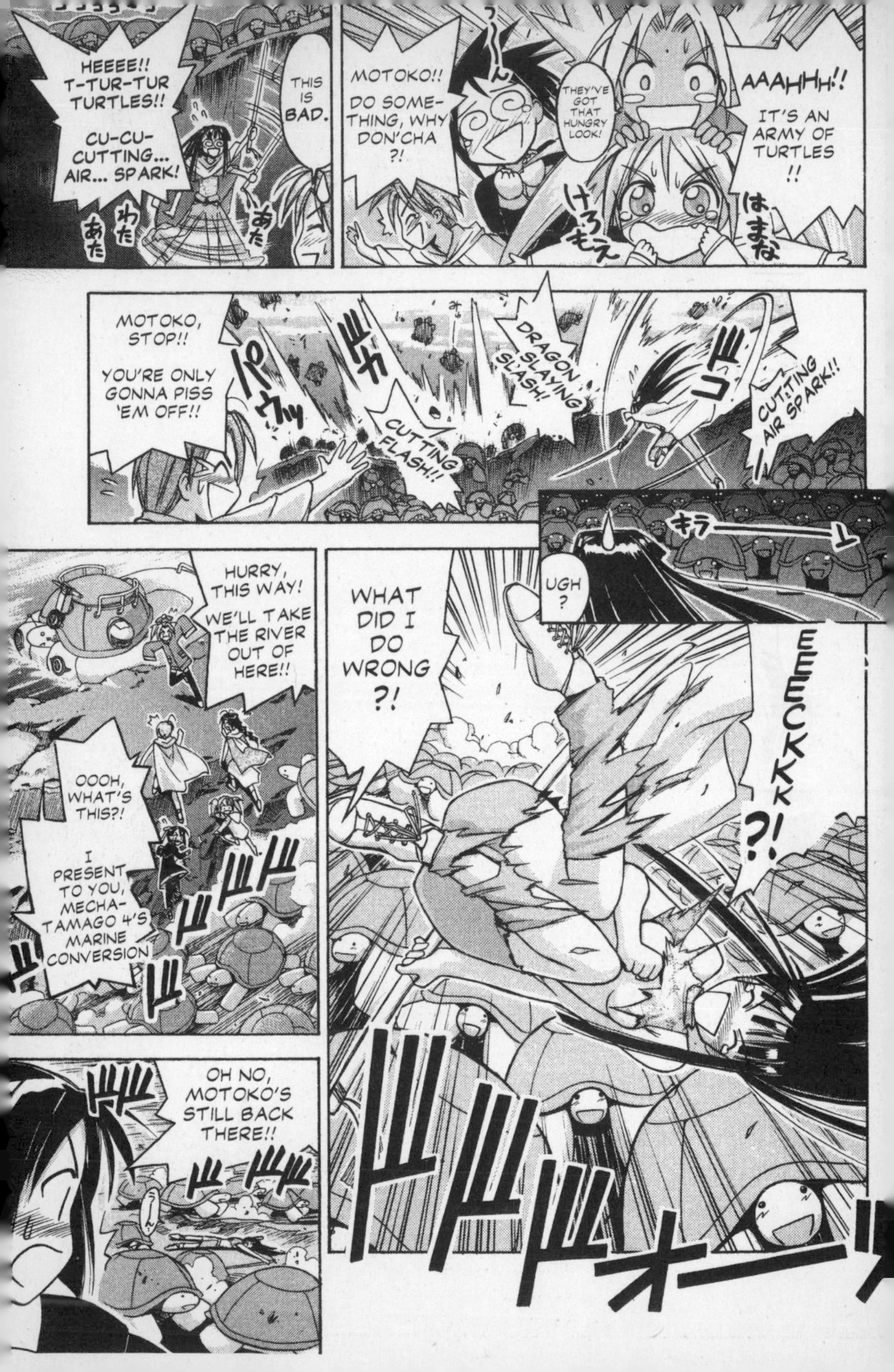

AAAHHH!!
IT'S AN ARMY OF TURTLES!!
THEY'VE GOT THAT HUNGRY LOOK!
はまな
けろもえ
MOTOKO!! DO SOME-THING, WHY DON'CHA?!
THIS IS BAD.
HEEEE!! T-TUR-TUR TURTLES!!
CU-CU-CUTTING... AIR... SPARK!
あた
わた
あた
CUTTING AIR SPARK!!
DRAGON SLAYING SLASH!
CUTTING FLASH!!
MOTOKO, STOP!!
YOU'RE ONLY GONNA PISS 'EM OFF!!
キラ
UGH?
WHAT DID I DO WRONG?!
EEECKKK?!
HURRY, THIS WAY!
WE'LL TAKE THE RIVER OUT OF HERE!!
OOOH, WHAT'S THIS?!
I PRESENT TO YOU, MECHA-TAMAGO 4'S MARINE CONVERSION
OH NO, MOTOKO'S STILL BACK THERE!!

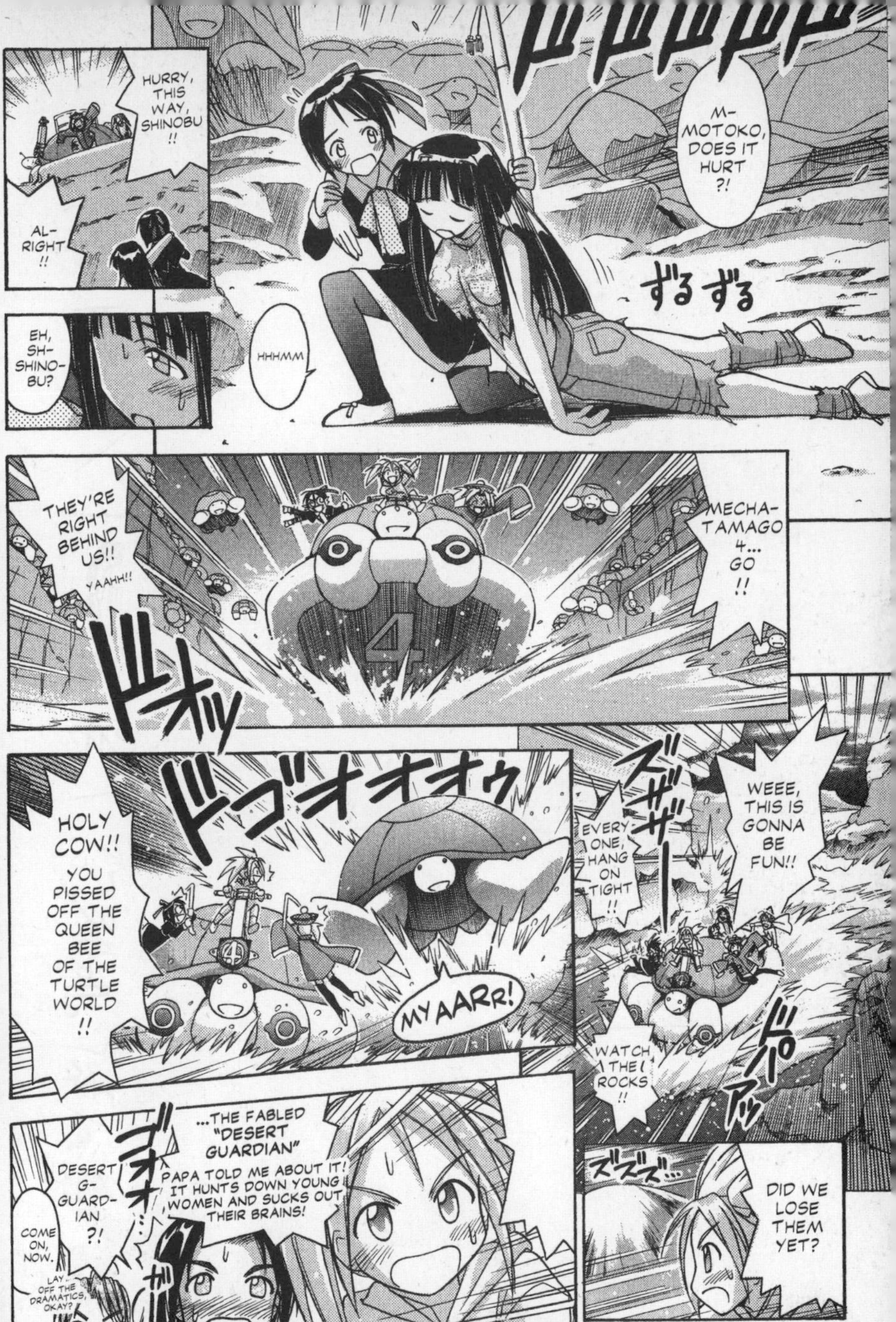
M-MOTOKO, DOES IT HURT ?!
ずるずる
HHHMM
HURRY, THIS WAY, SHINOBU !!
AL-RIGHT !!
EH, SH-SHINOBU?
MECHA-TAMAGO 4... GO !!
THEY'RE RIGHT BEHIND US!!
YAAHH!!
WEEE, THIS IS GONNA BE FUN!!
EVERY ONE, HANG ON TIGHT !!
WATCH THE ROCKS !!
HOLY COW!! YOU PISSED OFF THE QUEEN BEE OF THE TURTLE WORLD !!
MYAARr!
DID WE LOSE THEM YET?
...THE FABLED "DESERT GUARDIAN"
PAPA TOLD ME ABOUT IT! IT HUNTS DOWN YOUNG WOMEN AND SUCKS OUT THEIR BRAINS!
DESERT G-GUARDIAN ?!
COME ON, NOW.
LAY OFF THE DRAMATICS, OKAY?

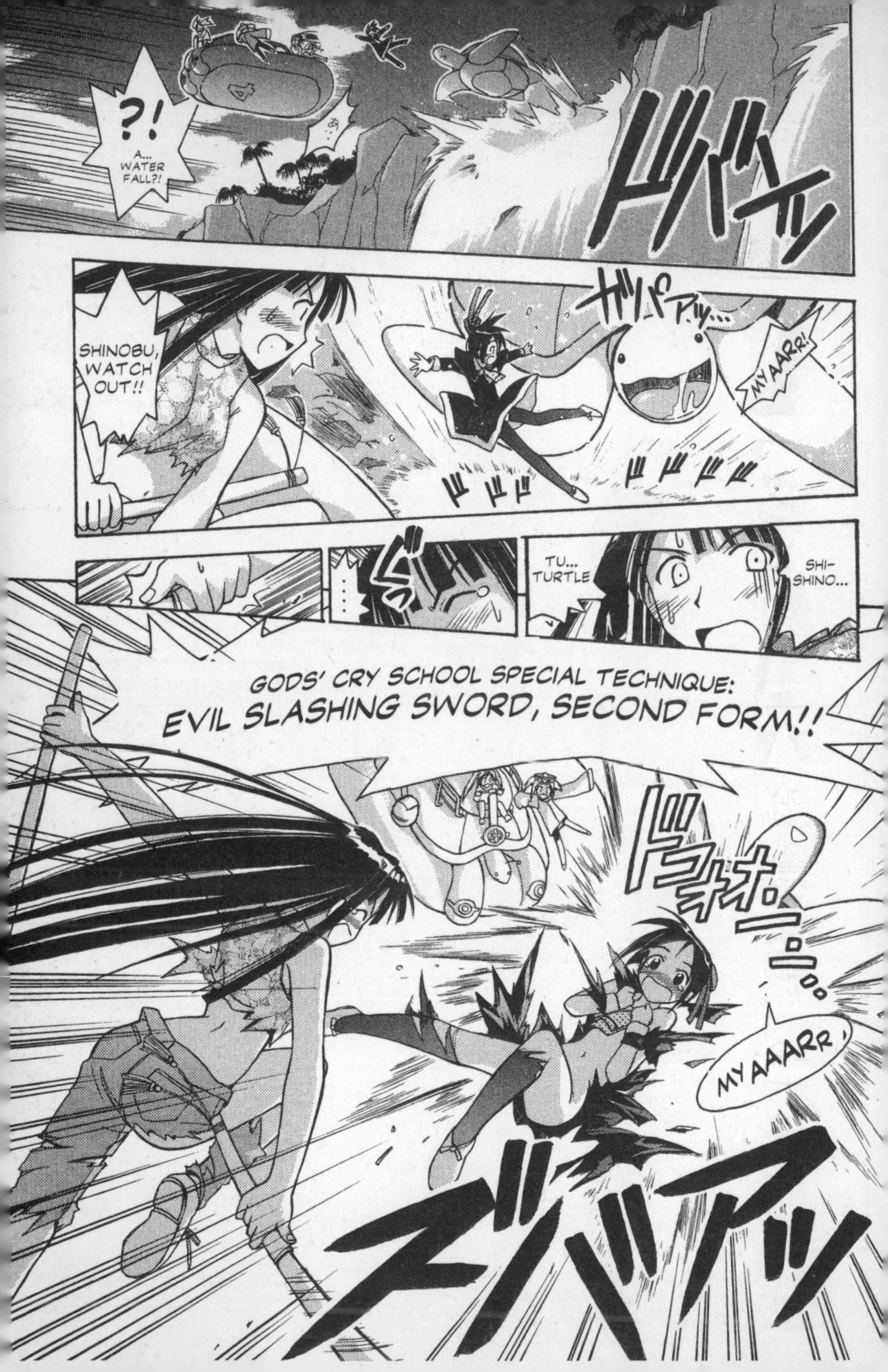

あ…
?!
A... WATER FALL?!
MYAARR!
SHINOBU, WATCH OUT!!
SHI-SHINO...
TU... TURTLE
......
GODS' CRY SCHOOL SPECIAL TECHNIQUE:
EVIL SLASHING SWORD, SECOND FORM!!
MYAAARR

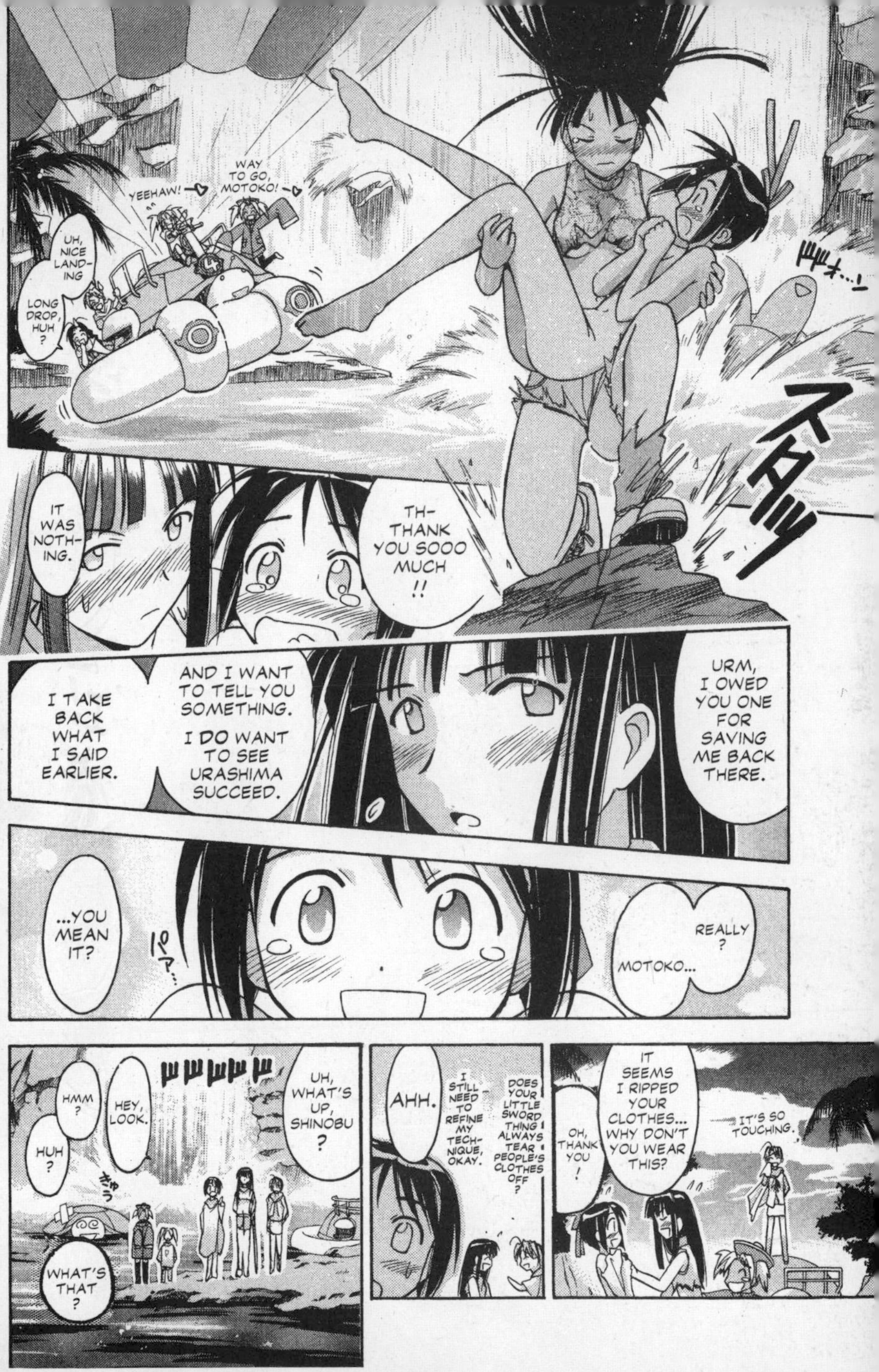
WAY TO GO, MOTOKO!
YEEHAW!
UH, NICE LANDING
LONG DROP, HUH?
スタッ
TH-THANK YOU SOOO MUCH!!
IT WAS NOTHING.
URM, I OWED YOU ONE FOR SAVING ME BACK THERE.
AND I WANT TO TELL YOU SOMETHING.
I DO WANT TO SEE URASHIMA SUCCEED.
I TAKE BACK WHAT I SAID EARLIER.
MOTOKO...
REALLY?
...YOU MEAN IT?
IT'S SO TOUCHING.
IT SEEMS I RIPPED YOUR CLOTHES... WHY DON'T YOU WEAR THIS?
OH, THANK YOU!
DOES YOUR LITTLE SWORD THING ALWAYS TEAR PEOPLE'S CLOTHES OFF?
I STILL NEED TO REFINE MY TECHNIQUE, OKAY.
AHH.
UH, WHAT'S UP, SHINOBU?
HEY, LOOK.
HMM?
HUH?
WHAT'S THAT?

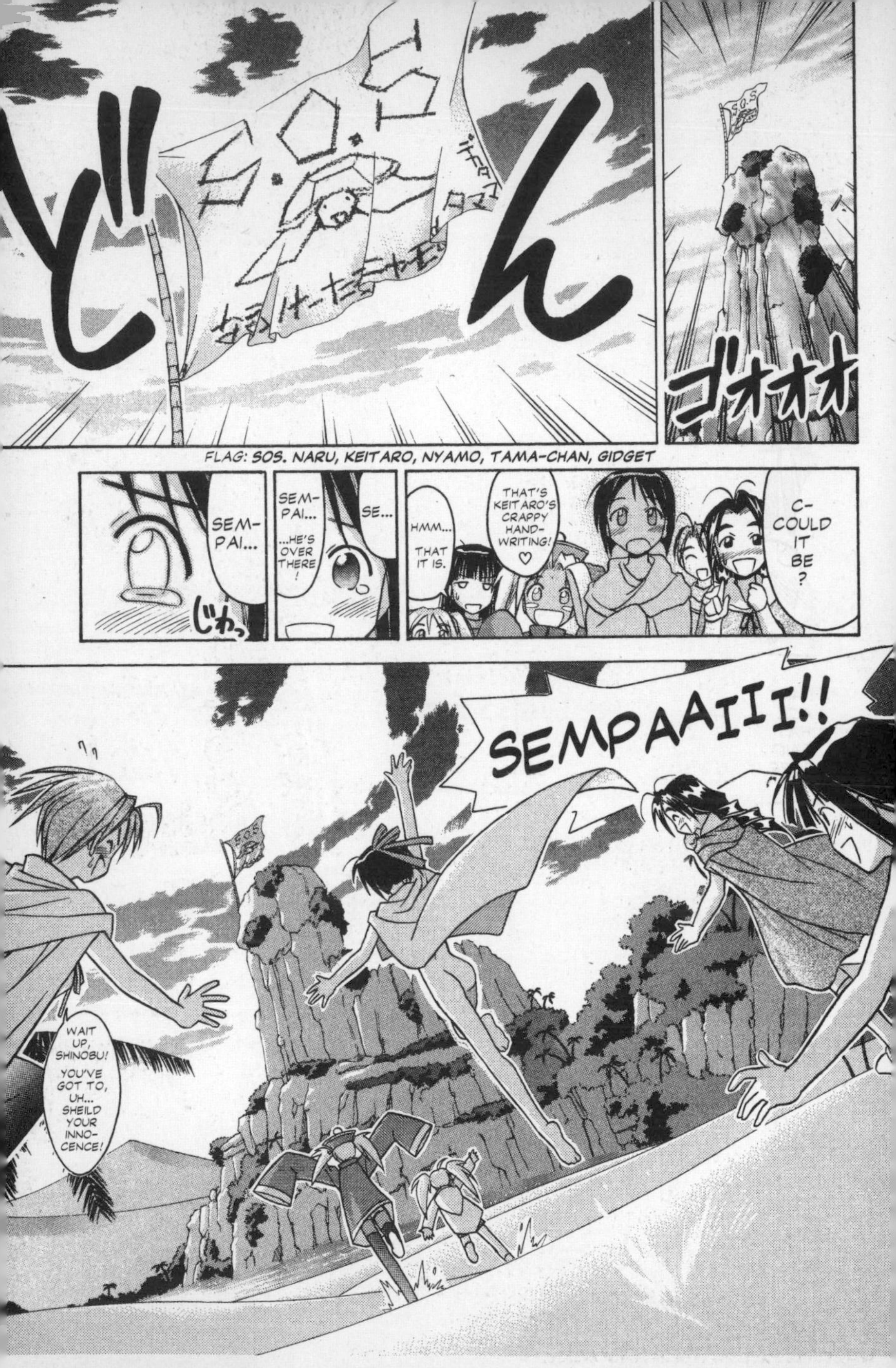
ゴオオオ
どん
FLAG: SOS. NARU, KEITARO, NYAMO, TAMA-CHAN, GIDGET
C-COULD IT BE?
THAT'S KEITARO'S CRAPPY HANDWRITING! ♡
HMM... THAT IT IS.
SE...
SEMPAI... ...HE'S OVER THERE!
SEM-PAI...
じわっ
SEMPAAIII!!
WAIT UP, SHINOBU! YOU'VE GOT TO, UH... SHEILD YOUR INNOCENCE!

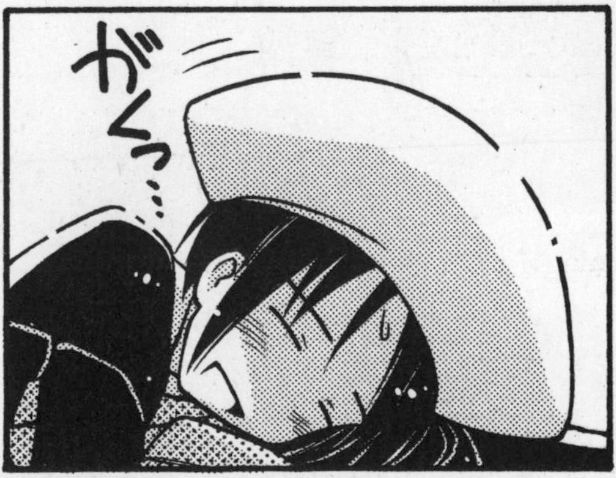
がくっ…

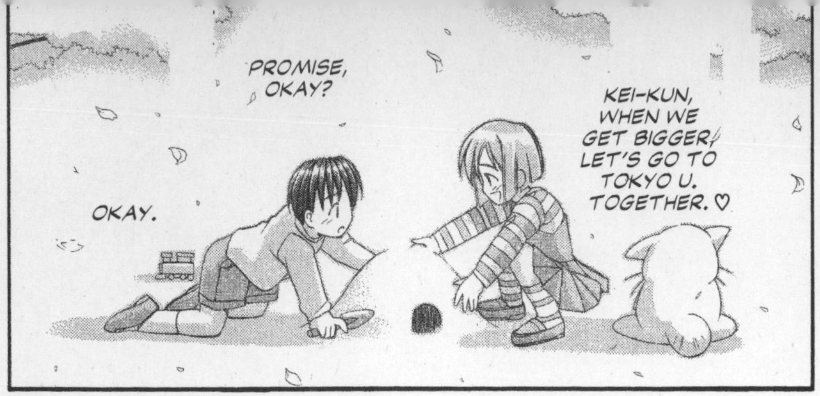
KEI-KUN, WHEN WE GET BIGGER, LET'S GO TO TOKYO U. TOGETHER. ♡
PROMISE, OKAY?
OKAY.

Love Hina

HINATA.66 Cherry Blossom Bloom in the Desert

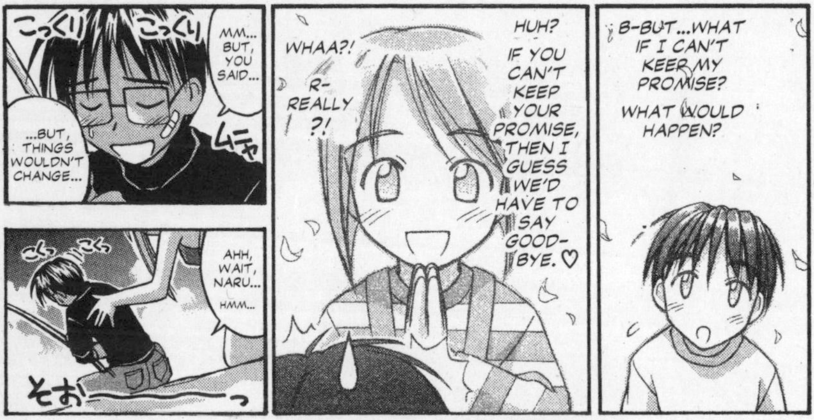
B-BUT...WHAT IF I CAN'T KEEP MY PROMISE?
WHAT WOULD HAPPEN?
HUH? IF YOU CAN'T KEEP YOUR PROMISE, THEN I GUESS WE'D HAVE TO SAY GOOD-BYE. ♡
WHAA?!
R-REALLY ?!
こっくり こっくり
MM... BUT, YOU SAID...
ムニャ
...BUT, THINGS WOULDN'T CHANGE...
AHH, WAIT, NARU... HMM...
こくっ こくっ
そお!っ

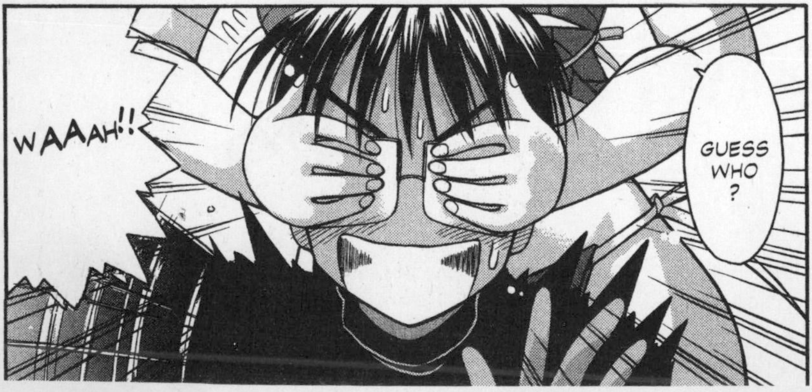
GUESS WHO ?
WAAAH!!

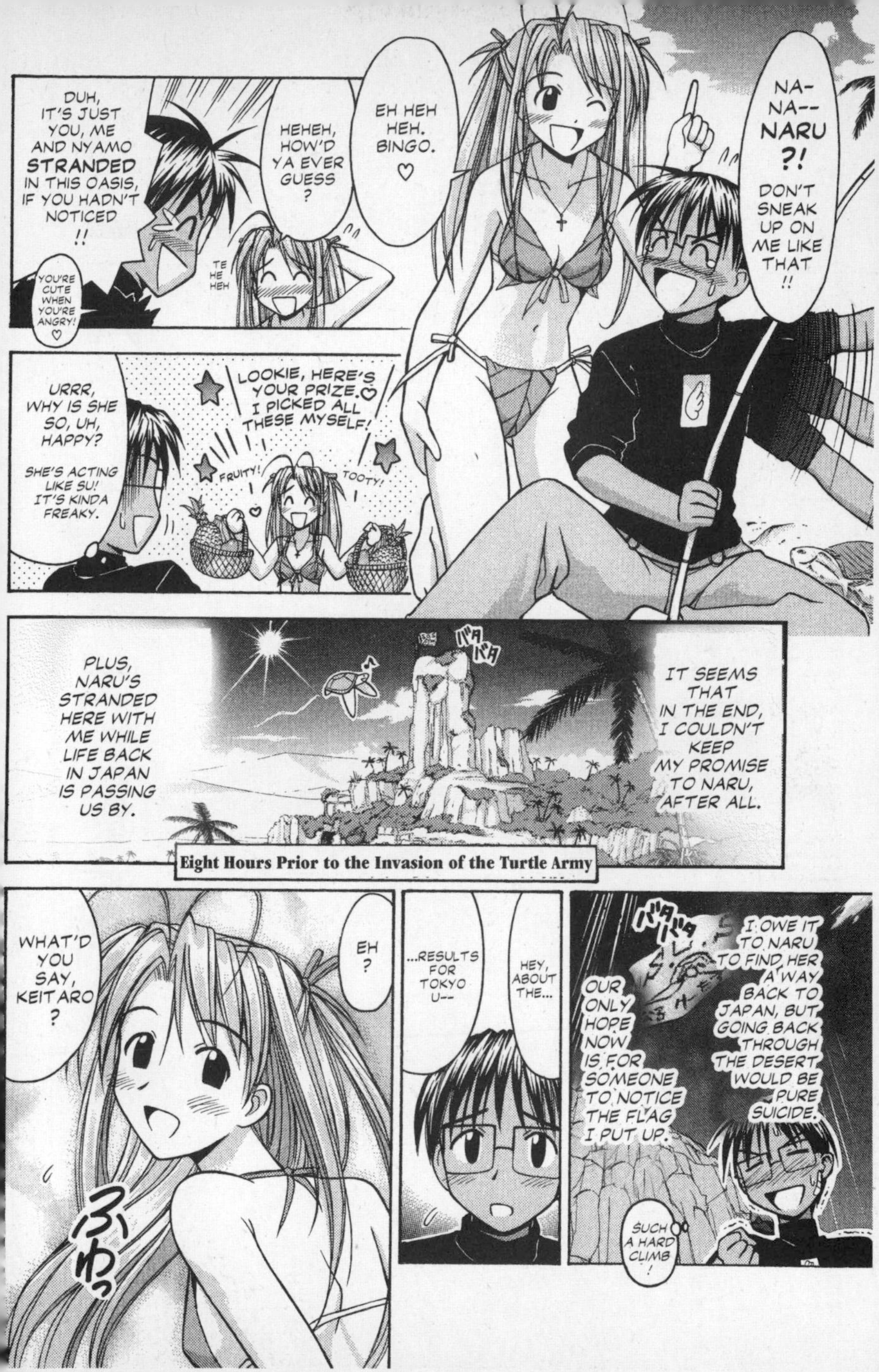
NA-NA--NARU ?!
DON'T SNEAK UP ON ME LIKE THAT !!
EH HEH HEH. BINGO. ♡
HEHEH, HOW'D YA EVER GUESS ?
DUH, IT'S JUST YOU, ME AND NYAMO STRANDED IN THIS OASIS, IF YOU HADN'T NOTICED !!
TE HE HEH
YOU'RE CUTE WHEN YOU'RE ANGRY! ♡
LOOKIE, HERE'S YOUR PRIZE.♡ I PICKED ALL THESE MYSELF!
TOOTY!
FRUITY!
URRR, WHY IS SHE SO, UH, HAPPY?
SHE'S ACTING LIKE SU! IT'S KINDA FREAKY.
IT SEEMS THAT IN THE END, I COULDN'T KEEP MY PROMISE TO NARU, AFTER ALL.
バタバタ
PLUS, NARU'S STRANDED HERE WITH ME WHILE LIFE BACK IN JAPAN IS PASSING US BY.
Eight Hours Prior to the Invasion of the Turtle Army
バタバタ
I OWE IT TO NARU TO FIND HER A WAY BACK TO JAPAN, BUT GOING BACK THROUGH THE DESERT WOULD BE PURE SUICIDE.
OUR ONLY HOPE NOW IS FOR SOMEONE TO NOTICE THE FLAG I PUT UP.
SUCH A HARD CLIMB !
HEY, ABOUT THE...
...RESULTS FOR TOKYO U--
EH ?
WHAT'D YOU SAY, KEITARO ?
ふわっ

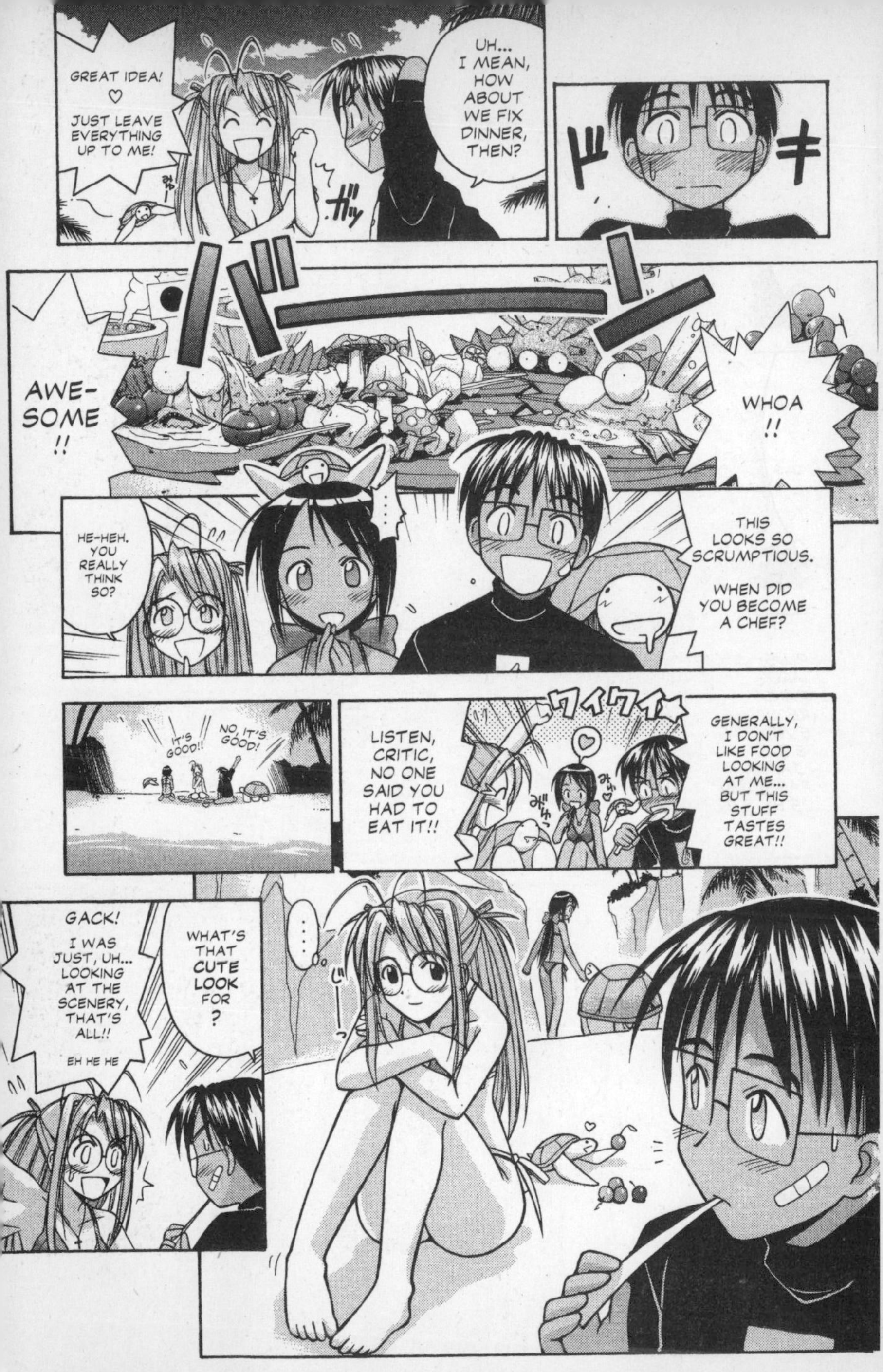

ドキ
UH... I MEAN, HOW ABOUT WE FIX DINNER, THEN?
GREAT IDEA! ♡ JUST LEAVE EVERYTHING UP TO ME!
バーン
WHOA !!
AWE-SOME !!
THIS LOOKS SO SCRUMPTIOUS. WHEN DID YOU BECOME A CHEF?
HE-HEH. YOU REALLY THINK SO?
ワイワイ
GENERALLY, I DON'T LIKE FOOD LOOKING AT ME... BUT THIS STUFF TASTES GREAT!!
LISTEN, CRITIC, NO ONE SAID YOU HAD TO EAT IT!!
NO, IT'S GOOD!
IT'S GOOD!!
WHAT'S THAT CUTE LOOK FOR?
GACK! I WAS JUST, UH... LOOKING AT THE SCENERY, THAT'S ALL!!
EH HE HE

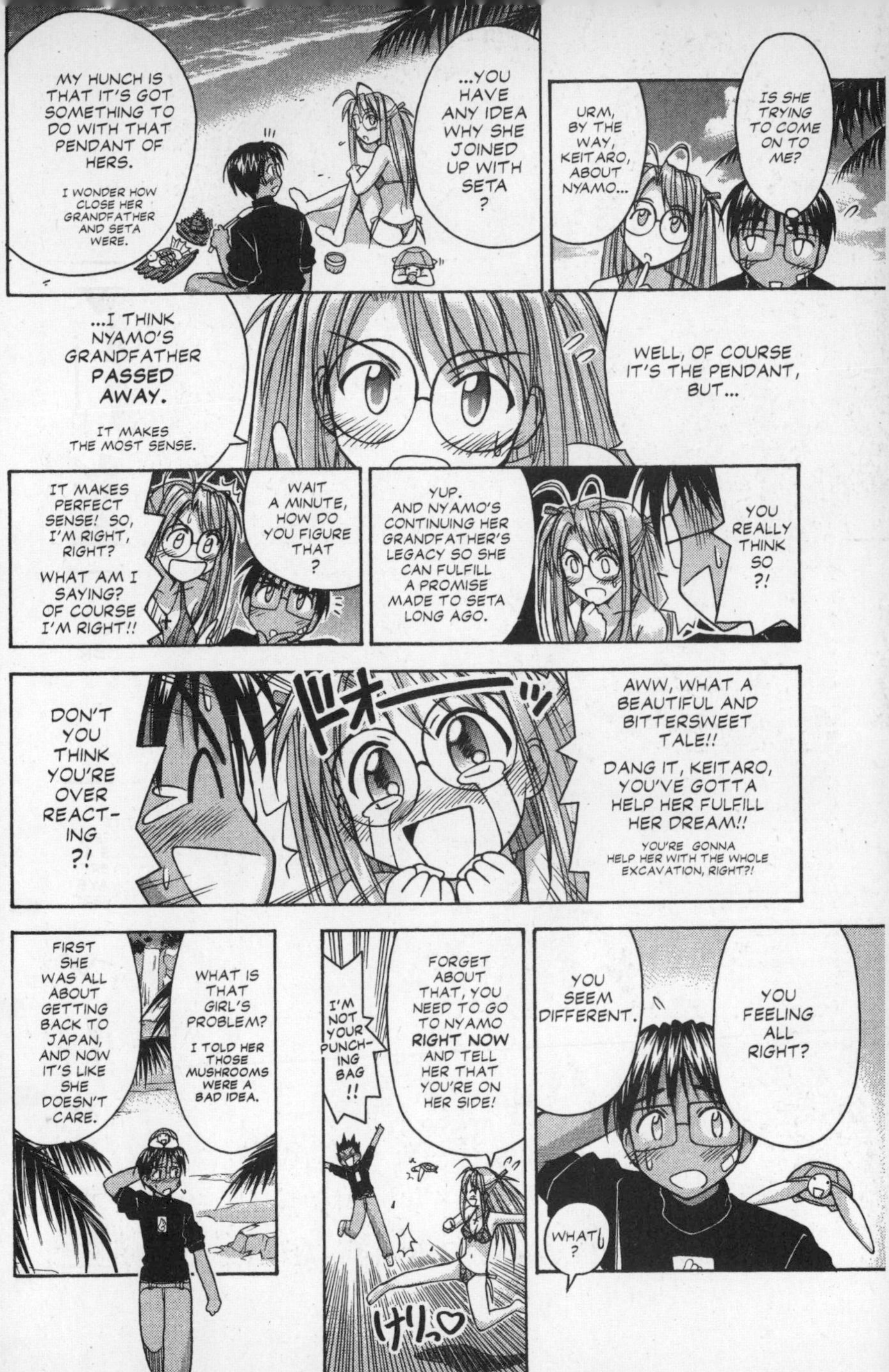
URM, BY THE WAY, KEITARO, ABOUT NYAMO...
IS SHE TRYING TO COME ON TO ME?
...YOU HAVE ANY IDEA WHY SHE JOINED UP WITH SETA?
MY HUNCH IS THAT IT'S GOT SOMETHING TO DO WITH THAT PENDANT OF HERS.
I WONDER HOW CLOSE HER GRANDFATHER AND SETA WERE.
WELL, OF COURSE IT'S THE PENDANT, BUT...
...I THINK NYAMO'S GRANDFATHER **PASSED AWAY.**
IT MAKES THE MOST SENSE.
YOU REALLY THINK SO?!
YUP. AND NYAMO'S CONTINUING HER GRANDFATHER'S LEGACY SO SHE CAN FULFILL A PROMISE MADE TO SETA LONG AGO.
WAIT A MINUTE, HOW DO YOU FIGURE THAT?
IT MAKES PERFECT SENSE! SO, I'M RIGHT, RIGHT?
WHAT AM I SAYING? OF COURSE I'M RIGHT!!
AWW, WHAT A BEAUTIFUL AND BITTERSWEET TALE!!
DANG IT, KEITARO, YOU'VE GOTTA HELP HER FULFILL HER DREAM!!
YOU'RE GONNA HELP HER WITH THE WHOLE EXCAVATION, RIGHT?!
ドオーッ
DON'T YOU THINK YOU'RE OVER REACT-ING?!
YOU FEELING ALL RIGHT?
YOU SEEM DIFFERENT.
WHAT?
FORGET ABOUT THAT, YOU NEED TO GO TO NYAMO **RIGHT NOW** AND TELL HER THAT YOU'RE ON HER SIDE!
I'M NOT YOUR PUNCH-ING BAG!!
けりっ♡
WHAT IS THAT GIRL'S PROBLEM?
I TOLD HER THOSE MUSHROOMS WERE A BAD IDEA.
FIRST SHE WAS ALL ABOUT GETTING BACK TO JAPAN, AND NOW IT'S LIKE SHE DOESN'T CARE.

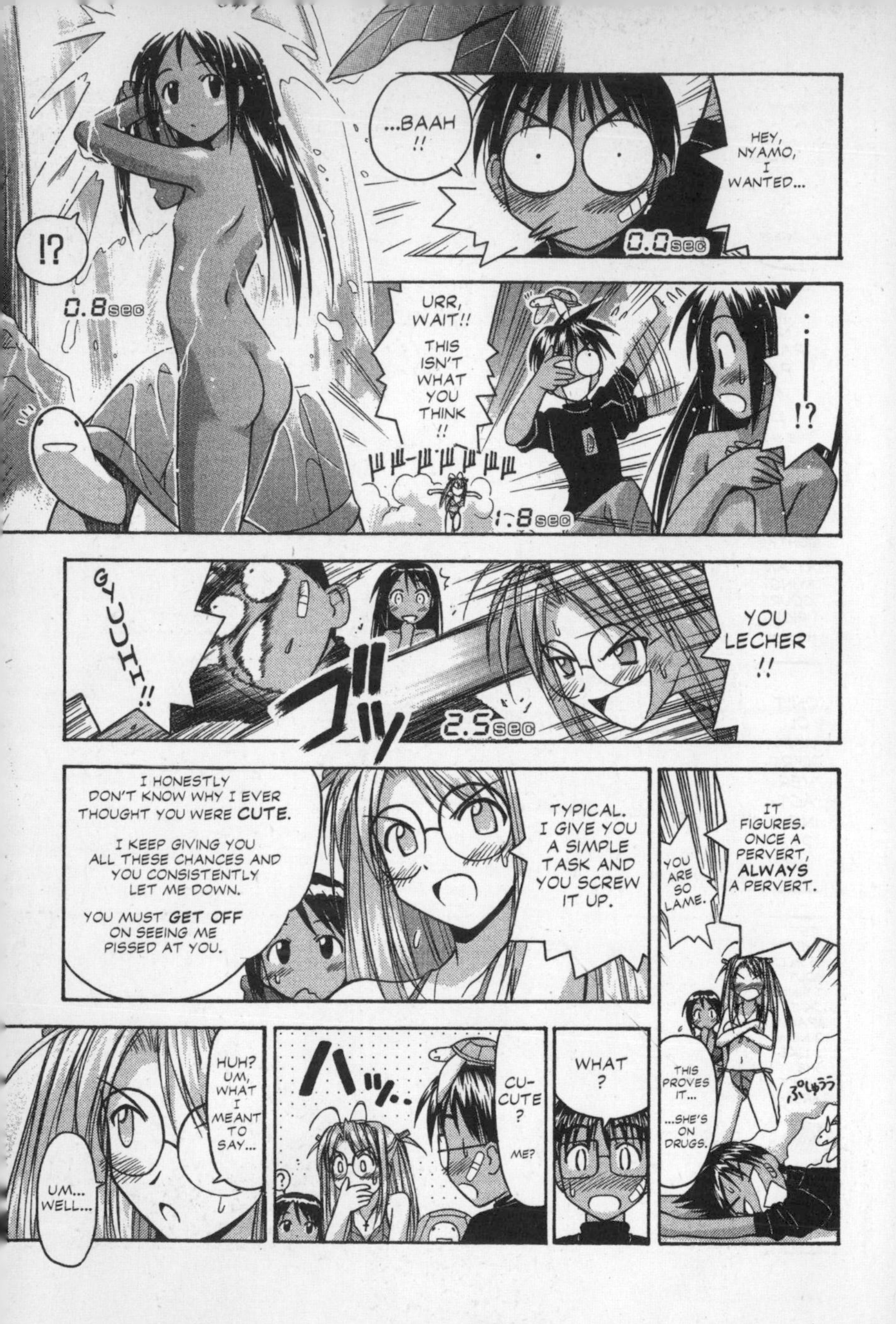
HEY, NYAMO, I WANTED...
...BAAH !!
0.0sec
...!?
URR, WAIT!!
THIS ISN'T WHAT YOU THINK !!
1.8sec
!?
0.8sec
YOU LECHER !!
2.5sec
GYUUII!!
IT FIGURES. ONCE A PERVERT, ALWAYS A PERVERT.
YOU ARE SO LAME.
THIS PROVES IT...
...SHE'S ON DRUGS.
ぷしゅうう
TYPICAL. I GIVE YOU A SIMPLE TASK AND YOU SCREW IT UP.
I HONESTLY DON'T KNOW WHY I EVER THOUGHT YOU WERE CUTE.
I KEEP GIVING YOU ALL THESE CHANCES AND YOU CONSISTENTLY LET ME DOWN.
YOU MUST GET OFF ON SEEING ME PISSED AT YOU.
WHAT ?
CU- CUTE ?
ME?
ハッ..
HUH? UM, WHAT I MEANT TO SAY...
UM... WELL...

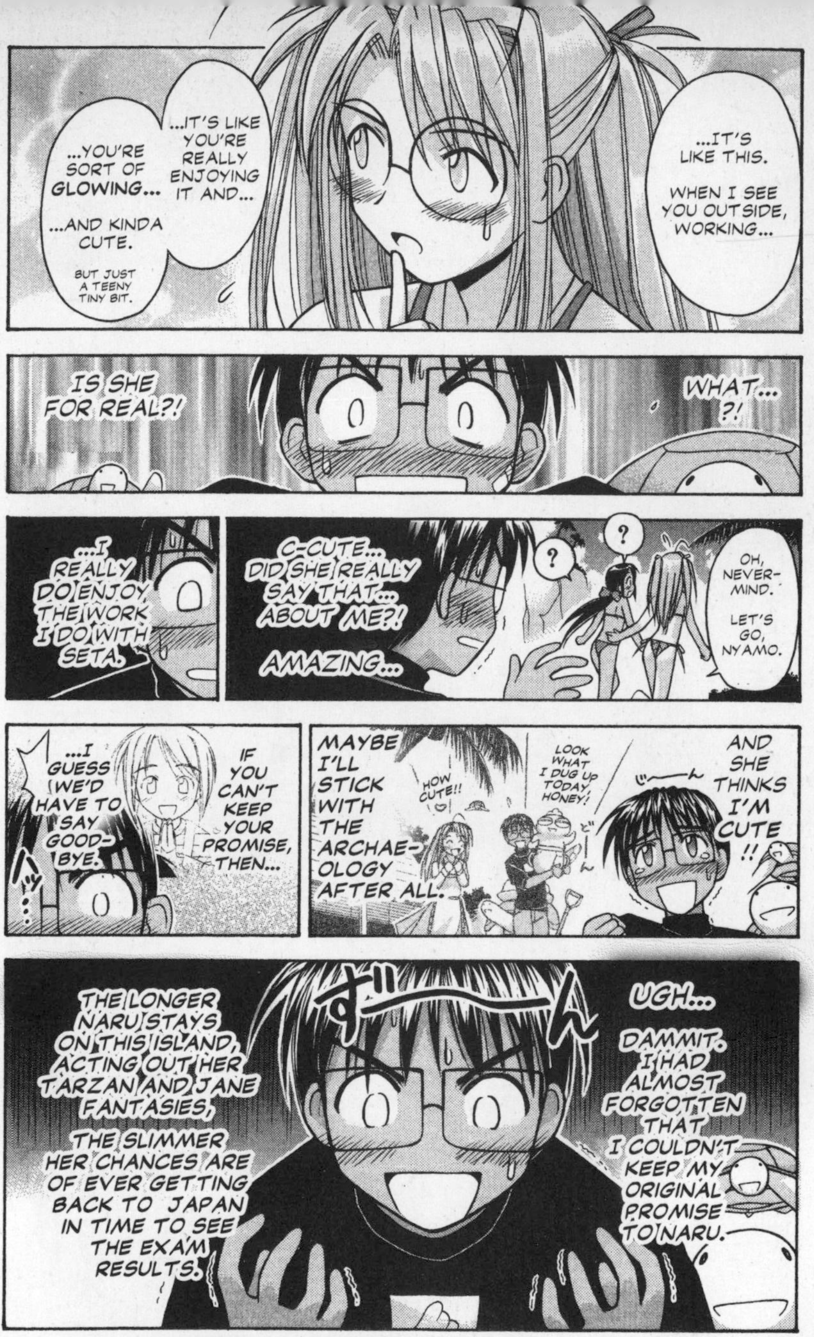
...IT'S LIKE THIS. WHEN I SEE YOU OUTSIDE, WORKING...
...IT'S LIKE YOU'RE REALLY ENJOYING IT AND...
...YOU'RE SORT OF GLOWING... ...AND KINDA CUTE.
BUT JUST A TEENY TINY BIT.
WHAT...?!
IS SHE FOR REAL?!
OH, NEVER-MIND. LET'S GO, NYAMO.
?
?
C-CUTE... DID SHE REALLY SAY THAT... ABOUT ME?!
AMAZING...
...I REALLY DO ENJOY THE WORK I DO WITH SETA.
AND SHE THINKS I'M CUTE!!
LOOK WHAT I DUG UP TODAY, HONEY!
HOW CUTE!!
MAYBE I'LL STICK WITH THE ARCHAEOLOGY AFTER ALL.
IF YOU CAN'T KEEP YOUR PROMISE, THEN...
...I GUESS WE'D HAVE TO SAY GOOD-BYE.
UGH...
DAMMIT. I HAD ALMOST FORGOTTEN THAT I COULDN'T KEEP MY ORIGINAL PROMISE TO NARU.
THE LONGER NARU STAYS ON THIS ISLAND, ACTING OUT HER TARZAN AND JANE FANTASIES,
THE SLIMMER HER CHANCES ARE OF EVER GETTING BACK TO JAPAN IN TIME TO SEE THE EXAM RESULTS.

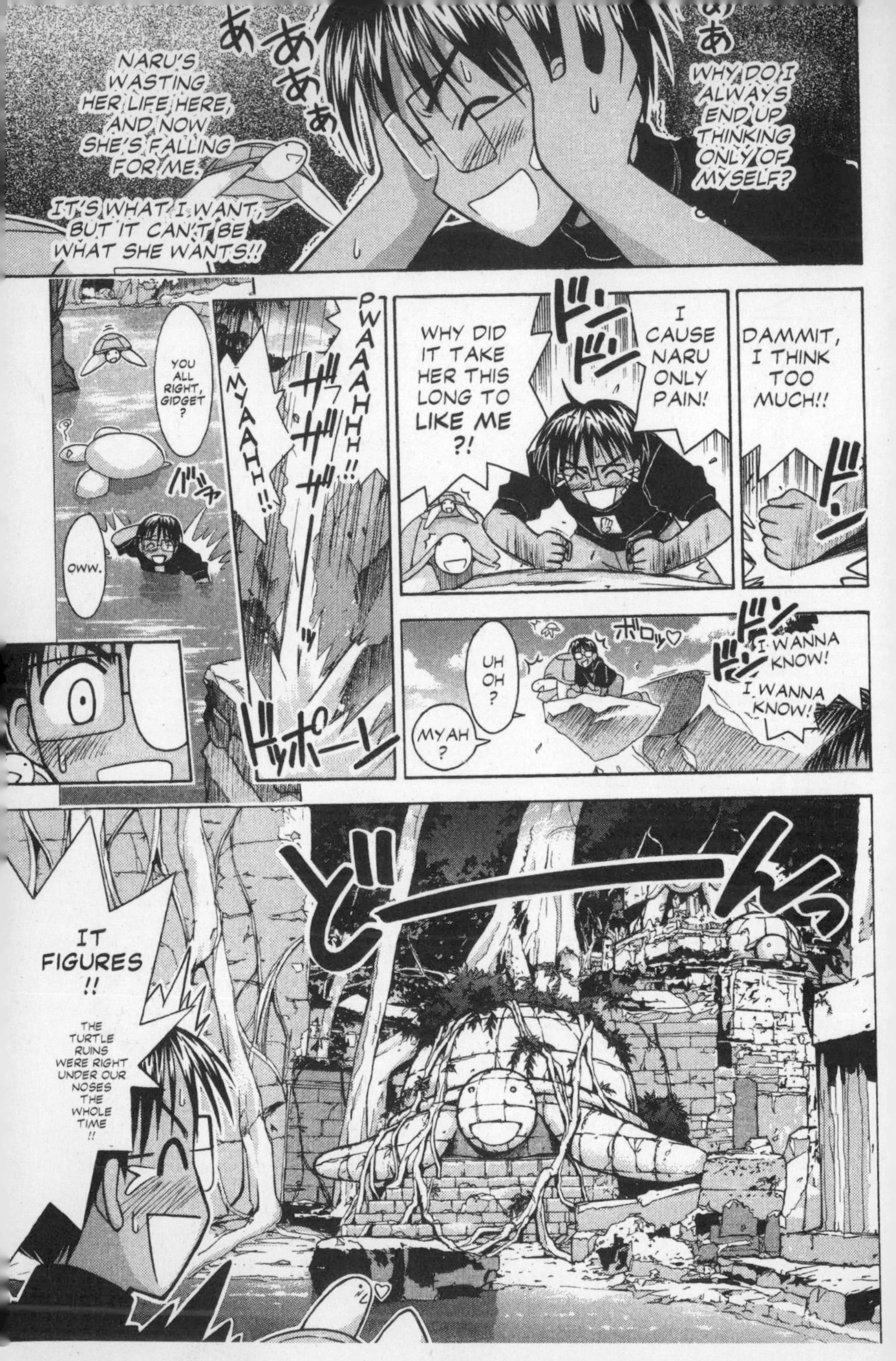
WHY DO I ALWAYS END UP THINKING ONLY OF MYSELF?
NARU'S WASTING HER LIFE HERE, AND NOW SHE'S FALLING FOR ME.
IT'S WHAT I WANT, BUT IT CAN'T BE WHAT SHE WANTS!!
DAMMIT, I THINK TOO MUCH!!
I CAUSE NARU ONLY PAIN!
WHY DID IT TAKE HER THIS LONG TO LIKE ME ?!
I WANNA KNOW!
I WANNA KNOW!
UH OH ?
MYAH ?
PWAAAAHHH!!
MYAAHH!!
YOU ALL RIGHT, GIDGET ?
OWW.
IT FIGURES !!
THE TURTLE RUINS WERE RIGHT UNDER OUR NOSES THE WHOLE TIME !!

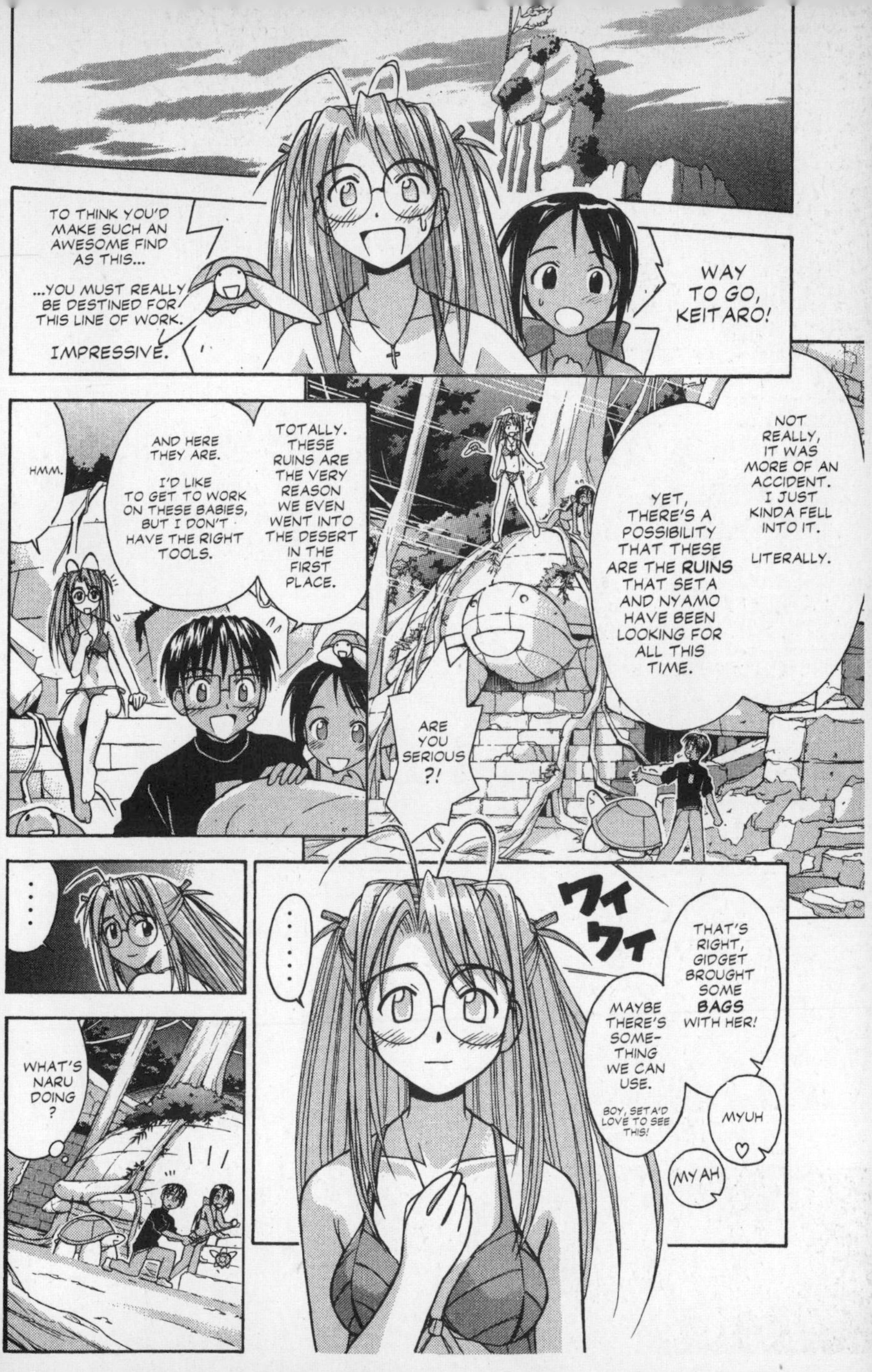

WAY TO GO, KEITARO!
TO THINK YOU'D MAKE SUCH AN AWESOME FIND AS THIS...
...YOU MUST REALLY BE DESTINED FOR THIS LINE OF WORK.
IMPRESSIVE.
NOT REALLY, IT WAS MORE OF AN ACCIDENT. I JUST KINDA FELL INTO IT.
LITERALLY.
YET, THERE'S A POSSIBILITY THAT THESE ARE THE **RUINS** THAT SETA AND NYAMO HAVE BEEN LOOKING FOR ALL THIS TIME.
ARE YOU SERIOUS ?!
TOTALLY. THESE RUINS ARE THE VERY REASON WE EVEN WENT INTO THE DESERT IN THE FIRST PLACE.
AND HERE THEY ARE.
I'D LIKE TO GET TO WORK ON THESE BABIES, BUT I DON'T HAVE THE RIGHT TOOLS.
HMM.
ワイワイ
THAT'S RIGHT, GIDGET BROUGHT SOME **BAGS** WITH HER!
MAYBE THERE'S SOME-THING WE CAN USE.
BOY, SETA'D LOVE TO SEE THIS!
MYUH ♡
MYAH
......
....
WHAT'S NARU DOING ?

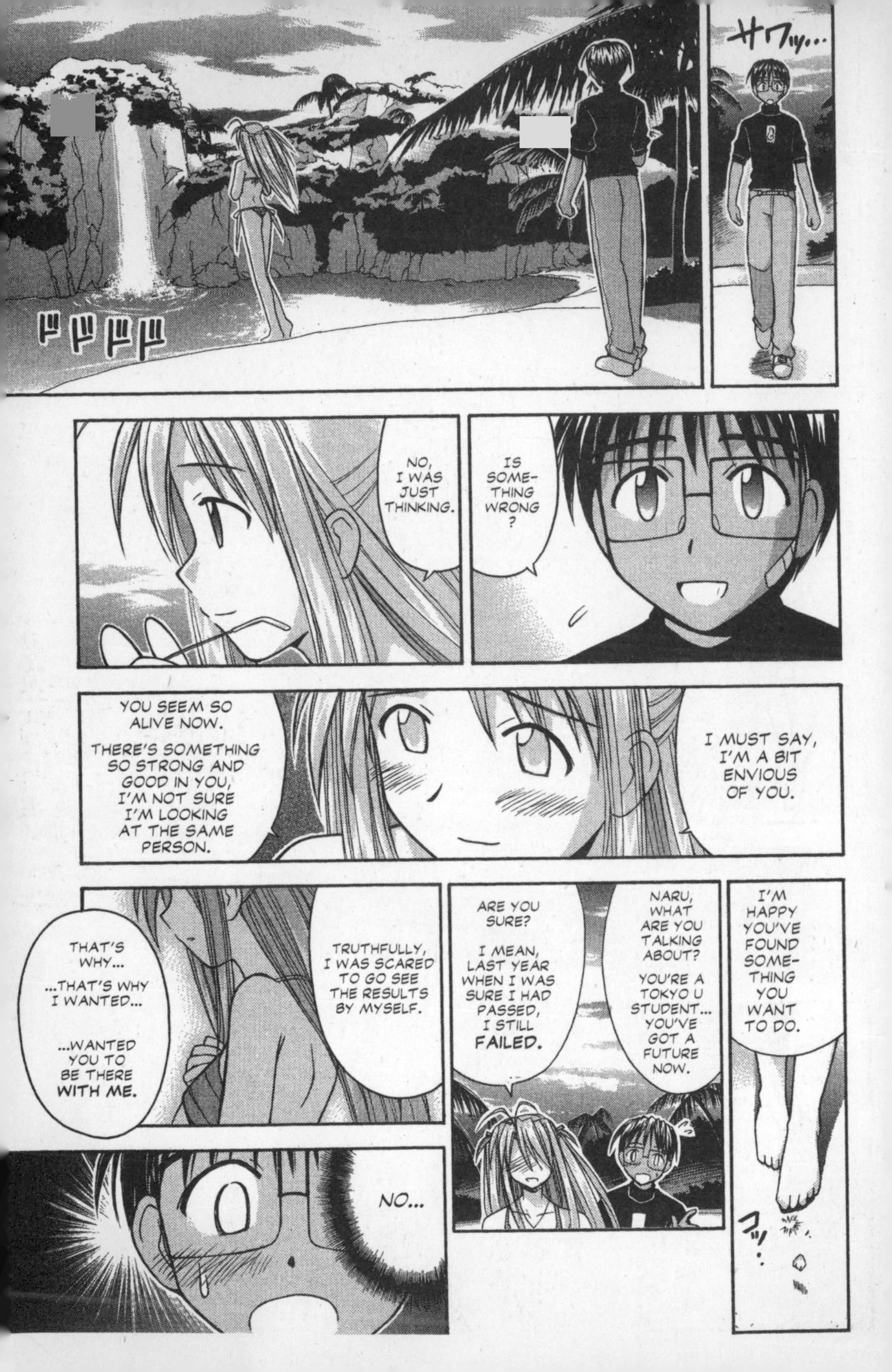
サワッ…
ドドドド
IS SOMETHING WRONG?
NO, I WAS JUST THINKING.
I MUST SAY, I'M A BIT ENVIOUS OF YOU.
YOU SEEM SO ALIVE NOW.
THERE'S SOMETHING SO STRONG AND GOOD IN YOU, I'M NOT SURE I'M LOOKING AT THE SAME PERSON.
I'M HAPPY YOU'VE FOUND SOMETHING YOU WANT TO DO.
NARU, WHAT ARE YOU TALKING ABOUT?
YOU'RE A TOKYO U STUDENT... YOU'VE GOT A FUTURE NOW.
ARE YOU SURE?
I MEAN, LAST YEAR WHEN I WAS SURE I HAD PASSED, I STILL **FAILED.**
TRUTHFULLY, I WAS SCARED TO GO SEE THE RESULTS BY MYSELF.
THAT'S WHY...
...THAT'S WHY I WANTED...
...WANTED YOU TO BE THERE **WITH ME.**
NO...

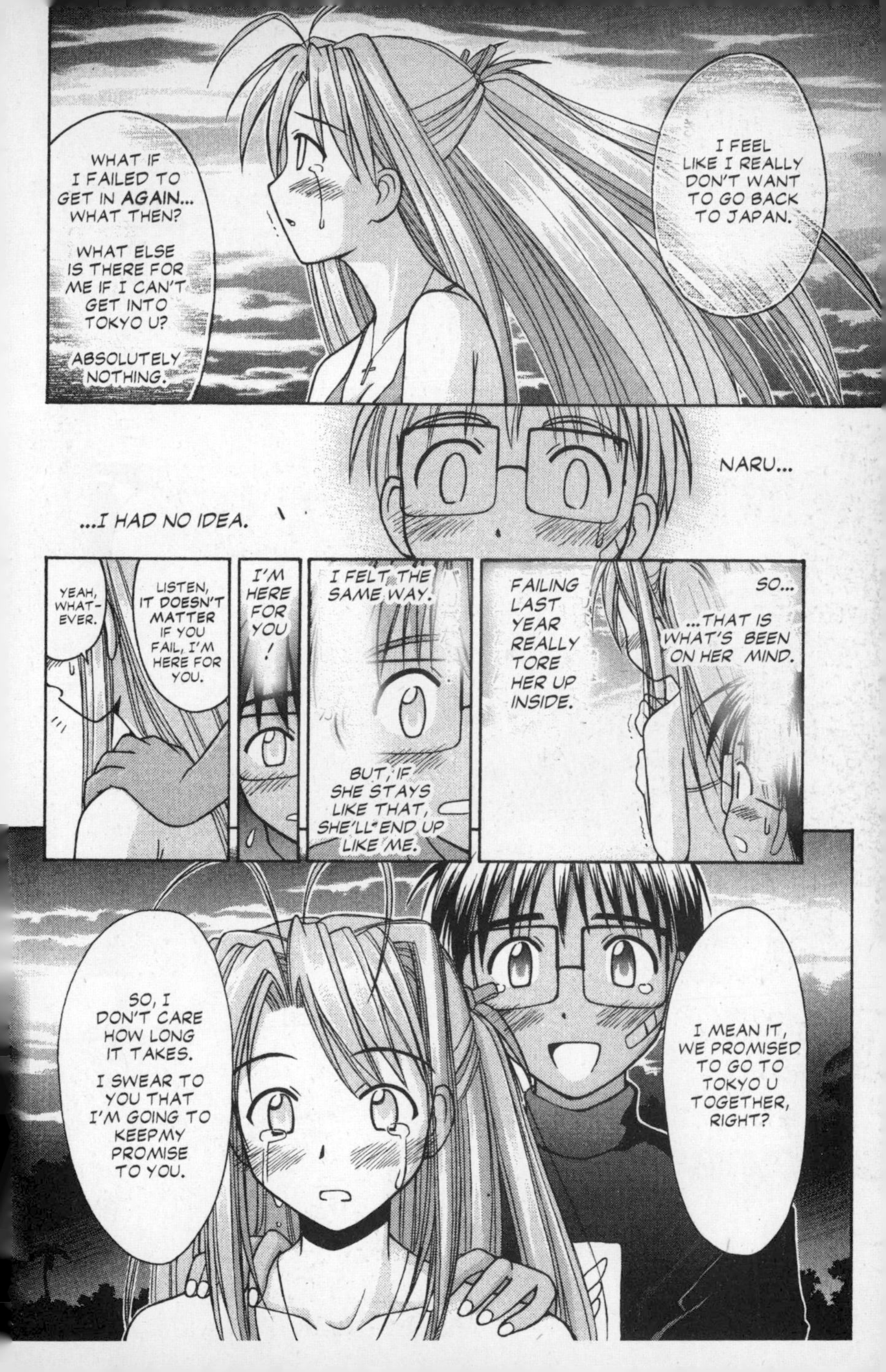
I FEEL LIKE I REALLY DON'T WANT TO GO BACK TO JAPAN.
WHAT IF I FAILED TO GET IN **AGAIN**... WHAT THEN?
WHAT ELSE IS THERE FOR ME IF I CAN'T GET INTO TOKYO U?
ABSOLUTELY NOTHING.
NARU...
...I HAD NO IDEA.
SO...
...THAT IS WHAT'S BEEN ON HER MIND.
FAILING LAST YEAR REALLY TORE HER UP INSIDE.
I FELT THE SAME WAY.
BUT, IF SHE STAYS LIKE THAT, SHE'LL END UP LIKE ME.
I'M HERE FOR YOU!
LISTEN, IT DOESN'T MATTER IF YOU FAIL, I'M HERE FOR YOU.
YEAH, WHATEVER.
I MEAN IT, WE PROMISED TO GO TO TOKYO U TOGETHER, RIGHT?
SO, I DON'T CARE HOW LONG IT TAKES.
I SWEAR TO YOU THAT I'M GOING TO KEEPMY PROMISE TO YOU.

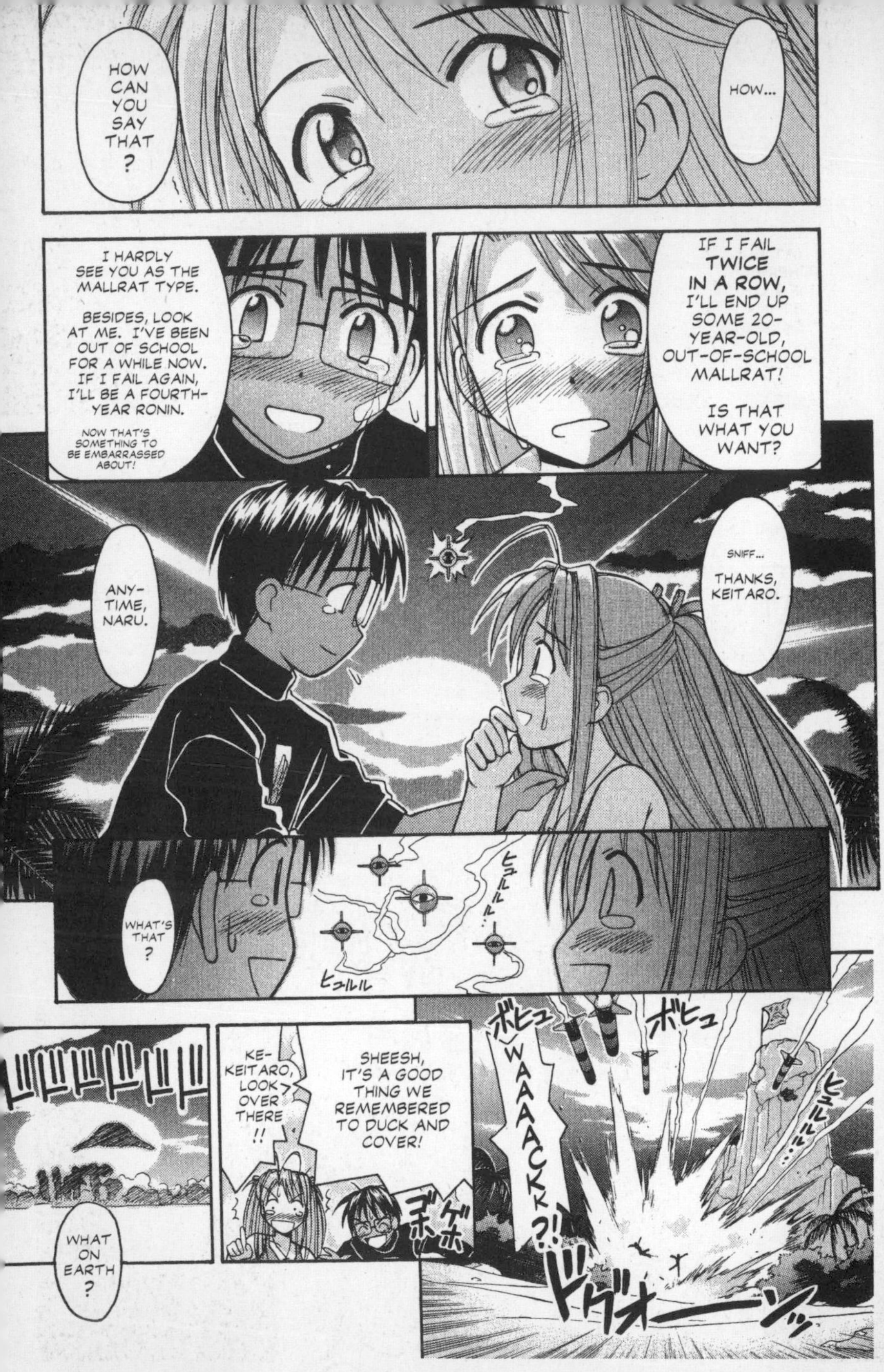
HOW...
HOW CAN YOU SAY THAT ?
IF I FAIL TWICE IN A ROW, I'LL END UP SOME 20-YEAR-OLD, OUT-OF-SCHOOL MALLRAT!
IS THAT WHAT YOU WANT?
I HARDLY SEE YOU AS THE MALLRAT TYPE.
BESIDES, LOOK AT ME. I'VE BEEN OUT OF SCHOOL FOR A WHILE NOW. IF I FAIL AGAIN, I'LL BE A FOURTH-YEAR RONIN.
NOW THAT'S SOMETHING TO BE EMBARRASSED ABOUT!
SNIFF...
THANKS, KEITARO.
ANY-TIME, NARU.
ヒュルルル…
WHAT'S THAT ?
ヒュルルル
ボヒュ
ボヒュ
WAAAACK?!
ヒュルルル…
ドグォーンッ
KE-KEITARO, LOOK OVER THERE !!
SHEESH, IT'S A GOOD THING WE REMEMBERED TO DUCK AND COVER!
ゲホ
ゴホ
ドドドドドドド
WHAT ON EARTH ?

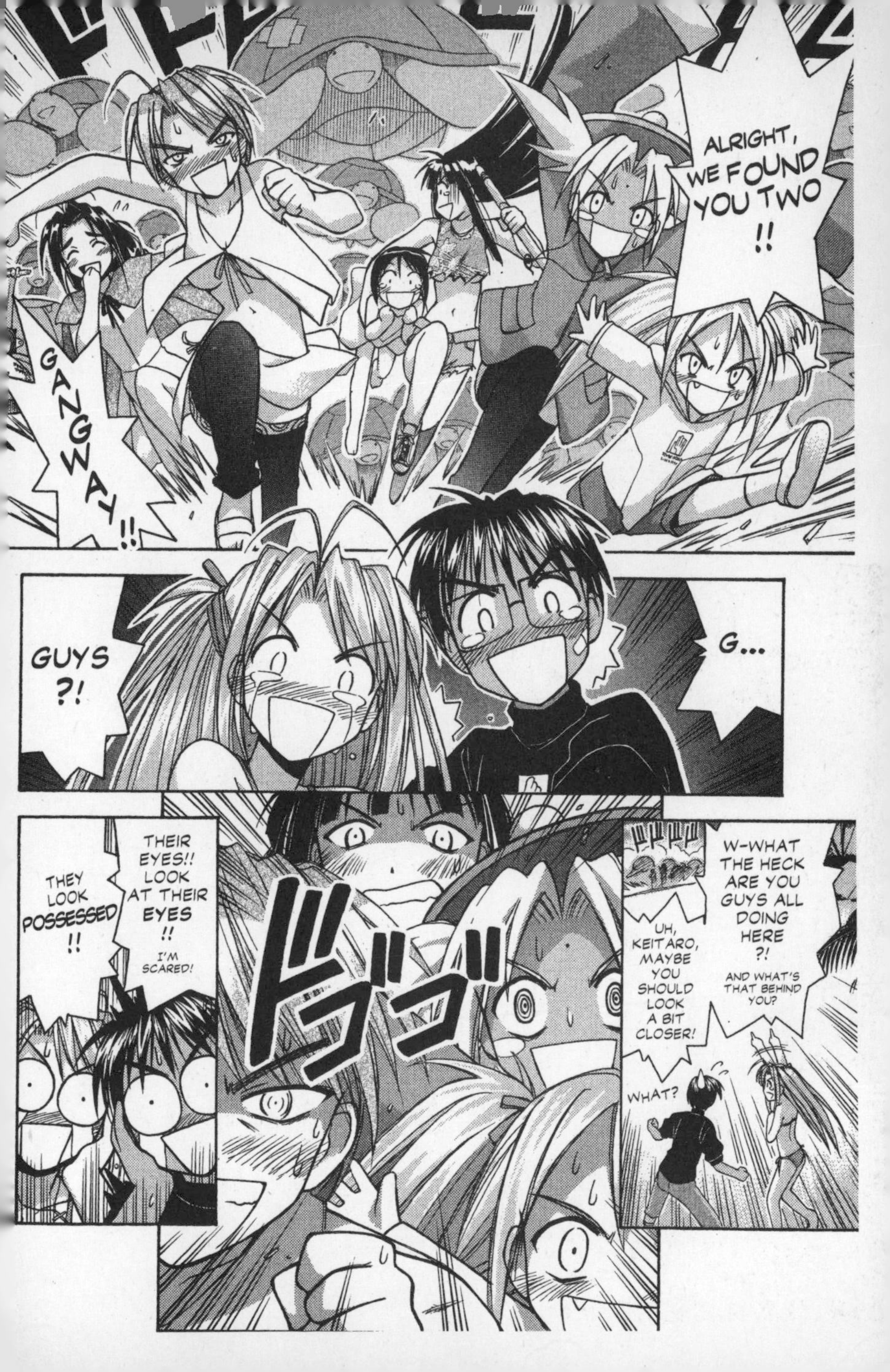
ALRIGHT, WE FOUND YOU TWO !!
GANGWAY !!
G...
GUYS ?!
W-WHAT THE HECK ARE YOU GUYS ALL DOING HERE ?!
AND WHAT'S THAT BEHIND YOU?
UH, KEITARO, MAYBE YOU SHOULD LOOK A BIT CLOSER!
WHAT?
THEIR EYES!! LOOK AT THEIR EYES !!
I'M SCARED!
THEY LOOK POSSESSED !!

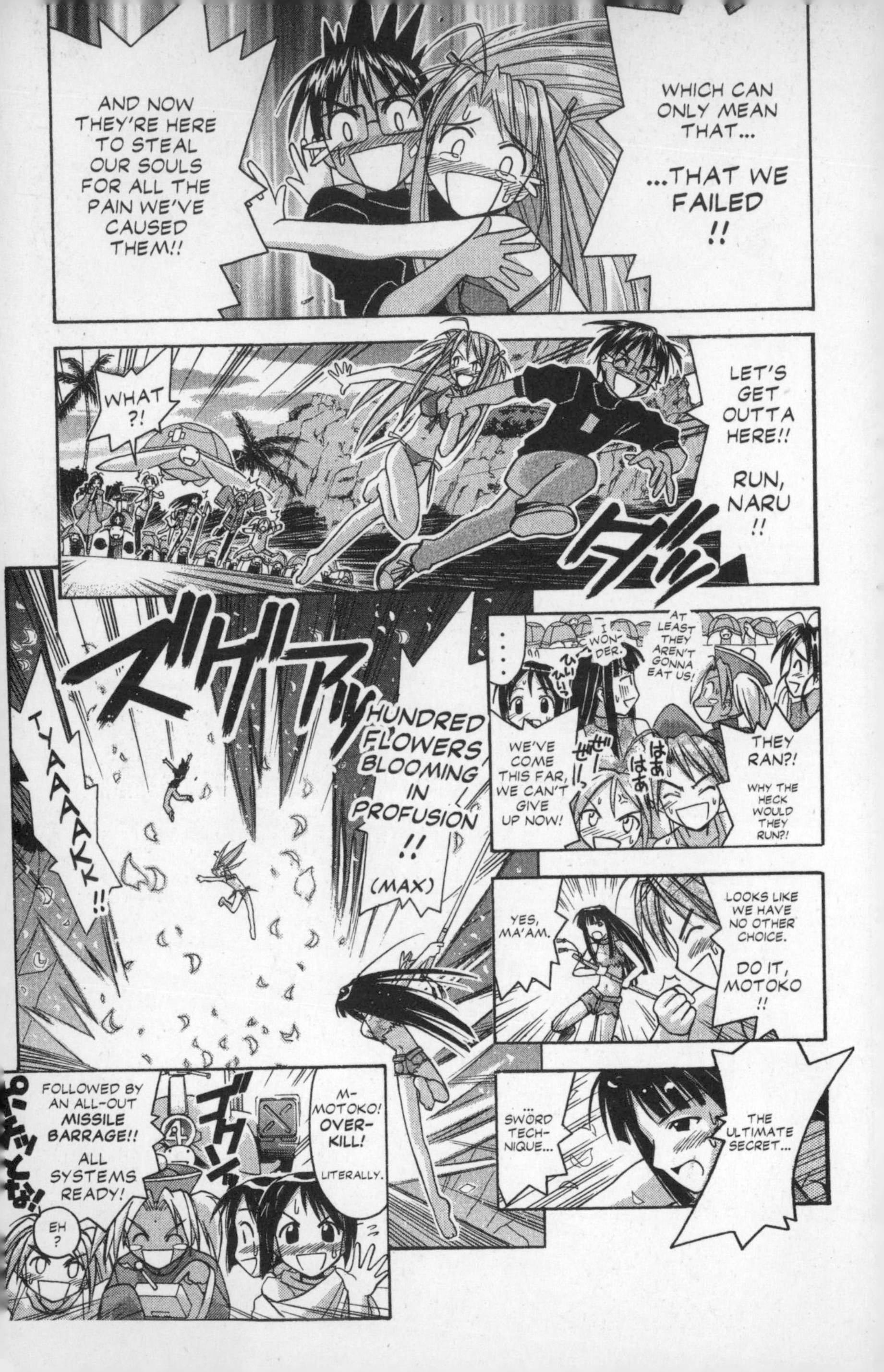
WHICH CAN ONLY MEAN THAT...
...THAT WE FAILED !!
AND NOW THEY'RE HERE TO STEAL OUR SOULS FOR ALL THE PAIN WE'VE CAUSED THEM!!
LET'S GET OUTTA HERE!!
RUN, NARU !!
WHAT ?!
AT LEAST THEY AREN'T GONNA EAT US!
I WONDER.
....
THEY RAN?!
WHY THE HECK WOULD THEY RUN?!
WE'VE COME THIS FAR, WE CAN'T GIVE UP NOW!
LOOKS LIKE WE HAVE NO OTHER CHOICE.
DO IT, MOTOKO !!
YES, MA'AM.
THE ULTIMATE SECRET...
...SWORD TECHNIQUE...
HUNDRED FLOWERS BLOOMING IN PROFUSION !!
(MAX)
AIYAAAAAKK !!
M-MOTOKO! OVER-KILL!
LITERALLY.
FOLLOWED BY AN ALL-OUT MISSILE BARRAGE!!
ALL SYSTEMS READY!
EH ?

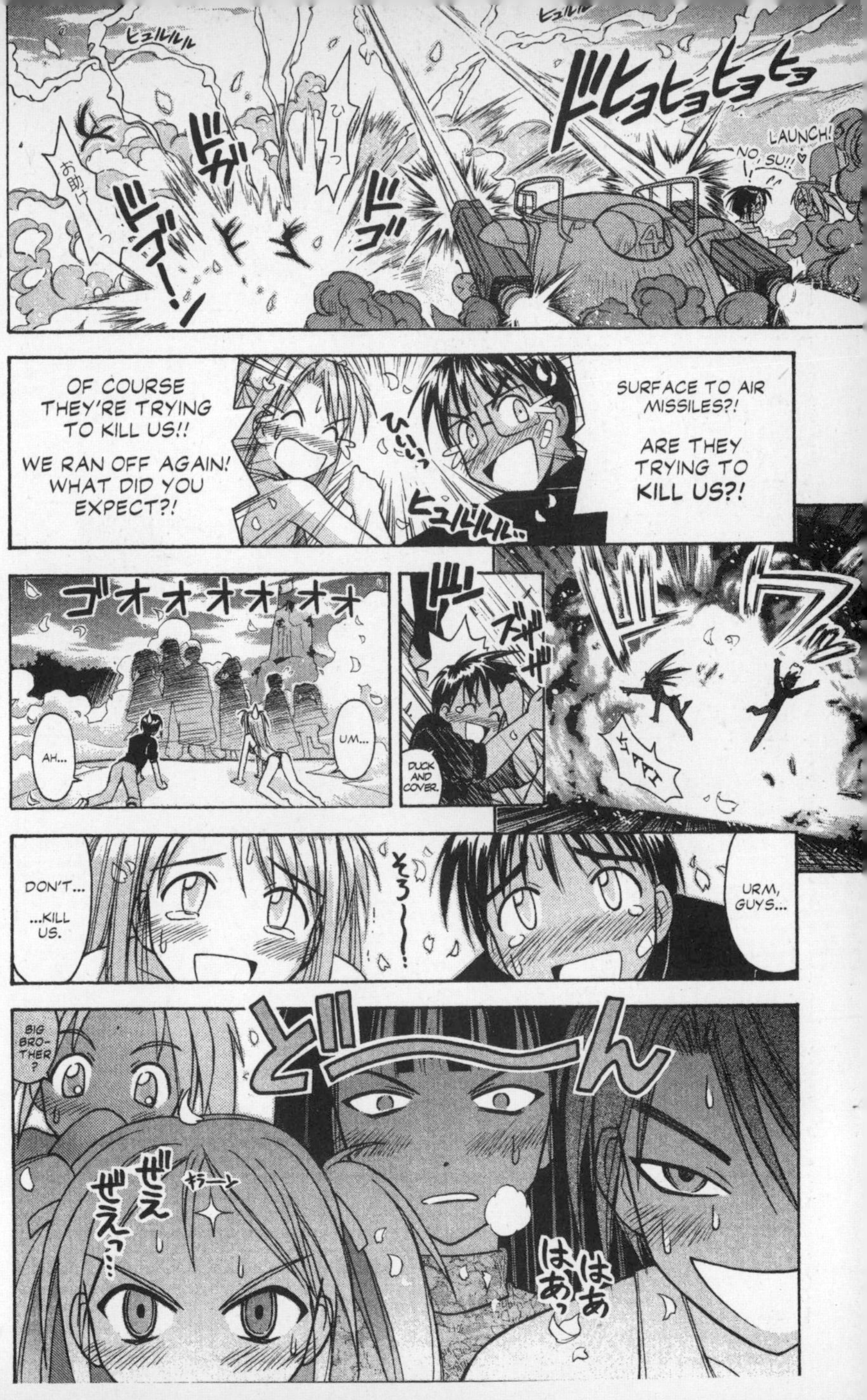

ヒュルルルル
ドヒョヒョヒョヒョ
LAUNCH!
NO, SU!!
ドゴ
ひーーっ
ドガ
ドゴーー!
お助けーっ
SURFACE TO AIR MISSILES?!
ARE THEY TRYING TO KILL US?!
ひいいっ
ヒュルルルル…
OF COURSE THEY'RE TRYING TO KILL US!!
WE RAN OFF AGAIN! WHAT DID YOU EXPECT?!
ズザザ
DUCK AND COVER.
ゴオオオオオオ
UM...
AH...
URM, GUYS...
そろ〜〜!
DON'T...
...KILL US.
どど〜〜ん
BIG BROTHER?
キラーン
ぜえぜえっ…
はあはあっ

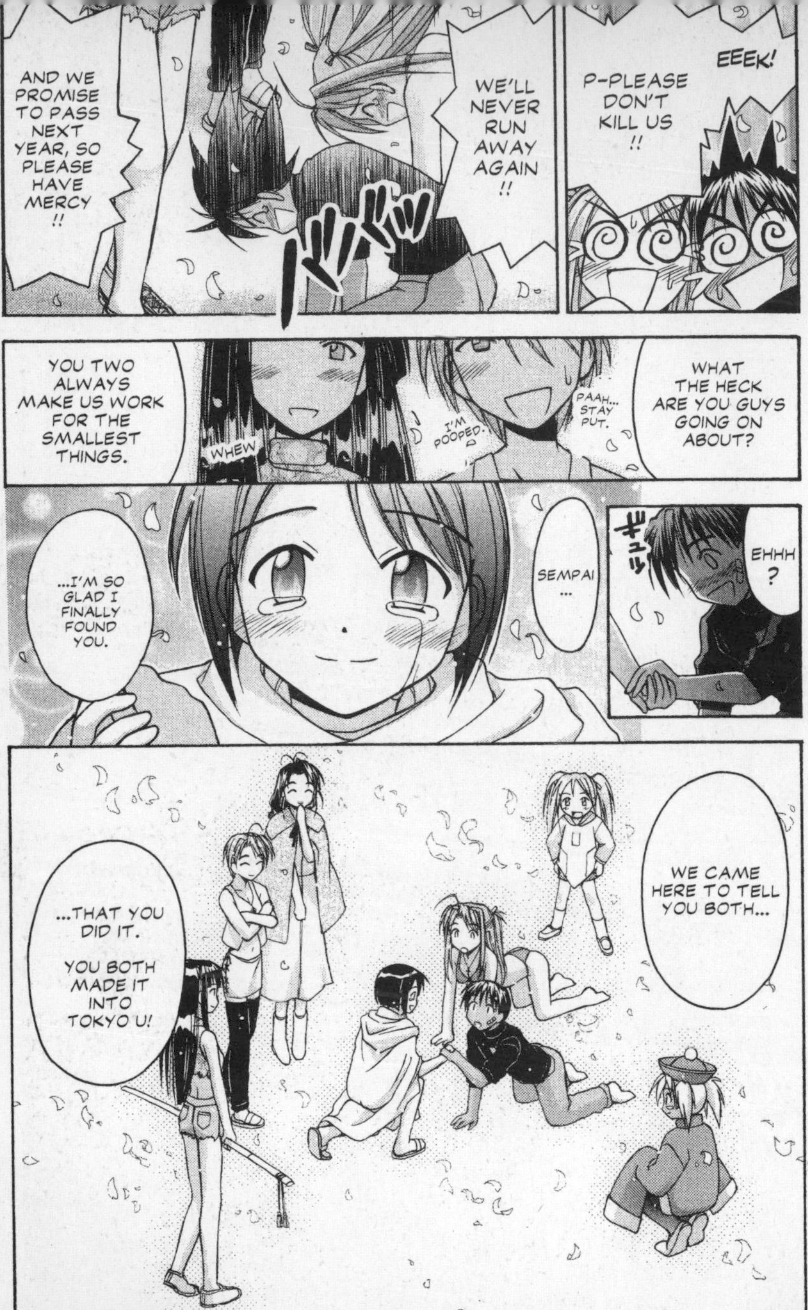
EEEK!
P-PLEASE DON'T KILL US !!
WE'LL NEVER RUN AWAY AGAIN !!
AND WE PROMISE TO PASS NEXT YEAR, SO PLEASE HAVE MERCY !!
WHAT THE HECK ARE YOU GUYS GOING ON ABOUT?
PAAH... STAY PUT.
I'M POOPED.
WHEW
YOU TWO ALWAYS MAKE US WORK FOR THE SMALLEST THINGS.
EHHH ?
SEMPAI ...
...I'M SO GLAD I FINALLY FOUND YOU.
WE CAME HERE TO TELL YOU BOTH...
...THAT YOU DID IT.
YOU BOTH MADE IT INTO TOKYO U!

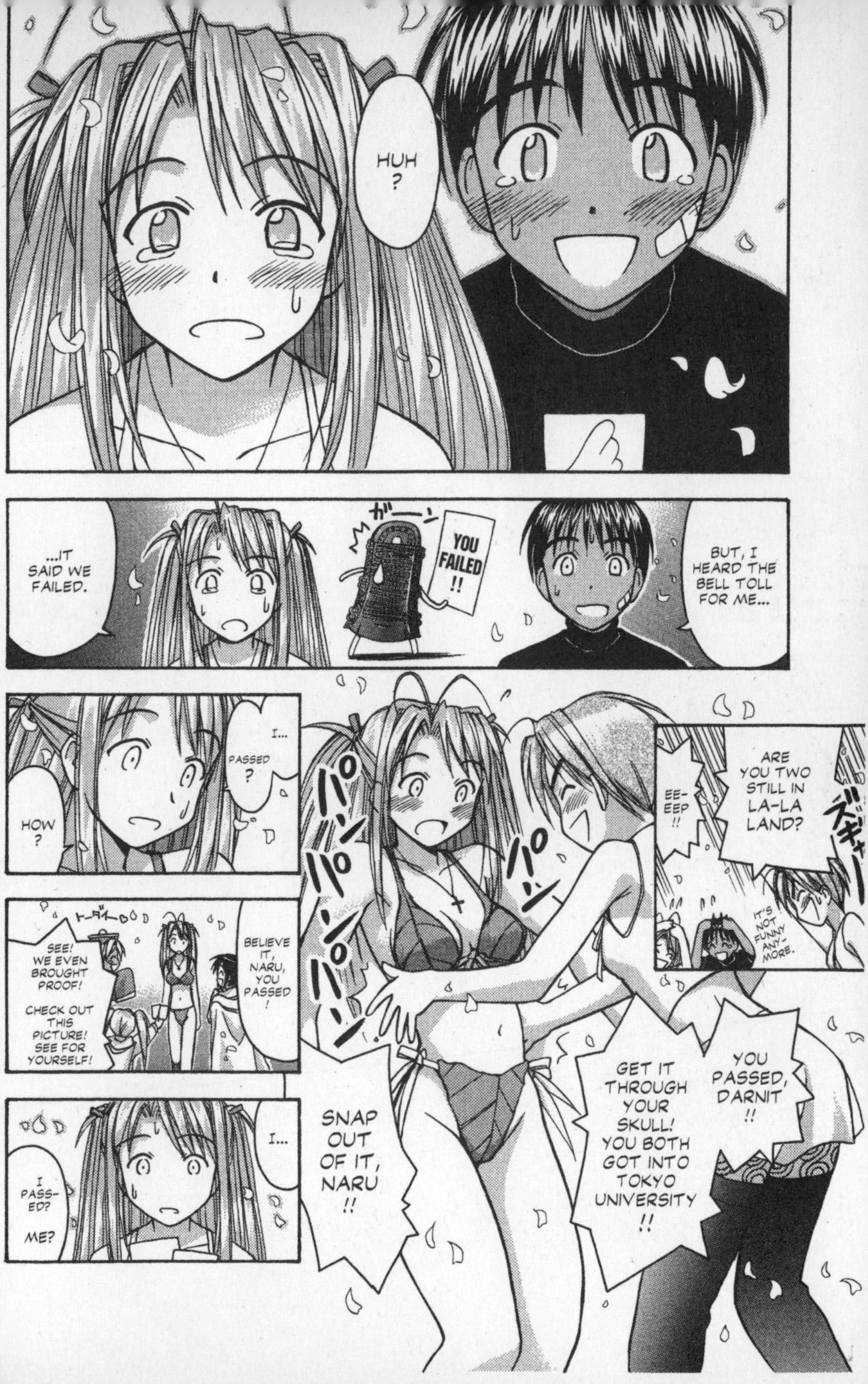
HUH ?
BUT, I HEARD THE BELL TOLL FOR ME...
YOU FAILED !!
...IT SAID WE FAILED.
I... PASSED ?
HOW ?
BELIEVE IT, NARU, YOU PASSED !
SEE! WE EVEN BROUGHT PROOF! CHECK OUT THIS PICTURE! SEE FOR YOURSELF!
I...
I PASS-ED?
ME?
YOU PASSED, DARNIT !!
GET IT THROUGH YOUR SKULL! YOU BOTH GOT INTO TOKYO UNIVERSITY !!
SNAP OUT OF IT, NARU !!
ARE YOU TWO STILL IN LA-LA LAND?
EE-EEP !!
IT'S NOT FUNNY ANY-MORE.

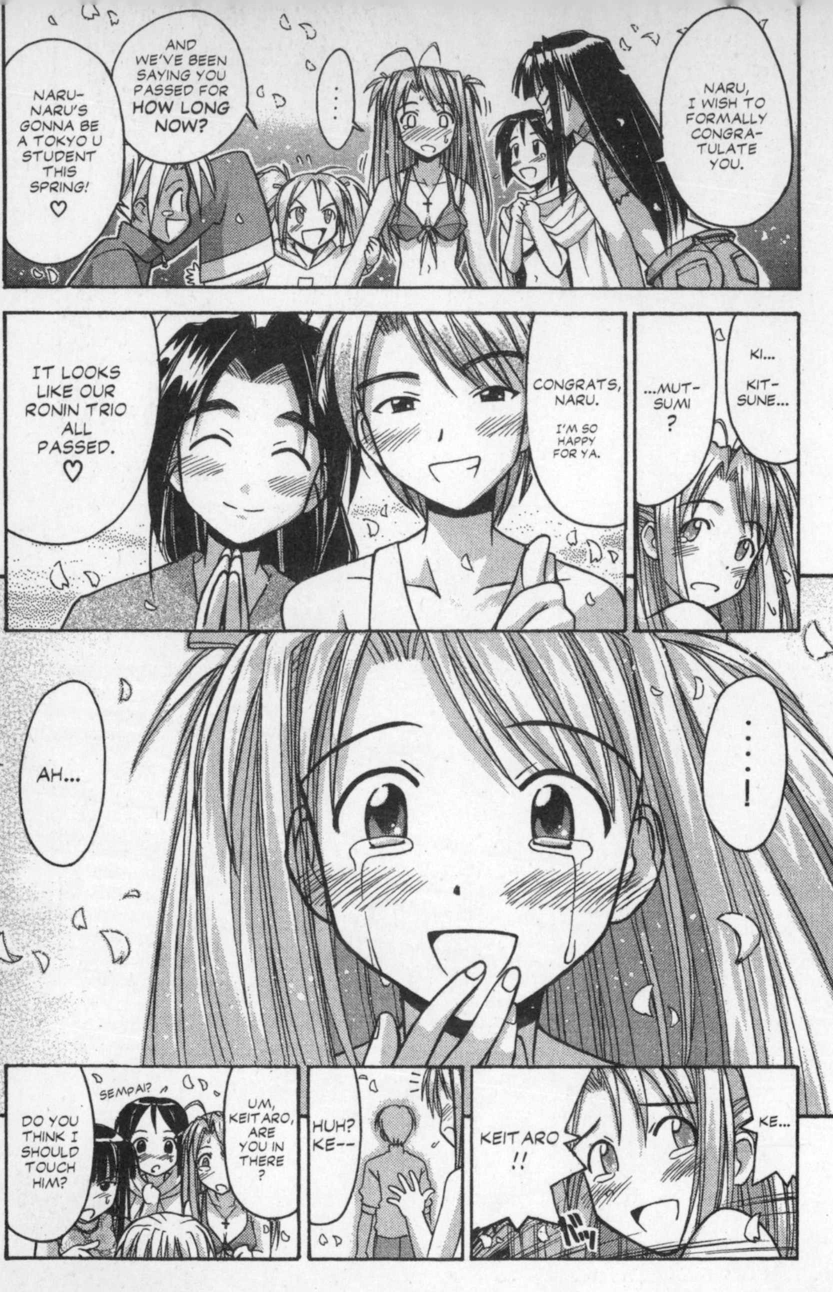
NARU, I WISH TO FORMALLY CONGRATULATE YOU.
....
AND WE'VE BEEN SAYING YOU PASSED FOR HOW LONG NOW?
NARU-NARU'S GONNA BE A TOKYO U STUDENT THIS SPRING! ♡
KI... KIT-SUNE...
...MUT-SUMI?
CONGRATS, NARU. I'M SO HAPPY FOR YA.
IT LOOKS LIKE OUR RONIN TRIO ALL PASSED. ♡
....!
AH...
KE...
KEITARO!!
HUH? KE--
UM, KEITARO, ARE YOU IN THERE?
SEMPAI?
DO YOU THINK I SHOULD TOUCH HIM?

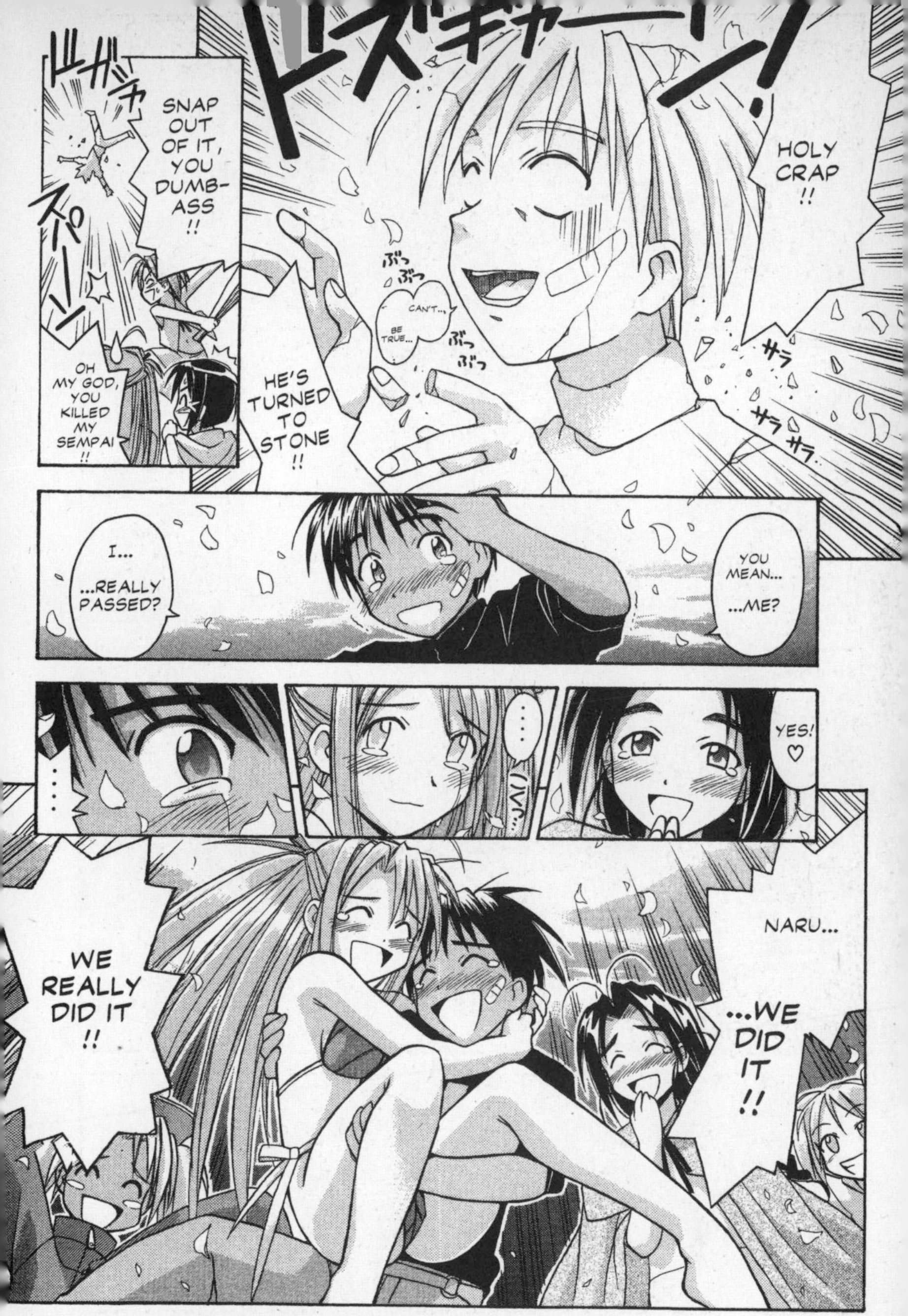
HOLY CRAP!!
ぶつ ぶつ
CAN'T... BE TRUE...
ぶつ ぶつ
HE'S TURNED TO STONE!!
サラ サラ サラ
SNAP OUT OF IT, YOU DUMB-ASS!!
OH MY GOD, YOU KILLED MY SEMPAI!!
YOU MEAN... ...ME?
I... ...REALLY PASSED?
YES! ♡
....
....
NARU...
...WE DID IT!!
WE REALLY DID IT!!

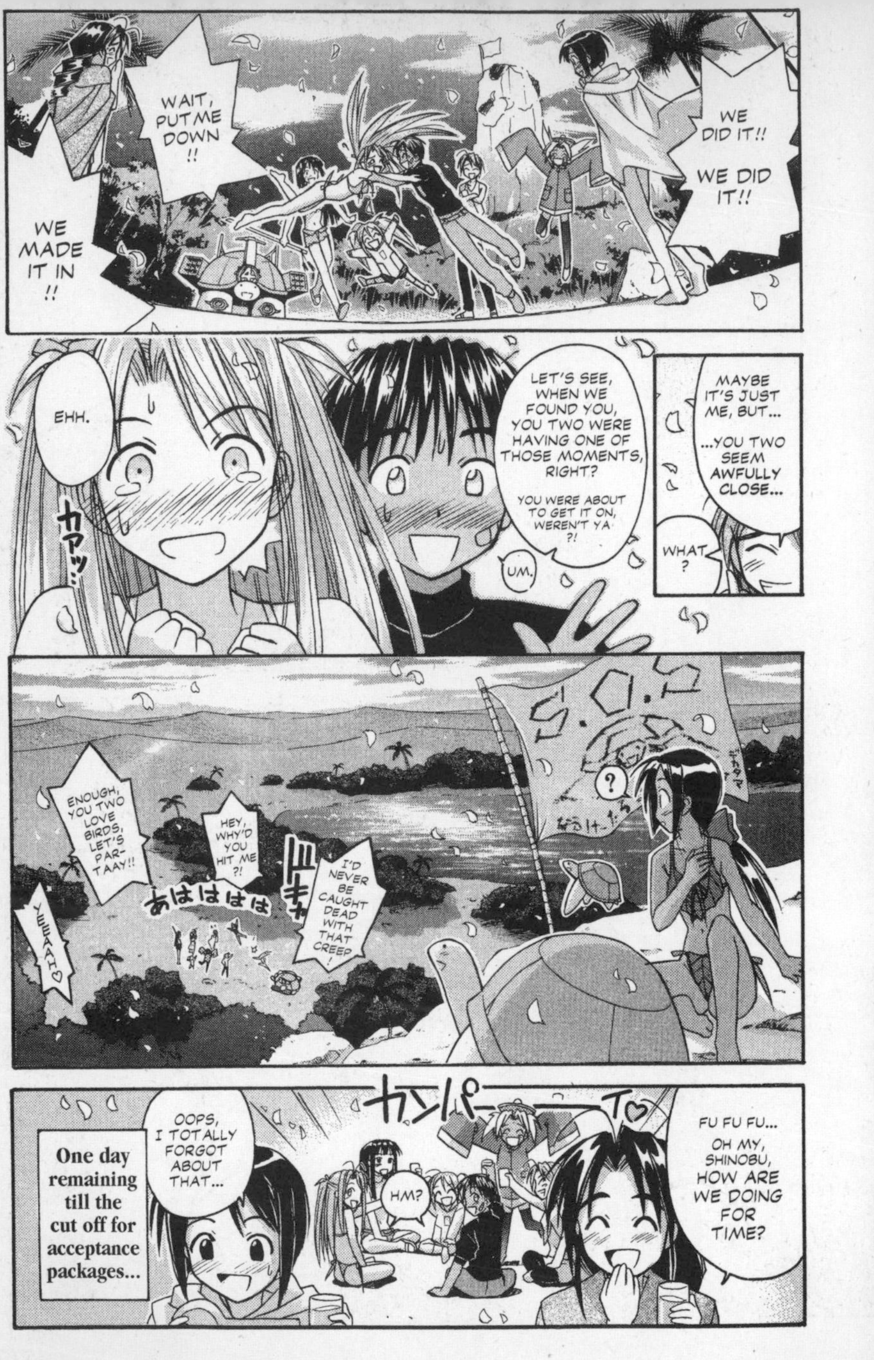
WE DID IT!!
WE DID IT!!
WAIT, PUT ME DOWN!!
WE MADE IT IN!!
MAYBE IT'S JUST ME, BUT... ...YOU TWO SEEM AWFULLY CLOSE...
WHAT?
LET'S SEE, WHEN WE FOUND YOU, YOU TWO WERE HAVING ONE OF THOSE MOMENTS, RIGHT?
YOU WERE ABOUT TO GET IT ON, WEREN'T YA?!
UM.
EHH.
カアッ…
?
I'D NEVER BE CAUGHT DEAD WITH THAT CREEP!
ドキャ
HEY, WHY'D YOU HIT ME?!
ENOUGH, YOU TWO LOVE BIRDS, LET'S PAR-TAAY!!
あはははは
YEEAAH♡
FU FU FU... OH MY, SHINOBU, HOW ARE WE DOING FOR TIME?
カンパーーイ♡
HM?
OOPS, I TOTALLY FORGOT ABOUT THAT...
One day remaining till the cut off for acceptance packages...

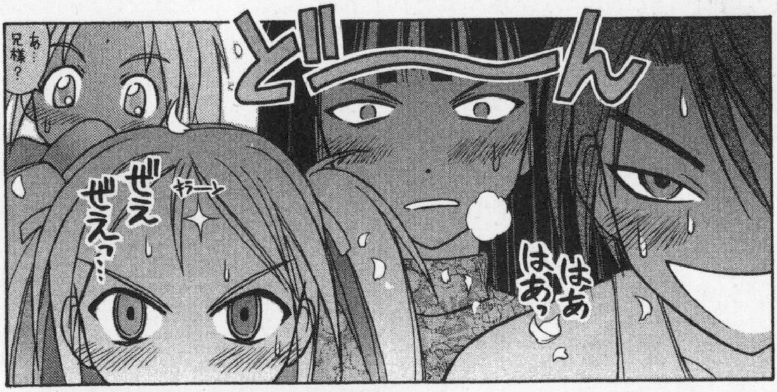
どーーん
はぁはぁっ
キラーン
ぜぇぜぇっ…
あ…兄様？

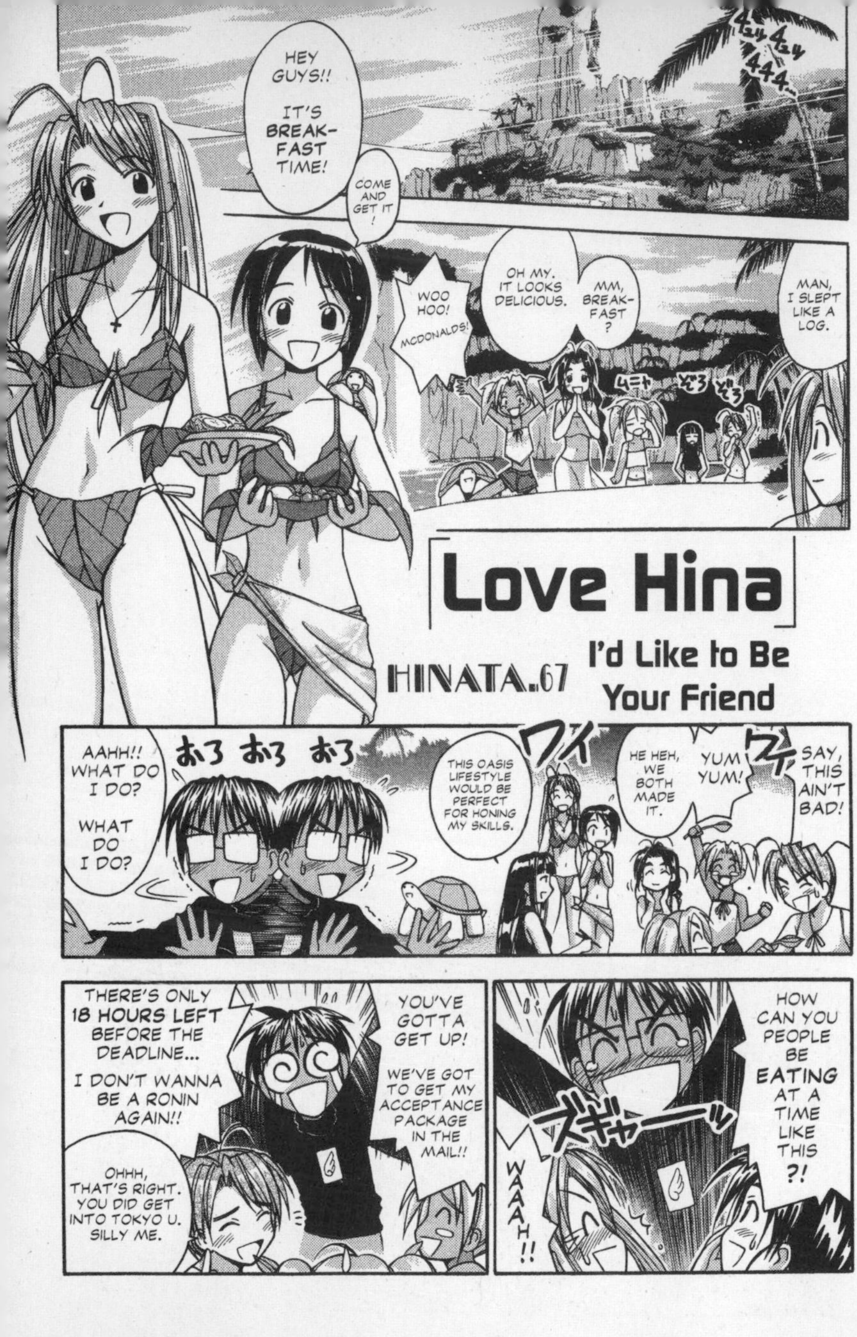
MAN, I SLEPT LIKE A LOG.
MM, BREAKFAST?
OH MY. IT LOOKS DELICIOUS.
WOO HOO! MCDONALDS!
ムニャ
ぞろ ぞろ
HEY GUYS!! IT'S BREAKFAST TIME!
COME AND GET IT!
Love Hina
HINATA.67
I'd Like to Be Your Friend
SAY, THIS AIN'T BAD!
ワイ ワイ
YUM YUM!
HE HEH, WE BOTH MADE IT.
THIS OASIS LIFESTYLE WOULD BE PERFECT FOR HONING MY SKILLS.
AAHH!! WHAT DO I DO? WHAT DO I DO?
おろ おろ おろ
HOW CAN YOU PEOPLE BE EATING AT A TIME LIKE THIS?!
ズギャーーッ
WAAAH!!
YOU'VE GOTTA GET UP!
WE'VE GOT TO GET MY ACCEPTANCE PACKAGE IN THE MAIL!!
THERE'S ONLY 18 HOURS LEFT BEFORE THE DEADLINE...
I DON'T WANNA BE A RONIN AGAIN!!
OHHH, THAT'S RIGHT. YOU DID GET INTO TOKYO U. SILLY ME.

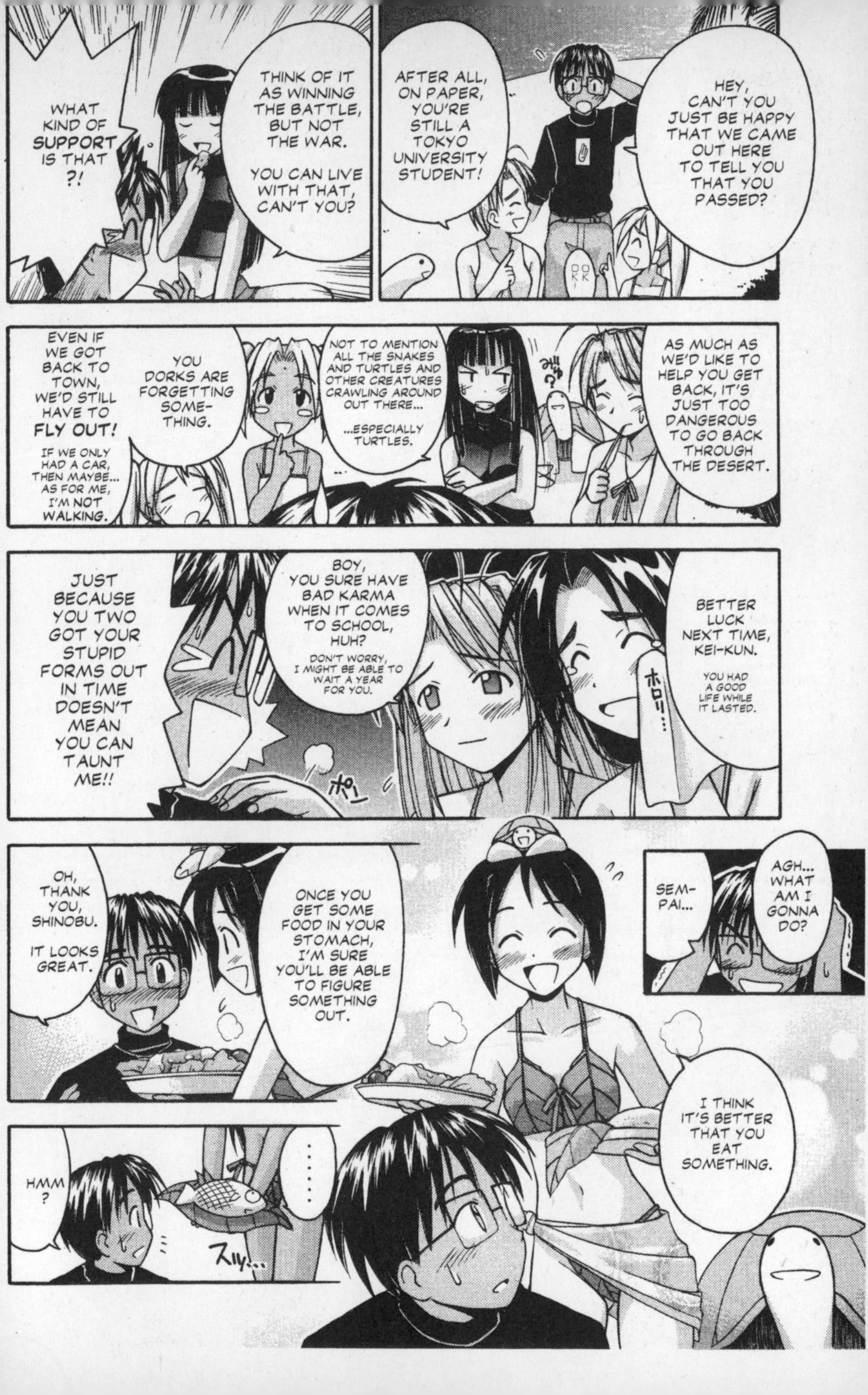
HEY, CAN'T YOU JUST BE HAPPY THAT WE CAME OUT HERE TO TELL YOU THAT YOU PASSED?
AFTER ALL, ON PAPER, YOU'RE STILL A TOKYO UNIVERSITY STUDENT!
THINK OF IT AS WINNING THE BATTLE, BUT NOT THE WAR.
YOU CAN LIVE WITH THAT, CAN'T YOU?
WHAT KIND OF SUPPORT IS THAT ?!
AS MUCH AS WE'D LIKE TO HELP YOU GET BACK, IT'S JUST TOO DANGEROUS TO GO BACK THROUGH THE DESERT.
NOT TO MENTION ALL THE SNAKES AND TURTLES AND OTHER CREATURES CRAWLING AROUND OUT THERE...
...ESPECIALLY TURTLES.
YOU DORKS ARE FORGETTING SOME-THING.
EVEN IF WE GOT BACK TO TOWN, WE'D STILL HAVE TO FLY OUT!
IF WE ONLY HAD A CAR, THEN MAYBE... AS FOR ME, I'M NOT WALKING.
BETTER LUCK NEXT TIME, KEI-KUN.
YOU HAD A GOOD LIFE WHILE IT LASTED.
ホロリ…
BOY, YOU SURE HAVE BAD KARMA WHEN IT COMES TO SCHOOL, HUH?
DON'T WORRY, I MIGHT BE ABLE TO WAIT A YEAR FOR YOU.
JUST BECAUSE YOU TWO GOT YOUR STUPID FORMS OUT IN TIME DOESN'T MEAN YOU CAN TAUNT ME!!
AGH... WHAT AM I GONNA DO?
SEM-PAI...
ONCE YOU GET SOME FOOD IN YOUR STOMACH, I'M SURE YOU'LL BE ABLE TO FIGURE SOMETHING OUT.
OH, THANK YOU, SHINOBU.
IT LOOKS GREAT.
I THINK IT'S BETTER THAT YOU EAT SOMETHING.
......
HMM ?

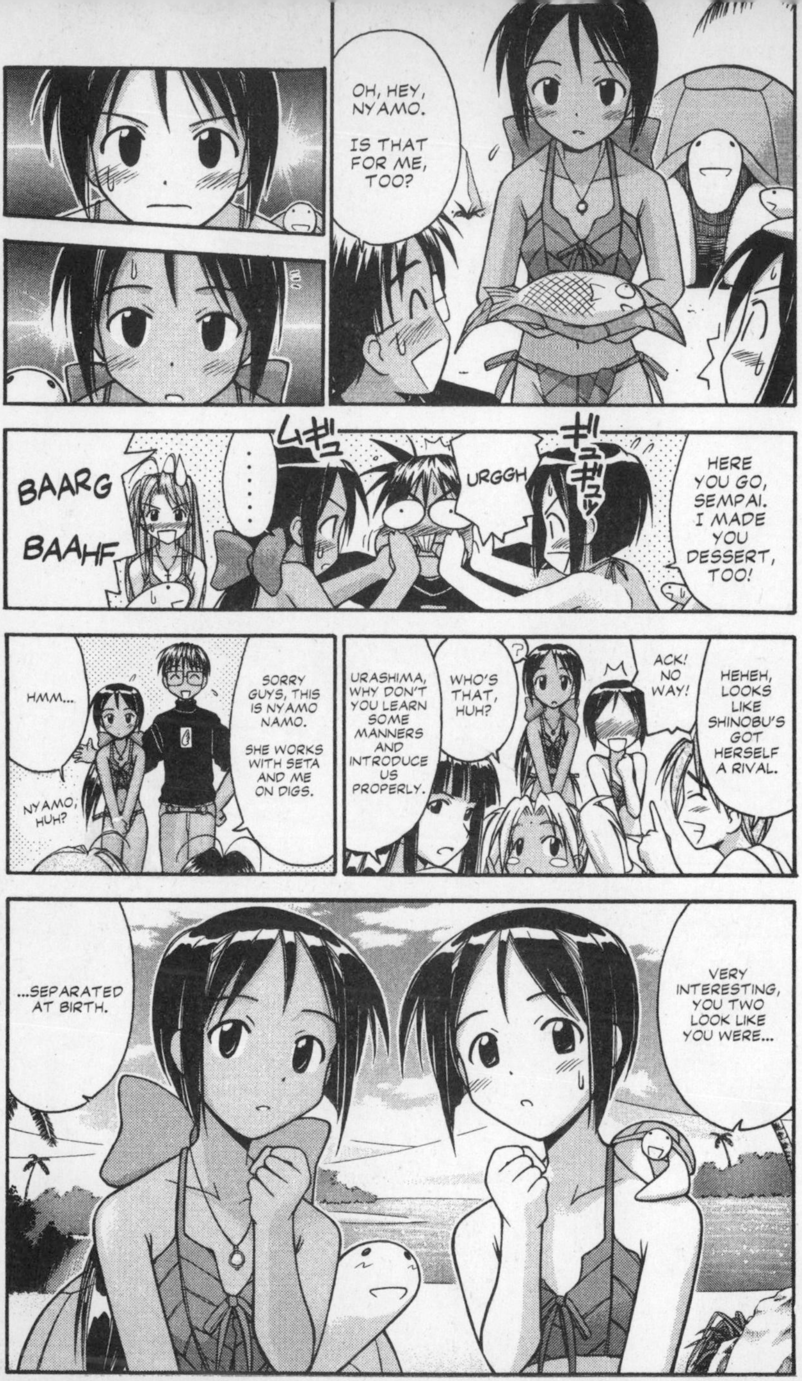
OH, HEY, NYAMO. IS THAT FOR ME, TOO?
HERE YOU GO, SEMPAI. I MADE YOU DESSERT, TOO!
ギュギュッ
URGGH
ムギュ
......
BAARG
BAAHF
HEHEH, LOOKS LIKE SHINOBU'S GOT HERSELF A RIVAL.
ACK! NO WAY!
WHO'S THAT, HUH?
URASHIMA, WHY DON'T YOU LEARN SOME MANNERS AND INTRODUCE US PROPERLY.
SORRY GUYS, THIS IS NYAMO NAMO. SHE WORKS WITH SETA AND ME ON DIGS.
HMM...
NYAMO, HUH?
VERY INTERESTING, YOU TWO LOOK LIKE YOU WERE...
...SEPARATED AT BIRTH.

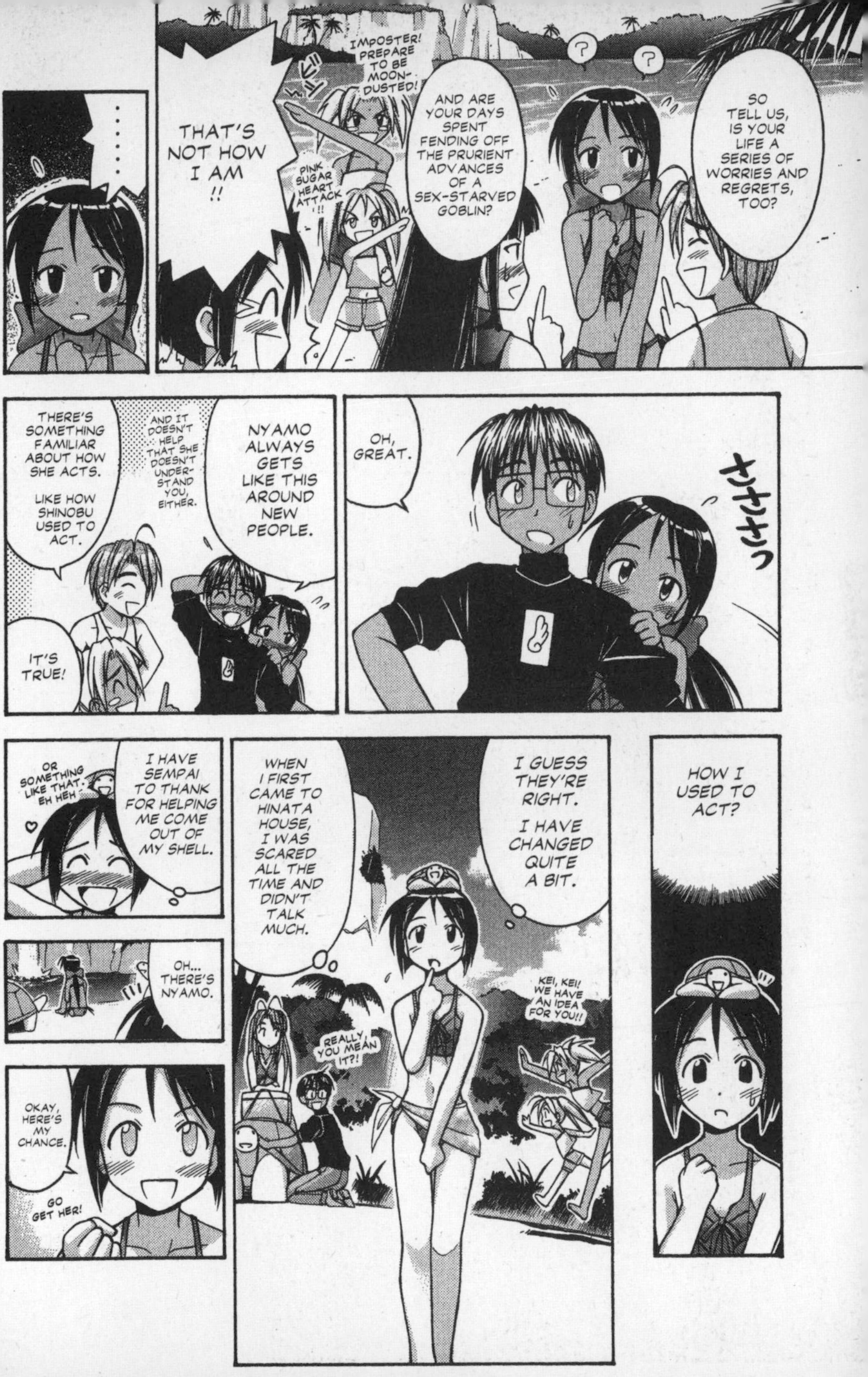
SO TELL US, IS YOUR LIFE A SERIES OF WORRIES AND REGRETS, TOO?
AND ARE YOUR DAYS SPENT FENDING OFF THE PRURIENT ADVANCES OF A SEX-STARVED GOBLIN?
IMPOSTER! PREPARE TO BE MOON-DUSTED!
PINK SUGAR HEART ATTACK!!
THAT'S NOT HOW I AM !!
......
さささっ
OH, GREAT.
NYAMO ALWAYS GETS LIKE THIS AROUND NEW PEOPLE.
AND IT DOESN'T HELP THAT SHE DOESN'T UNDER-STAND YOU, EITHER.
THERE'S SOMETHING FAMILIAR ABOUT HOW SHE ACTS. LIKE HOW SHINOBU USED TO ACT.
IT'S TRUE!
HOW I USED TO ACT?
I GUESS THEY'RE RIGHT. I HAVE CHANGED QUITE A BIT.
WHEN I FIRST CAME TO HINATA HOUSE, I WAS SCARED ALL THE TIME AND DIDN'T TALK MUCH.
KEI, KEI! WE HAVE AN IDEA FOR YOU!!
REALLY, YOU MEAN IT?!
I HAVE SEMPAI TO THANK FOR HELPING ME COME OUT OF MY SHELL.
OR SOMETHING LIKE THAT. EH HEH
OH... THERE'S NYAMO.
OKAY, HERE'S MY CHANCE.
GO GET HER!

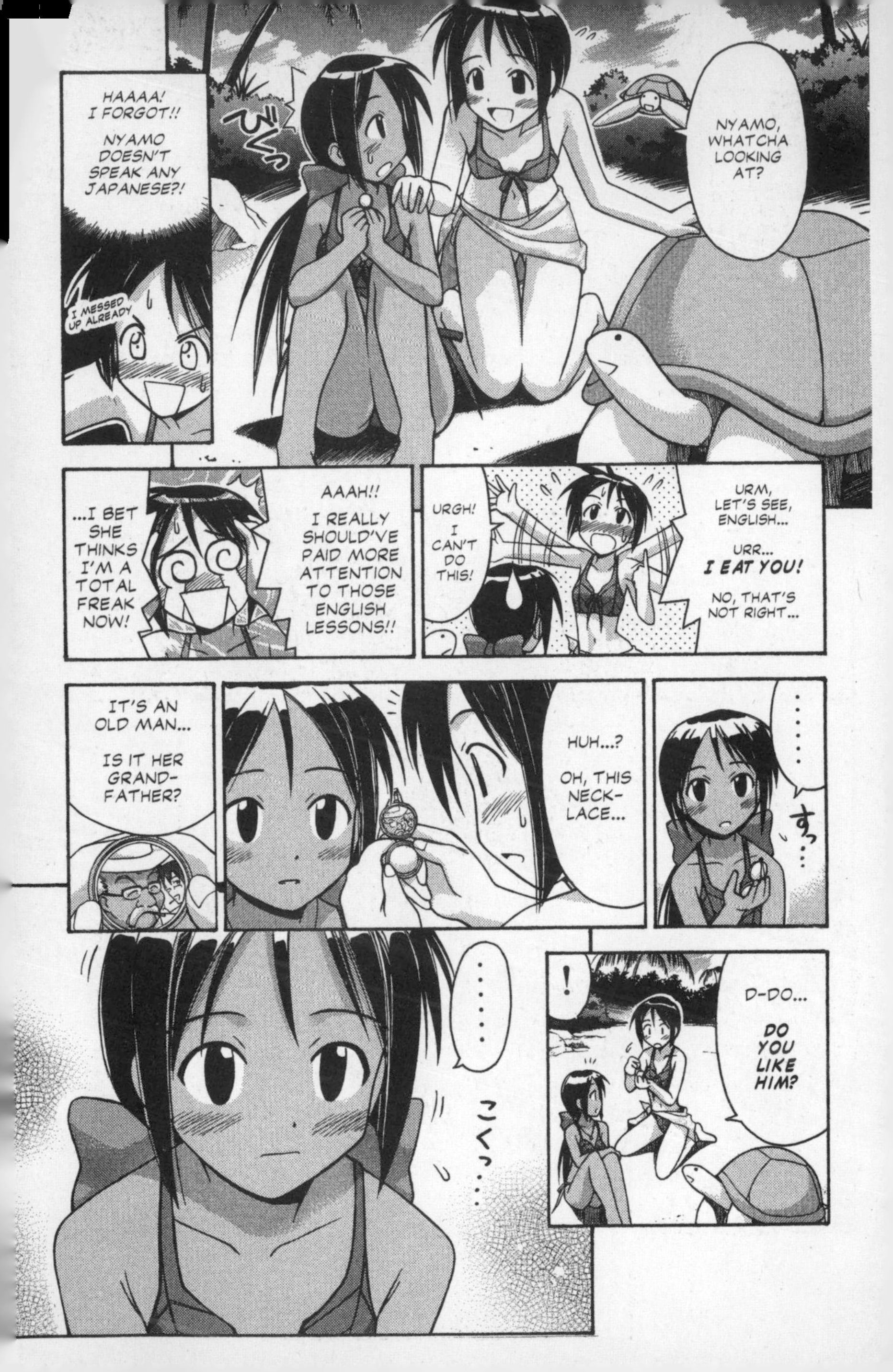
NYAMO, WHATCHA LOOKING AT?
HAAAA! I FORGOT!!
NYAMO DOESN'T SPEAK ANY JAPANESE?!
I MESSED UP ALREADY
URM, LET'S SEE, ENGLISH...
URR... **I EAT YOU!**
NO, THAT'S NOT RIGHT...
URGH! I CAN'T DO THIS!
AAAH!!
I REALLY SHOULD'VE PAID MORE ATTENTION TO THOSE ENGLISH LESSONS!!
...I BET SHE THINKS I'M A TOTAL FREAK NOW!
......
すっ...
HUH...?
OH, THIS NECK-LACE...
IT'S AN OLD MAN...
IS IT HER GRAND-FATHER?
!
D-DO...
DO YOU LIKE HIM?
......
こくっ...

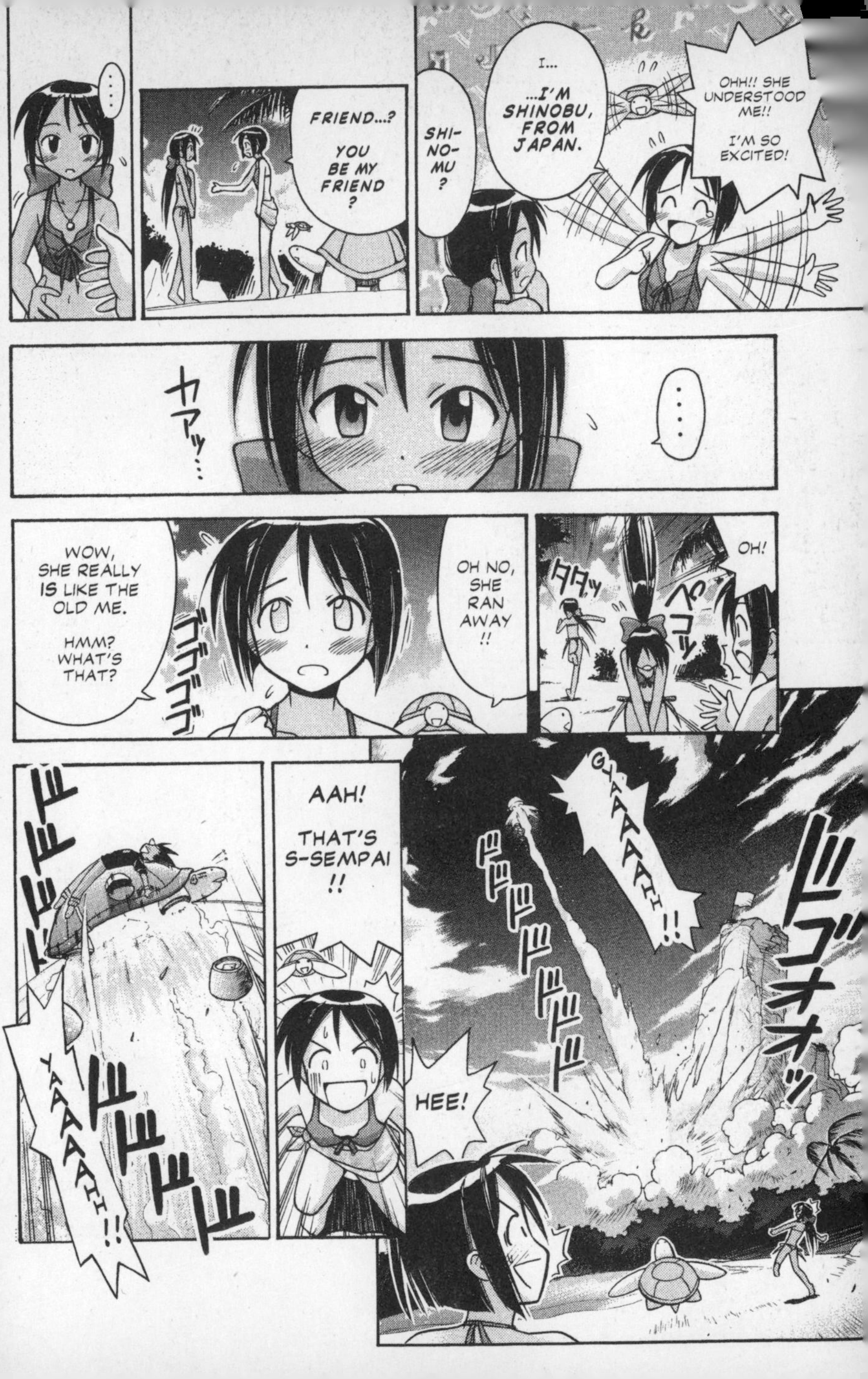
OHH!! SHE UNDERSTOOD ME!! I'M SO EXCITED!
I... ...I'M SHINOBU, FROM JAPAN.
SHI-NO-MU?
FRIEND...? YOU BE MY FRIEND?
....
....
ヤアッ…
OH!
ペコッ
タタッ
OH NO, SHE RAN AWAY!!
ゴゴゴゴ
WOW, SHE REALLY IS LIKE THE OLD ME. HMM? WHAT'S THAT?
ドゴオオッ
GYAAAAAAH!!
AAH! THAT'S S-SEMPAI!!
HEE!
YAAAAAAH!!

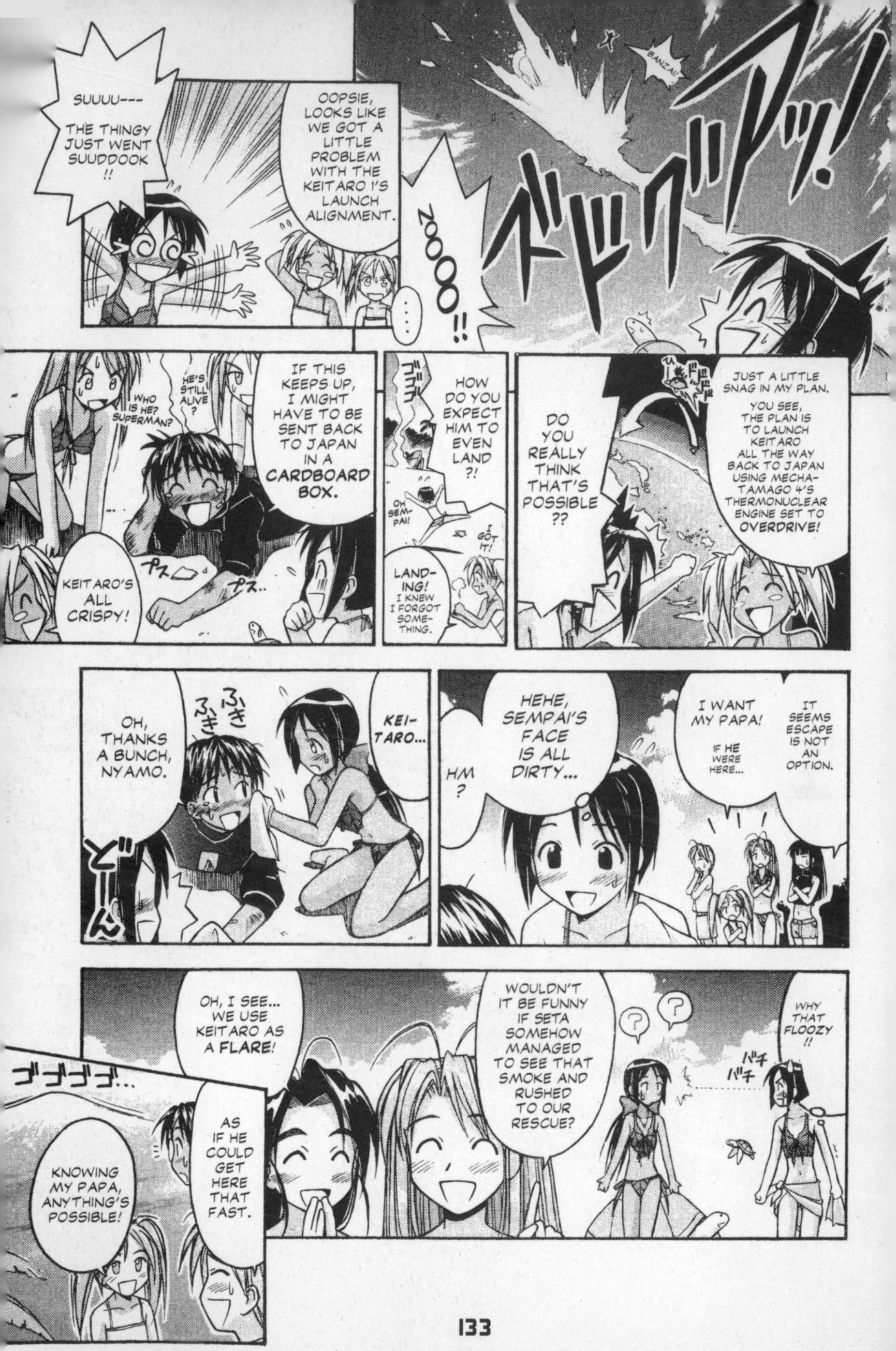
BANZAI!!
ZOOOO!!
OOPSIE, LOOKS LIKE WE GOT A LITTLE PROBLEM WITH THE KEITARO 1'S LAUNCH ALIGNMENT.
SUUUU--- THE THINGY JUST WENT SUUDDOOK !!
....
JUST A LITTLE SNAG IN MY PLAN. YOU SEE, THE PLAN IS TO LAUNCH KEITARO ALL THE WAY BACK TO JAPAN USING MECHA-TAMAGO 4'S THERMONUCLEAR ENGINE SET TO OVERDRIVE!
DO YOU REALLY THINK THAT'S POSSIBLE ??
HOW DO YOU EXPECT HIM TO EVEN LAND ?!
OH SEMPAI!
I GOT IT!
LANDING! I KNEW I FORGOT SOMETHING.
IF THIS KEEPS UP, I MIGHT HAVE TO BE SENT BACK TO JAPAN IN A CARDBOARD BOX.
HE'S STILL ALIVE ?
WHO IS HE? SUPERMAN?
KEITARO'S ALL CRISPY!
IT SEEMS ESCAPE IS NOT AN OPTION.
I WANT MY PAPA!
IF HE WERE HERE...
HEHE, SEMPAI'S FACE IS ALL DIRTY...
HM ?
KEI-TARO...
ふきふき
OH, THANKS A BUNCH, NYAMO.
WHY THAT FLOOZY !!
バチバチ
WOULDN'T IT BE FUNNY IF SETA SOMEHOW MANAGED TO SEE THAT SMOKE AND RUSHED TO OUR RESCUE?
OH, I SEE... WE USE KEITARO AS A FLARE!
AS IF HE COULD GET HERE THAT FAST.
KNOWING MY PAPA, ANYTHING'S POSSIBLE!

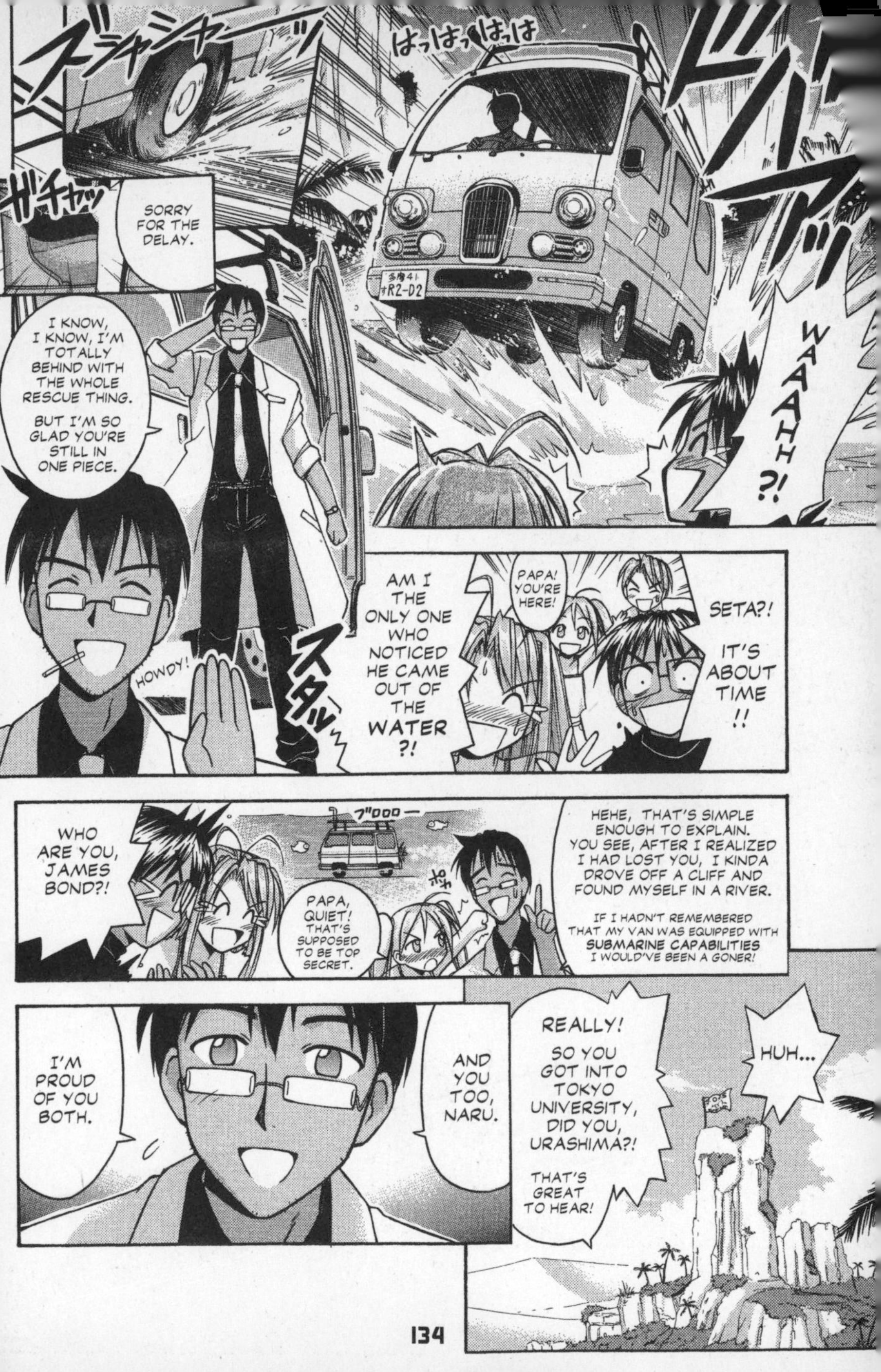
はっはっはっは
ズシャシャーッ
多摩41
す R2-D2
WAAAHH?!
ガチャッ
SORRY FOR THE DELAY.
I KNOW, I KNOW, I'M TOTALLY BEHIND WITH THE WHOLE RESCUE THING.
BUT I'M SO GLAD YOU'RE STILL IN ONE PIECE.
HOWDY!
SETA?!
IT'S ABOUT TIME!!
PAPA! YOU'RE HERE!
AM I THE ONLY ONE WHO NOTICED HE CAME OUT OF THE WATER?!
HEHE, THAT'S SIMPLE ENOUGH TO EXPLAIN. YOU SEE, AFTER I REALIZED I HAD LOST YOU, I KINDA DROVE OFF A CLIFF AND FOUND MYSELF IN A RIVER.
IF I HADN'T REMEMBERED THAT MY VAN WAS EQUIPPED WITH SUBMARINE CAPABILITIES I WOULD'VE BEEN A GONER!
ポッ
PAPA, QUIET! THAT'S SUPPOSED TO BE TOP SECRET.
WHO ARE YOU, JAMES BOND?!
HUH...
REALLY!
SO YOU GOT INTO TOKYO UNIVERSITY, DID YOU, URASHIMA?!
THAT'S GREAT TO HEAR!
AND YOU TOO, NARU.
I'M PROUD OF YOU BOTH.

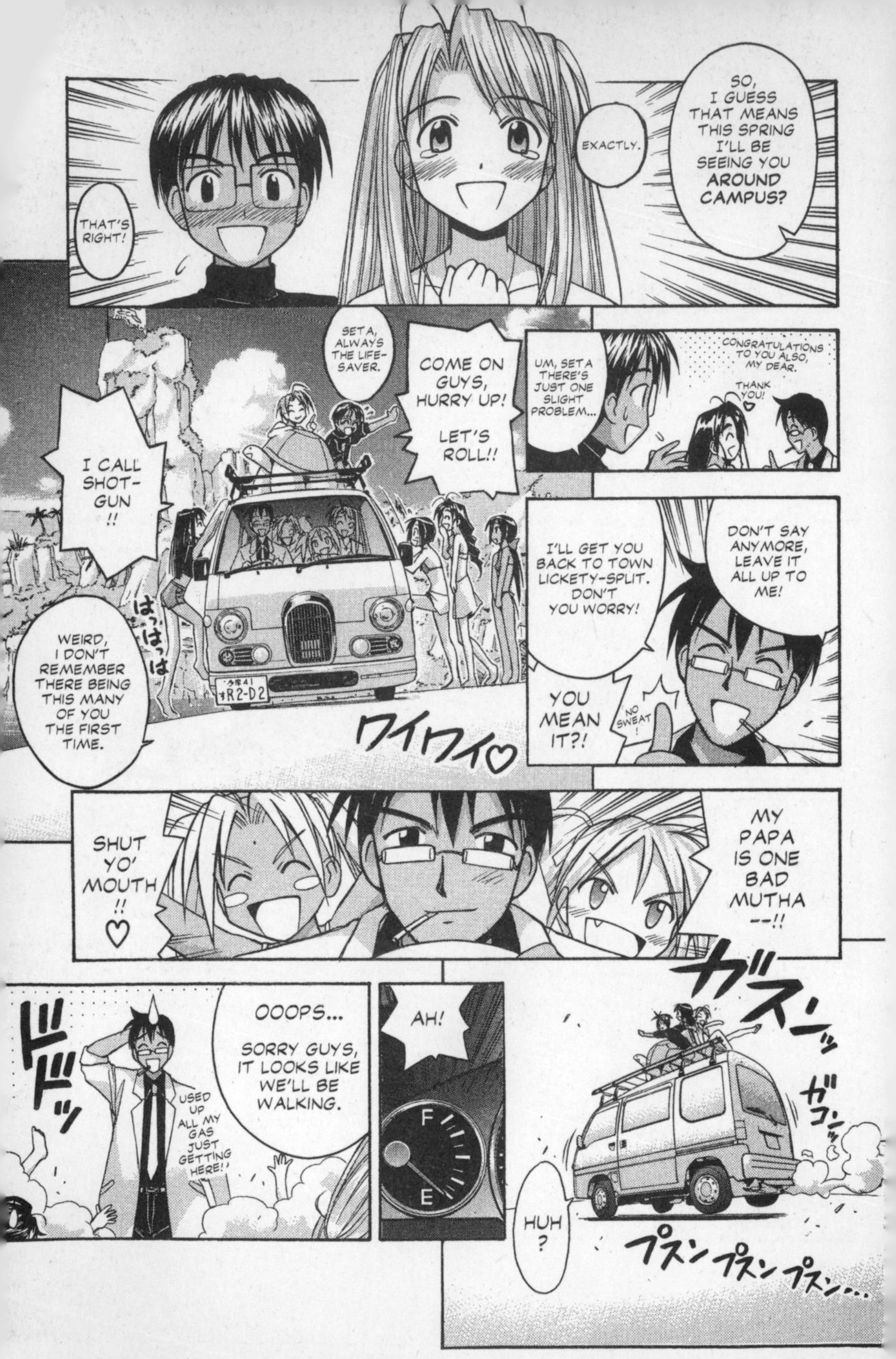
SO, I GUESS THAT MEANS THIS SPRING I'LL BE SEEING YOU AROUND CAMPUS?
EXACTLY.
THAT'S RIGHT!
CONGRATULATIONS TO YOU ALSO, MY DEAR.
THANK YOU! ♡
UM, SETA THERE'S JUST ONE SLIGHT PROBLEM...
DON'T SAY ANYMORE, LEAVE IT ALL UP TO ME!
I'LL GET YOU BACK TO TOWN LICKETY-SPLIT. DON'T YOU WORRY!
NO SWEAT!
YOU MEAN IT?!
COME ON GUYS, HURRY UP!
LET'S ROLL!!
SETA, ALWAYS THE LIFE-SAVER.
I CALL SHOT-GUN !!
R2-D2
はっはっは
WEIRD, I DON'T REMEMBER THERE BEING THIS MANY OF YOU THE FIRST TIME.
ワイワイ♡
MY PAPA IS ONE BAD MUTHA --!!
SHUT YO' MOUTH !! ♡
ガスンッ
ガコンッ
HUH ?
プスン プスン プスン...
AH!
F
E
OOOPS...
SORRY GUYS, IT LOOKS LIKE WE'LL BE WALKING.
USED UP ALL MY GAS JUST GETTING HERE!
ドドッ

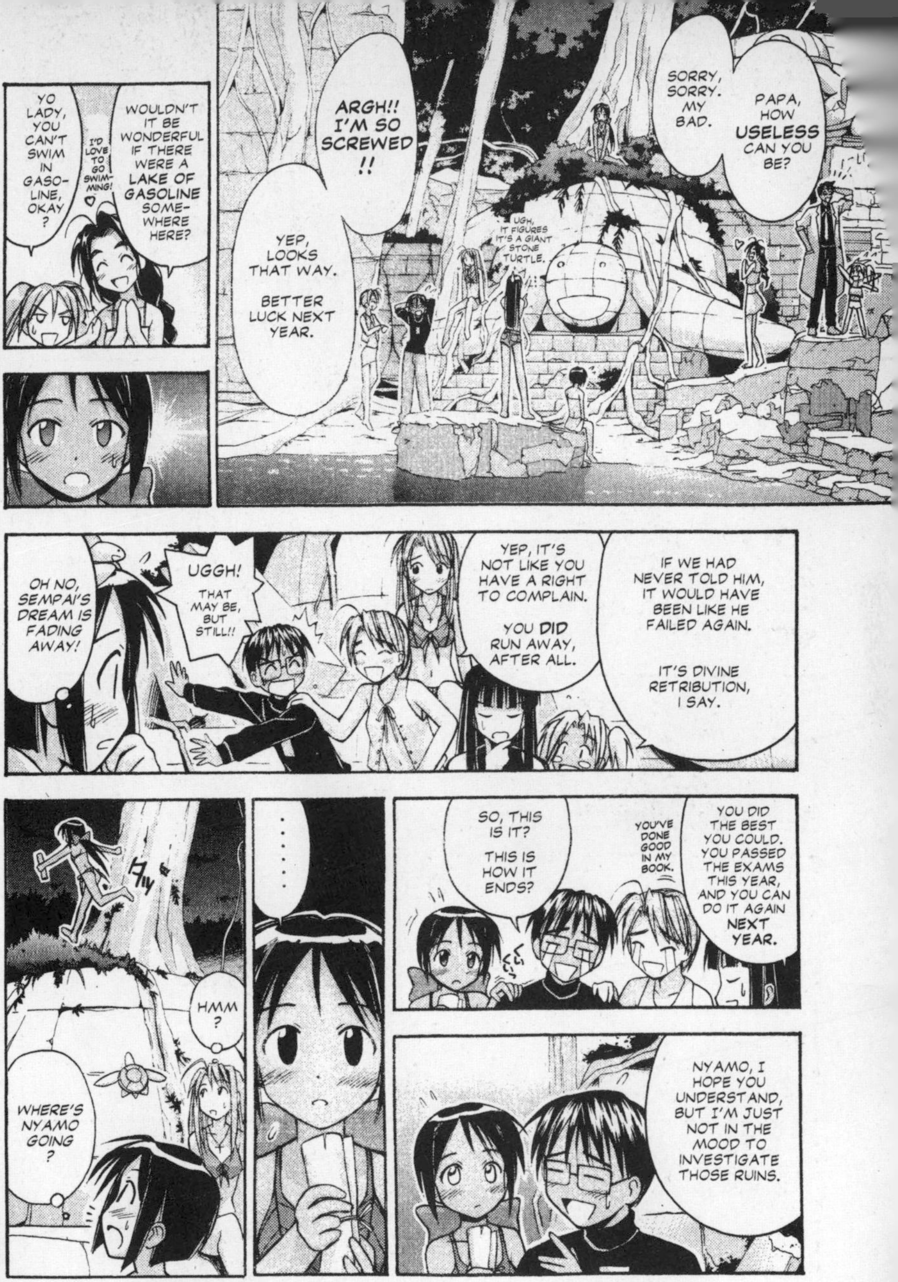
PAPA, HOW USELESS CAN YOU BE?
SORRY, SORRY. MY BAD.
ARGH!! I'M SO SCREWED!!
UGH, IT FIGURES IT'S A GIANT STONE TURTLE.
YEP, LOOKS THAT WAY.
BETTER LUCK NEXT YEAR.
WOULDN'T IT BE WONDERFUL IF THERE WERE A LAKE OF GASOLINE SOMEWHERE HERE?
I'D LOVE TO GO SWIMMING!
YO LADY, YOU CAN'T SWIM IN GASOLINE, OKAY?
IF WE HAD NEVER TOLD HIM, IT WOULD HAVE BEEN LIKE HE FAILED AGAIN.
IT'S DIVINE RETRIBUTION, I SAY.
YEP, IT'S NOT LIKE YOU HAVE A RIGHT TO COMPLAIN.
YOU DID RUN AWAY, AFTER ALL.
UGGH!
THAT MAY BE, BUT STILL!!
OH NO, SEMPAI'S DREAM IS FADING AWAY!
YOU DID THE BEST YOU COULD. YOU PASSED THE EXAMS THIS YEAR, AND YOU CAN DO IT AGAIN NEXT YEAR.
YOU'VE DONE GOOD IN MY BOOK.
SO, THIS IS IT?
THIS IS HOW IT ENDS?
NYAMO, I HOPE YOU UNDERSTAND, BUT I'M JUST NOT IN THE MOOD TO INVESTIGATE THOSE RUINS.
......
HMM?
WHERE'S NYAMO GOING?

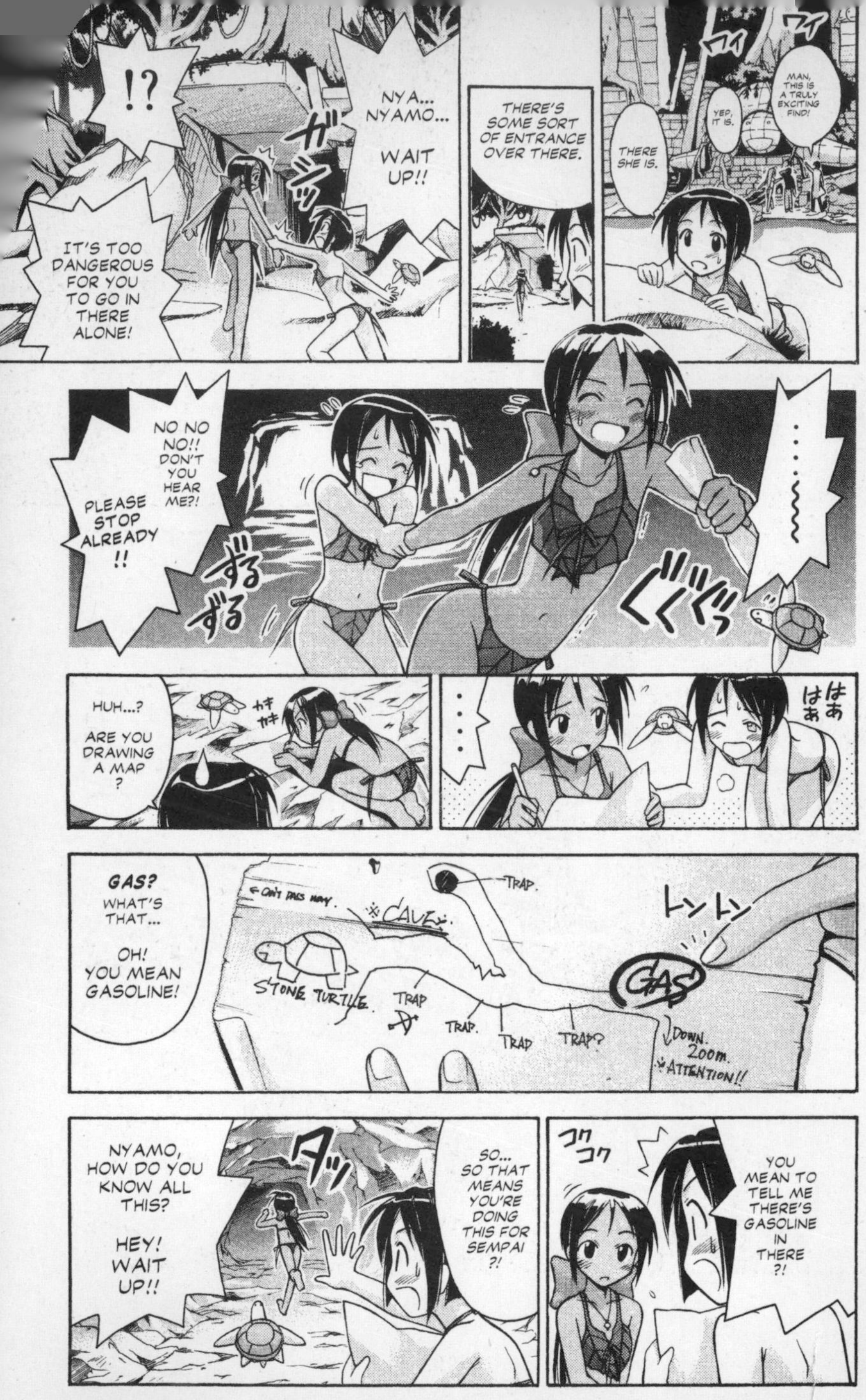
ワイ ワイ
MAN, THIS IS A TRULY EXCITING FIND!
YEP, IT IS.
THERE SHE IS.
THERE'S SOME SORT OF ENTRANCE OVER THERE.
NYA... NYAMO... WAIT UP!!
!?
ガシッ
IT'S TOO DANGEROUS FOR YOU TO GO IN THERE ALONE!
......~
NO NO NO!! DON'T YOU HEAR ME?!
PLEASE STOP ALREADY!!
ぐぐぐっ
ずる ずる
はあ はあ
....
カキ カキ
HUH...? ARE YOU DRAWING A MAP?
トントン
TRAP.
← CAN'T PASS WAY.
CAVE
STONE TURTLE
TRAP
TRAP.
TRAP
TRAP?
GAS
DOWN. 200m.
ATTENTION!!
GAS? WHAT'S THAT... OH! YOU MEAN GASOLINE!
コク コク
YOU MEAN TO TELL ME THERE'S GASOLINE IN THERE?!
SO... SO THAT MEANS YOU'RE DOING THIS FOR SEMPAI?!
ダッ
NYAMO, HOW DO YOU KNOW ALL THIS?
HEY! WAIT UP!!

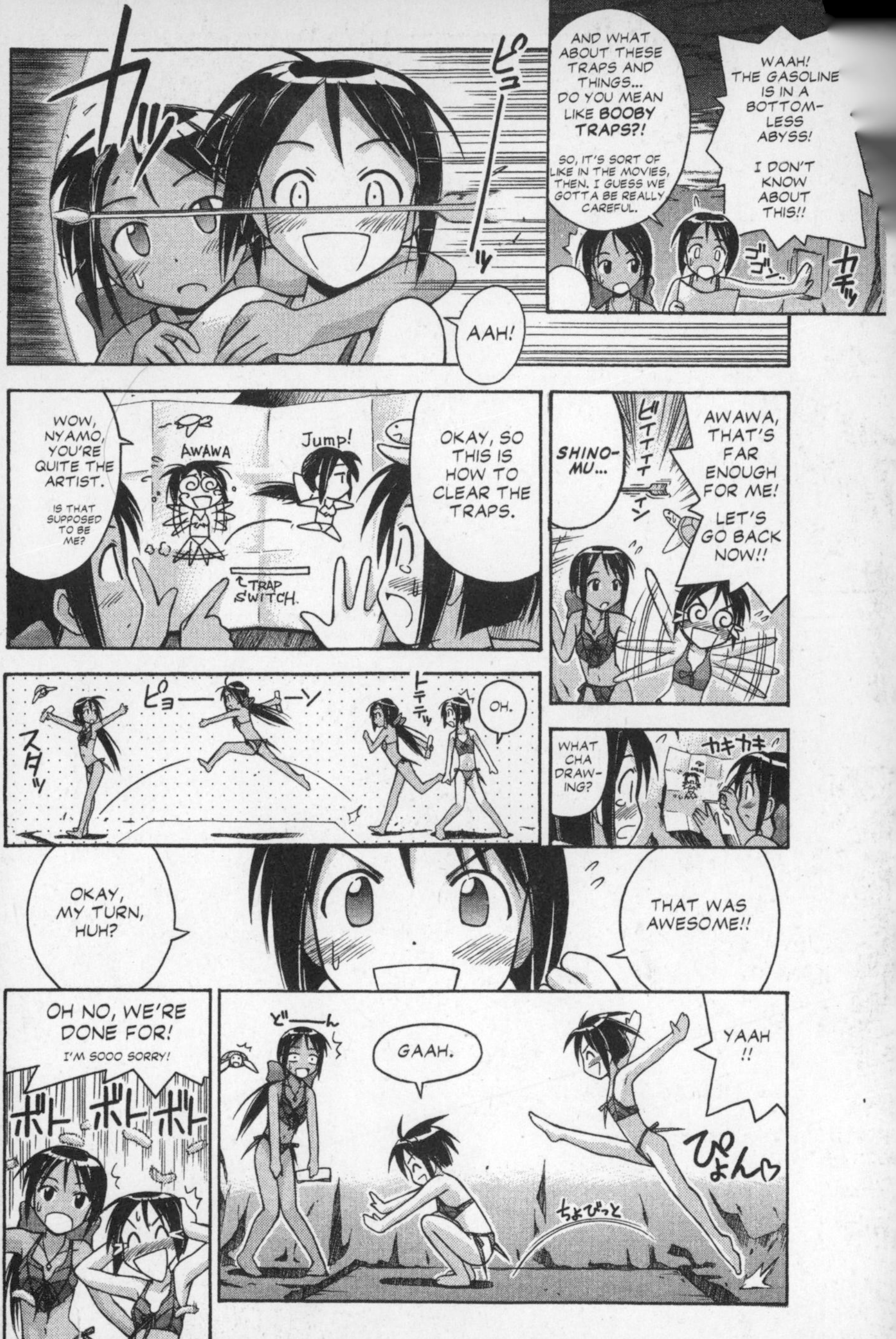
WAAH! THE GASOLINE IS IN A BOTTOM-LESS ABYSS!
I DON'T KNOW ABOUT THIS!!
AND WHAT ABOUT THESE TRAPS AND THINGS... DO YOU MEAN LIKE **BOOBY TRAPS?!**
SO, IT'S SORT OF LIKE IN THE MOVIES, THEN. I GUESS WE GOTTA BE REALLY CAREFUL.
カチッ
ゴゴン
ピュー
カッ
AAH!
AWAWA, THAT'S FAR ENOUGH FOR ME!
LET'S GO BACK NOW!!
SHINOMU...
OKAY, SO THIS IS HOW TO CLEAR THE TRAPS.
Jump!
AWAWA
WOW, NYAMO, YOU'RE QUITE THE ARTIST.
IS THAT SUPPOSED TO BE ME?
TRAP SWITCH.
カキカキ
WHAT CHA DRAW-ING?
OH.
トテテッ
ピョーーーン
スタッ
THAT WAS AWESOME!!
OKAY, MY TURN, HUH?
YAAH!!
ぴょん♡
ちょびっと
GAAH.
ど――ん
OH NO, WE'RE DONE FOR!
I'M SOOO SORRY!
ボトボトボト

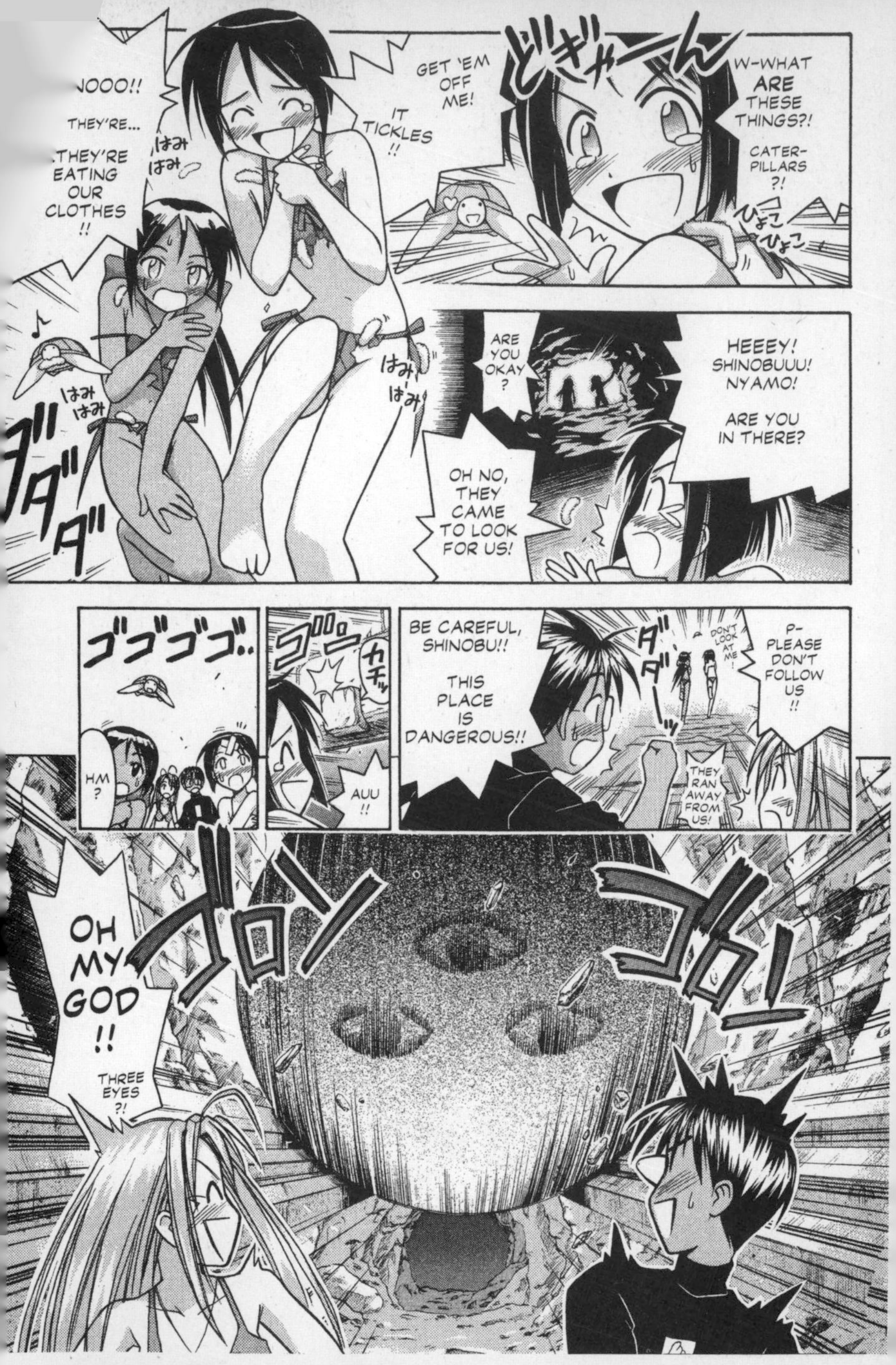
どぎゃーん
W-WHAT ARE THESE THINGS?!
CATER-PILLARS ?!
ひょこひょこ
HEEEY! SHINOBUUU! NYAMO!
ARE YOU IN THERE?
ARE YOU OKAY?
OH NO, THEY CAME TO LOOK FOR US!
GET 'EM OFF ME!
IT TICKLES!!
NOOO!!
THEY'RE...
...THEY'RE EATING OUR CLOTHES!!
はみはみ
はみはみ
はみはみ
ダダダ
P-PLEASE DON'T FOLLOW US!!
DON'T LOOK AT ME!
THEY RAN AWAY FROM US!
ダダーッ
BE CAREFUL, SHINOBU!!
THIS PLACE IS DANGEROUS!!
ゴー
カチッ
AUU!!
ゴゴゴゴ..
HM?
ゴロン
ゴロン
OH MY GOD!!
THREE EYES?!

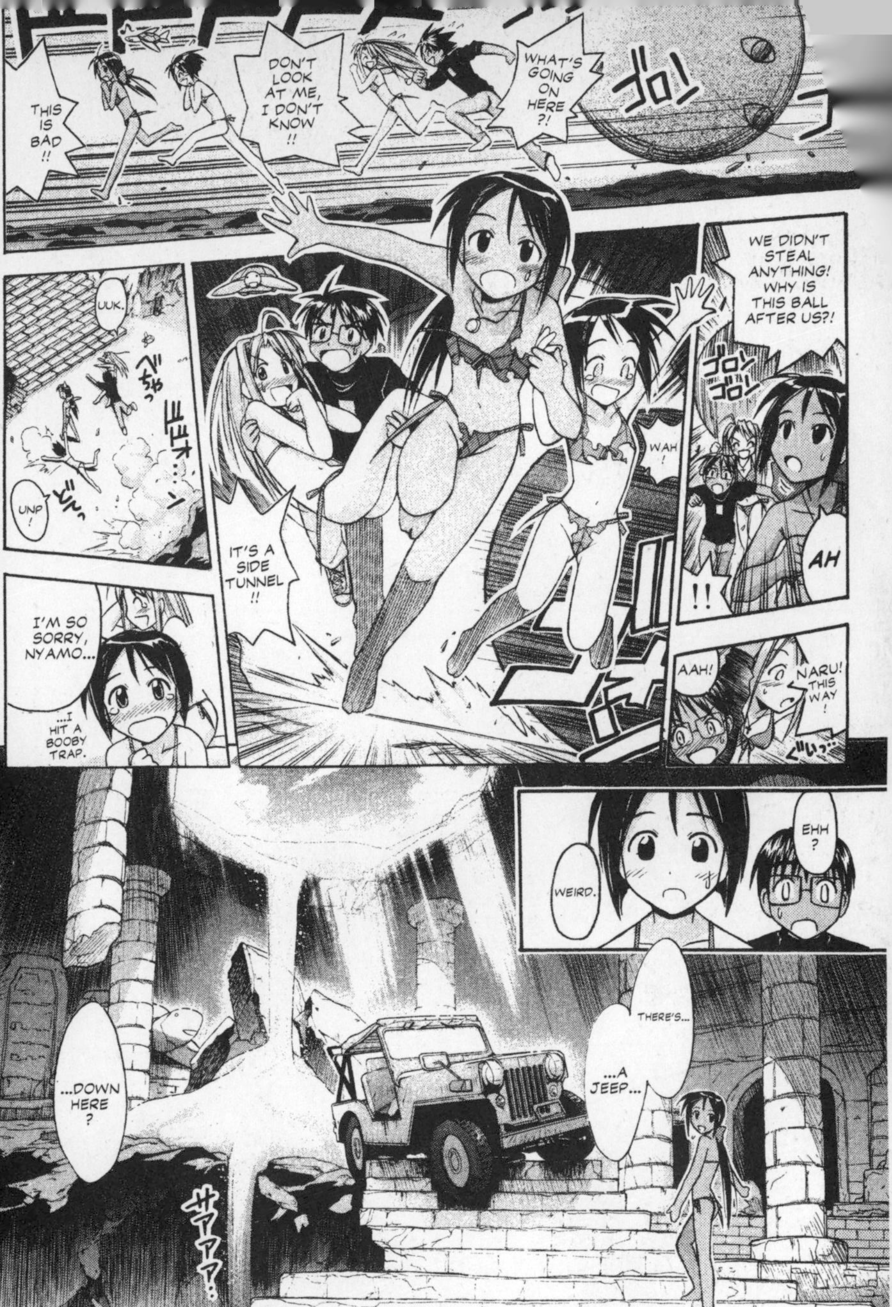

ゴロン
WHAT'S GOING ON HERE?!
DON'T LOOK AT ME, I DON'T KNOW!!
THIS IS BAD!!
WE DIDN'T STEAL ANYTHING! WHY IS THIS BALL AFTER US?!
ゴロン ゴロン
AH
!!
NARU! THIS WAY!
AAH!
WAH!
IT'S A SIDE TUNNEL!!
UUK.
UNP!
I'M SO SORRY, NYAMO...
...I HIT A BOOBY TRAP.
EHH?
WEIRD.
THERE'S...
...A JEEP...
...DOWN HERE?

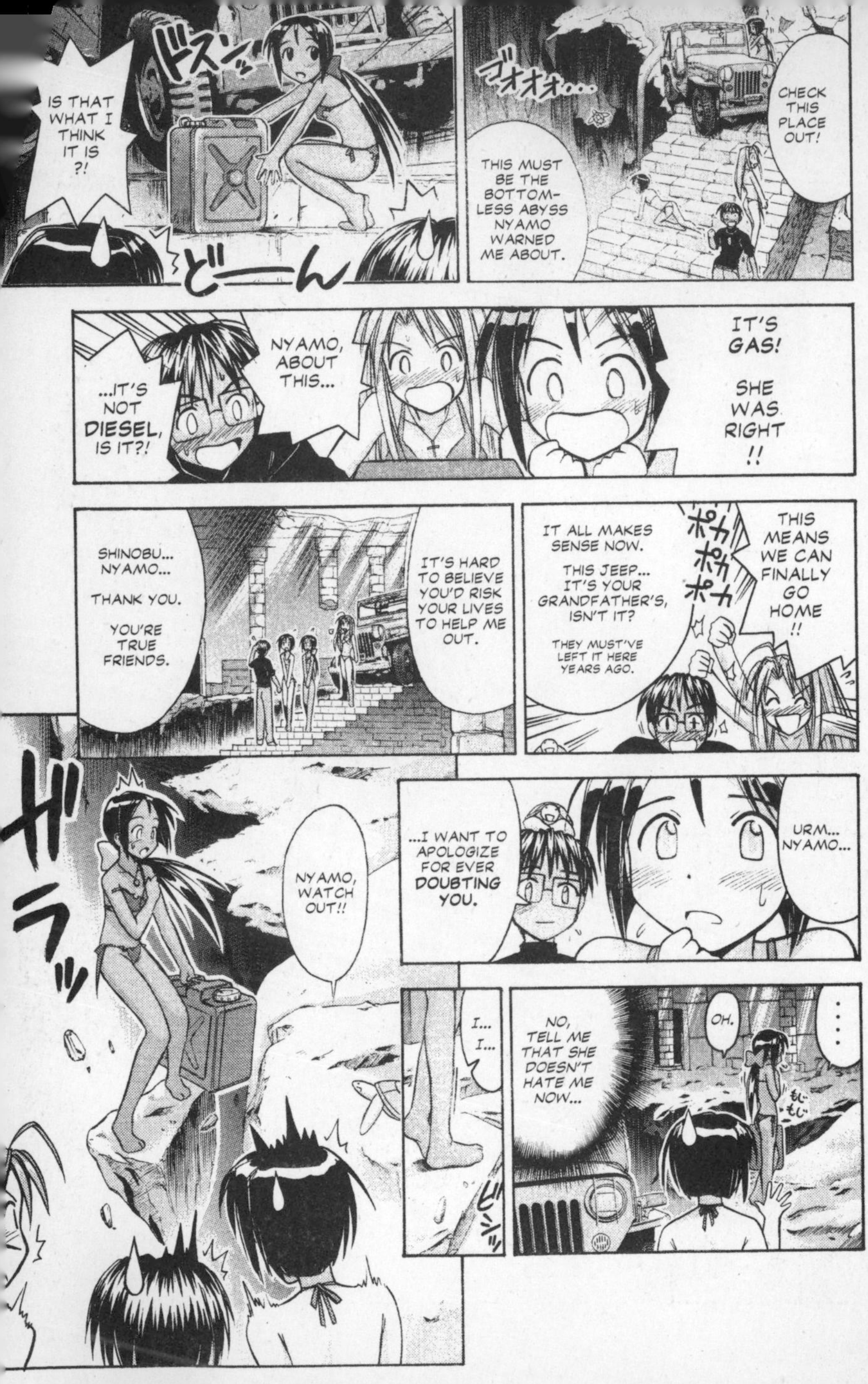

CHECK THIS PLACE OUT!
ゴオオオ...
THIS MUST BE THE BOTTOMLESS ABYSS NYAMO WARNED ME ABOUT.
ドスンッ
IS THAT WHAT I THINK IT IS ?!
どーん
IT'S GAS!
SHE WAS RIGHT !!
NYAMO, ABOUT THIS...
...IT'S NOT DIESEL, IS IT?!
THIS MEANS WE CAN FINALLY GO HOME !!
ポカポカポカ
IT ALL MAKES SENSE NOW.
THIS JEEP... IT'S YOUR GRANDFATHER'S, ISN'T IT?
THEY MUST'VE LEFT IT HERE YEARS AGO.
IT'S HARD TO BELIEVE YOU'D RISK YOUR LIVES TO HELP ME OUT.
SHINOBU... NYAMO...
THANK YOU.
YOU'RE TRUE FRIENDS.
URM... NYAMO...
...I WANT TO APOLOGIZE FOR EVER DOUBTING YOU.
...
OH.
もじもじ
NO, TELL ME THAT SHE DOESN'T HATE ME NOW...
I... I...
ビシッ
ガラッ
NYAMO, WATCH OUT!!

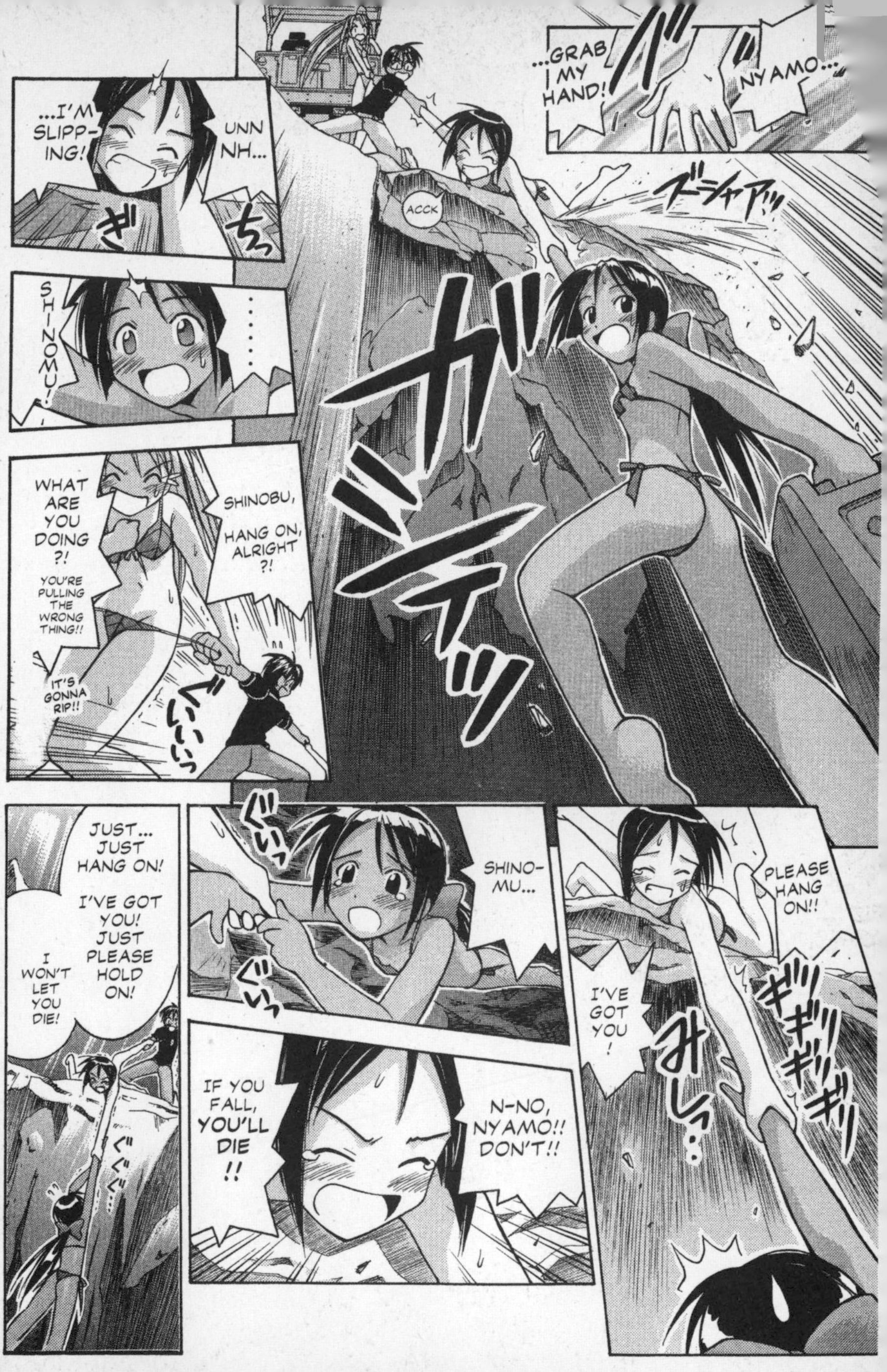

NYAMO...
...GRAB MY HAND!
ズシャア!!!
ACCK
ガシィッ
UNN NH...
...I'M SLIPP-ING!
ぎ
ちっ
......
SHINOMU!
SHINOBU, HANG ON, ALRIGHT?!
WHAT ARE YOU DOING?!
YOU'RE PULLING THE WRONG THING!!
IT'S GONNA RIP!!
ぐいいいっ
PLEASE HANG ON!!
I'VE GOT YOU!
ギギギギ
みしっ..
SHINO-MU...
ぐいっ
ぐいっ
N-NO, NYAMO!! DON'T!!
IF YOU FALL, YOU'LL DIE!!
JUST... JUST HANG ON!
I'VE GOT YOU! JUST PLEASE HOLD ON!
I WON'T LET YOU DIE!
ぐぐぐ...

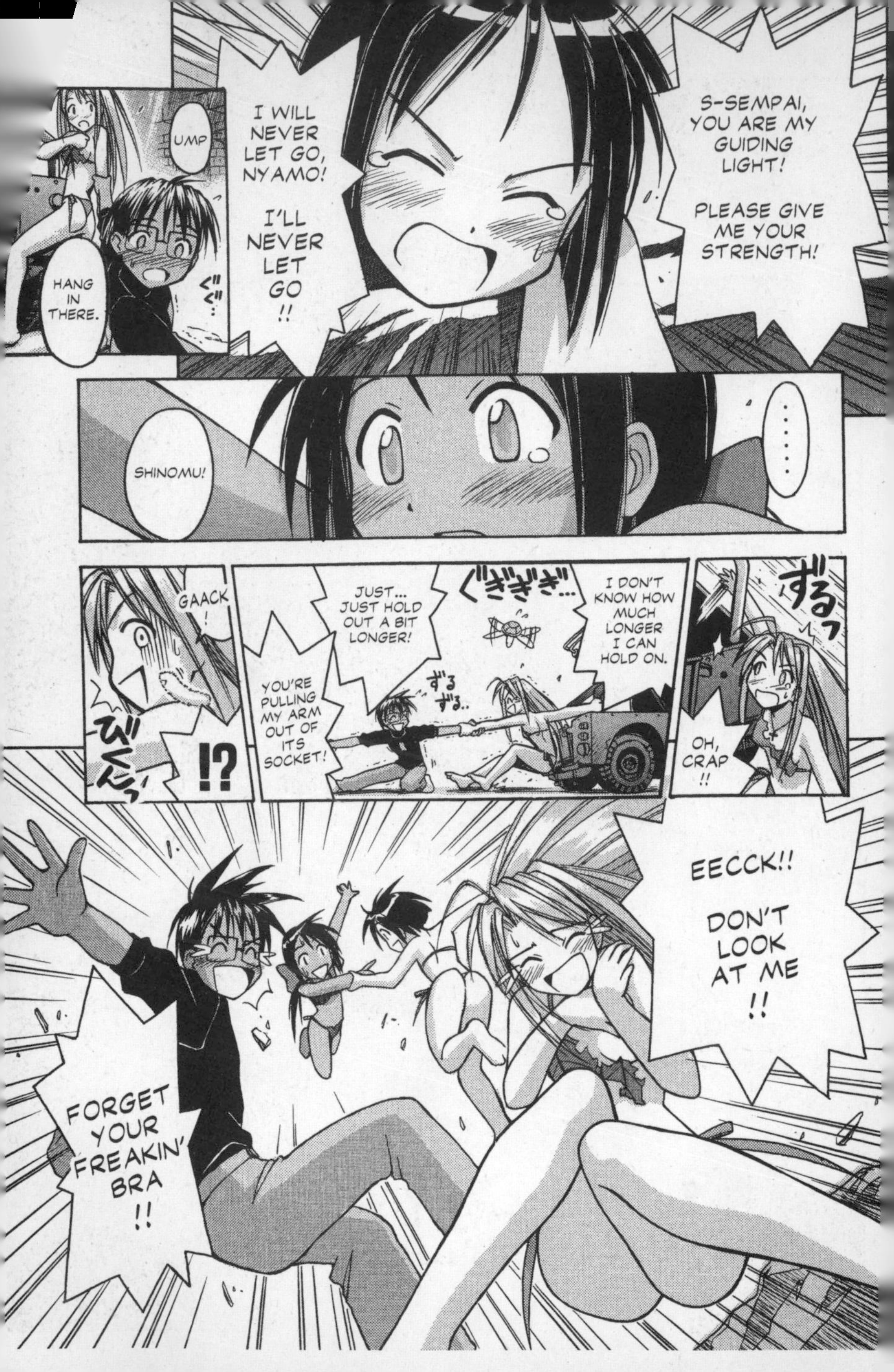
S-SEMPAI, YOU ARE MY GUIDING LIGHT!
PLEASE GIVE ME YOUR STRENGTH!
I WILL NEVER LET GO, NYAMO!
I'LL NEVER LET GO!!
UMP
ぐぐ..
HANG IN THERE.
......
SHINOMU!
ずるっ
OH, CRAP!!
ぐぎぎぎ...
I DON'T KNOW HOW MUCH LONGER I CAN HOLD ON.
JUST... JUST HOLD OUT A BIT LONGER!
ずるずる..
YOU'RE PULLING MY ARM OUT OF ITS SOCKET!
GAACK!
びくんっ
!?
EECCK!!
DON'T LOOK AT ME!!
FORGET YOUR FREAKIN' BRA!!

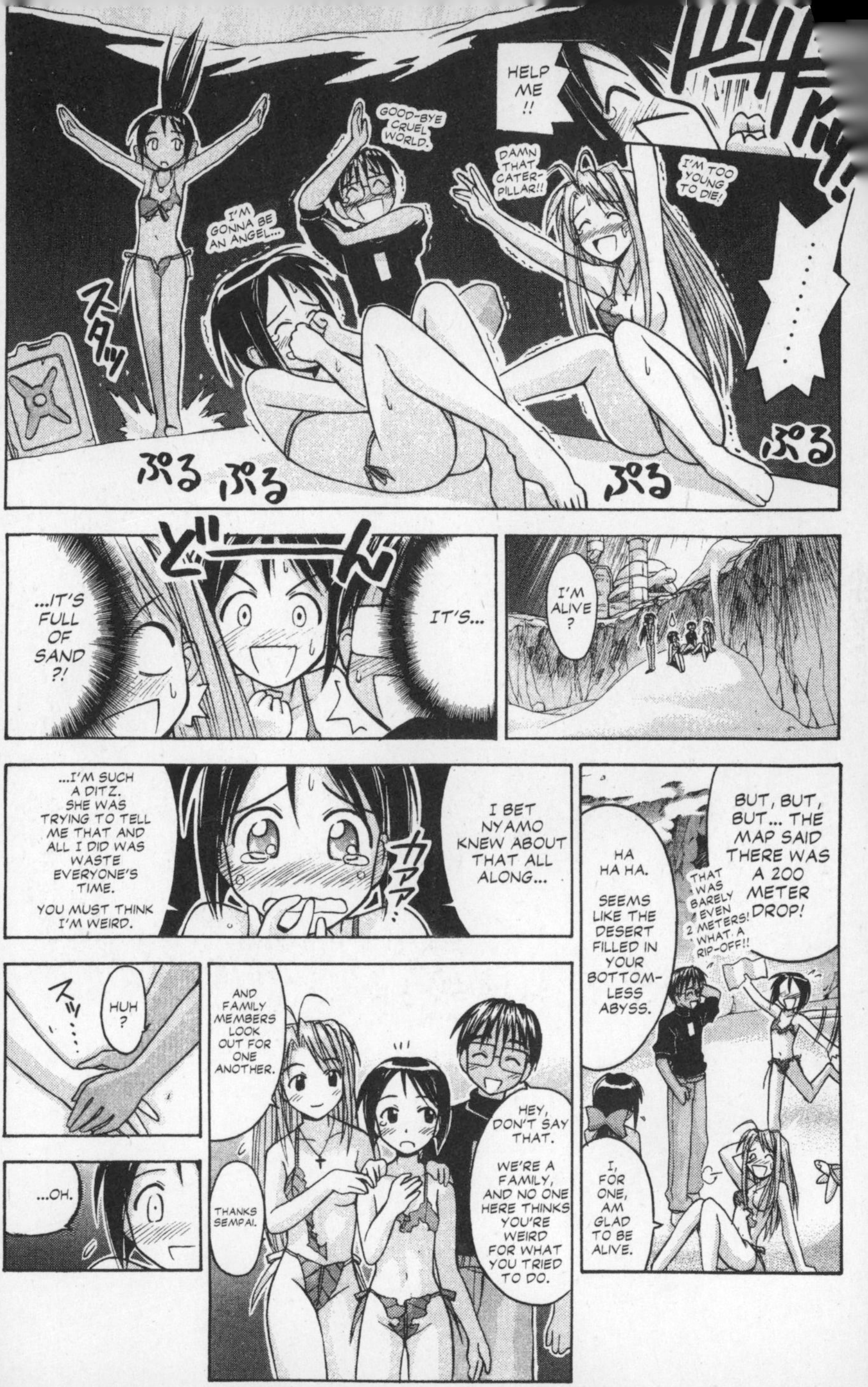
HELP ME !!
I'M TOO YOUNG TO DIE!
DAMN THAT CATER-PILLAR!!
GOOD-BYE CRUEL WORLD.
I'M GONNA BE AN ANGEL...
ぷる
ぷる
ぷる ぷる
I'M ALIVE ?
IT'S...
...IT'S FULL OF SAND ?!
BUT, BUT, BUT... THE MAP SAID THERE WAS A 200 METER DROP!
THAT WAS BARELY EVEN 2 METERS! WHAT A RIP-OFF!!
HA HA HA.
SEEMS LIKE THE DESERT FILLED IN YOUR BOTTOM-LESS ABYSS.
I, FOR ONE, AM GLAD TO BE ALIVE.
I BET NYAMO KNEW ABOUT THAT ALL ALONG...
...I'M SUCH A DITZ. SHE WAS TRYING TO TELL ME THAT AND ALL I DID WAS WASTE EVERYONE'S TIME.
YOU MUST THINK I'M WEIRD.
HEY, DON'T SAY THAT.
WE'RE A FAMILY, AND NO ONE HERE THINKS YOU'RE WEIRD FOR WHAT YOU TRIED TO DO.
AND FAMILY MEMBERS LOOK OUT FOR ONE ANOTHER.
THANKS SEMPAI.
HUH ?
...OH.

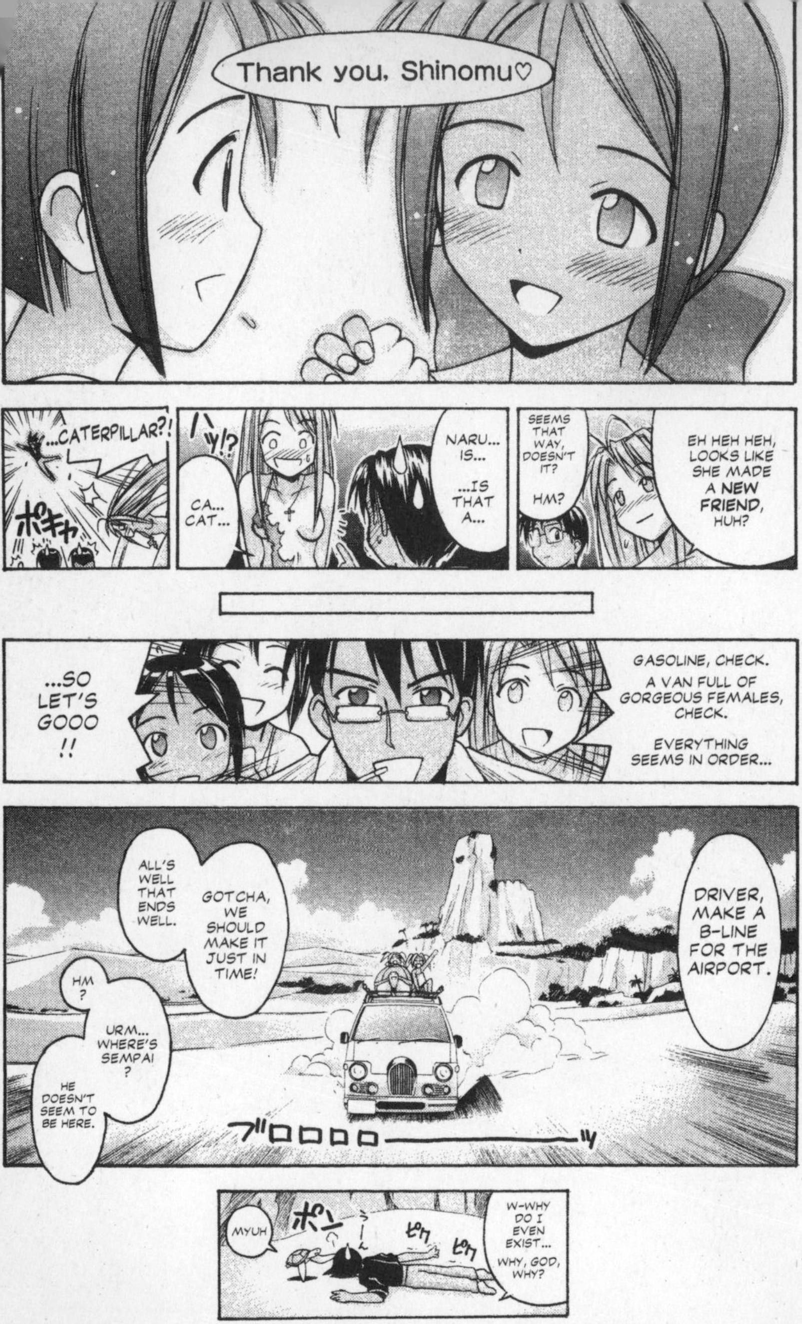
Thank you, Shinomu♡
EH HEH HEH, LOOKS LIKE SHE MADE A NEW FRIEND, HUH?
SEEMS THAT WAY, DOESN'T IT?
HM?
NARU... IS...
...IS THAT A...
ハッ!?
CA... CAT...
...CATERPILLAR?!
ポキャ
GASOLINE, CHECK.
A VAN FULL OF GORGEOUS FEMALES, CHECK.
EVERYTHING SEEMS IN ORDER...
...SO LET'S GOOO!!
DRIVER, MAKE A B-LINE FOR THE AIRPORT.
GOTCHA, WE SHOULD MAKE IT JUST IN TIME!
ALL'S WELL THAT ENDS WELL.
HM?
URM... WHERE'S SEMPAI?
HE DOESN'T SEEM TO BE HERE.
ブロロロロ――ッ
W-WHY DO I EVEN EXIST...
WHY, GOD, WHY?
ピク ピク
うーん
ポン
MYUH

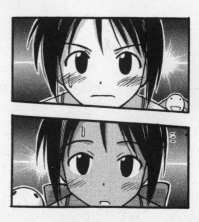

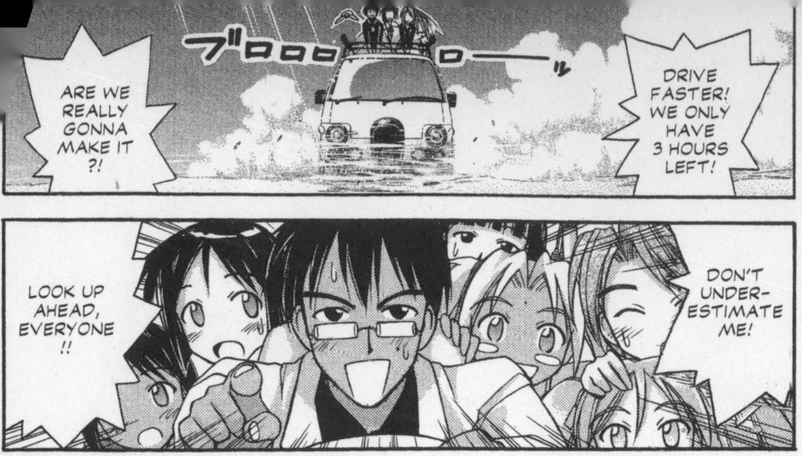
DRIVE FASTER! WE ONLY HAVE 3 HOURS LEFT!
ARE WE REALLY GONNA MAKE IT ?!
DON'T UNDER-ESTIMATE ME!
LOOK UP AHEAD, EVERYONE !!

Love Hina

HINATA.68 From Pararakelse With Love (Part I)

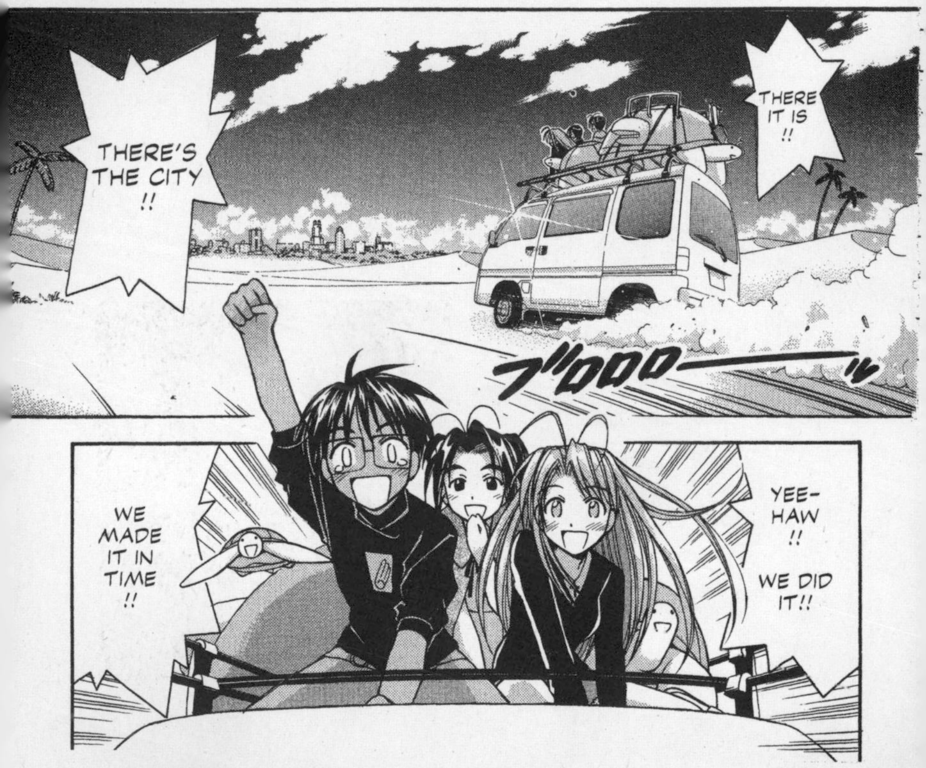
THERE IT IS !!
THERE'S THE CITY !!
YEE-HAW !!
WE DID IT!!
WE MADE IT IN TIME !!

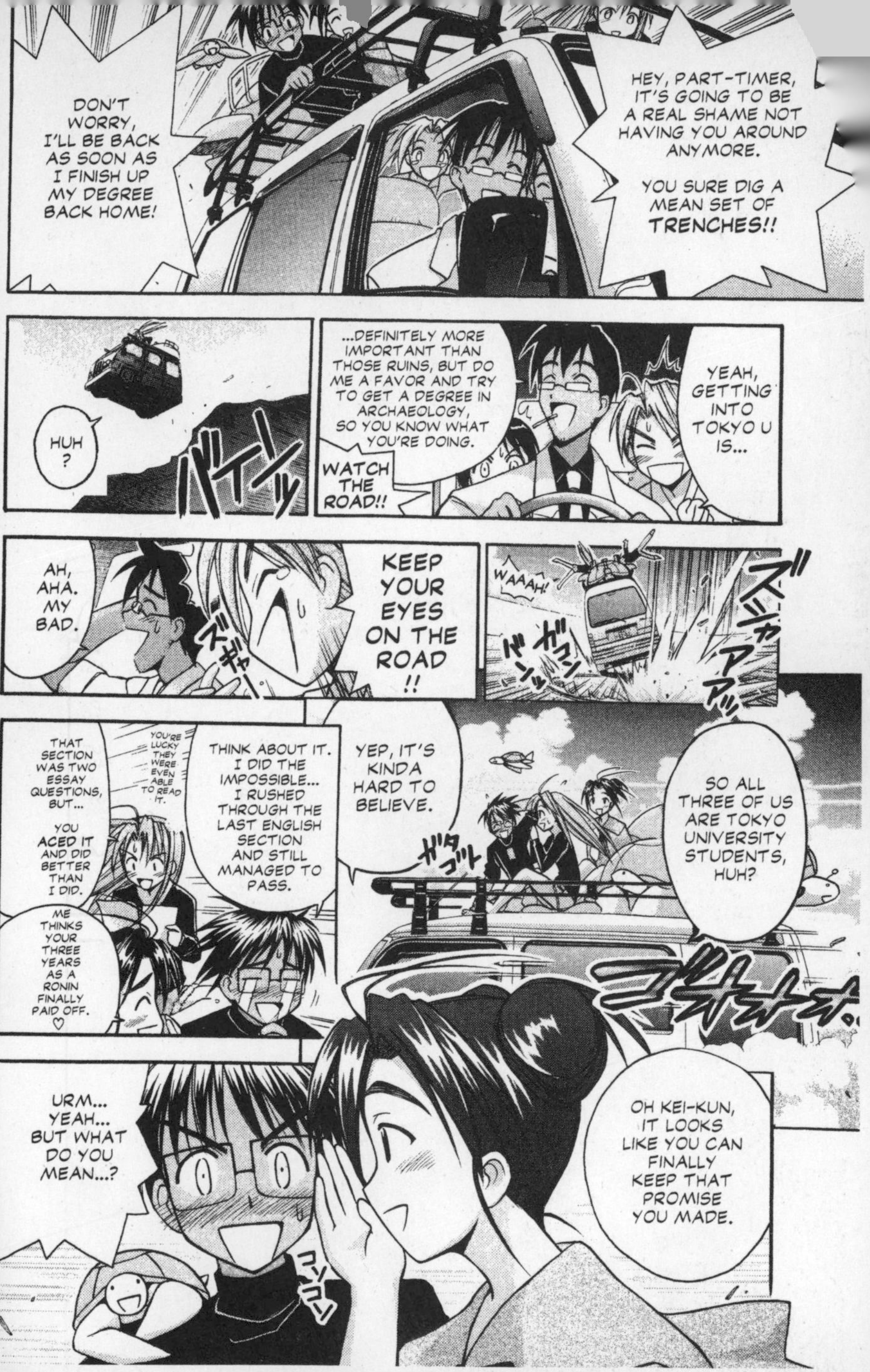
HEY, PART-TIMER, IT'S GOING TO BE A REAL SHAME NOT HAVING YOU AROUND ANYMORE.
YOU SURE DIG A MEAN SET OF TRENCHES!!
DON'T WORRY, I'LL BE BACK AS SOON AS I FINISH UP MY DEGREE BACK HOME!
YEAH, GETTING INTO TOKYO U IS...
...DEFINITELY MORE IMPORTANT THAN THOSE RUINS, BUT DO ME A FAVOR AND TRY TO GET A DEGREE IN ARCHAEOLOGY, SO YOU KNOW WHAT YOU'RE DOING.
WATCH THE ROAD!!
HUH?
WAAAH!
KEEP YOUR EYES ON THE ROAD!!
AH, AHA. MY BAD.
SO ALL THREE OF US ARE TOKYO UNIVERSITY STUDENTS, HUH?
YEP, IT'S KINDA HARD TO BELIEVE.
THINK ABOUT IT. I DID THE IMPOSSIBLE... I RUSHED THROUGH THE LAST ENGLISH SECTION AND STILL MANAGED TO PASS.
YOU'RE LUCKY THEY WERE EVEN ABLE TO READ IT.
THAT SECTION WAS TWO ESSAY QUESTIONS, BUT... YOU ACED IT AND DID BETTER THAN I DID.
ME THINKS YOUR THREE YEARS AS A RONIN FINALLY PAID OFF. ♡
OH KEI-KUN, IT LOOKS LIKE YOU CAN FINALLY KEEP THAT PROMISE YOU MADE.
URM... YEAH... BUT WHAT DO YOU MEAN...?

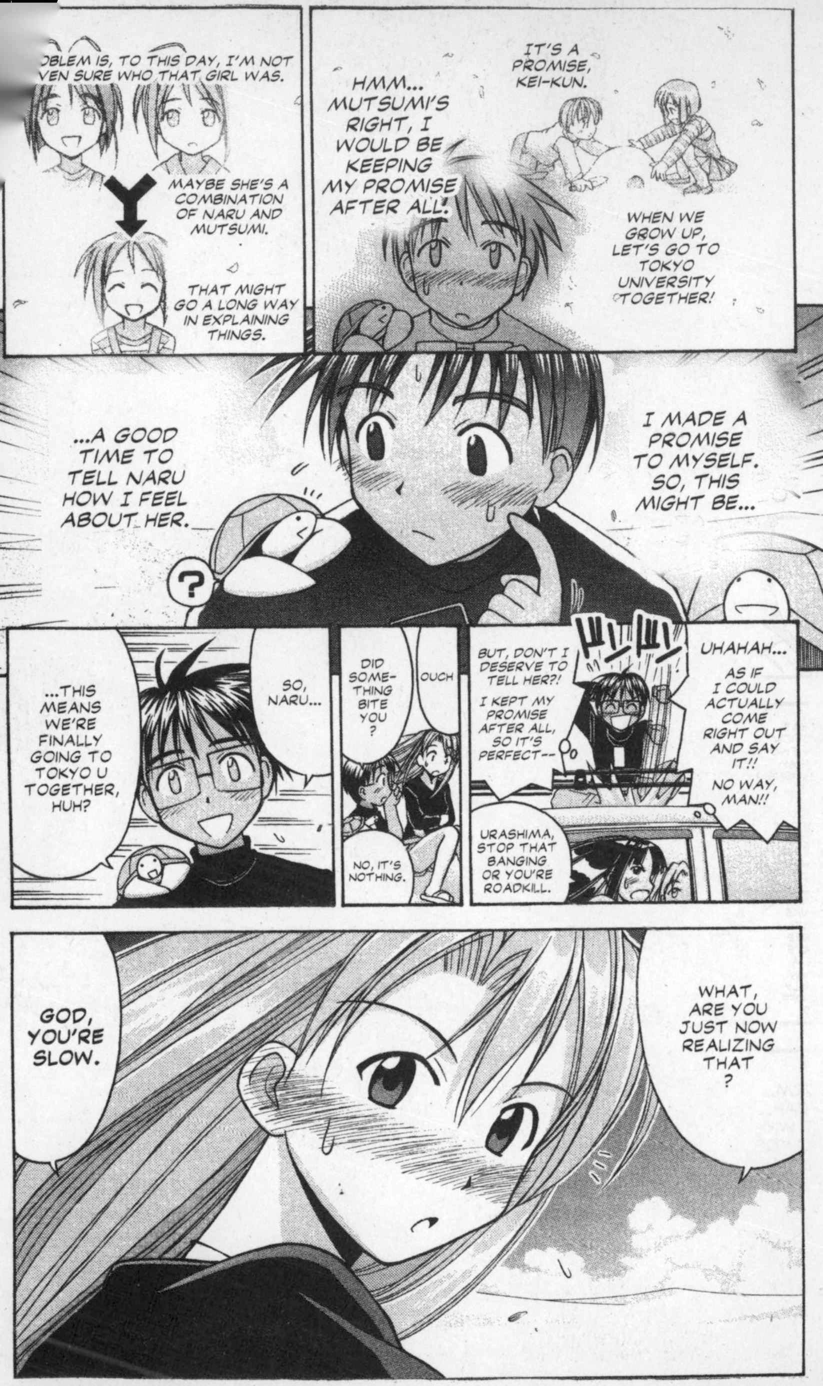
IT'S A PROMISE, KEI-KUN.
WHEN WE GROW UP, LET'S GO TO TOKYO UNIVERSITY TOGETHER!
HMM... MUTSUMI'S RIGHT, I WOULD BE KEEPING MY PROMISE AFTER ALL.
OBLEM IS, TO THIS DAY, I'M NOT VEN SURE WHO THAT GIRL WAS.
MAYBE SHE'S A COMBINATION OF NARU AND MUTSUMI.
THAT MIGHT GO A LONG WAY IN EXPLAINING THINGS.
I MADE A PROMISE TO MYSELF. SO, THIS MIGHT BE...
...A GOOD TIME TO TELL NARU HOW I FEEL ABOUT HER.
?
UHAHAH...
AS IF I COULD ACTUALLY COME RIGHT OUT AND SAY IT!!
NO WAY, MAN!!
BUT, DON'T I DESERVE TO TELL HER?!
I KEPT MY PROMISE AFTER ALL, SO IT'S PERFECT--
URASHIMA, STOP THAT BANGING OR YOU'RE ROADKILL.
OUCH
DID SOMETHING BITE YOU?
NO, IT'S NOTHING.
SO, NARU...
...THIS MEANS WE'RE FINALLY GOING TO TOKYO U TOGETHER, HUH?
WHAT, ARE YOU JUST NOW REALIZING THAT?
GOD, YOU'RE SLOW.

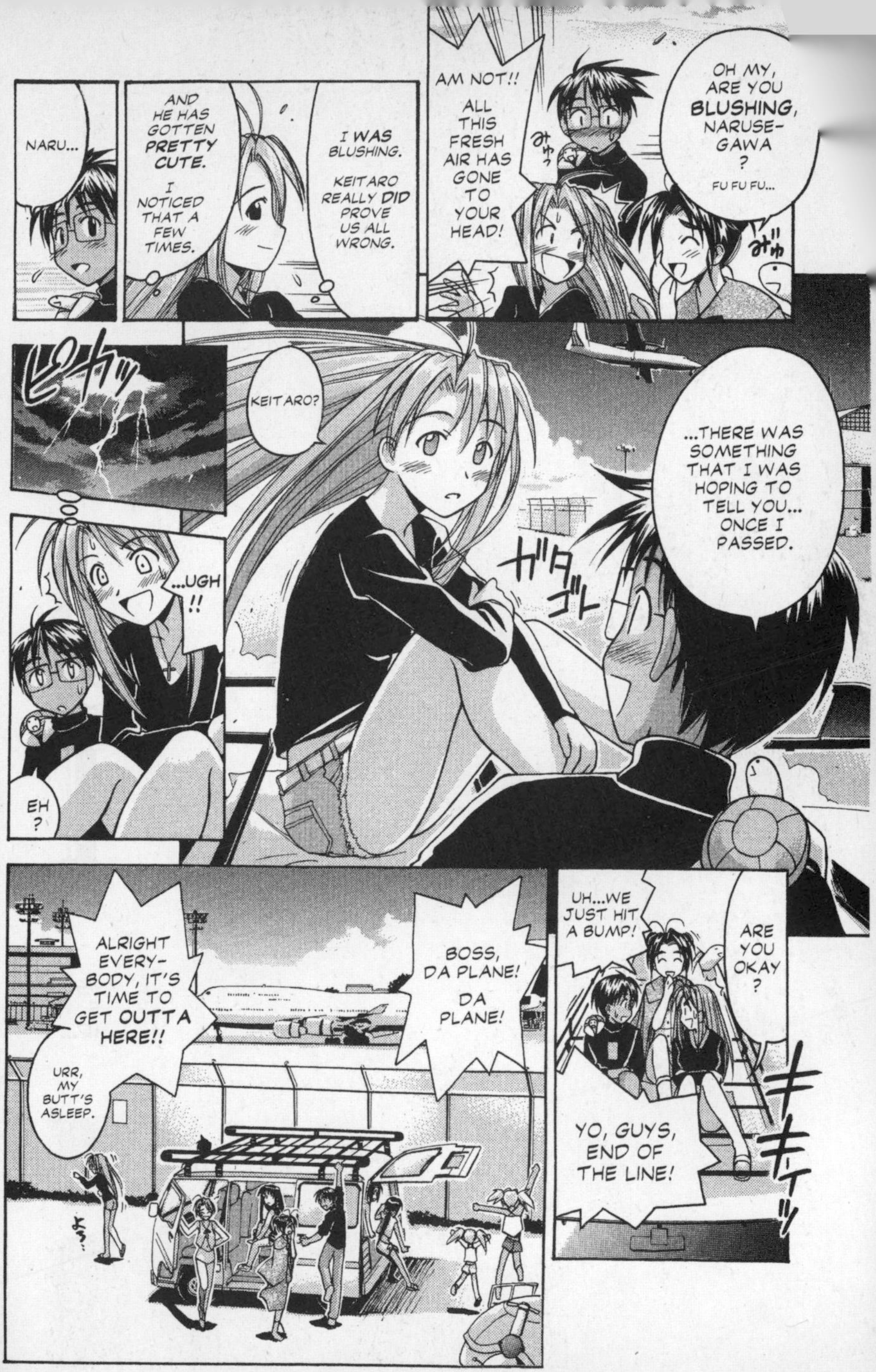
OH MY, ARE YOU BLUSHING, NARUSE-GAWA?
FU FU FU...
AM NOT!!
ALL THIS FRESH AIR HAS GONE TO YOUR HEAD!
I WAS BLUSHING.
KEITARO REALLY DID PROVE US ALL WRONG.
AND HE HAS GOTTEN PRETTY CUTE.
I NOTICED THAT A FEW TIMES.
NARU...
...THERE WAS SOMETHING THAT I WAS HOPING TO TELL YOU... ONCE I PASSED.
KEITARO?
...UGH!!
EH?
ARE YOU OKAY?
UH...WE JUST HIT A BUMP!
YO, GUYS, END OF THE LINE!
BOSS, DA PLANE!
DA PLANE!
ALRIGHT EVERYBODY, IT'S TIME TO GET OUTTA HERE!!
URR, MY BUTT'S ASLEEP.

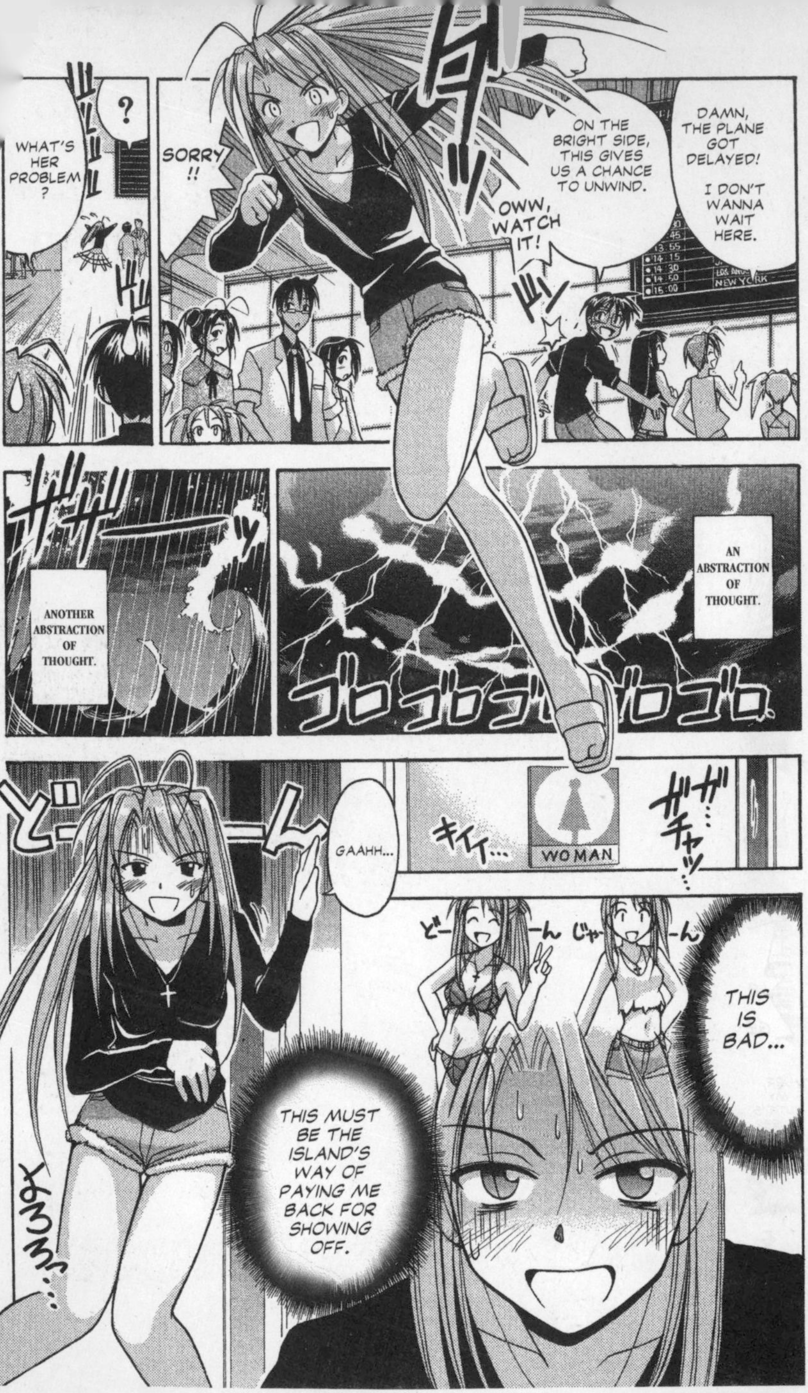
DAMN, THE PLANE GOT DELAYED!
I DON'T WANNA WAIT HERE.
ON THE BRIGHT SIDE, THIS GIVES US A CHANCE TO UNWIND.
OWW, WATCH IT!
SORRY!!
?
WHAT'S HER PROBLEM?
AN ABSTRACTION OF THOUGHT.
ANOTHER ABSTRACTION OF THOUGHT.
WOMAN
GAAHH...
THIS IS BAD...
THIS MUST BE THE ISLAND'S WAY OF PAYING ME BACK FOR SHOWING OFF.

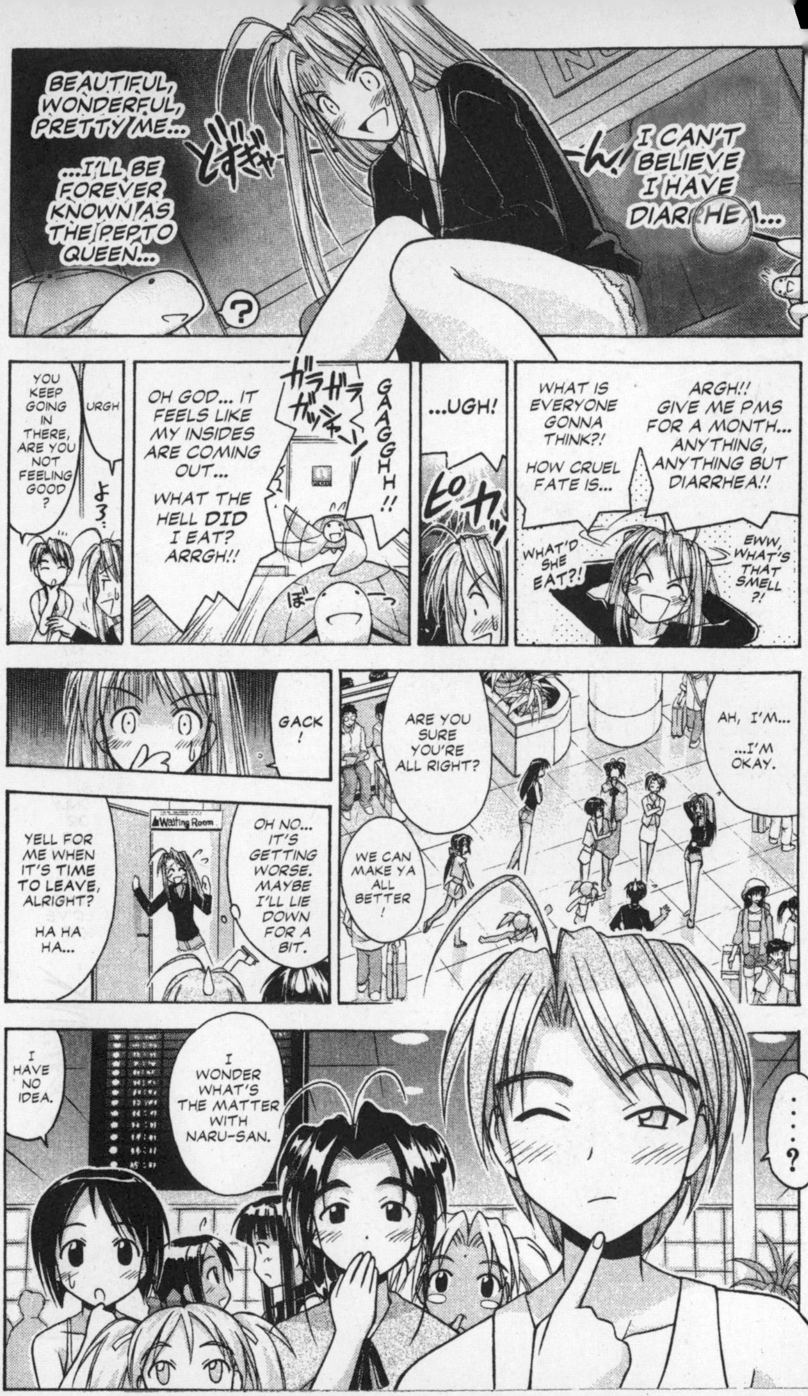

I CAN'T BELIEVE I HAVE DIARRHEA...
ん!
どずぎゃー
BEAUTIFUL, WONDERFUL, PRETTY ME...
...I'LL BE FOREVER KNOWN AS THE PEPTO QUEEN...
?
ARGH!! GIVE ME PMS FOR A MONTH... ANYTHING, ANYTHING BUT DIARRHEA!!
WHAT IS EVERYONE GONNA THINK?!
HOW CRUEL FATE IS...
EWW, WHAT'S THAT SMELL?!
WHAT'D SHE EAT?!
...UGH!
ピカッ
GAAGGH!!
ガラガラガッシャーン
OH GOD... IT FEELS LIKE MY INSIDES ARE COMING OUT...
WHAT THE HELL DID I EAT? ARRGH!!
ぼー
URGH
YOU KEEP GOING IN THERE, ARE YOU NOT FEELING GOOD?
よろ...
AH, I'M...
...I'M OKAY.
ARE YOU SURE YOU'RE ALL RIGHT?
WE CAN MAKE YA ALL BETTER!
GACK!
OH NO... IT'S GETTING WORSE. MAYBE I'LL LIE DOWN FOR A BIT.
Waiting Room
YELL FOR ME WHEN IT'S TIME TO LEAVE, ALRIGHT?
HA HA HA...
...?
I WONDER WHAT'S THE MATTER WITH NARU-SAN.
I HAVE NO IDEA.

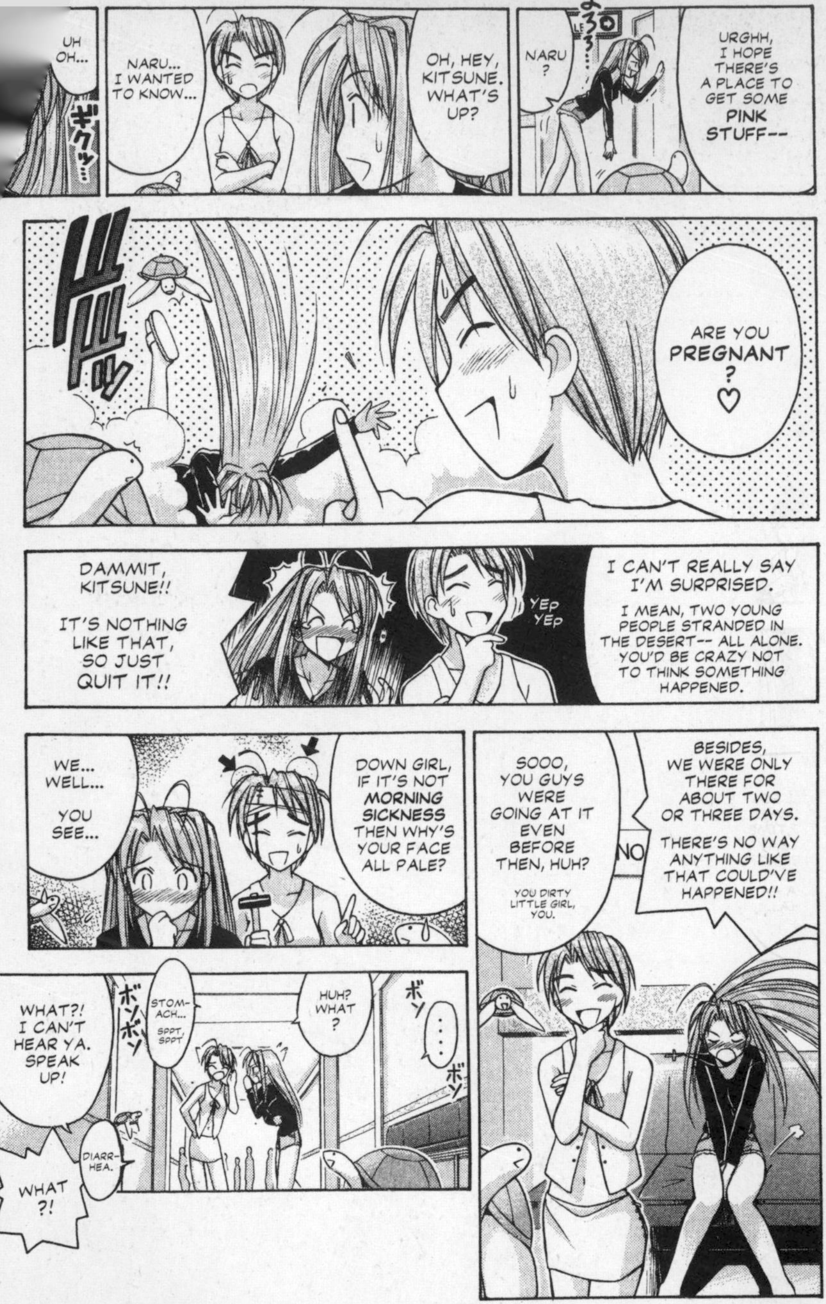

よろろ…
URGHH, I HOPE THERE'S A PLACE TO GET SOME PINK STUFF--
NARU?
OH, HEY, KITSUNE. WHAT'S UP?
NARU... I WANTED TO KNOW...
UH OH...
ギクッ…
ARE YOU PREGNANT? ♡
I CAN'T REALLY SAY I'M SURPRISED.
I MEAN, TWO YOUNG PEOPLE STRANDED IN THE DESERT-- ALL ALONE. YOU'D BE CRAZY NOT TO THINK SOMETHING HAPPENED.
YEP YEP
DAMMIT, KITSUNE!!
IT'S NOTHING LIKE THAT, SO JUST QUIT IT!!
BESIDES, WE WERE ONLY THERE FOR ABOUT TWO OR THREE DAYS.
THERE'S NO WAY ANYTHING LIKE THAT COULD'VE HAPPENED!!
SOOO, YOU GUYS WERE GOING AT IT EVEN BEFORE THEN, HUH?
YOU DIRTY LITTLE GIRL, YOU.
DOWN GIRL, IF IT'S NOT MORNING SICKNESS THEN WHY'S YOUR FACE ALL PALE?
WE... WELL...
YOU SEE...
ボソ
ボソ
HUH? WHAT?
STOM-ACH...
SPPT, SPPT
ボソボソ
WHAT?! I CAN'T HEAR YA. SPEAK UP!
DIARR-HEA.
WHAT?!

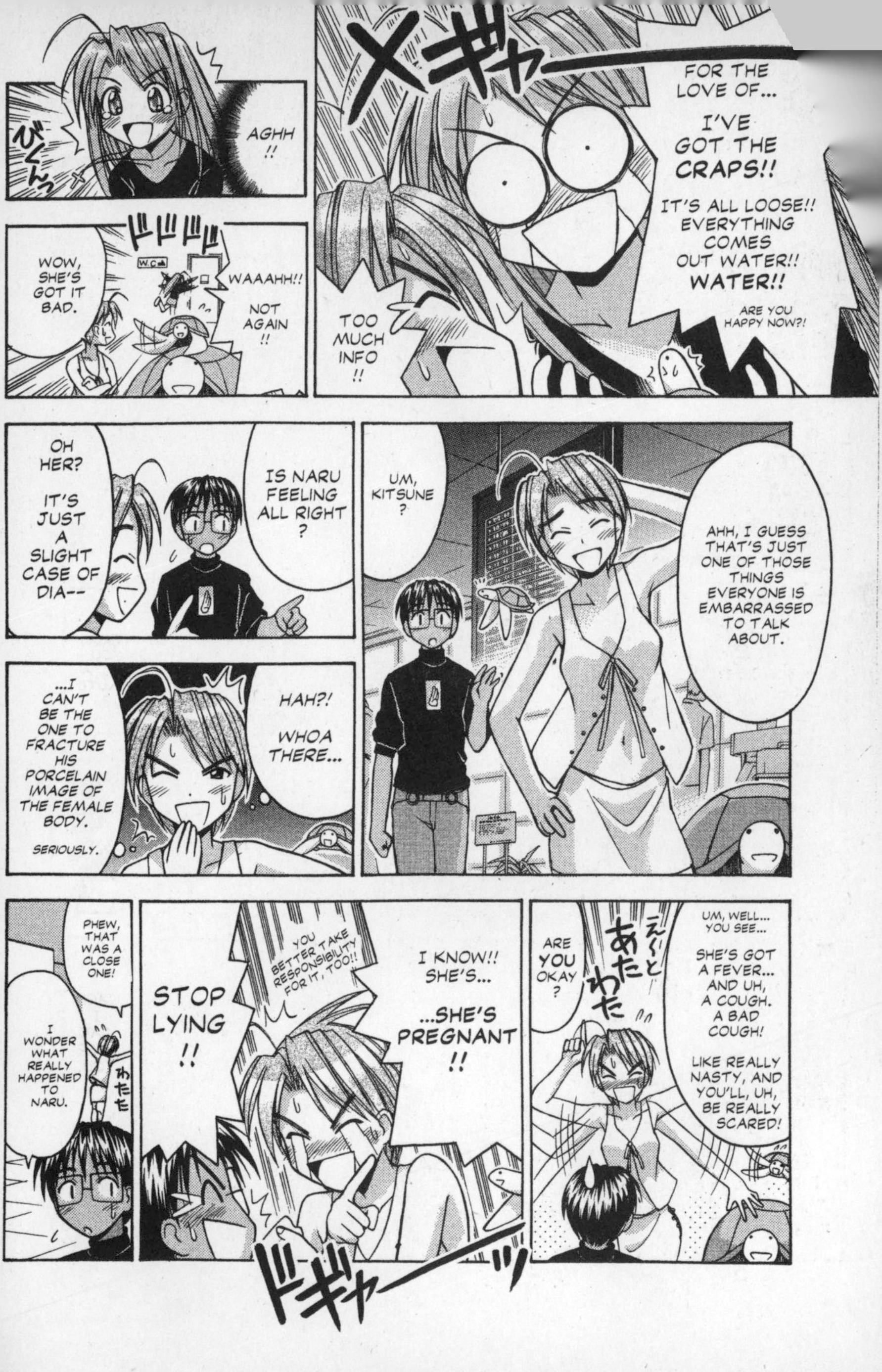
メギャー
FOR THE LOVE OF...
I'VE GOT THE CRAPS!!
IT'S ALL LOOSE!! EVERYTHING COMES OUT WATER!! WATER!!
ARE YOU HAPPY NOW?!
TOO MUCH INFO !!
びくんっ
AGHH !!
ドドドド
W.C.
WAAAHH!!
NOT AGAIN !!
WOW, SHE'S GOT IT BAD.
UM, KITSUNE ?
AHH, I GUESS THAT'S JUST ONE OF THOSE THINGS EVERYONE IS EMBARRASSED TO TALK ABOUT.
IS NARU FEELING ALL RIGHT ?
OH HER?
IT'S JUST A SLIGHT CASE OF DIA--
HAH?!
WHOA THERE...
...I CAN'T BE THE ONE TO FRACTURE HIS PORCELAIN IMAGE OF THE FEMALE BODY.
SERIOUSLY.
えーと
あたわた
ARE YOU OKAY ?
UM, WELL... YOU SEE...
SHE'S GOT A FEVER... AND UH, A COUGH. A BAD COUGH!
LIKE REALLY NASTY, AND YOU'LL, UH, BE REALLY SCARED!
I KNOW!! SHE'S...
...SHE'S PREGNANT !!
YOU BETTER TAKE RESPONSIBILITY FOR IT, TOO!!
STOP LYING !!
ドギャーッ
PHEW, THAT WAS A CLOSE ONE!
I WONDER WHAT REALLY HAPPENED TO NARU.
わたた

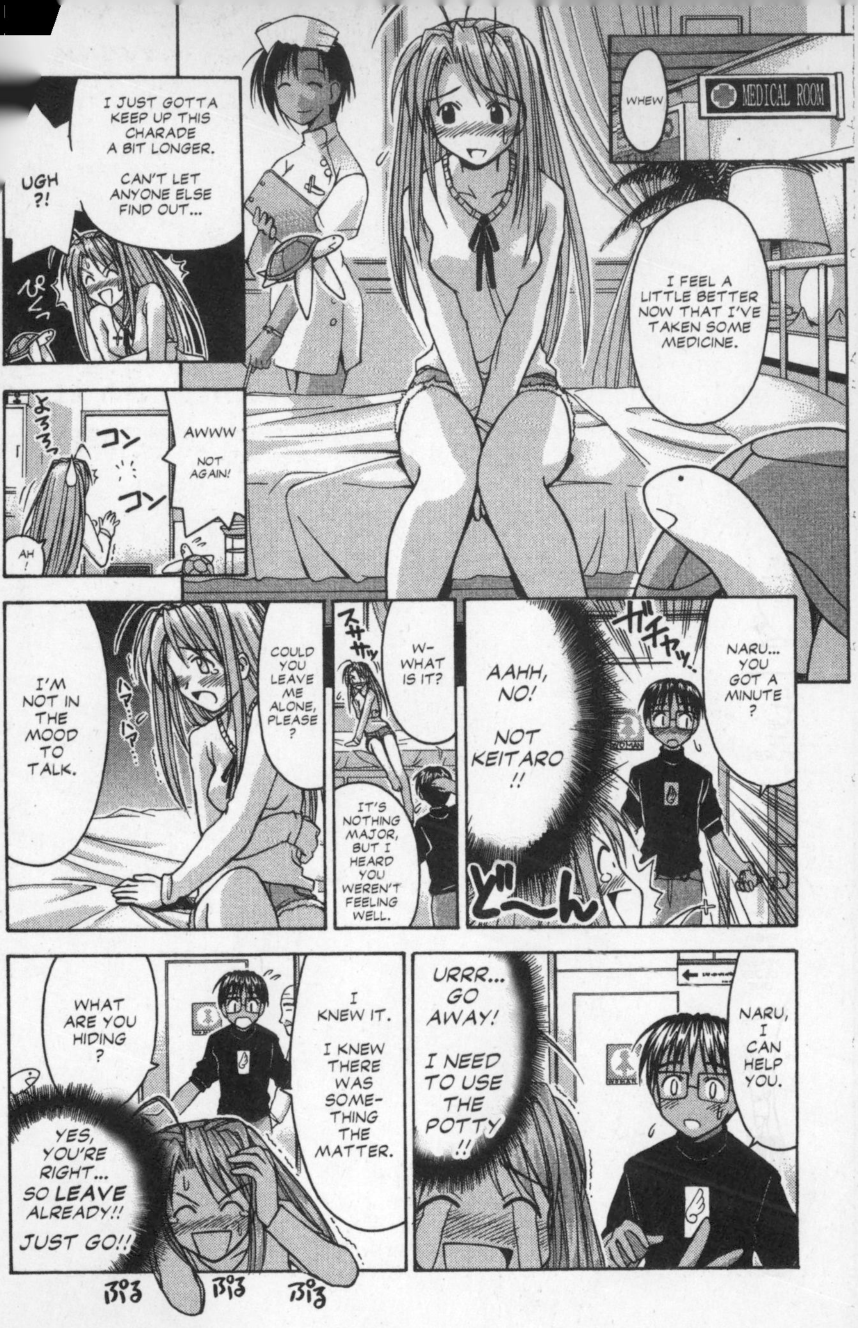
MEDICAL ROOM
WHEW
I FEEL A LITTLE BETTER NOW THAT I'VE TAKEN SOME MEDICINE.
I JUST GOTTA KEEP UP THIS CHARADE A BIT LONGER.
CAN'T LET ANYONE ELSE FIND OUT...
UGH ?!
ぴくっ
AWWW
NOT AGAIN!
よろろっ
コン
コン
AH !
NARU... YOU GOT A MINUTE ?
ガチャッ
AAHH, NO!
NOT KEITARO !!
どーん
W-WHAT IS IT?
スサササッ
IT'S NOTHING MAJOR, BUT I HEARD YOU WEREN'T FEELING WELL.
COULD YOU LEAVE ME ALONE, PLEASE ?
I'M NOT IN THE MOOD TO TALK.
NARU, I CAN HELP YOU.
URRR... GO AWAY!
I NEED TO USE THE POTTY !!
I KNEW IT.
I KNEW THERE WAS SOMETHING THE MATTER.
WHAT ARE YOU HIDING ?
YES, YOU'RE RIGHT... SO LEAVE ALREADY!!
JUST GO!!
ぷる ぷる ぷる

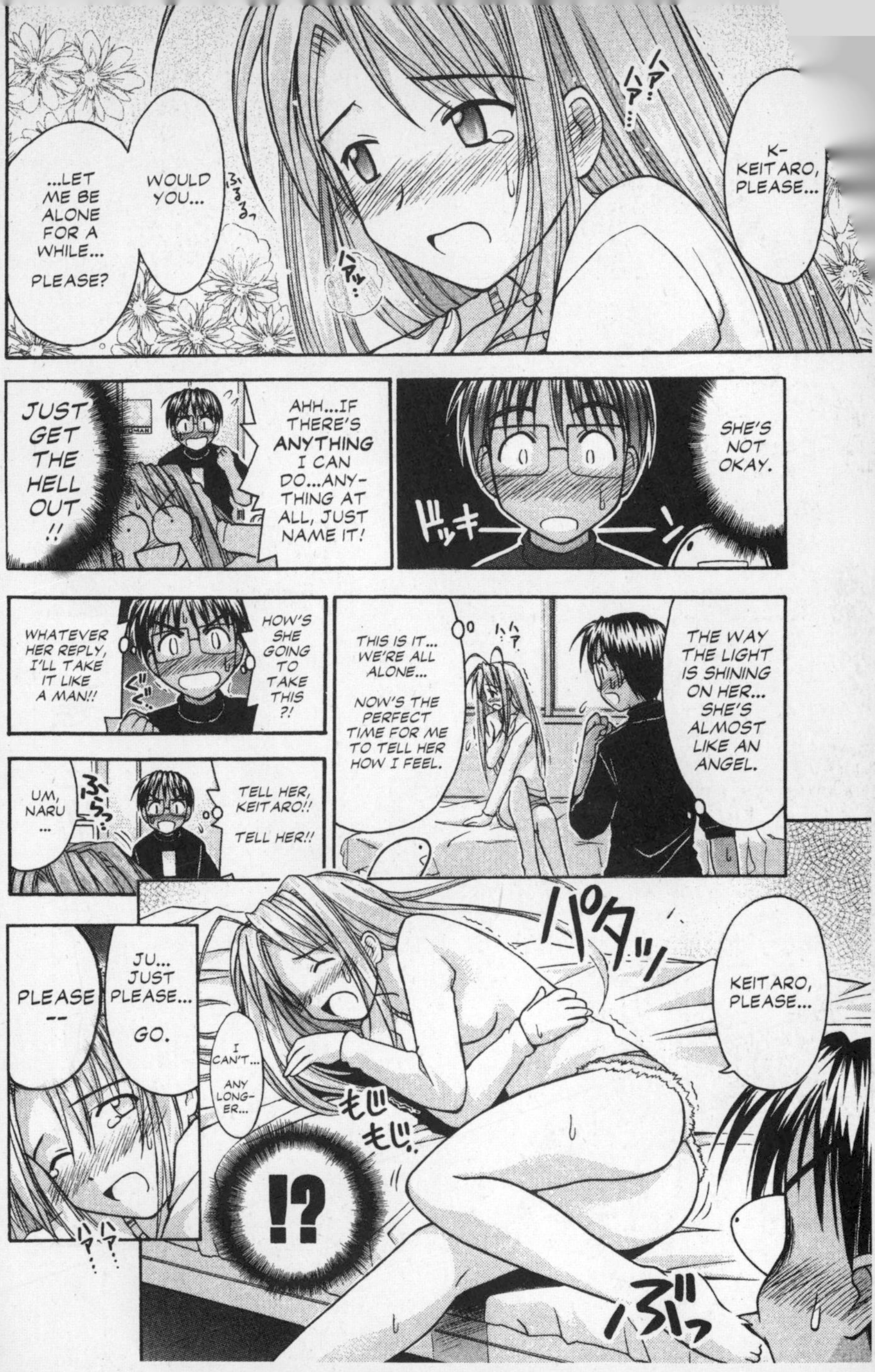
K-KEITARO, PLEASE...
WOULD YOU...
...LET ME BE ALONE FOR A WHILE... PLEASE?
SHE'S NOT OKAY.
ドッキーン
AHH...IF THERE'S ANYTHING I CAN DO...ANYTHING AT ALL, JUST NAME IT!
JUST GET THE HELL OUT!!
THE WAY THE LIGHT IS SHINING ON HER... SHE'S ALMOST LIKE AN ANGEL.
THIS IS IT... WE'RE ALL ALONE... NOW'S THE PERFECT TIME FOR ME TO TELL HER HOW I FEEL.
HOW'S SHE GOING TO TAKE THIS?!
WHATEVER HER REPLY, I'LL TAKE IT LIKE A MAN!!
TELL HER, KEITARO!! TELL HER!!
UM, NARU ...
KEITARO, PLEASE...
パタッ
I CAN'T... ANY LONGER...
もじもじ
!?
ぶっ
JU... JUST PLEASE... GO.
PLEASE --

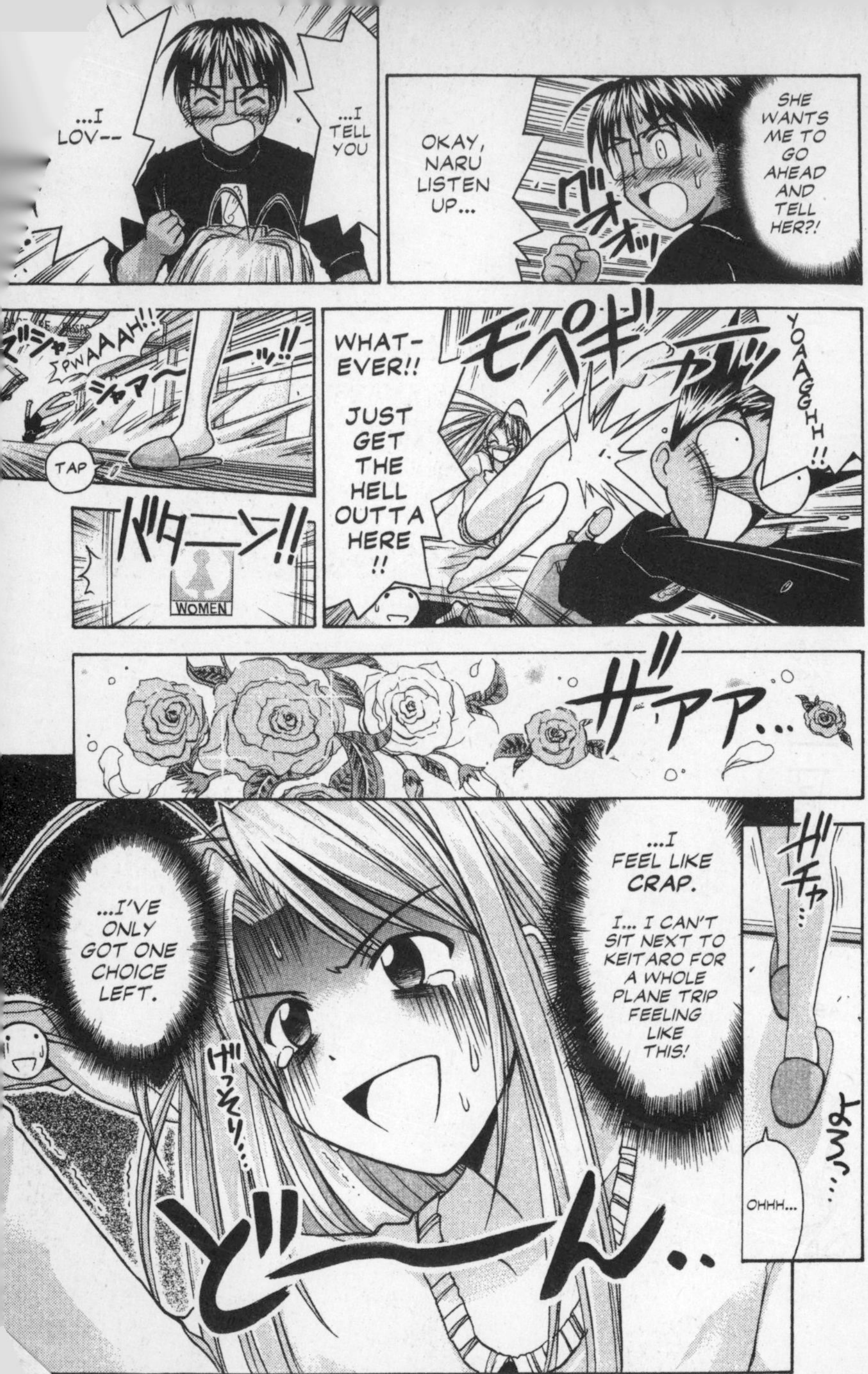
SHE WANTS ME TO GO AHEAD AND TELL HER?!
OKAY, NARU LISTEN UP...
...I TELL YOU
...I LOV--
YOAAGGHH!!
WHAT-EVER!!
JUST GET THE HELL OUTTA HERE!!
PWAAAAH!!
TAP
WOMEN
...I FEEL LIKE CRAP.
I... I CAN'T SIT NEXT TO KEITARO FOR A WHOLE PLANE TRIP FEELING LIKE THIS!
...I'VE ONLY GOT ONE CHOICE LEFT.
OHHH...

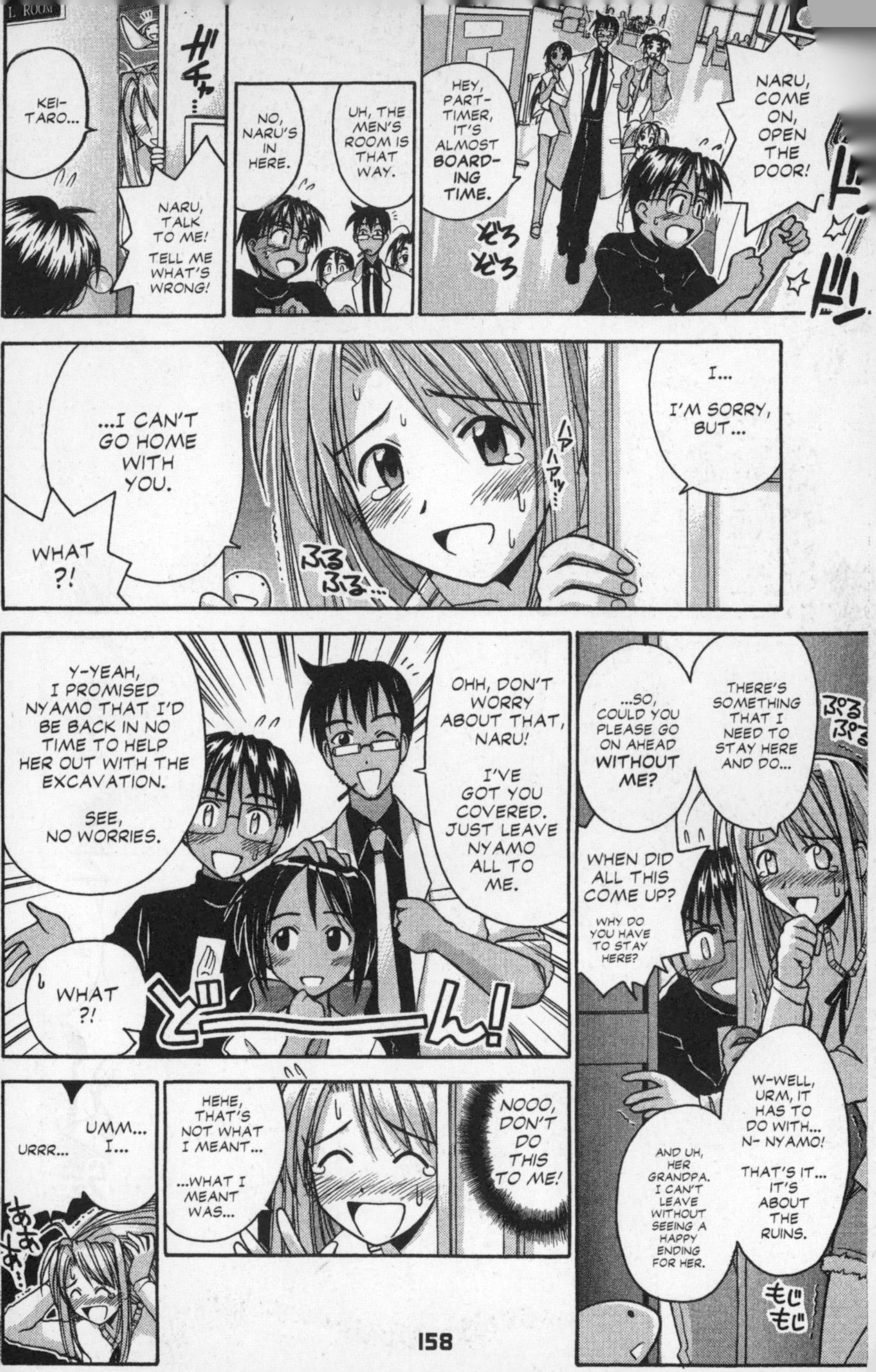
NARU, COME ON, OPEN THE DOOR!
HEY, PART-TIMER, IT'S ALMOST BOARDING TIME.
ぞろぞろ
UH, THE MEN'S ROOM IS THAT WAY.
NO, NARU'S IN HERE.
ガチャ…
KEI-TARO...
NARU, TALK TO ME! TELL ME WHAT'S WRONG!
I... I'M SORRY, BUT...
ハァハァッ…
...I CAN'T GO HOME WITH YOU.
ふるふる…
WHAT ?!
ぷるぷる
THERE'S SOMETHING THAT I NEED TO STAY HERE AND DO...
...SO, COULD YOU PLEASE GO ON AHEAD WITHOUT ME?
WHEN DID ALL THIS COME UP?
WHY DO YOU HAVE TO STAY HERE?
W-WELL, URM, IT HAS TO DO WITH... N- NYAMO! THAT'S IT... IT'S ABOUT THE RUINS.
AND UH, HER GRANDPA. I CAN'T LEAVE WITHOUT SEEING A HAPPY ENDING FOR HER.
もじもじ
OHH, DON'T WORRY ABOUT THAT, NARU! I'VE GOT YOU COVERED. JUST LEAVE NYAMO ALL TO ME.
Y-YEAH, I PROMISED NYAMO THAT I'D BE BACK IN NO TIME TO HELP HER OUT WITH THE EXCAVATION. SEE, NO WORRIES.
どーーん!
WHAT ?!
NOOO, DON'T DO THIS TO ME!
HEHE, THAT'S NOT WHAT I MEANT... ...WHAT I MEANT WAS...
UMM... I...
URRR...

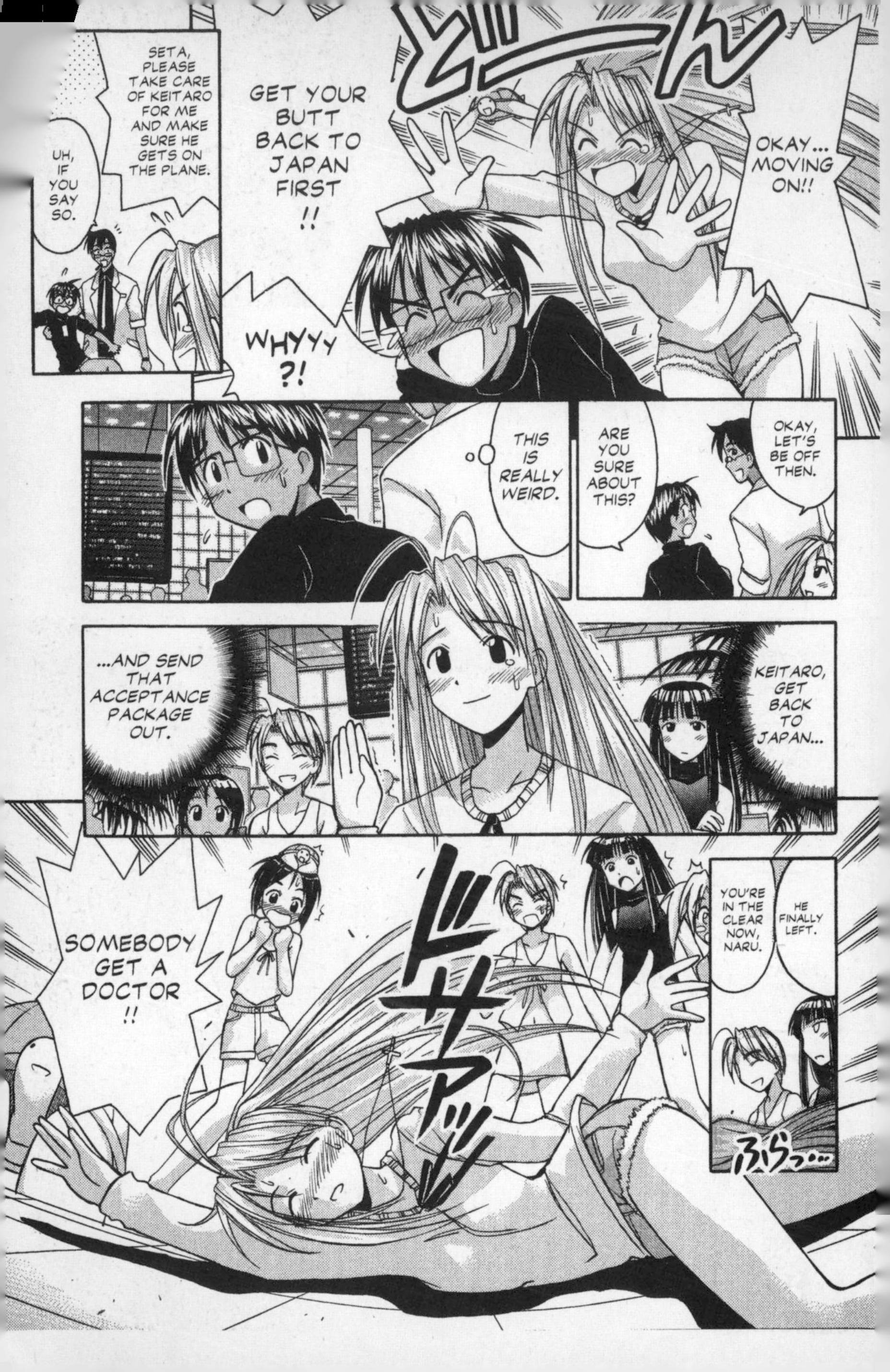
どーん
OKAY... MOVING ON!!
GET YOUR BUTT BACK TO JAPAN FIRST!!
WHYYY?!
SETA, PLEASE TAKE CARE OF KEITARO FOR ME AND MAKE SURE HE GETS ON THE PLANE.
UH, IF YOU SAY SO.
OKAY, LET'S BE OFF THEN.
ARE YOU SURE ABOUT THIS?
THIS IS REALLY WEIRD.
KEITARO, GET BACK TO JAPAN...
...AND SEND THAT ACCEPTANCE PACKAGE OUT.
HE FINALLY LEFT.
YOU'RE IN THE CLEAR NOW, NARU.
ふらっ…
ドサァッ
SOMEBODY GET A DOCTOR!!

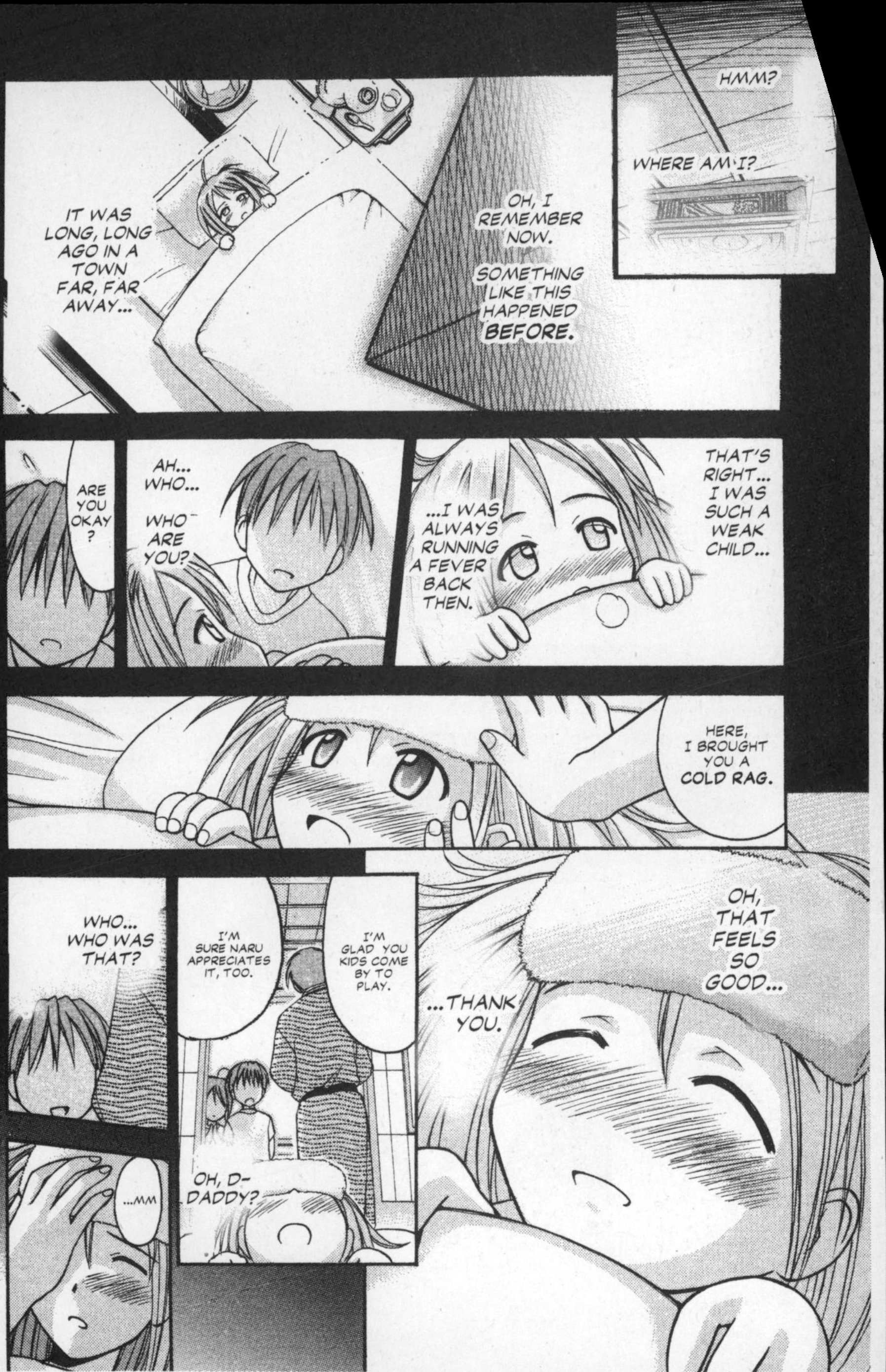
HMM?
WHERE AM I?
OH, I REMEMBER NOW.
SOMETHING LIKE THIS HAPPENED BEFORE.
IT WAS LONG, LONG AGO IN A TOWN FAR, FAR AWAY...
THAT'S RIGHT... I WAS SUCH A WEAK CHILD...
...I WAS ALWAYS RUNNING A FEVER BACK THEN.
AH... WHO...
WHO ARE YOU?
ARE YOU OKAY?
HERE, I BROUGHT YOU A COLD RAG.
OH, THAT FEELS SO GOOD...
...THANK YOU.
I'M GLAD YOU KIDS COME BY TO PLAY.
I'M SURE NARU APPRECIATES IT, TOO.
OH, D-DADDY?
WHO... WHO WAS THAT?
...MM

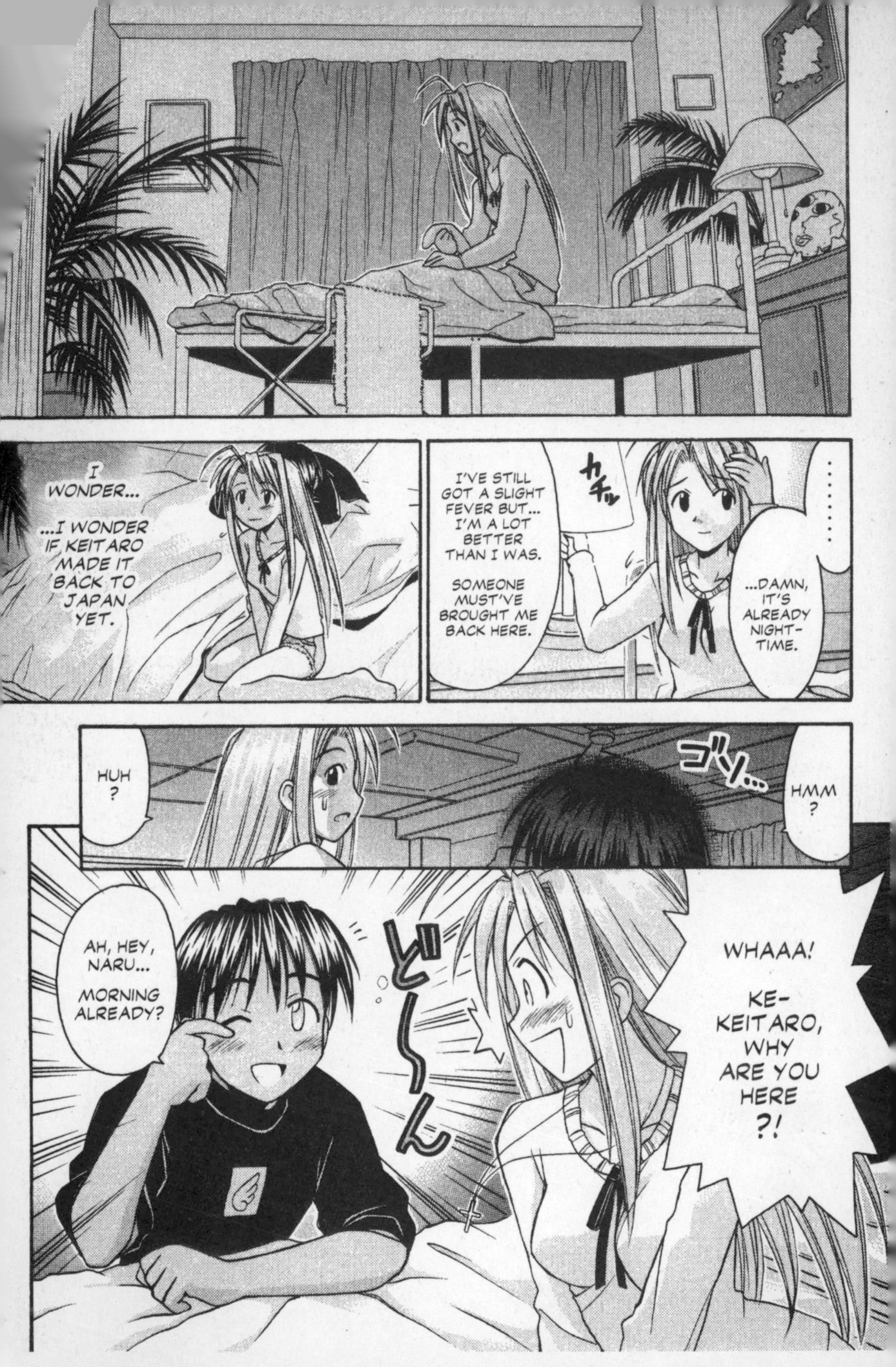
....
...DAMN, IT'S ALREADY NIGHT-TIME.
カチッ
I'VE STILL GOT A SLIGHT FEVER BUT... I'M A LOT BETTER THAN I WAS.
SOMEONE MUST'VE BROUGHT ME BACK HERE.
I WONDER...
...I WONDER IF KEITARO MADE IT BACK TO JAPAN YET.
HMM?
ゴソ...
HUH?
WHAAA!
KE-KEITARO, WHY ARE YOU HERE?!
どーん
AH, HEY, NARU...
MORNING ALREADY?

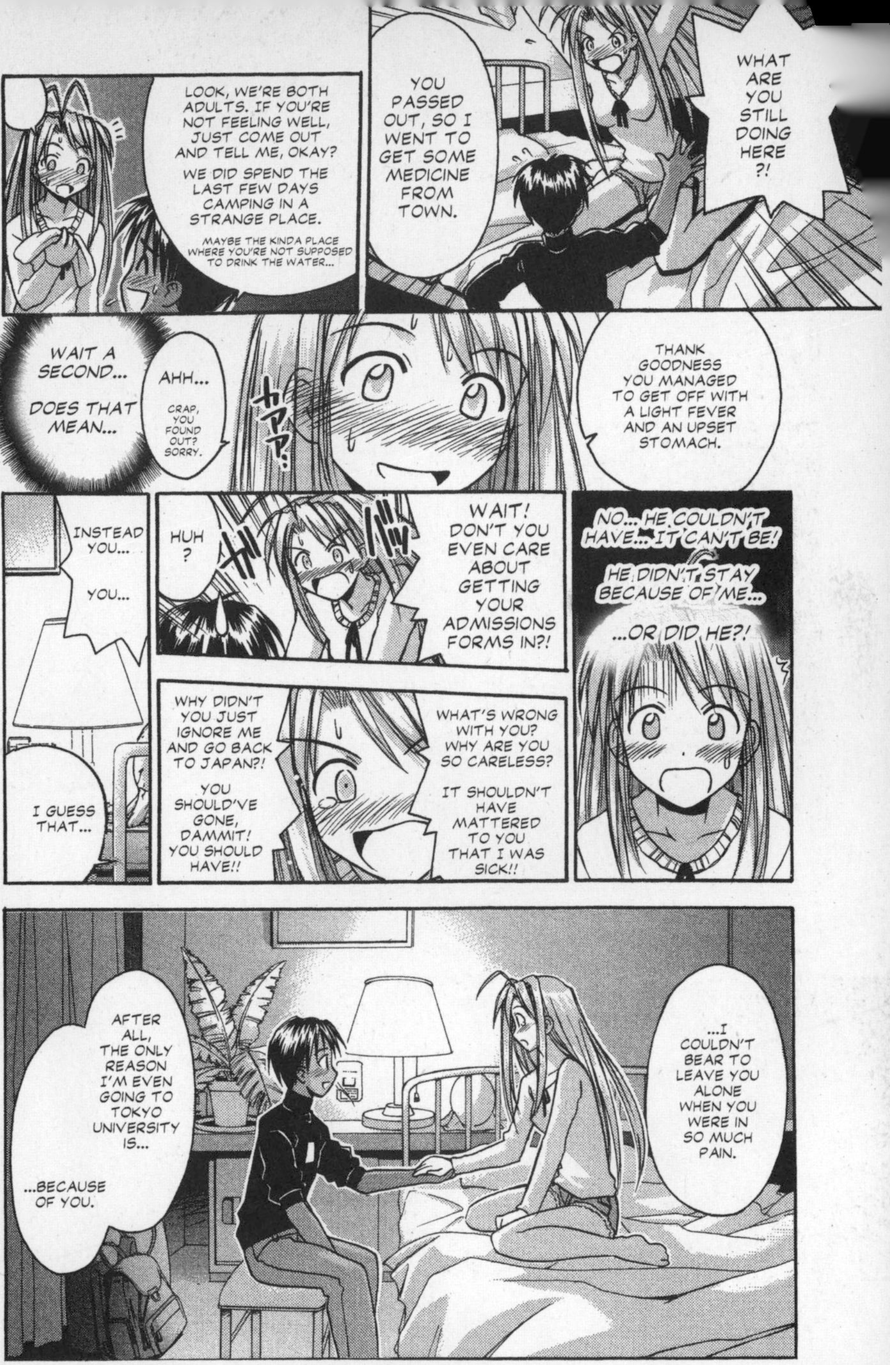

WHAT ARE YOU STILL DOING HERE?!
YOU PASSED OUT, SO I WENT TO GET SOME MEDICINE FROM TOWN.
LOOK, WE'RE BOTH ADULTS. IF YOU'RE NOT FEELING WELL, JUST COME OUT AND TELL ME, OKAY?
WE DID SPEND THE LAST FEW DAYS CAMPING IN A STRANGE PLACE.
MAYBE THE KINDA PLACE WHERE YOU'RE NOT SUPPOSED TO DRINK THE WATER...
THANK GOODNESS YOU MANAGED TO GET OFF WITH A LIGHT FEVER AND AN UPSET STOMACH.
AHH...
CRAP, YOU FOUND OUT? SORRY.
WAIT A SECOND...
DOES THAT MEAN...
NO... HE COULDN'T HAVE... IT CAN'T BE!
HE DIDN'T STAY BECAUSE OF ME...
...OR DID HE?!
WAIT! DON'T YOU EVEN CARE ABOUT GETTING YOUR ADMISSIONS FORMS IN?!
HUH?
WHAT'S WRONG WITH YOU? WHY ARE YOU SO CARELESS?
IT SHOULDN'T HAVE MATTERED TO YOU THAT I WAS SICK!!
WHY DIDN'T YOU JUST IGNORE ME AND GO BACK TO JAPAN?!
YOU SHOULD'VE GONE, DAMMIT! YOU SHOULD HAVE!!
INSTEAD YOU...
YOU...
I GUESS THAT...
...I COULDN'T BEAR TO LEAVE YOU ALONE WHEN YOU WERE IN SO MUCH PAIN.
AFTER ALL, THE ONLY REASON I'M EVEN GOING TO TOKYO UNIVERSITY IS...
...BECAUSE OF YOU.

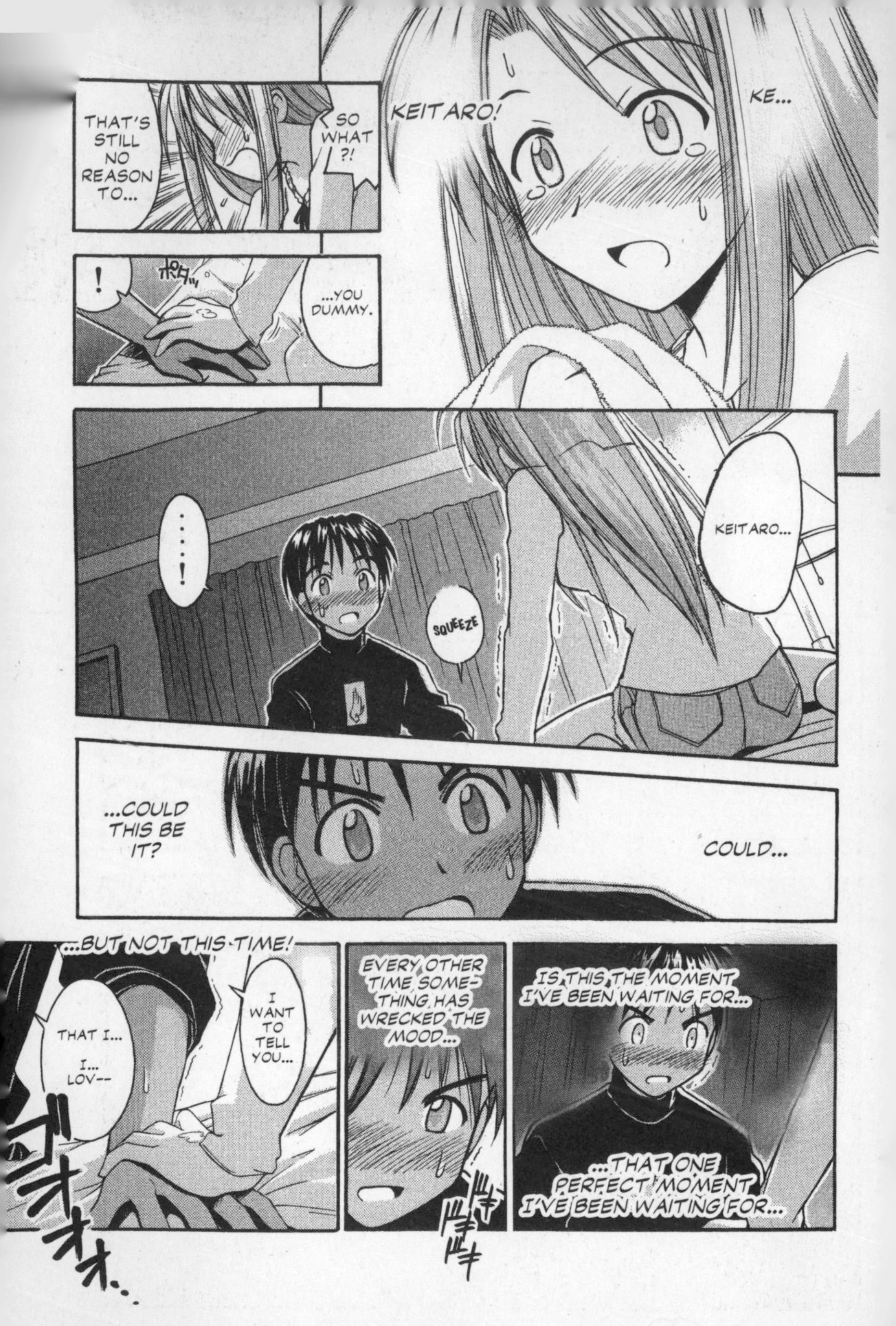
KE...
KEITARO!
SO WHAT ?!
THAT'S STILL NO REASON TO...
...YOU DUMMY.
!
KEITARO...
SQUEEZE
....!
COULD...
...COULD THIS BE IT?
IS THIS THE MOMENT I'VE BEEN WAITING FOR...
...THAT ONE PERFECT MOMENT I'VE BEEN WAITING FOR...
EVERY OTHER TIME SOME-THING HAS WRECKED THE MOOD...
...BUT NOT THIS TIME!
I WANT TO TELL YOU...
THAT I... I... LOV--

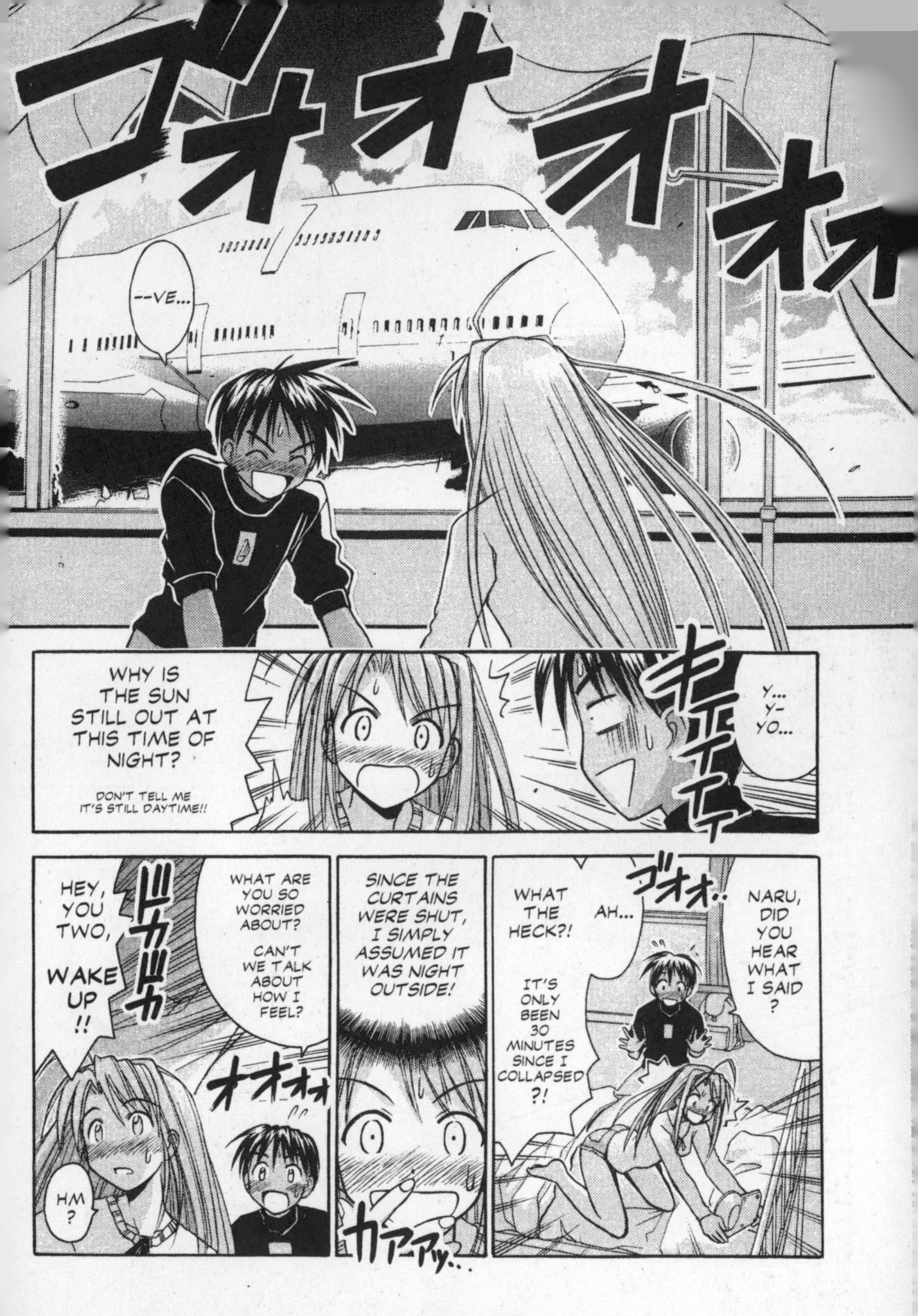
ゴオオオオ
--VE...
Y... Y-YO...
WHY IS THE SUN STILL OUT AT THIS TIME OF NIGHT?
DON'T TELL ME IT'S STILL DAYTIME!!
NARU, DID YOU HEAR WHAT I SAID?
ゴオオ..
AH...
WHAT THE HECK?!
IT'S ONLY BEEN 30 MINUTES SINCE I COLLAPSED?!
SINCE THE CURTAINS WERE SHUT, I SIMPLY ASSUMED IT WAS NIGHT OUTSIDE!
WHAT ARE YOU SO WORRIED ABOUT?
CAN'T WE TALK ABOUT HOW I FEEL?
HEY, YOU TWO, WAKE UP!!
HM?

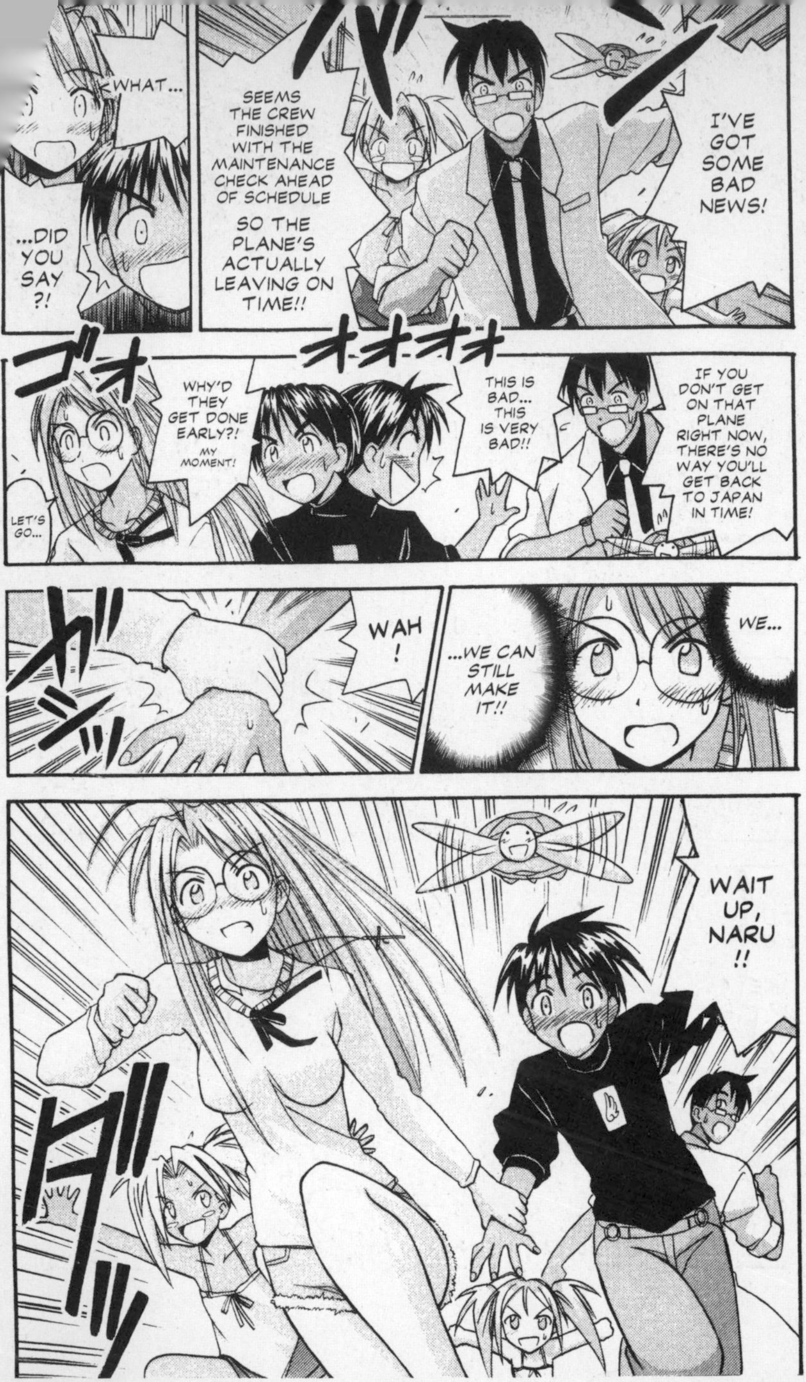
I'VE GOT SOME BAD NEWS!
SEEMS THE CREW FINISHED WITH THE MAINTENANCE CHECK AHEAD OF SCHEDULE
SO THE PLANE'S ACTUALLY LEAVING ON TIME!!
WHAT...
...DID YOU SAY?!
ゴオオオオオ
IF YOU DON'T GET ON THAT PLANE RIGHT NOW, THERE'S NO WAY YOU'LL GET BACK TO JAPAN IN TIME!
THIS IS BAD... THIS IS VERY BAD!!
WHY'D THEY GET DONE EARLY?!
MY MOMENT!
LET'S GO...
WE...
...WE CAN STILL MAKE IT!!
WAH!
ガシッ
WAIT UP, NARU!!
ダッ

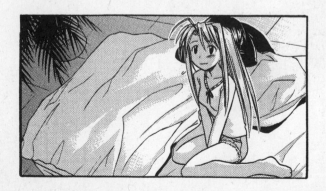

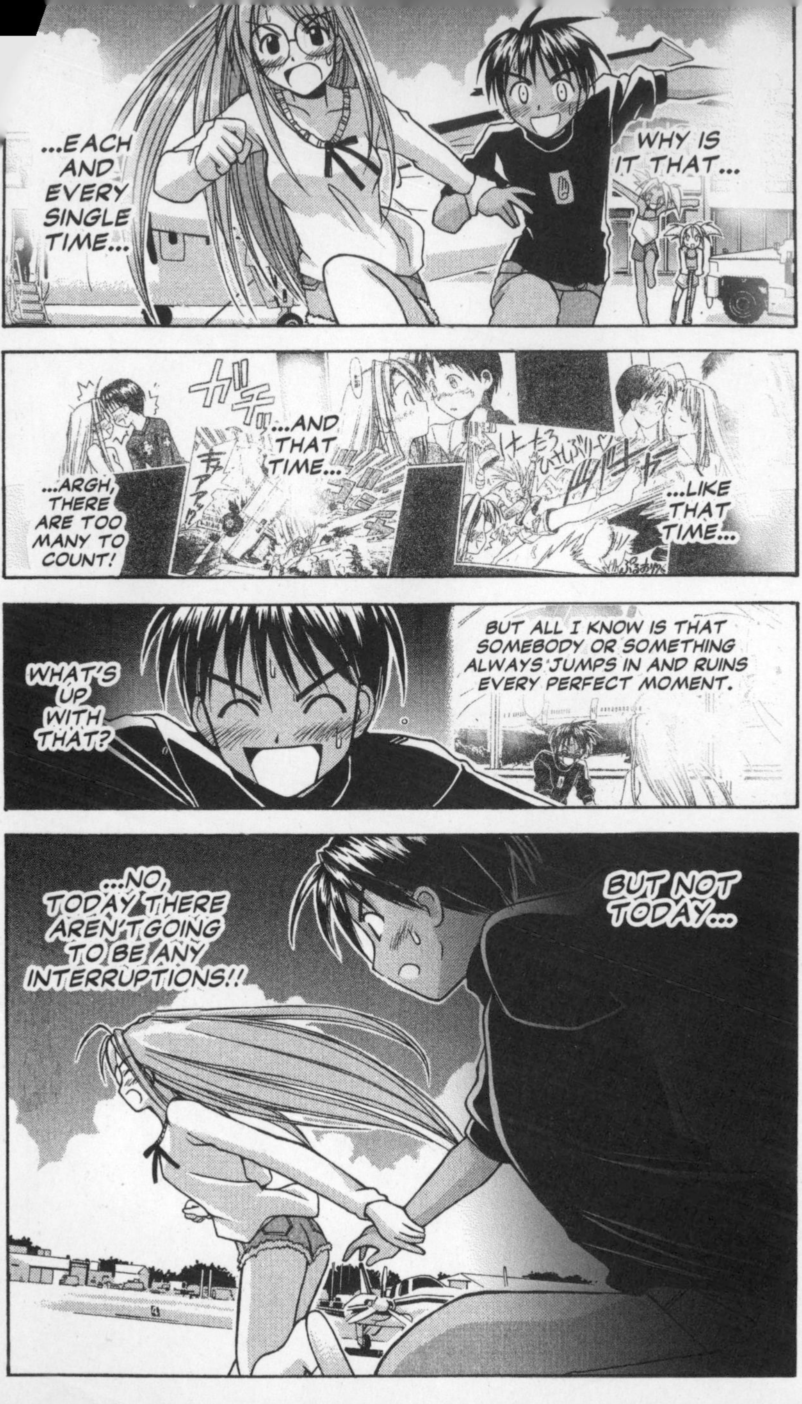
WHY IS IT THAT...
...EACH AND EVERY SINGLE TIME...
...LIKE THAT TIME...
...AND THAT TIME...
...ARGH, THERE ARE TOO MANY TO COUNT!
BUT ALL I KNOW IS THAT SOMEBODY OR SOMETHING ALWAYS JUMPS IN AND RUINS EVERY PERFECT MOMENT.
WHAT'S UP WITH THAT?
BUT NOT TODAY...
...NO, TODAY THERE AREN'T GOING TO BE ANY INTERRUPTIONS!!

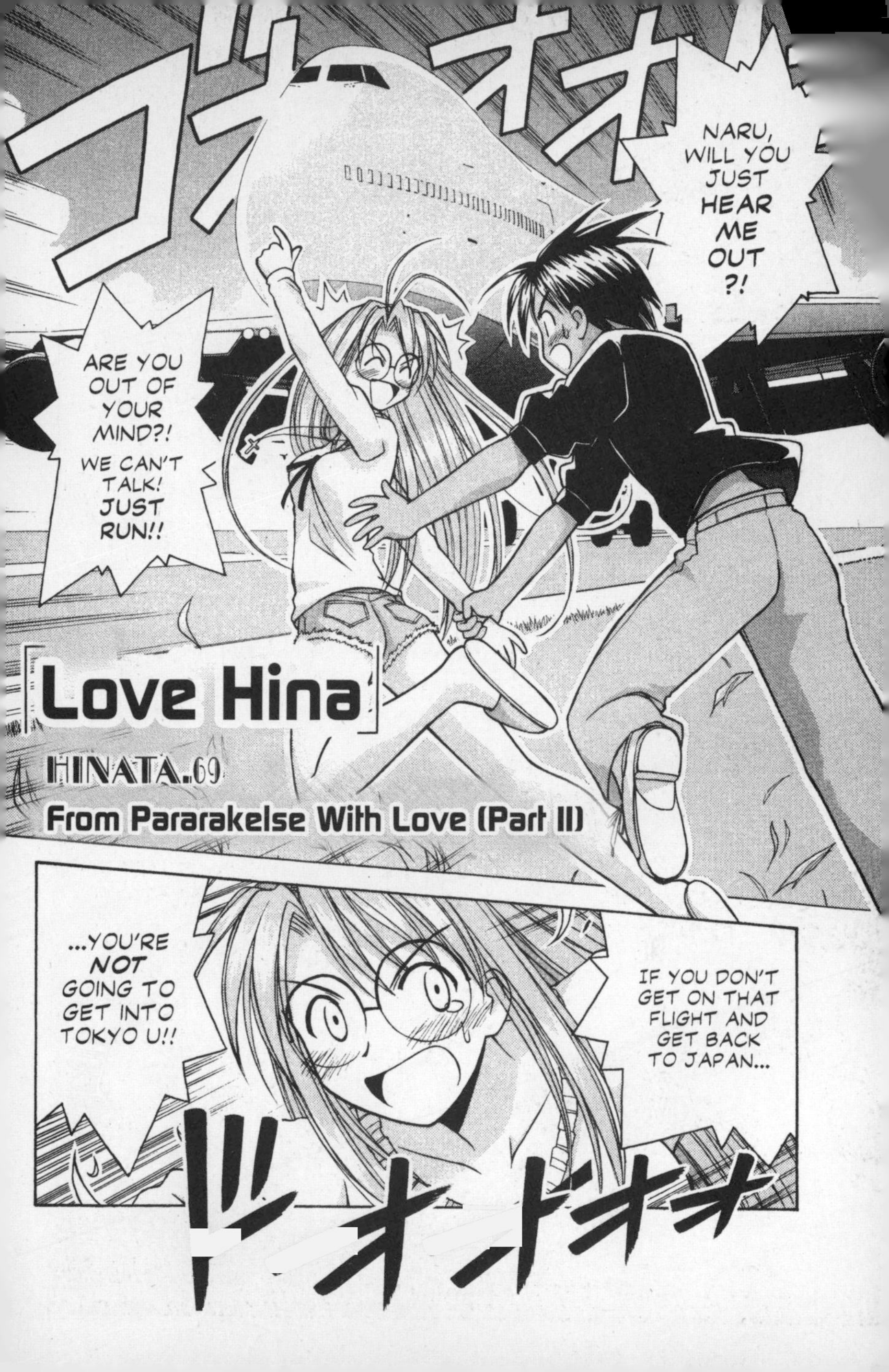
NARU, WILL YOU JUST HEAR ME OUT?!
ARE YOU OUT OF YOUR MIND?!
WE CAN'T TALK! JUST RUN!!
Love Hina
HINATA.69
From Pararakelse With Love (Part II)
IF YOU DON'T GET ON THAT FLIGHT AND GET BACK TO JAPAN...
...YOU'RE NOT GOING TO GET INTO TOKYO U!!

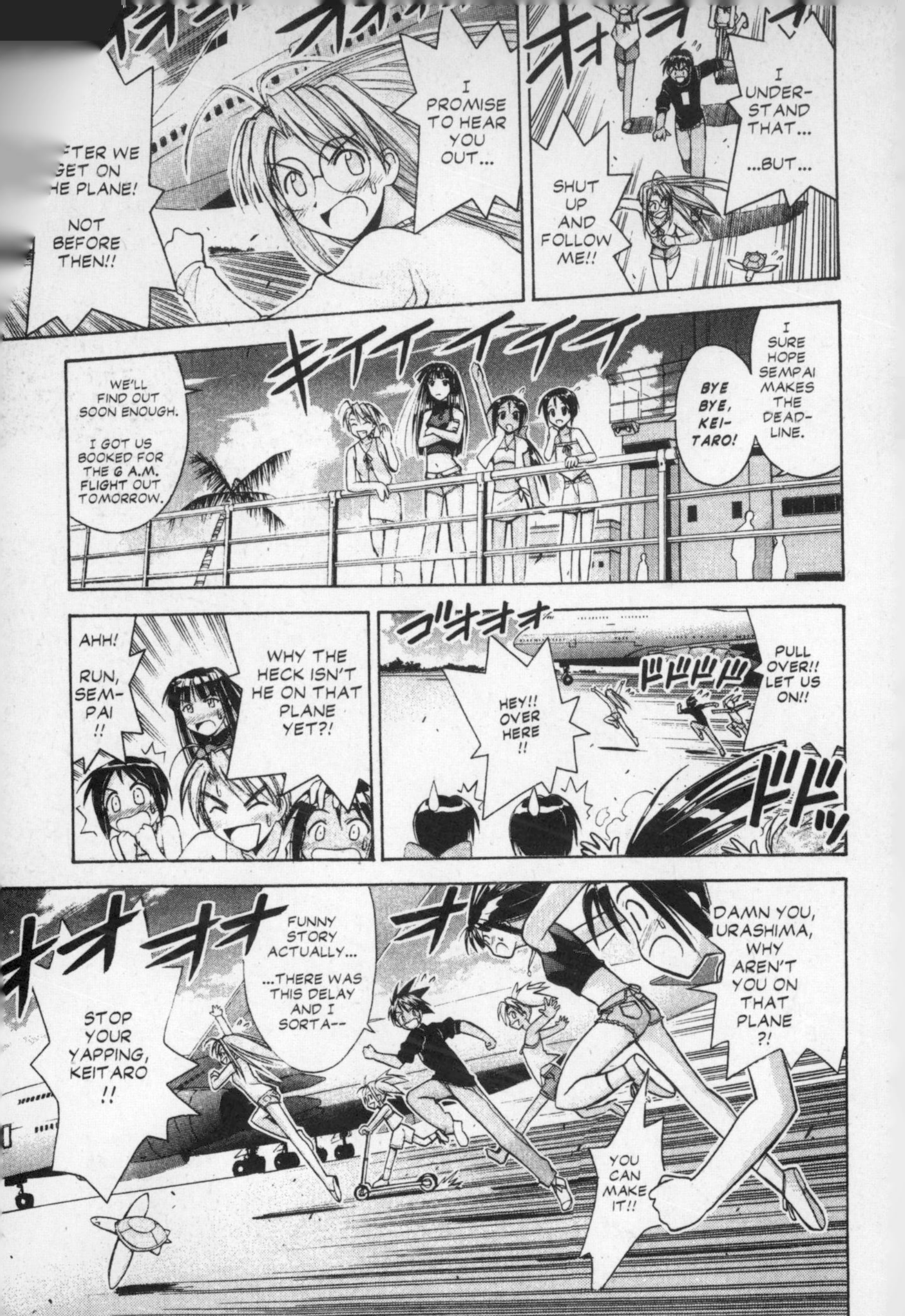
I UNDER-STAND THAT...
...BUT...
SHUT UP AND FOLLOW ME!!
I PROMISE TO HEAR YOU OUT...
FTER WE GET ON HE PLANE!
NOT BEFORE THEN!!
I SURE HOPE SEMPAI MAKES THE DEAD-LINE.
BYE BYE, KEI-TARO!
WE'LL FIND OUT SOON ENOUGH.
I GOT US BOOKED FOR THE 6 A.M. FLIGHT OUT TOMORROW.
PULL OVER!! LET US ON!!
HEY!! OVER HERE!!
WHY THE HECK ISN'T HE ON THAT PLANE YET?!
AHH!
RUN, SEM-PAI!!
DAMN YOU, URASHIMA, WHY AREN'T YOU ON THAT PLANE?!
YOU CAN MAKE IT!!
FUNNY STORY ACTUALLY...
...THERE WAS THIS DELAY AND I SORTA--
STOP YOUR YAPPING, KEITARO!!

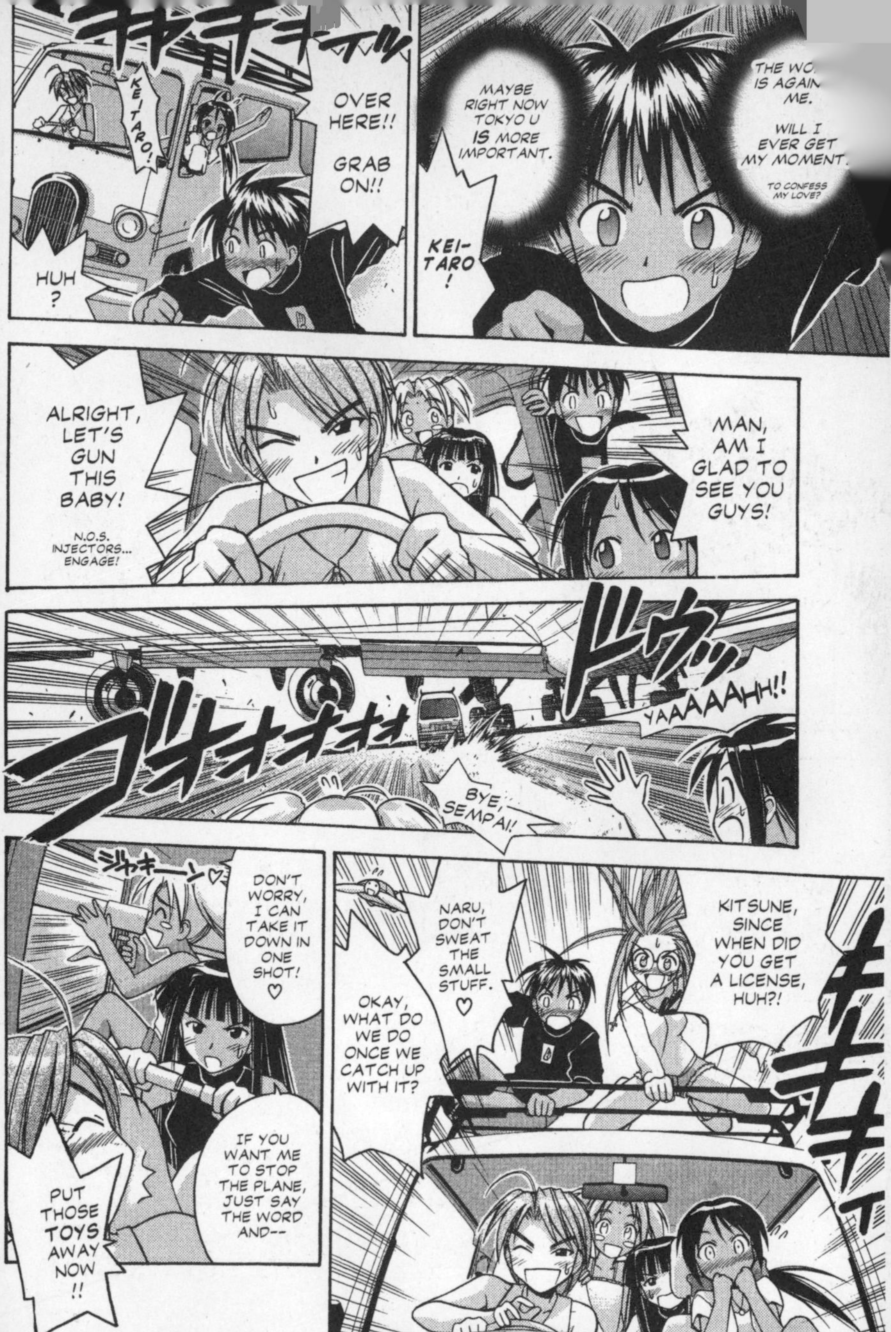
THE WO
IS AGAIN
ME.
WILL I EVER GET MY MOMENT
TO CONFESS MY LOVE?
MAYBE RIGHT NOW TOKYO U IS MORE IMPORTANT.
KEI-TARO!
KEITARO!
OVER HERE!!
GRAB ON!!
HUH?
MAN, AM I GLAD TO SEE YOU GUYS!
ALRIGHT, LET'S GUN THIS BABY!
N.O.S. INJECTORS... ENGAGE!
YAAAAAHH!!
BYE, SEMPAI!
KITSUNE, SINCE WHEN DID YOU GET A LICENSE, HUH?!
NARU, DON'T SWEAT THE SMALL STUFF. ♡
OKAY, WHAT DO WE DO ONCE WE CATCH UP WITH IT?
DON'T WORRY, I CAN TAKE IT DOWN IN ONE SHOT! ♡
IF YOU WANT ME TO STOP THE PLANE, JUST SAY THE WORD AND--
PUT THOSE TOYS AWAY NOW!!

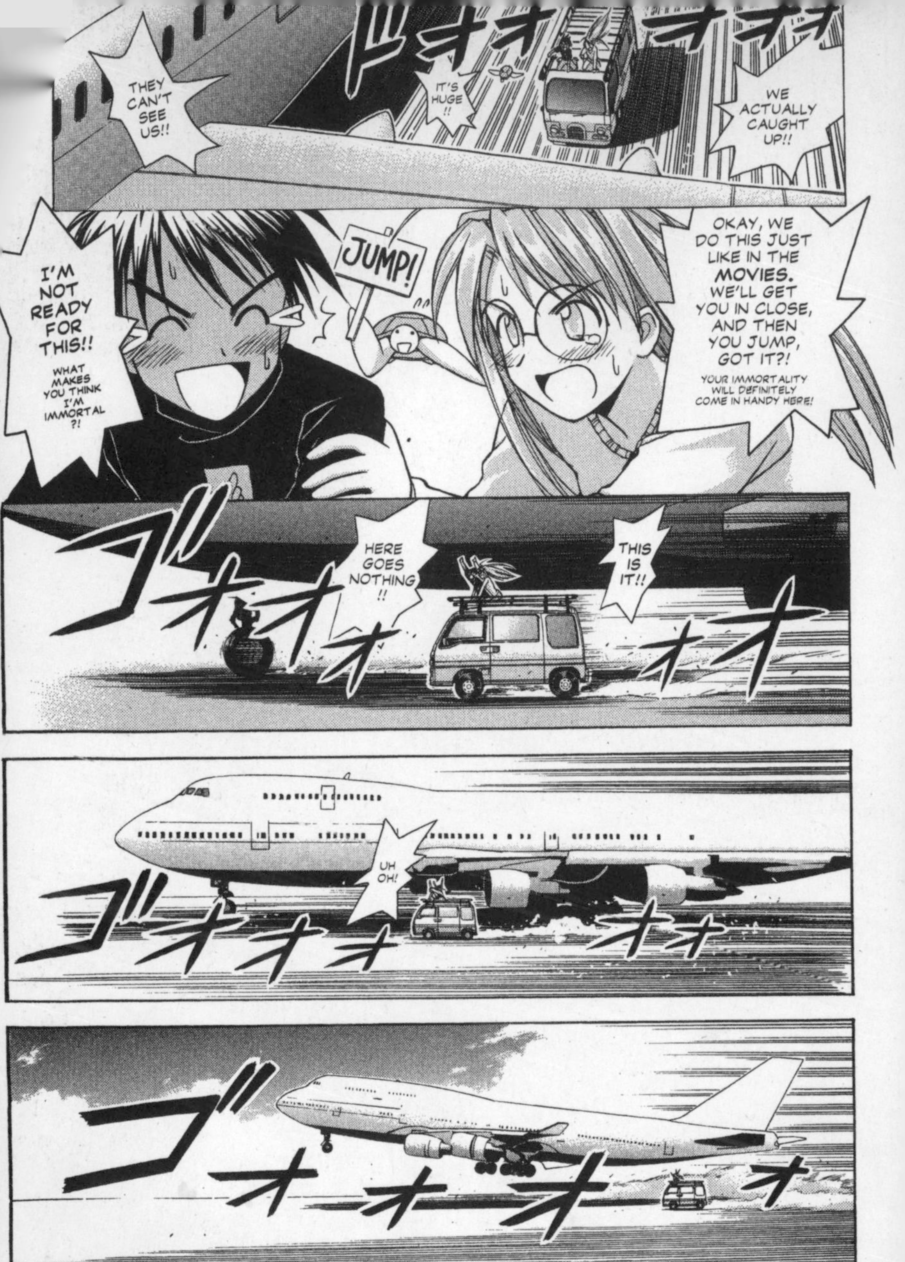
WE ACTUALLY CAUGHT UP!!
IT'S HUGE!!
THEY CAN'T SEE US!!
OKAY, WE DO THIS JUST LIKE IN THE MOVIES. WE'LL GET YOU IN CLOSE, AND THEN YOU JUMP, GOT IT?!
YOUR IMMORTALITY WILL DEFINITELY COME IN HANDY HERE!
JUMP!
I'M NOT READY FOR THIS!!
WHAT MAKES YOU THINK I'M IMMORTAL?!
THIS IS IT!!
HERE GOES NOTHING!!
UH OH!

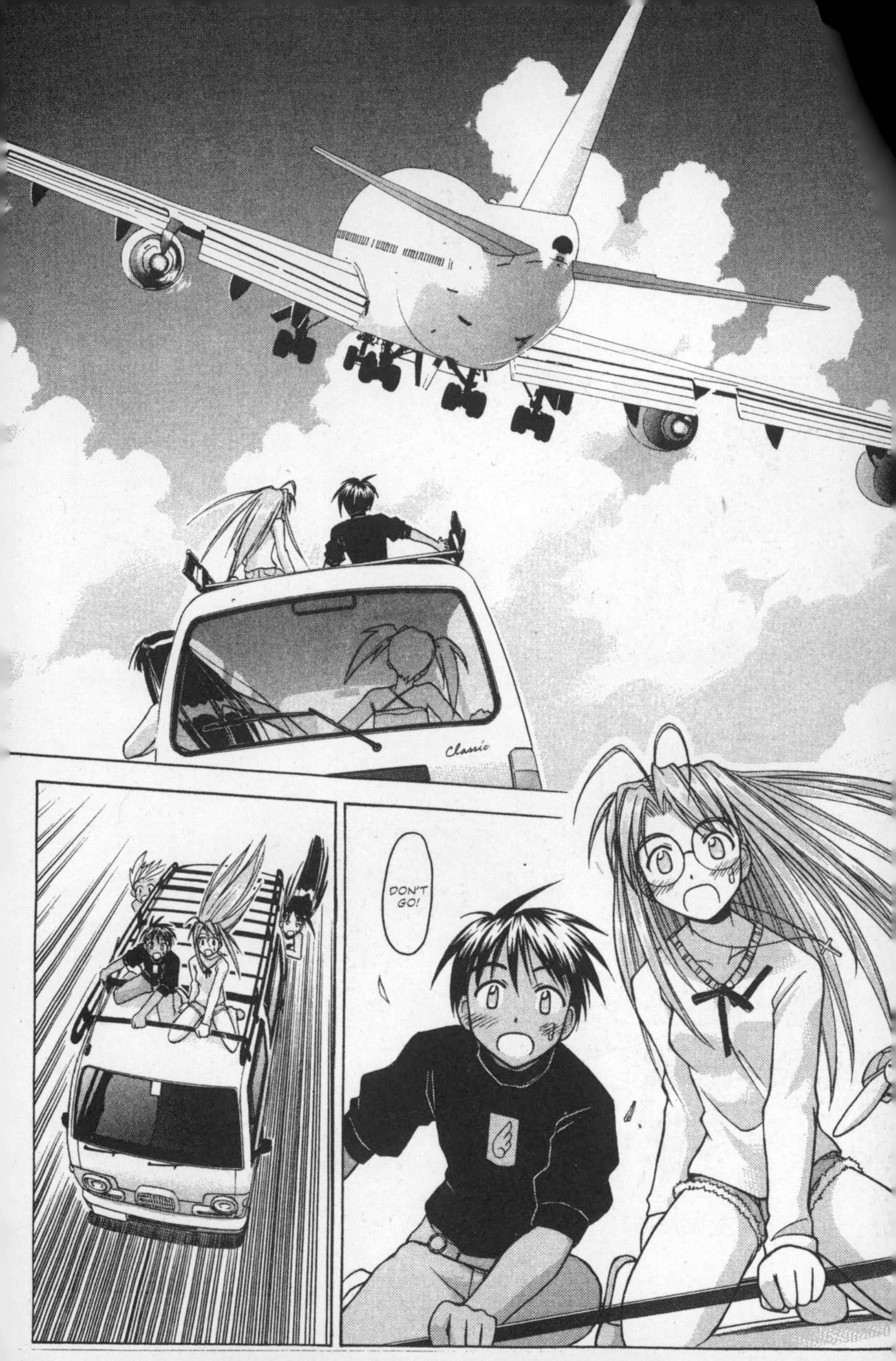
Classic
DON'T GO!

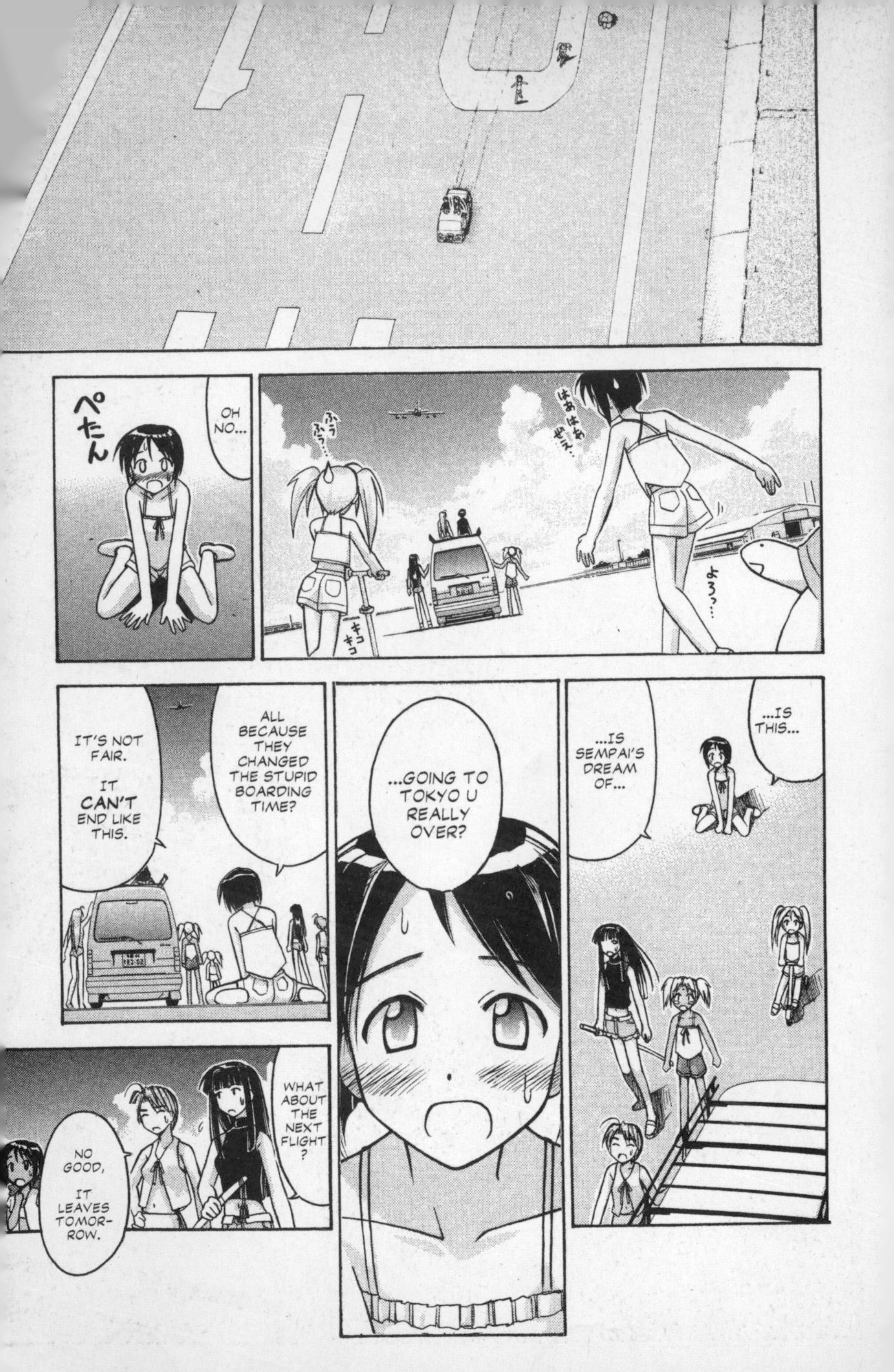

はあはあ ぜえ…
ふうふう…
よろっ…
キコキコ
ぺたん
OH NO...
...IS THIS...
...IS SEMPAI'S DREAM OF...
...GOING TO TOKYO U REALLY OVER?
ALL BECAUSE THEY CHANGED THE STUPID BOARDING TIME?
IT'S NOT FAIR. IT CAN'T END LIKE THIS.
WHAT ABOUT THE NEXT FLIGHT?
NO GOOD, IT LEAVES TOMOR-ROW.

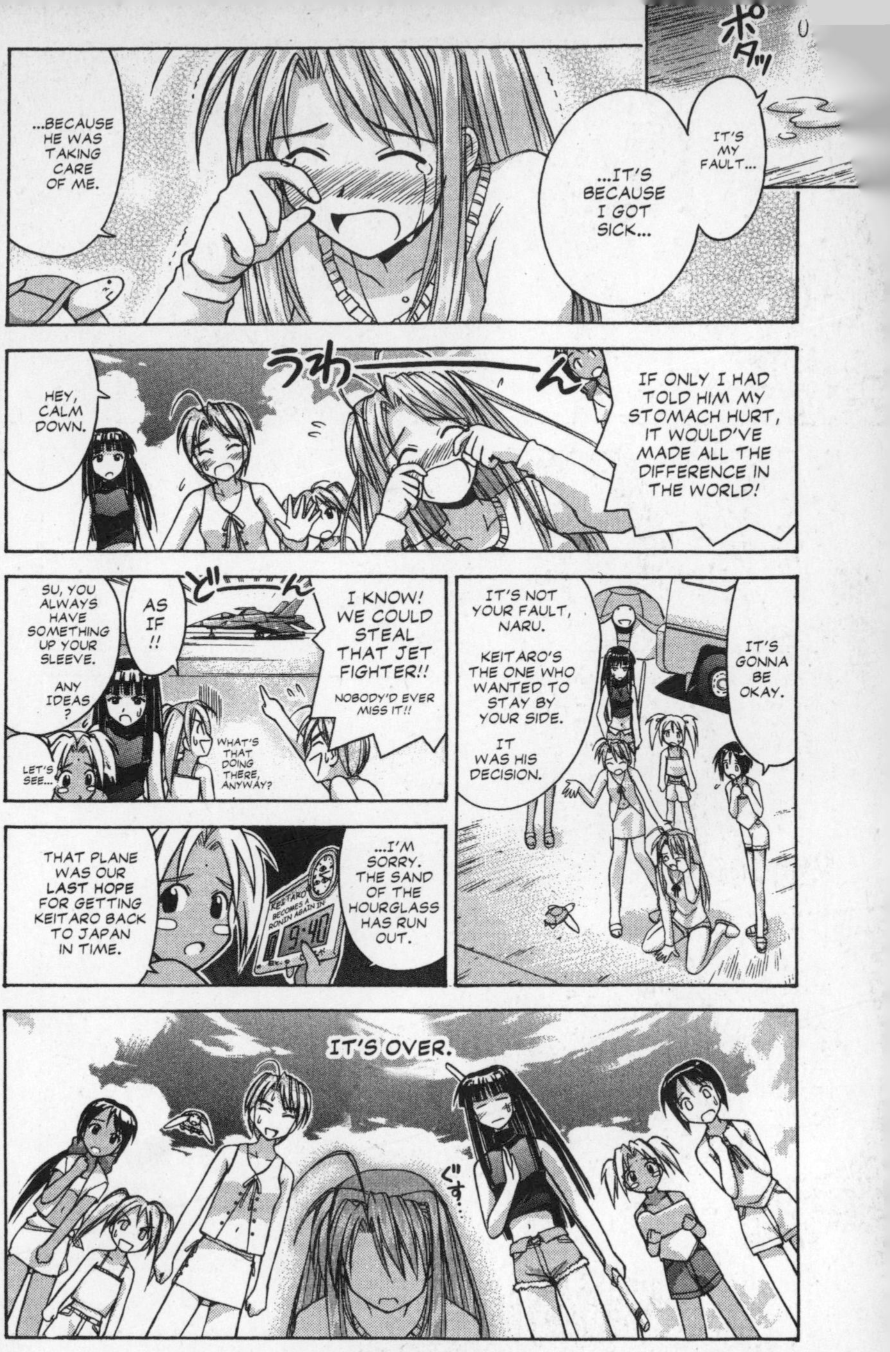
ポタッ
IT'S MY FAULT...
...IT'S BECAUSE I GOT SICK...
...BECAUSE HE WAS TAKING CARE OF ME.
うわーーーーん
IF ONLY I HAD TOLD HIM MY STOMACH HURT, IT WOULD'VE MADE ALL THE DIFFERENCE IN THE WORLD!
HEY, CALM DOWN.
IT'S GONNA BE OKAY.
IT'S NOT YOUR FAULT, NARU.
KEITARO'S THE ONE WHO WANTED TO STAY BY YOUR SIDE.
IT WAS HIS DECISION.
どーん
I KNOW! WE COULD STEAL THAT JET FIGHTER!!
NOBODY'D EVER MISS IT!!
AS IF!!
WHAT'S THAT DOING THERE, ANYWAY?
SU, YOU ALWAYS HAVE SOMETHING UP YOUR SLEEVE.
ANY IDEAS?
LET'S SEE...
...I'M SORRY. THE SAND OF THE HOURGLASS HAS RUN OUT.
KEITARO BECOMES A RONIN AGAIN IN
9:40
THAT PLANE WAS OUR LAST HOPE FOR GETTING KEITARO BACK TO JAPAN IN TIME.
IT'S OVER.
ぐす...

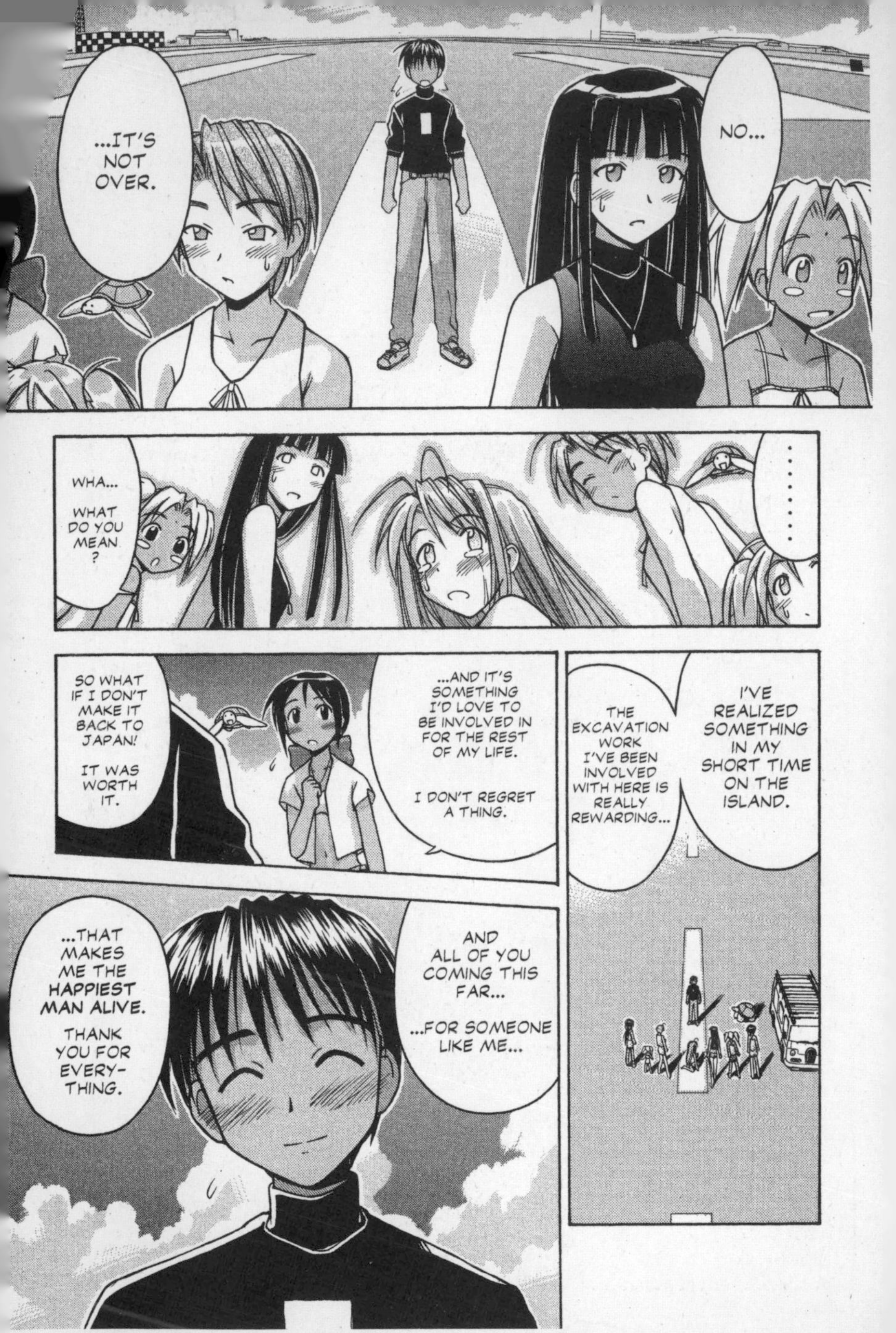
NO...
...IT'S NOT OVER.
......
WHA... WHAT DO YOU MEAN?
I'VE REALIZED SOMETHING IN MY SHORT TIME ON THE ISLAND.
THE EXCAVATION WORK I'VE BEEN INVOLVED WITH HERE IS REALLY REWARDING...
...AND IT'S SOMETHING I'D LOVE TO BE INVOLVED IN FOR THE REST OF MY LIFE.
I DON'T REGRET A THING.
SO WHAT IF I DON'T MAKE IT BACK TO JAPAN!
IT WAS WORTH IT.
AND ALL OF YOU COMING THIS FAR...
...FOR SOMEONE LIKE ME...
...THAT MAKES ME THE **HAPPIEST MAN ALIVE.**
THANK YOU FOR EVERY-THING.

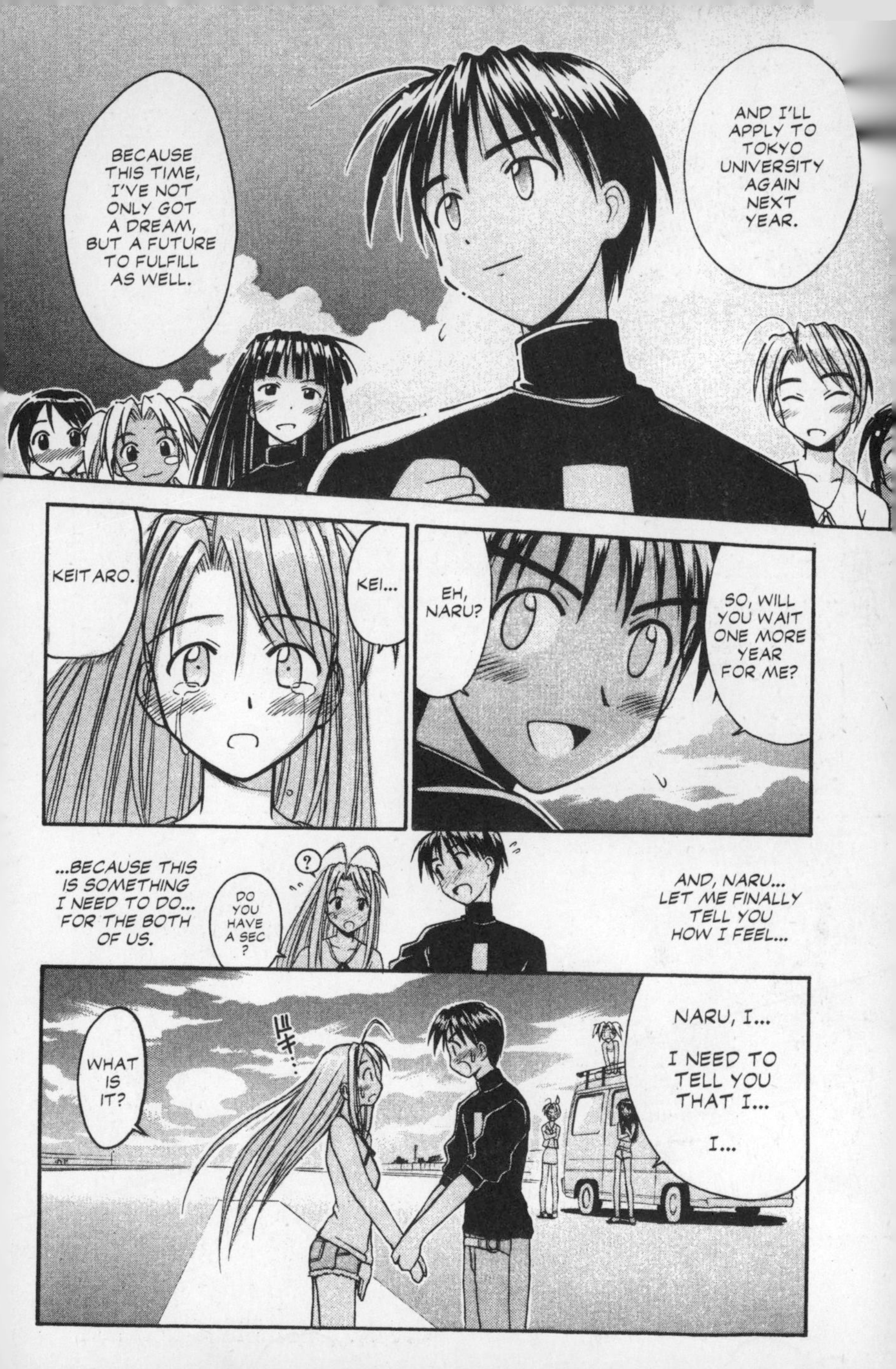
AND I'LL APPLY TO TOKYO UNIVERSITY AGAIN NEXT YEAR.
BECAUSE THIS TIME, I'VE NOT ONLY GOT A DREAM, BUT A FUTURE TO FULFILL AS WELL.
SO, WILL YOU WAIT ONE MORE YEAR FOR ME?
EH, NARU?
KEI...
KEITARO.
AND, NARU... LET ME FINALLY TELL YOU HOW I FEEL...
DO YOU HAVE A SEC?
?
...BECAUSE THIS IS SOMETHING I NEED TO DO... FOR THE BOTH OF US.
NARU, I...
I NEED TO TELL YOU THAT I...
I...
WHAT IS IT?

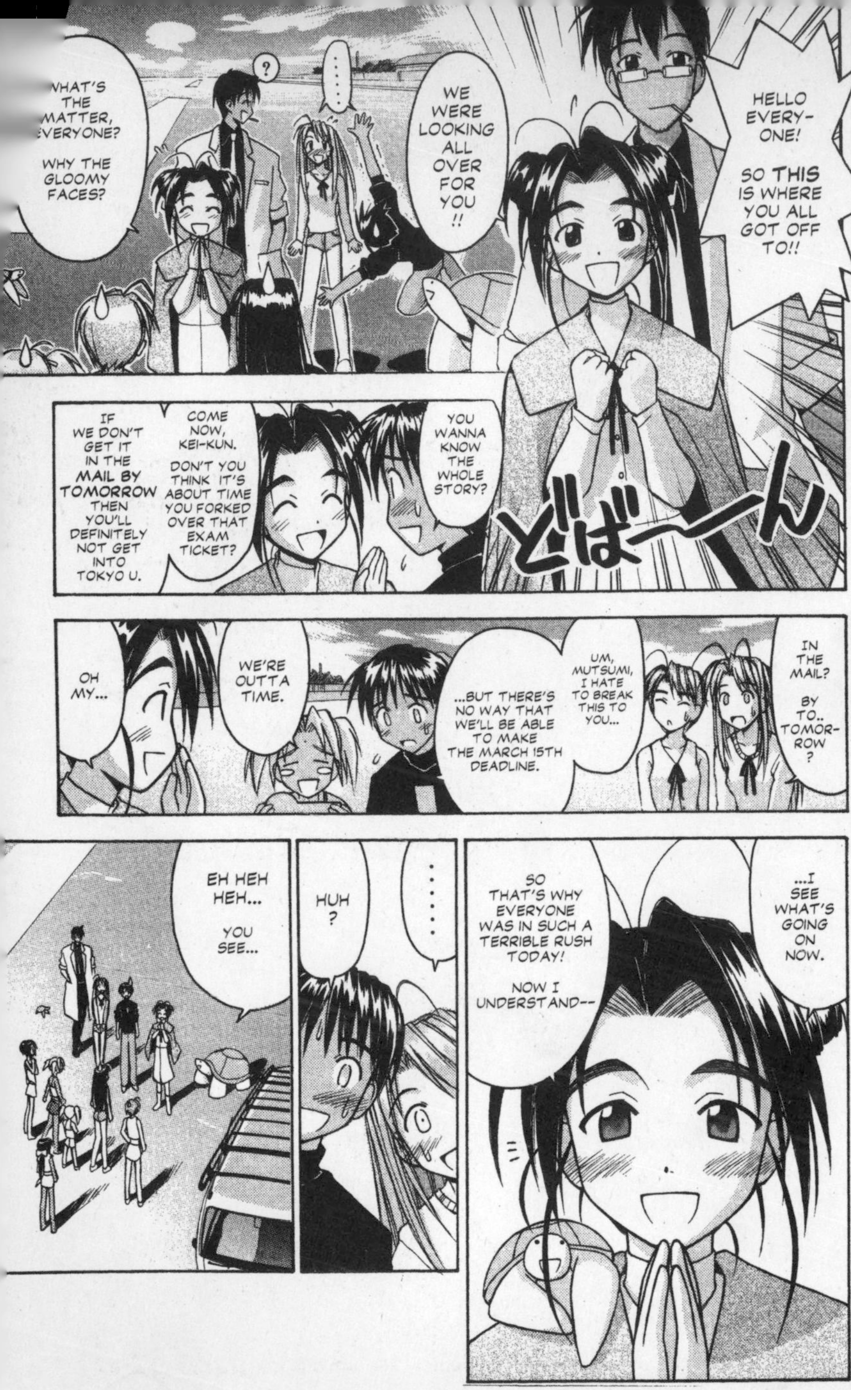
HELLO EVERYONE!
SO THIS IS WHERE YOU ALL GOT OFF TO!!
どばーーん
WE WERE LOOKING ALL OVER FOR YOU!!
......
?
WHAT'S THE MATTER, EVERYONE?
WHY THE GLOOMY FACES?
YOU WANNA KNOW THE WHOLE STORY?
COME NOW, KEI-KUN.
DON'T YOU THINK IT'S ABOUT TIME YOU FORKED OVER THAT EXAM TICKET?
IF WE DON'T GET IT IN THE MAIL BY TOMORROW THEN YOU'LL DEFINITELY NOT GET INTO TOKYO U.
IN THE MAIL?
BY TO.. TOMOR-ROW?
UM, MUTSUMI, I HATE TO BREAK THIS TO YOU...
...BUT THERE'S NO WAY THAT WE'LL BE ABLE TO MAKE THE MARCH 15TH DEADLINE.
WE'RE OUTTA TIME.
OH MY...
...I SEE WHAT'S GOING ON NOW.
SO THAT'S WHY EVERYONE WAS IN SUCH A TERRIBLE RUSH TODAY!
NOW I UNDERSTAND--
......
HUH?
EH HEH HEH...
YOU SEE...

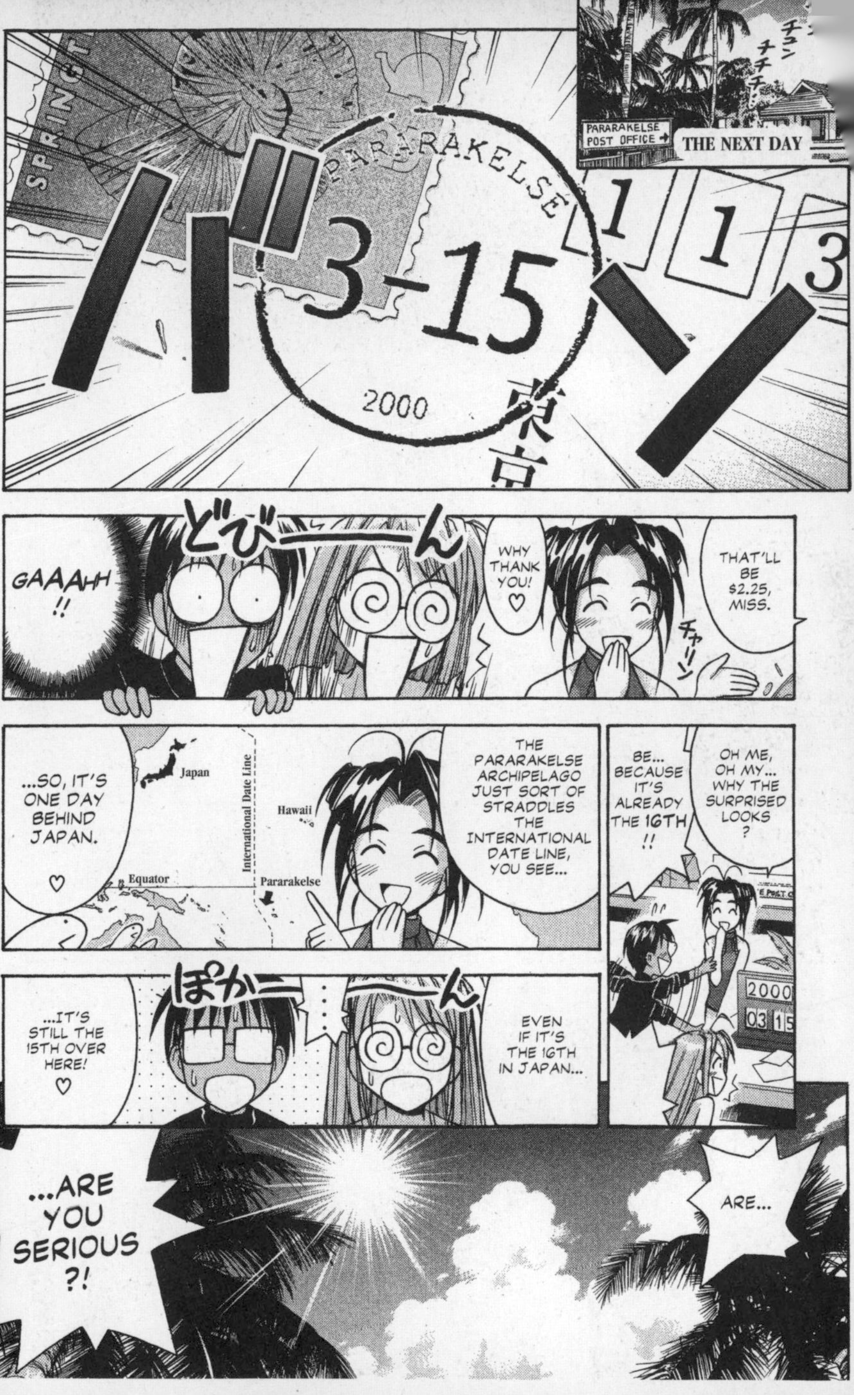
チュン
チチチ…
PARARAKELSE POST OFFICE →
THE NEXT DAY
SPRINGT
PARARAKELSE
3-15
2000
1 1 3
東京
バン
THAT'LL BE $2.25, MISS.
チャリン
WHY THANK YOU! ♡
どびーーーん
GAAAHH !!
OH ME, OH MY... WHY THE SURPRISED LOOKS ?
BE... BECAUSE IT'S ALREADY THE 16TH !!
2000
03 15
THE PARARAKELSE ARCHIPELAGO JUST SORT OF STRADDLES THE INTERNATIONAL DATE LINE, YOU SEE...
International Date Line
Hawaii
Japan
Pararakelse
Equator
...SO, IT'S ONE DAY BEHIND JAPAN. ♡
EVEN IF IT'S THE 16TH IN JAPAN...
ぽかーーーん
...IT'S STILL THE 15TH OVER HERE! ♡
ARE...
...ARE YOU SERIOUS ?!

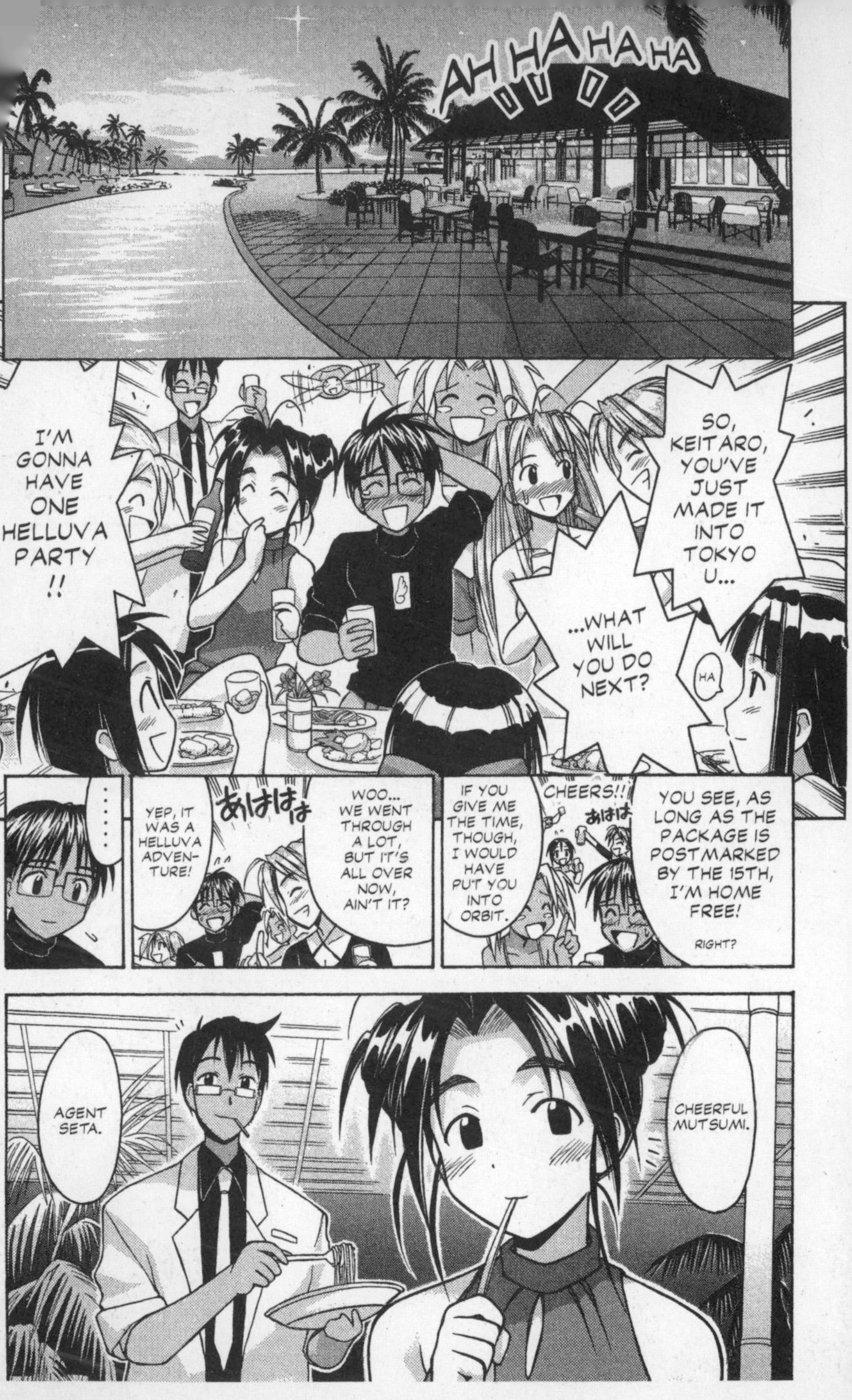
AH HA HA HA HA
SO, KEITARO, YOU'VE JUST MADE IT INTO TOKYO U...
HA
...WHAT WILL YOU DO NEXT?
I'M GONNA HAVE ONE HELLUVA PARTY!!
YOU SEE, AS LONG AS THE PACKAGE IS POSTMARKED BY THE 15TH, I'M HOME FREE!
RIGHT?
あはは
CHEERS!!
IF YOU GIVE ME THE TIME, THOUGH, I WOULD HAVE PUT YOU INTO ORBIT.
WOO... WE WENT THROUGH A LOT, BUT IT'S ALL OVER NOW, AIN'T IT?
あははは
YEP, IT WAS A HELLUVA ADVENTURE!
......
CHEERFUL MUTSUMI.
AGENT SETA.

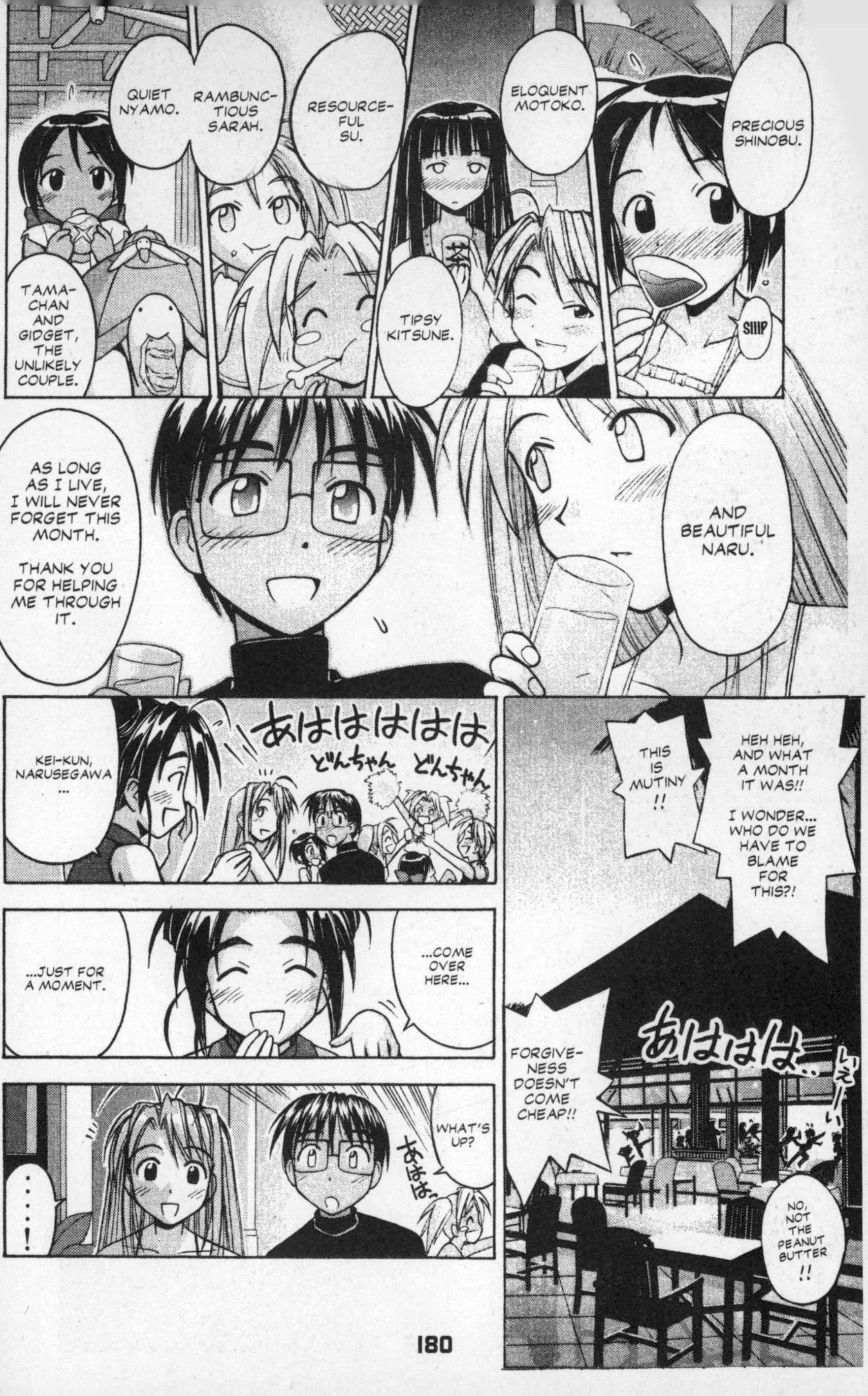
PRECIOUS SHINOBU.
SIIIP
ELOQUENT MOTOKO.
TIPSY KITSUNE.
RESOURCE-FUL SU.
RAMBUNC-TIOUS SARAH.
QUIET NYAMO.
TAMA-CHAN AND GIDGET, THE UNLIKELY COUPLE.
AND BEAUTIFUL NARU.
AS LONG AS I LIVE, I WILL NEVER FORGET THIS MONTH.
THANK YOU FOR HELPING ME THROUGH IT.
HEH HEH, AND WHAT A MONTH IT WAS!!
I WONDER... WHO DO WE HAVE TO BLAME FOR THIS?!
THIS IS MUTINY!!
あははは…
いえーい
FORGIVE-NESS DOESN'T COME CHEAP!!
NO, NOT THE PEANUT BUTTER!!
あははははは
どんちゃん どんちゃん
KEI-KUN, NARUSEGAWA ...
...COME OVER HERE...
...JUST FOR A MOMENT.
WHAT'S UP?
あはは…
......!

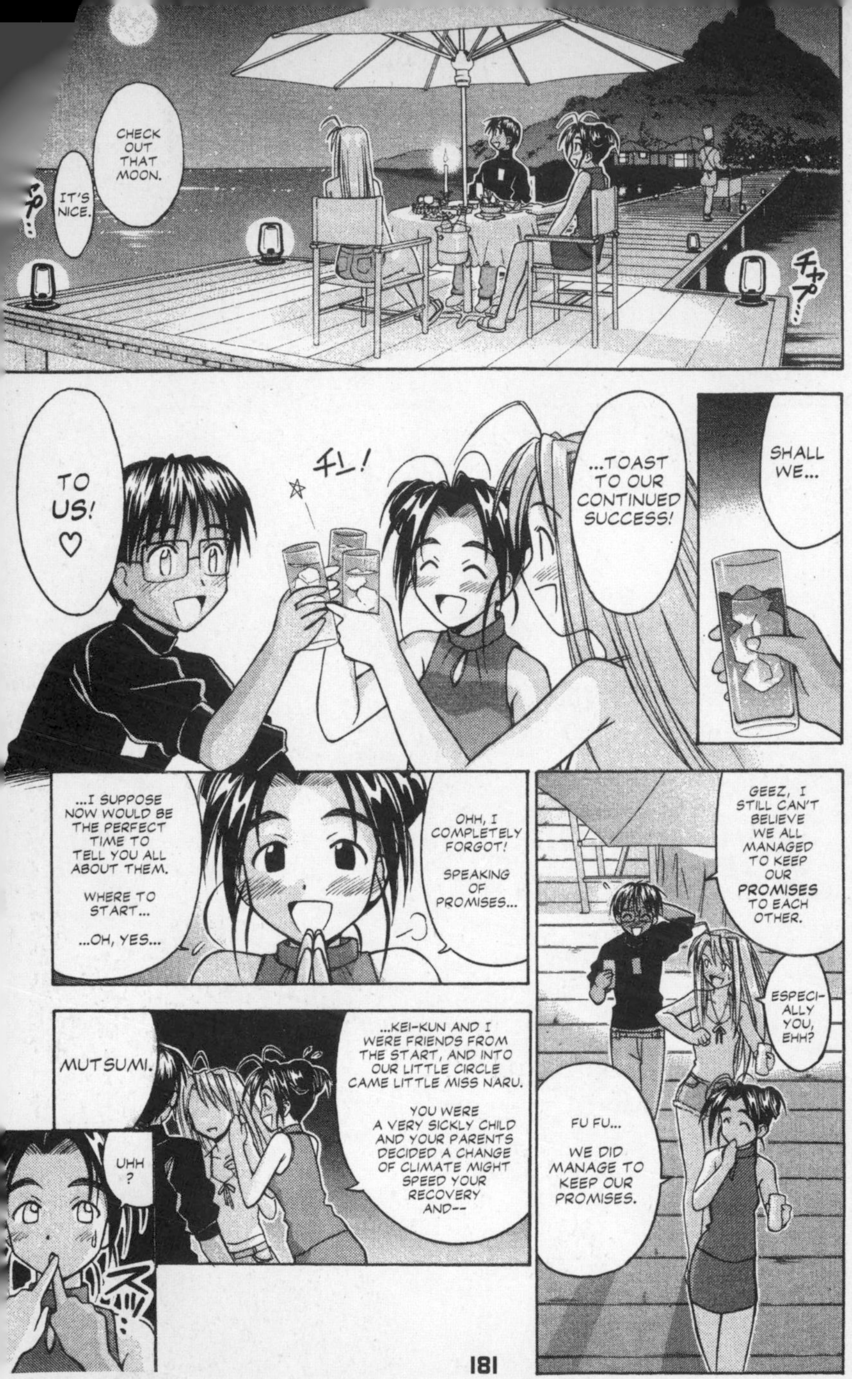

チャプ...
CHECK OUT THAT MOON.
IT'S NICE.
SHALL WE...
...TOAST TO OUR CONTINUED SUCCESS!
チン!
TO US! ♡
GEEZ, I STILL CAN'T BELIEVE WE ALL MANAGED TO KEEP OUR PROMISES TO EACH OTHER.
ESPECIALLY YOU, EHH?
FU FU... WE DID MANAGE TO KEEP OUR PROMISES.
OHH, I COMPLETELY FORGOT! SPEAKING OF PROMISES...
...I SUPPOSE NOW WOULD BE THE PERFECT TIME TO TELL YOU ALL ABOUT THEM. WHERE TO START... ...OH, YES...
...KEI-KUN AND I WERE FRIENDS FROM THE START, AND INTO OUR LITTLE CIRCLE CAME LITTLE MISS NARU. YOU WERE A VERY SICKLY CHILD AND YOUR PARENTS DECIDED A CHANGE OF CLIMATE MIGHT SPEED YOUR RECOVERY AND--
MUTSUMI.
UHH ?

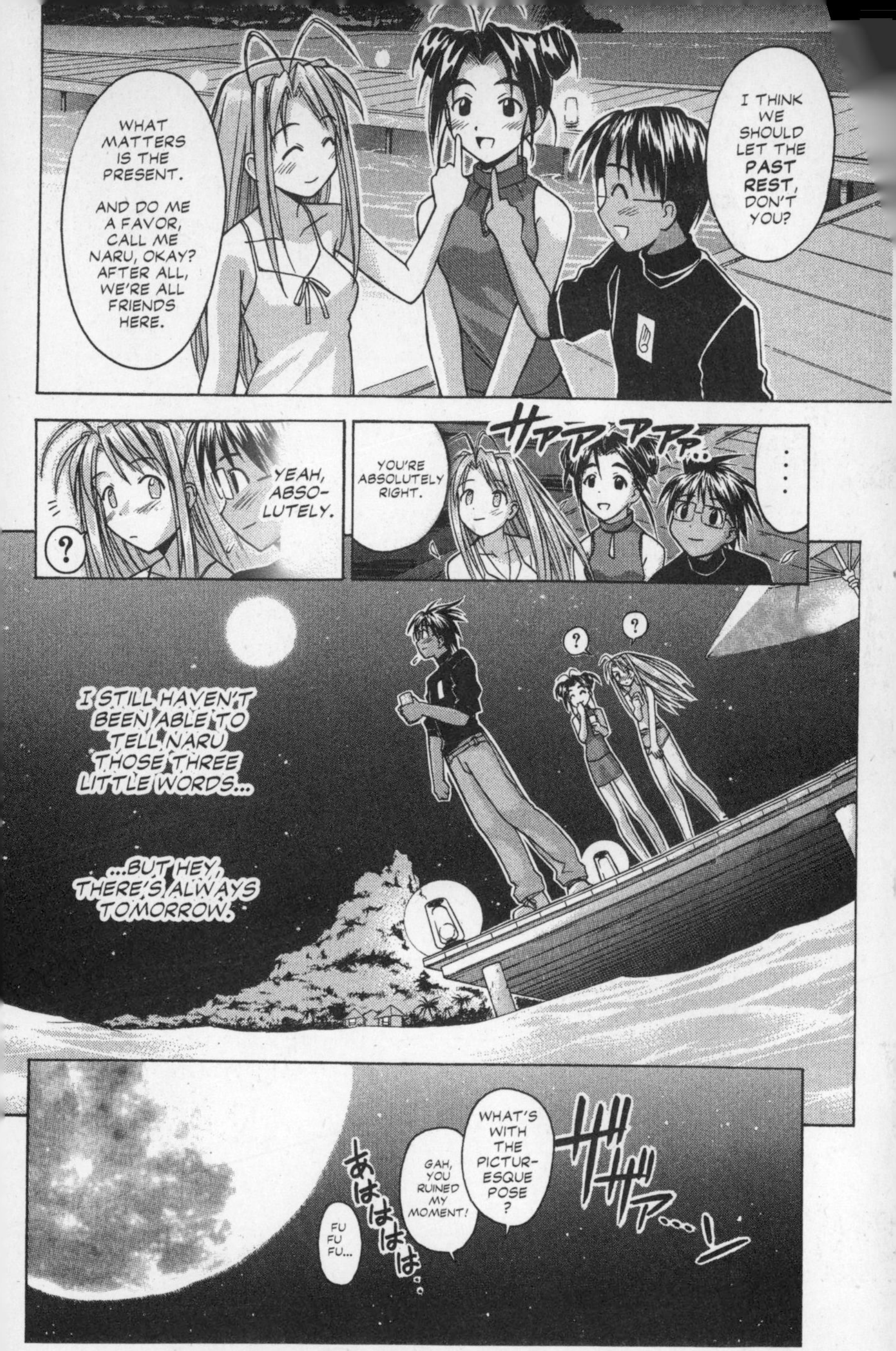
I THINK WE SHOULD LET THE PAST REST, DON'T YOU?
WHAT MATTERS IS THE PRESENT.
AND DO ME A FAVOR, CALL ME NARU, OKAY? AFTER ALL, WE'RE ALL FRIENDS HERE.
サァァ アァァ..
. . . .
YOU'RE ABSOLUTELY RIGHT.
YEAH, ABSO-LUTELY.
?
I STILL HAVEN'T BEEN ABLE TO TELL NARU THOSE THREE LITTLE WORDS...
...BUT HEY, THERE'S ALWAYS TOMORROW.
?
?
ザザァ...
WHAT'S WITH THE PICTURE-ESQUE POSE?
GAH, YOU RUINED MY MOMENT!
あははは
FU FU FU...

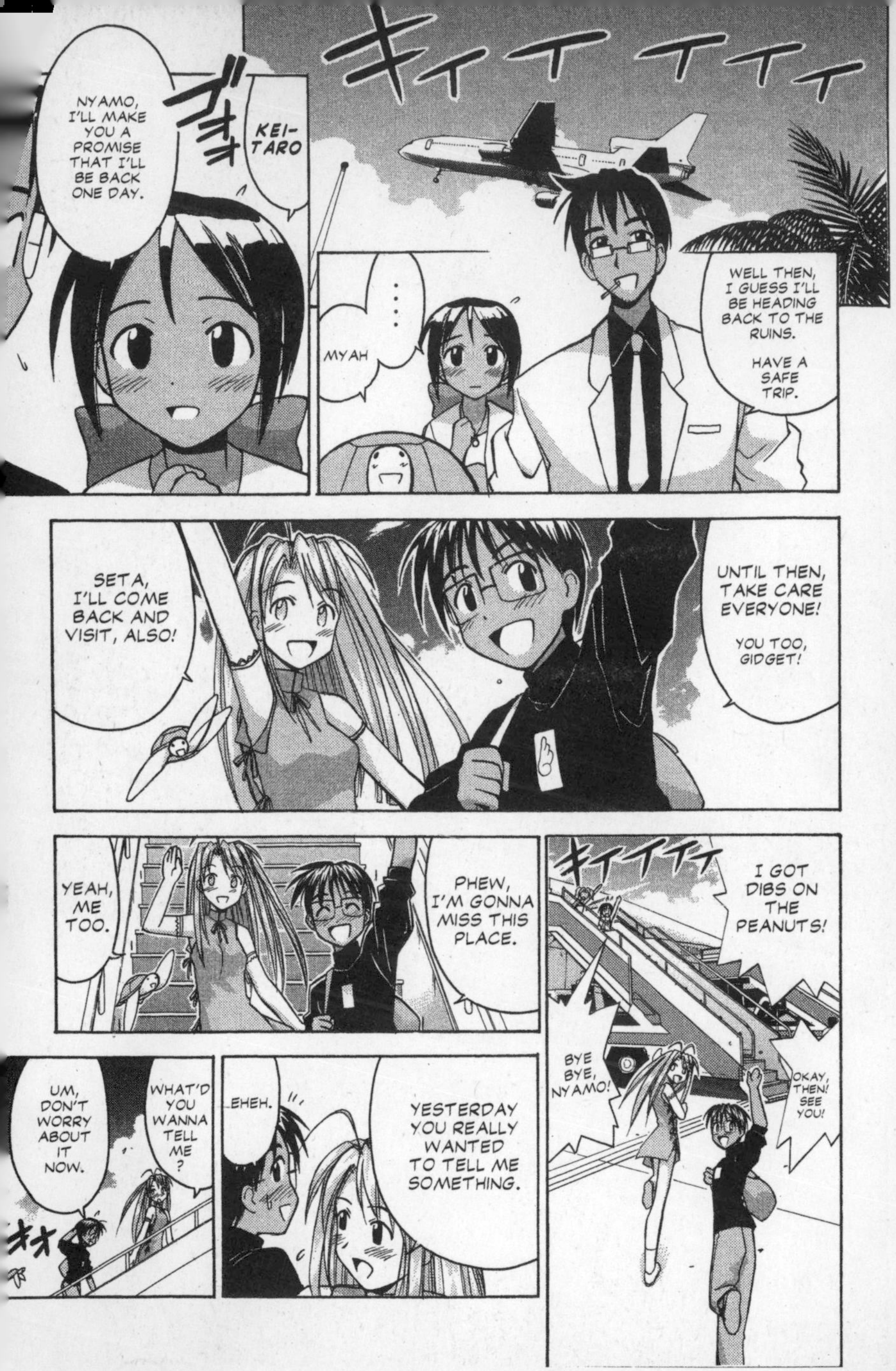
キイイ イイイ
WELL THEN, I GUESS I'LL BE HEADING BACK TO THE RUINS.
HAVE A SAFE TRIP.
...... MYAH
ゴォォ
KEI-TARO
NYAMO, I'LL MAKE YOU A PROMISE THAT I'LL BE BACK ONE DAY.
UNTIL THEN, TAKE CARE EVERYONE!
YOU TOO, GIDGET!
SETA, I'LL COME BACK AND VISIT, ALSO!
キイイイイイ
I GOT DIBS ON THE PEANUTS!
OKAY, THEN! SEE YOU!
BYE BYE, NYAMO!
PHEW, I'M GONNA MISS THIS PLACE.
YEAH, ME TOO.
YESTERDAY YOU REALLY WANTED TO TELL ME SOMETHING.
EHEH.
WHAT'D YOU WANNA TELL ME?
UM, DON'T WORRY ABOUT IT NOW.
オオ

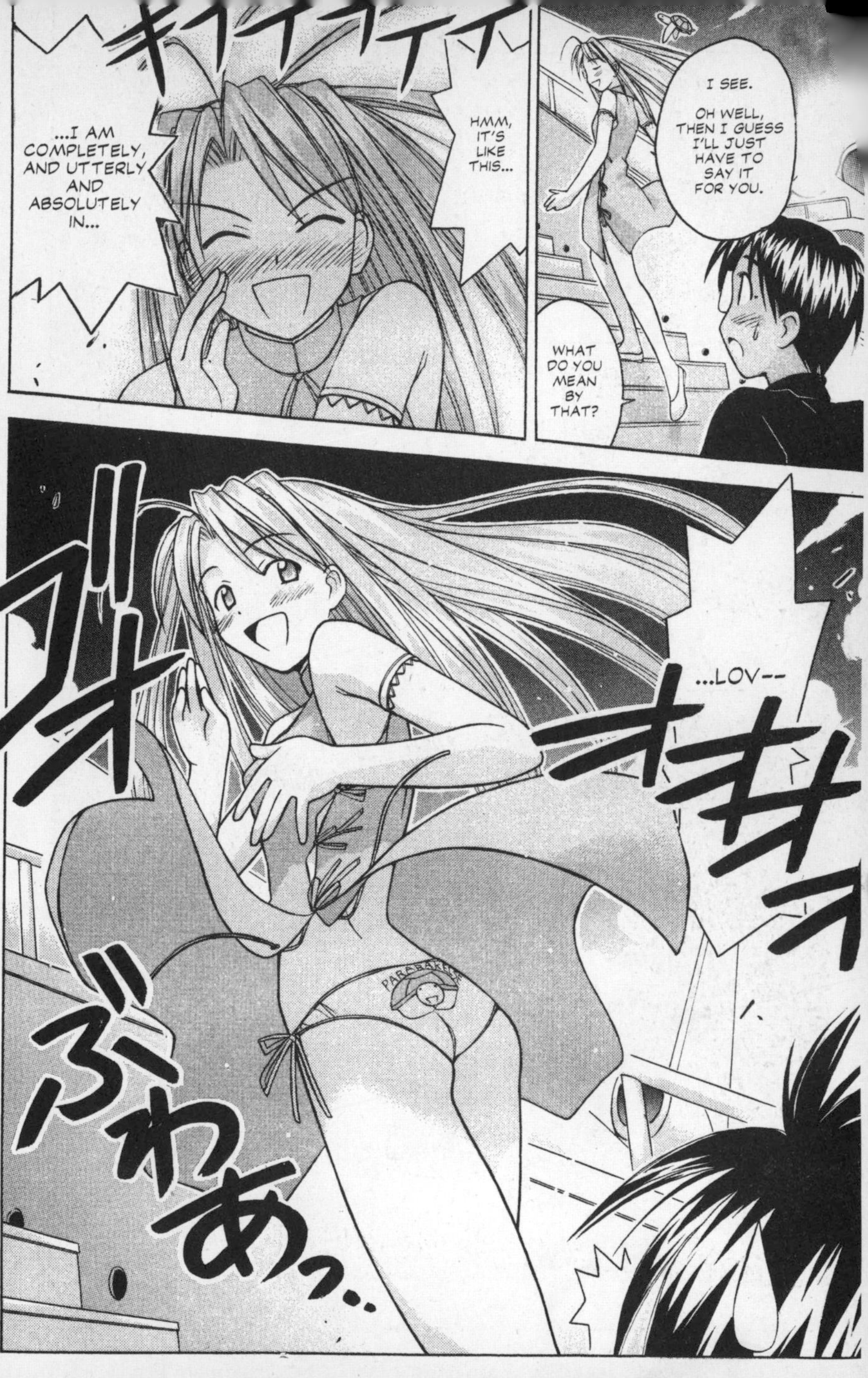

I SEE.
OH WELL, THEN I GUESS I'LL JUST HAVE TO SAY IT FOR YOU.
WHAT DO YOU MEAN BY THAT?
HMM, IT'S LIKE THIS...
...I AM COMPLETELY, AND UTTERLY AND ABSOLUTELY IN...
...LOV--
ぶわあっ...

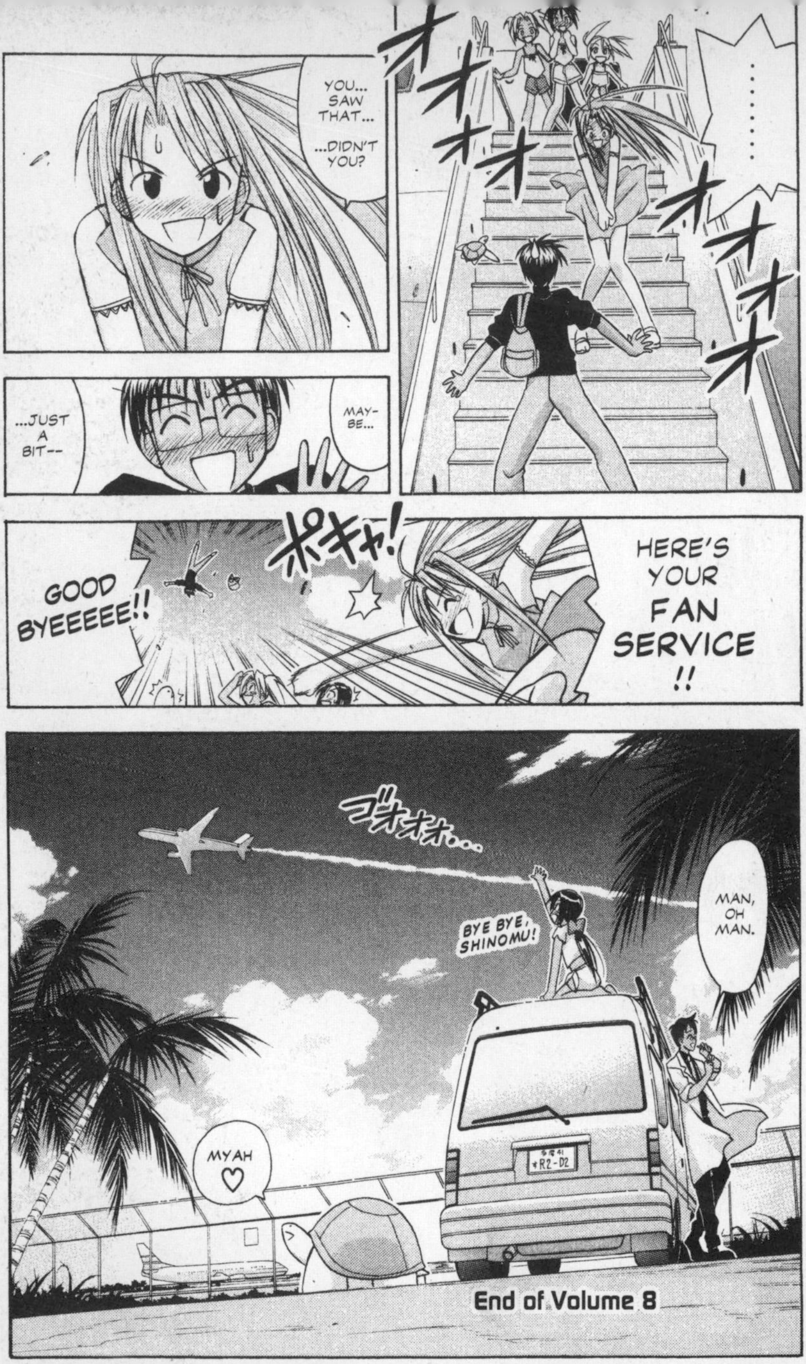
......
オオオオオオオオオ
YOU... SAW THAT... ...DIDN'T YOU?
MAY-BE...
...JUST A BIT--
HERE'S YOUR FAN SERVICE !!
ポキャ!
GOOD BYEEEEE!!
ゴオオオ...
MAN, OH MAN.
BYE BYE, SHINOMU!
MYAH ♡
End of Volume 8

STAFF

Ken Akamatsu
Takashi Takemoto
Kenichi Nakamura
Takaaki Miyahara
Masaki Ohyama
Yumiko Shinohara

EDITOR

Noboru Ohno
Tomoyuki Shiratsuchi
Yasushi Yamanaka

KC Editor

Shinichiro Yoshihara

Love Hina

Preview for Volume 9

Against all odds and despite repeated failings, Keitaro has finally passed the Tokyo University entrance exam, the road to his salvation coming to a triumphant end. Or has it? He'll soon learn that he still has a long way to go before things really start looking up for him - before he even has a chance to step onto the university grounds, a building falls on him, breaks his leg and sends him to the hospital! And to make matters worse for him, Miss Todai Pageant representatives scout Naru to be a contestant, attention that leads her away physically and emotionally from the Hinata den. Faced with losing her forever, can Keitaro finally tell Naru how he feels?

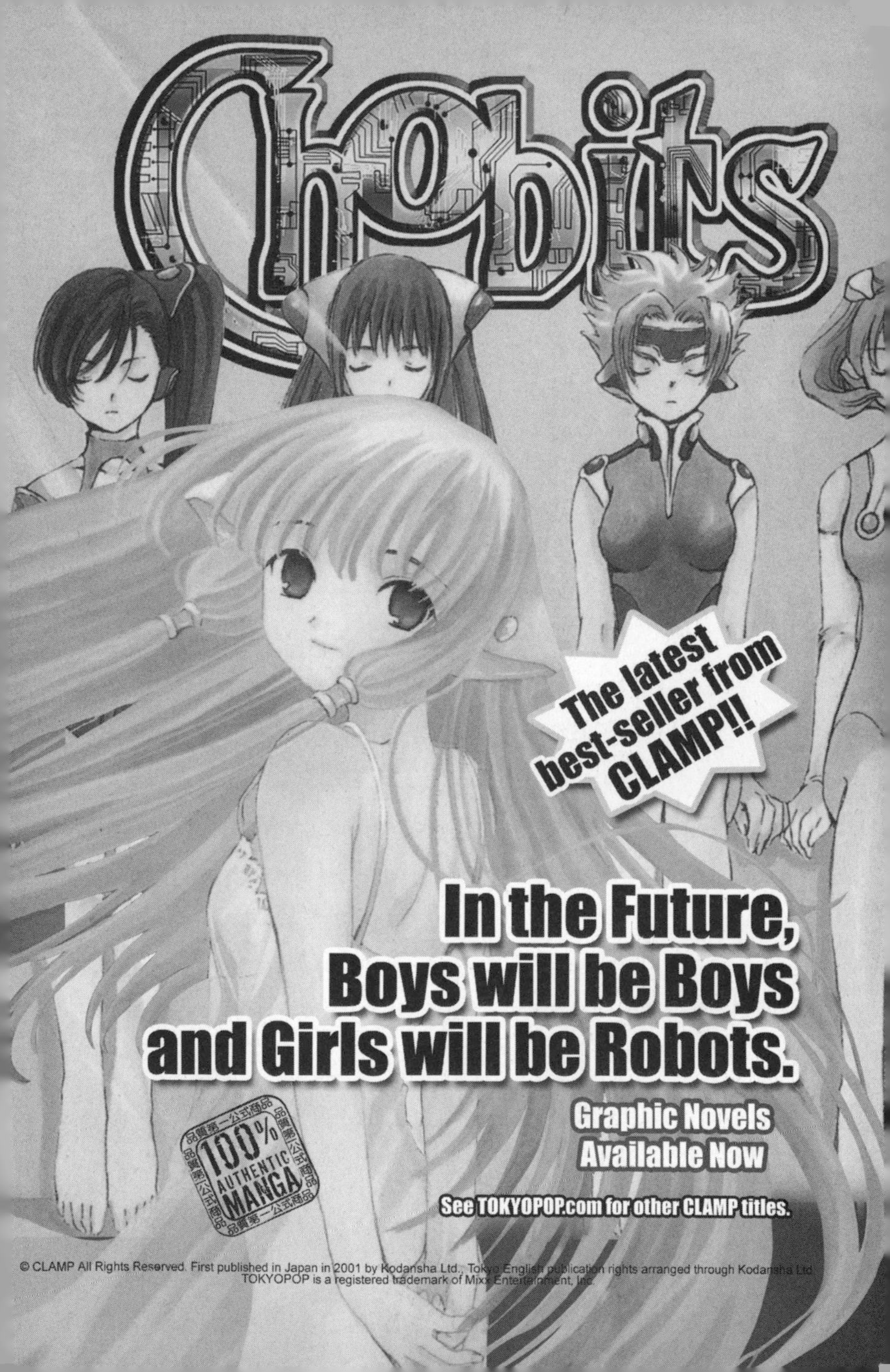
Chobits
The latest best-seller from CLAMP!!
In the Future, Boys will be Boys and Girls will be Robots.
Graphic Novels Available Now
100% AUTHENTIC MANGA
See TOKYOPOP.com for other CLAMP titles.

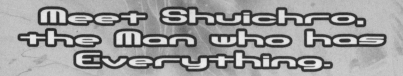
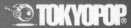

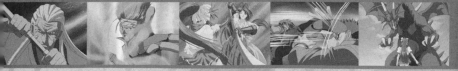
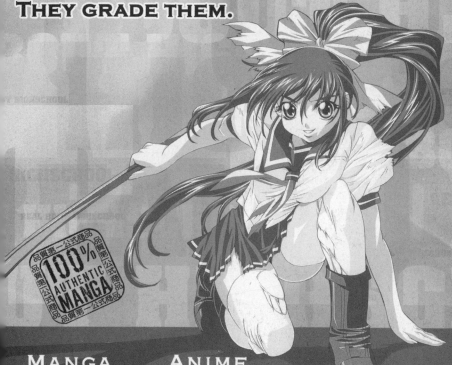

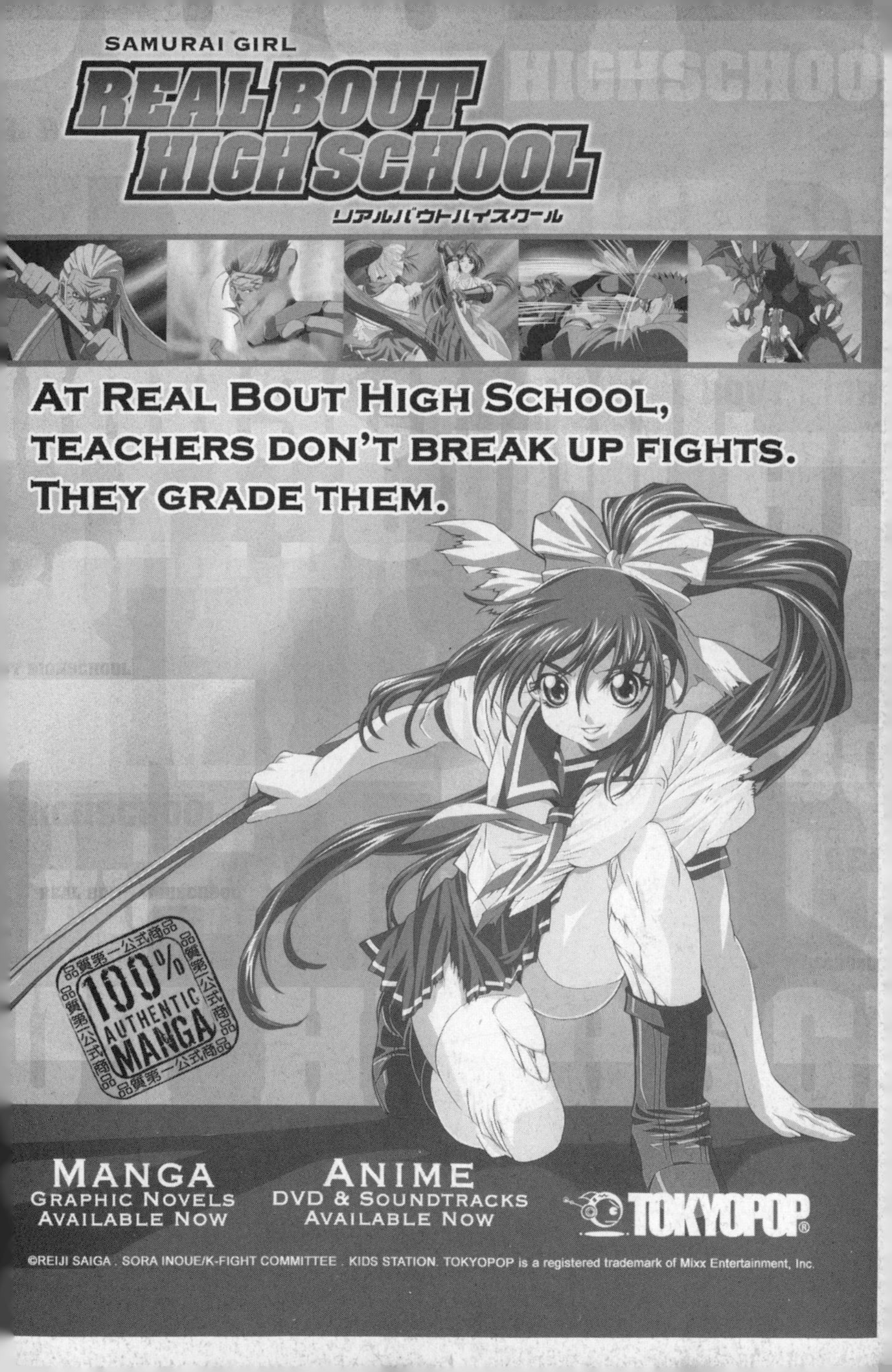

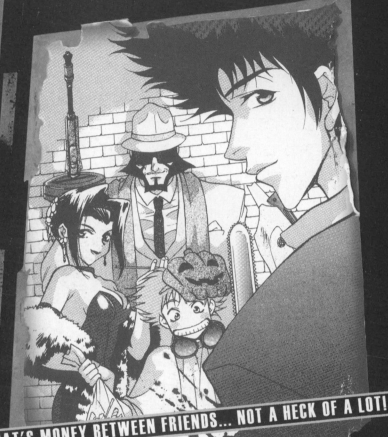

STOP!

This is the back of the book.
You wouldn't want to spoil a great ending!

This book is printed "manga-style," in the authentic Japanese right-to-left format. Since none of the artwork has been flipped or altered, readers get to experience the story just as the creator intended. You've been asking for it, so TOKYOPOP® delivered: authentic, hot-off-the-press, and far more fun!

DIRECTIONS

If this is your first time reading manga-style, here's a quick guide to help you understand how it works.

It's easy... just start in the top right panel and follow the numbers. Have fun, and look for more 100% authentic manga from TOKYOPOP®!

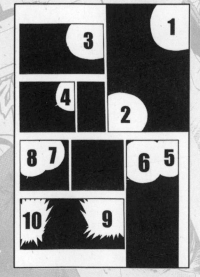

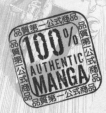